YOUR GUIDE FOR DEFENDING THE BIBLE

THIRD EDITION

Self-Education of the Bible Made Easy

Edward D. Andrews

YOUR GUIDE FOR DEFENDING THE BIBLE

Self-Education of the Bible Made Easy

Edward D. Andrews

Christian Publishing House
Cambridge, Ohio

Copyright © 2016 Edward D. Andrews

All rights reserved. Except for brief quotations in articles, other publications, book reviews, and blogs, no part of this book may be reproduced in any manner without prior written permission from the publishers. For information, write, support@christianpublishers.org

Unless otherwise stated, Scripture quotations are from Updated American Standard Version (UASV) Copyright © 2022 by Christian Publishing House

YOUR GUIDE FOR DEFENDING THE BIBLE: Self-Education of the Bible Made Easy by Edward D. Andrews

ISBN-10: 1945757345

ISBN-13: 978-1945757341

Table of Contents

Book Description 7

Preface 9

Introduction 11

SECTION 1 BIBLICAL INTERPRETATION 13

CHAPTER 1 The Basics of Conservative Objective Historical Grammatical Method of Interpretation 14

CHAPTER 2 The Basics of Liberal-Moderate Subjective Historical Critical Method of Biblical Interpretation 21

CHAPTER 3 The Basics of Conservative Biblical Exegesis 29

CHAPTER 4 The History of Higher Criticism—Its Assault on the Bible? 38

CHAPTER 5 Interpreting Different Genres 94

CHAPTER 6 Interpreting New Testament Writers Use of the Old Testament 124

SECTION 2 BIBLE TRANSLATION PHILOSOPHY 132

CHAPTER 7 The Steps of the Bible Translation Process 133

CHAPTER 8 Defining the Terms of the Bible Translation Debate 160

CHAPTER 9 How the Bible Came to Down to Us 181

CHAPTER 10 Manuscript Discoveries to Help Establish the Bible Text 200

SECTION 3 TEXTUAL CRITICISM OF THE OLD AND NEW TESTAMENT 212

CHAPTER 11 Introduction to Textual Criticism 214

CHAPTER 12 Principles of Textual Criticism 230

CHAPTER 13 The New Testament Textual Criticism 251

CHAPTER 14 Applying Textual Criticism 268

CHAPTER 15 The Future of Textual Criticism 285

SECTION 4 BIBLE DIFFICULTIES 300

CHAPTER 16 Bible Difficulties Explained 301

CHAPTER 17 View of Bible Difficulties 333

CHAPTER 18 Some Types of Bible Difficulties 338

CHAPTER 19 Dealing With Bible Difficulties 349

SECTION 5 HOW TO STUDY THE BIBLE 352

CHAPTER 20 Unlocking the Treasures of Scripture 353

CHAPTER 21 Digging Deeper: Advanced Bible Study Methods 362

CHAPTER 22 Applying God's Word to Your Life 371

SECTION 6 CHRISTIAN APOLOGETICS 379

CHAPTER 23 Introduction to Christian Apologetics 380

CHAPTER 24 Being Prepared to Make a Defense 389

CHAPTER 25 Contend for the Faith 397

CHAPTER 26 Reasoning from the Scriptures 405

SECTION 7 CHRISTIAN EVANGELISM 413

CHAPTER 27 Using Persuasion to Reach the Heart of Our Listeners ... 414

CHAPTER 28 Speak the Word of God with Boldness 422

CHAPTER 29 Skillfully Using the Word of God 430

CHAPTER 30 Giving Reasonable, Rational, and Persuasive Answers When We Share God's Word 440

SECTION 8 BIBLICAL ARCHAEOLOGY 452

CHAPTER 31 Unearthing the Past: Introduction to Biblical Archaeology 453

CHAPTER 32 Exploring Ancient Sites: Archaeological Excavations 463

CHAPTER 33 Biblical Archaeology and Faith: Implications for Believers 464

CHAPTER 34 Some Major Sites and Finds 473

Bibliography 489

YOUR GUIDE FOR DEFENDING THE BIBLE

Book Description

In today's shifting spiritual landscape, the authority and relevance of the Bible have come under intense scrutiny. *YOUR GUIDE FOR DEFENDING THE BIBLE: Self-Education of the Bible Made Easy* emerges as an indispensable resource tailored for both seasoned believers and those grappling with the big questions about the Bible's integrity, authenticity, and practicality.

Structured in eight comprehensive sections, this book equips you with the necessary tools to navigate the complex world of biblical interpretation, translation philosophies, textual criticism, and beyond.

Section 1 lays the groundwork for understanding the conservative objective historical-grammatical method of biblical interpretation, offering a counter-view by exploring the liberal-moderate historical-critical approach.

In **Section 2**, delve into the intricacies of Bible translation, exploring key terms and processes that have guided how the Holy Scriptures have been rendered in various languages over the centuries.

Section 3 is a deep dive into the realm of textual criticism of both the Old and New Testaments, a vital field that has played an essential role in restoring and preserving the biblical text.

Section 4 tackles Bible difficulties head-on. Gain keen insights into the various types of difficulties and how to effectively deal with them, strengthening your confidence in Scripture's reliability.

Section 5 serves as a practical guide to unlocking the treasures of Scripture, helping you dig deeper into the text and apply its truths to your life.

In **Section 6**, the focus shifts to Christian Apologetics. Learn how to be prepared to make a defense for your faith and how to reason from the Scriptures in a manner that is both reasonable and persuasive.

Section 7 transitions into the art of Christian evangelism, presenting methods to effectively communicate the Gospel message and speak the Word of God with boldness.

Finally, **Section 8** takes you on an archaeological expedition, offering insights into how the physical remnants of ancient civilizations provide ancillary support for the biblical narrative.

With its rigorous scholarship, practical applications, and unwavering commitment to a conservative viewpoint, *YOUR GUIDE FOR DEFENDING THE BIBLE* serves as a go-to manual for anyone seeking a deeply informed and faith-affirming understanding of the Scriptures. Aided by a comprehensive bibliography, this guide is your one-stop-shop for biblical knowledge, designed to help you navigate and appreciate the complex yet awe-inspiring world of the Bible.

Whether you're a pastor, student of theology, or layperson, this guide is designed to arm you with the knowledge, tactics, and confidence needed to defend the reliability and eternal relevance of the Bible.

Preface

Dear Reader,

The journey through the pages of the Bible is as much an intellectual expedition as it is a spiritual one. However, that journey can be fraught with questions, challenges, and objections that range from textual ambiguities to ethical dilemmas. In our present age, where skepticism often casts a long shadow over faith, and where misinformation can easily replace sound doctrine, a robust, grounded, and informed understanding of the Bible is not just beneficial—it's essential.

The idea for *YOUR GUIDE FOR DEFENDING THE BIBLE: Self-Education of the Bible Made Easy* was born out of a heartfelt concern for those struggling to reconcile their faith with the scholarly, ethical, and social questions that arise in the context of the Bible. Additionally, there has been a long-standing need for a resource that doesn't merely espouse dogma, but carefully, rationally, and faithfully examines the critical aspects that contribute to the understanding and application of the Bible.

The purpose of this guide is to bridge the gap between academic scrutiny and personal faith, providing readers with the intellectual armament they need to not only defend the Bible but also enrich their own understanding of it. In doing so, the book addresses multiple facets of biblical knowledge and study, from hermeneutics to archaeology, and from apologetics to evangelism.

One distinguishing feature of this work is its unwavering commitment to the conservative objective historical-grammatical method of interpretation. You won't find subjectivity here; only a robust, systematic, and empirical approach to understanding the Word of God. However, that doesn't mean the book shies away from exploring alternative perspectives—rather, it critically examines them to equip readers with a well-rounded view.

Another notable focus is on the practical application of the Bible. The book is not merely a theoretical discourse but offers actionable guidance on how to apply the Bible's teachings and principles in everyday life. This makes it an invaluable resource for pastors, ministry leaders, and laypersons alike, who can benefit from its insights in their personal spiritual journey as well as in their roles as spiritual leaders within the community.

It is my hope that this book will serve as a reliable companion in your quest for biblical literacy. Whether you are looking to deepen your personal study, engage in effective evangelism, or be well-equipped to stand your ground in faith-based conversations, this guide offers a comprehensive, in-depth approach that respects both the text and the reader's intellect. Thank you for allowing me to be part of your spiritual and intellectual journey through the complexities, challenges, and eternal rewards that come with diving deep into the Word of God.

May your pursuit of biblical truth be as enlightening as it is transformative.

Buckle up for an enlightening journey through the annals of Scripture and the depths of faith.

Warmly in Christ,

Edward D. Andrews

Author of 220+ books and the Chief Translator of the Updated American Standard Version

YOUR GUIDE FOR DEFENDING THE BIBLE

Introduction

Welcome to a transformative endeavor—a quest to not only grasp the Bible as a religious text but also to engage it as an intellectual masterpiece deserving of rigorous analysis and thoughtful reflection. If you've picked up *YOUR GUIDE FOR DEFENDING THE BIBLE: Self-Education of the Bible Made Easy*, you're not merely interested in passive faith; you're seeking an active, robust, and well-rounded understanding of the Scriptures that will stand the test of inquiry and skepticism. You're eager for a faith that isn't blind but is instead illuminated by the lamp of reason, research, and thorough understanding.

What makes the Bible a unique book in the annals of history? Is it merely a compilation of mythological stories, as some critics claim? Is it simply an inspirational piece, a collection of moral tales, or is it something much more profound, something divinely orchestrated? The forthcoming pages are designed to take you through this very exploration, offering a detailed roadmap of the essential doctrines, debates, and discoveries that have shaped the Bible as we know it today.

The structure of this book is carefully crafted to guide you through a multi-faceted approach to biblical understanding. Beginning with the fundamentals of interpretation, we will delve into the conservative objective historical-grammatical method, examining its principles, merits, and applications. Understanding the techniques for reading the Bible is crucial for anyone who wants to appreciate the layers and depths that it offers.

As we progress, you'll find sections dedicated to the principles and debates surrounding Bible translation, providing a clear-eyed view of how the Word of God has been rendered in various languages and cultures across history. Manuscript evidence and the science of textual criticism will also find its place, addressing some of the most crucial questions regarding the integrity and reliability of the Bible text.

Yet, understanding the Bible isn't merely an academic exercise; it has profound practical implications. Thus, this book also dedicates significant attention to tackling Bible difficulties, offering a rational framework for addressing seeming contradictions or ethical quandaries presented in the Scriptures. Moreover, the guide dives into advanced methods for personal Bible study and practical application, ensuring that the knowledge gained isn't sterile but is vibrant and life-altering.

The later sections open up the universe of Christian apologetics and evangelism. These are especially crafted for those who are not content with just internalizing their faith but are passionate about sharing it, defending it, and discussing it in the marketplace of ideas. Finally, a special focus on biblical archaeology offers a grounding in the physical world, exploring how the Bible stands up against the hard evidence of historical finds.

By the end of this guide, you won't just be a "reader" of the Bible; you will be a student, a critic, an apologist, and most importantly, a more fortified believer. Embark on this journey with an open mind and a willing heart, and you'll find that the Bible isn't just a book—it's an expansive, enriching, and eternal world of its own.

YOUR GUIDE FOR DEFENDING THE BIBLE

SECTION 1 BIBLICAL INTERPRETATION

Digging Deeper

We put books here on this subject if one is interested in taking the subject deeper. This section gives you foundational knowledge to evangelize or engage people in conversation.

INTERPRETING THE BIBLE: Introduction to Biblical Hermeneutics by Edward D Andrews (2016)

https://www.amazon.com/dp/1945757078

BIBLICAL EXEGESIS: Biblical Criticism on Trial by Edward Andrews (2023)

https://www.amazon.com/dp/B0CBZHDFP9

BIBLICAL APOCALYPTICS HANDBOOK: A Study of the Most Important Revelations that God and Christ Disclosed in the Bible by Edward D. Andrews (2023)

https://www.amazon.com/dp/B0C9S5HKTD

Edward D. Andrews

CHAPTER 1 The Basics of Conservative Objective Historical Grammatical Method of Interpretation

Defining the Objective Historical-Grammatical Method

The objective Historical-Grammatical Method (HGM) of Biblical interpretation stands as a cornerstone for conservative Biblical scholarship. Unlike subjective approaches that may be tainted by various secular ideologies, the HGM is rooted in an unwavering commitment to the authority and inerrancy of Scripture. The key tenet here is to discern the meaning of the text as the original authors intended and as the initial audience would have understood it, considering both its historical context and its grammatical structure. This chapter will serve as a guidepost for understanding the basics of this essential method.

Authority and Inerrancy of Scripture

The HGM begins with the premise that the Bible is both authoritative and inerrant. This stands in contrast to modern critical methodologies that often treat the Bible as merely a human product subjected to historical, social, and ideological scrutiny. By affirming the Bible's divine inspiration, the HGM upholds its timeless relevance and ultimate authority.

Textual Honesty

The HGM emphasizes a "text-first" approach. The text itself, in its original languages and contexts, provides the necessary boundaries within which interpretation occurs. This eliminates subjective tendencies to impose on the text what isn't there. For example, while one may be tempted to read 21st-century issues into first-century texts, such eisegesis is avoided in favor of letting the text "speak" on its own terms. This aligns with the exhortation in 2 Timothy 2:15 to "rightly handle the word of truth."

YOUR GUIDE FOR DEFENDING THE BIBLE

Historical Context

The HGM pays close attention to the historical backdrop against which a given text was written. This includes the cultural, social, political, and religious factors that influenced its composition. Understanding the historical setting is vital in interpreting texts like the Mosaic Law or Pauline Epistles, which were written to specific audiences facing unique challenges. This is not to reduce Scripture to a mere cultural artifact but to recognize that God spoke through human authors in particular circumstances to communicate universal truths.

Grammatical Analysis

Here, words are analyzed based on their root meanings, forms, and syntactical relationships. Tenses, moods, voices of verbs, and the relationships of clauses and phrases to one another all come into play. The aim is to understand how language works within specific texts to convey meaning. This grammatical rigor serves as an additional safeguard against subjective interpretations.

The Centrality of Exegesis

Exegesis is the extraction of meaning from the text as opposed to eisegesis, where one reads their own preconceptions into the text. When exegesis is conducted within the framework of HGM, the interpreter is less likely to veer off into the realms of speculation, allegory, or subjective bias.

Critique of Alternative Methods

In contrast, the critical methodologies often applied in liberal-moderate biblical criticism are inherently flawed and speculative. They subject the text to an ideological grid that distorts its meaning. Whether it is the Historical-Critical Method, which is often applied subjectively, or form criticism, which attempts to identify the "life situations" behind the texts, these approaches dilute the authority of the Scripture. While they claim to be objective, they often reflect external biases such as secular humanism and Enlightenment rationalism, resulting in an interpretation far removed from the text's original intent.

A Return to Faithfulness

The HGM offers an antidote to the subjective and ideologically skewed practices of modern biblical criticism. It serves both as an affirmation of the divine authority and inerrancy of Scripture and as a reliable methodology that honors the text's original context and language. The aim is not merely academic but spiritual: to equip the body of Christ with a sound understanding of God's Word, thereby strengthening faith and fostering obedience to the divine will.

Thus, the Historical-Grammatical Method is not just an academic exercise; it is a commitment to faithfully handling the Word of God, illuminating its timeless truths for the edification of the Church and the glory of God.

The Importance of Context in Interpretation

Principles and Rules Governing Objective Historical-Grammatical Interpretation

Understanding context is pivotal in applying the Historical-Grammatical Method (HGM) of Biblical interpretation. The Bible, though a divine revelation, was penned by human authors who were products of their specific historical, cultural, and linguistic settings. Hence, the interpretation of Scripture cannot ignore these essential contexts if one aims to ascertain the original intent of the authors and thereby understand the authoritative message of Scripture.

Literary Context

To understand any given passage, it's essential to consider what comes before and after it. Often, verses cannot be fully understood in isolation. For example, Paul's declaration that "For by grace you have been saved through faith. And this is not your own doing; it is the gift of God, not a result of works, so that no one may boast" (Ephesians 2:8-9, ESV) gains fuller meaning when seen within the larger discussion of Jew-Gentile relationships and the unity of the Church.

Scriptural Context

Every verse is part of a chapter, every chapter part of a book, and every book part of the entire canon. Hence, the context of a verse in its chapter, its book, and ultimately the whole Bible is indispensable for accurate interpretation. Take the principle of "an eye for an eye" (Exodus 21:24). By itself, it seems like a mandate for vengeance, but when read alongside Jesus' teaching in the Sermon on the Mount (Matthew 5:38-39), its role as a limitation on retribution becomes clearer.

YOUR GUIDE FOR DEFENDING THE BIBLE

Historical and Cultural Context

Understanding the time and culture a text emerged from helps clarify its meaning. This is evident in texts like 1 Corinthians 11:4-16, where Paul discusses head coverings. This passage makes more sense when understood within the Greco-Roman and Jewish cultural milieu, where head coverings had specific cultural and symbolic significances.

Theological Context

The HGM is concerned with the consistency of the biblical message. It acknowledges that God's revelation was given progressively and must be understood in that unfolding theological framework. A text like Genesis 15:6, which speaks of Abram's faith being counted as righteousness, can be fully appreciated only when placed within the broader framework of biblical theology, including Paul's treatment of faith and righteousness in Romans.

Immediate Context

Consider the word "law" in Romans. It can refer to Mosaic Law, the broader Old Testament, or even a principle of behavior (Rom. 7:21-23). Understanding what Paul means in each instance requires a close look at the immediate context.

Cohesiveness of the Biblical Message

It's essential to note that Scripture interprets Scripture. For example, understanding the concept of the "Sabbath rest" is greatly enriched when one considers its presentation from Genesis to Revelation. From the creation account in Genesis 2:1-3 to the eschatological rest mentioned in Revelation 14:13, one can trace a cohesive, divine narrative.

Language and Syntax

Understanding the original languages (Hebrew, Aramaic, and Greek) aids in ascertaining the precise meanings of words, syntactical nuances, and idioms that might not be fully captured in translation. For example, the Greek term 'agape' and 'philia' both translated as 'love' in English, have subtle differences that are crucial for correct interpretation.

The Fallacy of Proof-texting

In avoiding the pitfalls of proof-texting—taking verses out of context to prove a point—the HGM insists on a comprehensive understanding of the biblical message. For example, using James 2:24 ("You see that a person is justified by works and not by faith alone") to argue against the doctrine of justification by faith would be misleading without considering its broader context and other Scriptural teachings on justification.

Caution Against Subjective Methods

Other methods like allegorical or typological interpretations often distort the clear meaning of the text by importing external ideas into it. The HGM keeps interpretation grounded in what can be objectively determined from the text itself.

In essence, context serves as a protective boundary against the distortion of Scripture, ensuring its original meaning is conveyed as intended by its authors. Through understanding the multiple layers of context—literary, historical, cultural, theological, and linguistic—the HGM enables interpreters to arrive at interpretations that are both faithful to the original text and deeply respectful of its divine Author. This not only equips the Christian community to "rightly handle the word of truth" (2 Timothy 2:15) but also serves as a safeguard against the biases and distortions that are rife in other, less objective methods of interpretation.

Practical Application: Case Studies and Examples

The historical-grammatical method of interpretation offers a disciplined and rigorous framework for Biblical interpretation. This conservative approach is underpinned by a profound respect for the authority and inerrancy of Scripture. It seeks to comprehend the original meaning intended by the Biblical authors through careful study of linguistic, historical, and cultural elements. This chapter outlines the principles behind this method and provides practical applications through case studies.

The Objective Historical-Grammatical Method Explained

In essence, this method involves three primary steps:

1. **Observation**: Scrutinize the text to understand its explicit and implicit meanings.
2. **Interpretation**: Determine what the text meant to the original audience, taking into account the language, culture, and historical context.
3. **Application**: Understand the principles the text articulates and how they can be faithfully applied today.

YOUR GUIDE FOR DEFENDING THE BIBLE

Case Study 1: Genesis 1 — The Creation Account

The creation account in Genesis 1 is often subjected to varying interpretations. Using the historical-grammatical method, one observes the text's emphasis on the divine ordering of the cosmos over six "days." The Hebrew term "yom" can mean a literal 24-hour day or a period; context must guide the interpretation.

Case Study 2: Matthew 24:40-41 — The "Left Behind"

This text about one person being "taken" and the other "left" has been interpreted differently across the theological spectrum. The context here is eschatological, tied to Christ's Second Coming. In contrast to fanciful speculations or allegorical readings, the historical-grammatical approach observes that being "taken" or "left" was understood within a Jewish framework of divine judgment and salvation at the end of the age.

Case Study 3: Romans 9-11 — Israel and Divine Election

Paul's discourse here is theological and deals with questions of God's sovereignty and human responsibility. Using the historical-grammatical method, we understand Paul was addressing a mostly Gentile audience familiar with Jewish history. Romans 9-11 deals with the issue of Israel's current unbelief and future restoration in the eschatological plan of God. Here, both the historical context (Israel's national history) and the immediate context (the theological argument Paul is making) are essential for accurate interpretation.

Case Study 4: 1 Timothy 2:12 — Women in Ministry

Paul's prohibition against a woman teaching or having authority over a man has generated debate. However, the historical-grammatical method considers the historical situation that Paul was addressing—a young Ephesian church bombarded by false teachings, some of which apparently came from women. It's crucial to note that this does not establish a universal principle that women are not allowed to teach in all contexts.

Case Study 5: 1 Corinthians 7:1-40 — Principles of Marriage and Singleness

Paul's advice about marriage, divorce, and singleness is often applied prescriptively. However, the historical-grammatical method would take into account that Paul was responding to specific questions from the Corinthians, which were culturally and historically conditioned. This gives valuable context to phrases like "it is good for a man not to touch a woman" (v. 1), allowing for a balanced understanding that neither demonizes marriage nor idolizes singleness.

Case Study 6: Acts 2:38 — Baptism and the Gift of the Holy Spirit

Peter's command to repent, be baptized, and receive the gift of the Holy Spirit is sometimes interpreted in a way that links salvation strictly with water baptism. However, examining it through a historical-grammatical lens indicates that Peter was addressing a Jewish audience familiar with baptism as a ritual act of purification. The emphasis is on repentance and faith, which are symbolized and confirmed through baptism but not exclusively tied to it.

The historical-grammatical method provides a robust framework for interpreting Scripture. Its primary advantage is its commitment to discovering the original meaning of the text, rooted in its linguistic, historical, and cultural backdrop. By focusing on what the Biblical authors intended to communicate, we can apply the timeless truths of Scripture to contemporary life responsibly and faithfully. This approach serves as a bulwark against interpretative methodologies that compromise the inerrancy and authority of Scripture, thereby affirming the essential doctrines of the Christian faith.

CHAPTER 2 The Basics of Liberal-Moderate Subjective Historical Critical Method of Biblical Interpretation

Defining the Subjective Historical-Critical Method

The historical-critical method of biblical interpretation stands in stark contrast to the historical-grammatical method. Whereas the latter emphasizes the objective evaluation of texts based on linguistic, historical, and cultural factors, the historical-critical method often incorporates a variety of speculative approaches. These speculative methodologies are generally rooted in broader ideological systems, such as secular humanism and Enlightenment rationalism. Below is an overview of the subjective historical-critical method.

The Historical-Critical Method Defined

The historical-critical method employs several sub-methods like form criticism, redaction criticism, and source criticism. It operates under the assumption that the biblical text is a product of human history and, therefore, should be dissected using the same critical tools applied to any other historical documents. Unlike the conservative viewpoint, which upholds the divine inspiration and inerrancy of Scripture, the historical-critical approach often views the Bible as a flawed and errant human creation.

Criticisms and Sub-Methods

1. **Literary Criticism**: Examines the genre and literary features of the text but often leads to a de-emphasis on the historical context or the original meaning. For instance, the narrative of the Exodus could be dissected into literary forms without regard for its historical significance to the Israelites and their understanding of God.
2. **Form Criticism**: This focuses on the oral traditions behind the text. It assumes that Biblical texts, like the Gospels, are compilations of smaller

units of oral tradition. However, this risks neglecting the coherent message of entire books.

3. **Redaction Criticism**: This method looks at how editors (or 'redactors') might have shaped or manipulated the text. In the Gospel accounts, for instance, it assumes that each Gospel writer selectively edited the material to serve a theological or community-based agenda.

4. **Source Criticism**: This method attempts to discern the different sources that were used to compile a particular book. For example, it claims that the first five books of the Bible, the Torah, were not authored by Moses but were compiled from various sources, commonly referred to as J, E, D, and P. This standpoint directly conflicts with the traditional Jewish and Christian understanding of Mosaic authorship.

Ideological Underpinnings

The historical-critical method is often influenced by external philosophical frameworks. It frequently adopts a skeptical approach to the supernatural, mirroring the Enlightenment's emphasis on human reason. These ideologies distance biblical interpretation from the realm of faith and move it into the sphere of speculative human thought.

Implications for Interpretation

Applying the historical-critical method can lead to conclusions that significantly differ from traditional understandings. For instance, the Virgin Birth or Christ's Resurrection could be considered as theological constructs rather than historical events. Similarly, important doctrines, like the divinity of Christ or the concept of atonement, can be diluted or outright dismissed.

The Impact on the Church and Individual Believers

The liberal-moderate use of the historical-critical method has been contentious, leading to division within denominations and theological circles. It has undermined the faith of many by challenging the veracity and authority of Scripture, leading to a "pick and choose" approach to biblical truths. Such an approach destabilizes the foundational tenets of Christianity, including the authority of Scripture and the basic tenets of Christian doctrine.

The historical-critical method represents a subjective and ideologically-driven approach to biblical interpretation. Unlike the historical-grammatical method, which is rooted in an unwavering commitment to the authority and inerrancy of Scripture, the historical-critical method is fraught with speculative endeavors that often serve to distance the text from its original meaning and context. Its prevalence in modern academia stands as a warning to those committed to a more conservative, objective approach, highlighting the need for constant vigilance in the field of biblical interpretation.

The Role of Reader Subjectivity

Reader subjectivity occupies a prominent role in the liberal-moderate subjective historical-critical method of biblical interpretation. In contrast to the objective, text-centered approach of the historical-grammatical method, reader subjectivity allows the interpreter's own experiences, cultural background, and ideological leanings to play a vital role in understanding the biblical text. This chapter examines the emphasis on reader subjectivity in the historical-critical method and its consequences for biblical interpretation.

The Role of Reader Subjectivity Defined

In the historical-critical approach, the reader's perspective, cultural background, and ideological beliefs are not just acknowledged but are often celebrated as contributing factors in the interpretive process. The focus shifts from what the text says to how different readers perceive the text. This departs markedly from the Apostle Paul's exhortation to Timothy to "rightly handle the word of truth" (2 Timothy 2:15, ESV).

Subjectivity in Various Sub-Methods

1. **Literary Criticism**: Subjectivity enters as readers may focus on elements like plot, characters, and literary devices while often neglecting the message the original authors intended to communicate.

2. **Form Criticism**: The reader's cultural lens might significantly influence the identification and interpretation of different 'forms' or genres within the text.

3. **Redaction Criticism**: Personal beliefs may guide the reader in attributing motives to the supposed redactors, often reflecting the interpreter's own worldview more than the text itself.

4. **Source Criticism**: Reader subjectivity often shapes the hypothetical sources that are proposed, frequently in a manner that aligns with the critic's ideological stance.

Ideological Influence

The subjective nature of the historical-critical method often reflects the broader ideological systems it originates from. If one's worldview denies the supernatural, miracles like the parting of the Red Sea are naturally interpreted as literary constructs rather than historical events. Reader subjectivity, therefore, does not operate in a vacuum but is significantly colored by external ideologies.

Scriptural Examples: The Pitfalls of Subjectivity

1. **The Resurrection of Christ**: A reader inclined to deny the supernatural might interpret the Resurrection as a symbolic event, thereby neglecting the apostolic testimony and the foundational role of the Resurrection in Christian doctrine (1 Corinthians 15:14-19).
2. **Creation Account**: The narrative of a six-day creation in Genesis 1 might be seen through the lens of evolutionary theory, thereby undermining the text's straightforward presentation of divine creation.
3. **Atonement**: The sacrificial death of Christ could be reinterpreted as a mere example of selfless love, sidelining its central role as a propitiation for human sin (Romans 3:25).

Consequences for the Church and Individual Believers

The emphasis on reader subjectivity has contributed to a relativistic approach to Scripture, where personal feelings or experiences can easily override the text's original intent. This has led to widespread theological divergence, weakened doctrinal clarity, and even apostasy.

Countering Reader Subjectivity: The Need for an Objective Approach

To counter the pitfalls of reader subjectivity, one must adhere to an objective method that is grounded in the text and its original context. This aligns with the Bereans, who were commended for carefully examining the Scriptures daily to see if what they were taught was true (Acts 17:11).

While reader subjectivity might seem to democratize biblical interpretation, it introduces a range of problems that can lead to a distortion of the text. Far from being an asset, unchecked subjectivity is a liability that can pull one away from the foundational truths of Scripture. Its rise and prevalence should serve as a cautionary tale, reaffirming the need for a more objective, text-centered approach like the historical-grammatical method. This objective approach not only respects the text but also honors Jehovah, the God of truth, who inspired it (2 Timothy 3:16).

Principles Governing Subjective Historical-Critical Interpretation

Understanding the underlying principles that govern subjective historical-critical interpretation can shed light on its limitations and biases. This chapter aims to delineate these principles and offer Scriptural examples to highlight the pitfalls of this approach.

Principle 1: Human Autonomy Over Divine Authority

One fundamental principle of the historical-critical method is the elevation of human reasoning above divine authority. This is contrary to the Scriptural admonition to "lean not on your own understanding" (Proverbs 3:5, ESV). By situating human intellect as the final arbiter, the historical-critical method places itself at odds with the notion of divine revelation and inspiration (2 Timothy 3:16).

Principle 2: Tentativeness and Uncertainty

The historical-critical method often embraces uncertainty, rejecting the idea of an absolute truth. This contradicts Christ's statement that God's word is truth (John 17:17). Skepticism is nurtured, and conclusions are rarely considered definitive, leading to an unstable foundation for faith.

Principle 3: Presentism

Presentism implies that current cultural and moral norms should be used as a lens to interpret ancient texts. For instance, Paul's views on gender roles or slavery are often critiqued using contemporary ethical standards. Such an approach can lead to anachronistic readings and overlooks Paul's cultural and historical context.

Principle 4: Relativism and Reader-Centeredness

This principle highlights the role of the reader's perspective in determining meaning. It thereby undermines the author's intended message, a phenomenon that Paul warned against (Galatians 1:6-9).

Scriptural Examples

1. **Virgin Birth**: Isaiah's prophecy about a virgin giving birth to Emmanuel (Isaiah 7:14) is often dismissed as a mistranslation or mythologization. However, the Gospel of Matthew clearly affirms this as fulfilled prophecy (Matthew 1:22-23).

2. **The Exodus**: The historical-critical method often considers the Exodus narrative as a legendary account rather than a historical event. This diminishes the monumental act of Jehovah liberating His people (Exodus 14).
3. **Pauline Authorship**: The principle of tentativeness undermines the traditional understanding that Paul authored all the letters attributed to him, including the often-disputed Hebrews. Questioning Pauline authorship, however, conflicts with the internal evidence and early Church tradition.
4. **Resurrection Accounts**: By employing a principle of skepticism, the resurrection accounts in the Gospels are often seen as conflicting and therefore unreliable. This overlooks the core Christian doctrine that Christ was raised from the dead (1 Corinthians 15:14).

Consequences for the Church

1. **Erosion of Doctrinal Integrity**: The application of these principles erodes core doctrines like the Deity of Christ, the historicity of biblical events, and the future judgment, undermining the faith once delivered to the saints (Jude 1:3).
2. **Confusion among Believers**: The ambiguity and relativism endorsed by the historical-critical method can lead to confusion, drawing believers away from the straightforward teachings of Scripture.

An Objective Alternative: The Historical-Grammatical Method

An objective approach like the historical-grammatical method avoids these pitfalls. It seeks to understand the original meaning intended by the author, respecting both the divine and human elements of Scripture. This method aligns more closely with Paul's exhortation to Timothy to correctly handle the word of truth (2 Timothy 2:15).

The principles governing the subjective historical-critical interpretation—human autonomy, tentativeness, presentism, and relativism—stand in stark contrast to a conservative, objective approach to Scripture. These principles often lead to interpretations that are at odds with the intended meaning of the text and its Author. As such, an objective, text-centered approach, which respects the authority and inerrancy of Scripture, remains the best tool for faithful biblical interpretation. It allows for an exegetical method that aligns with the inherent nature of the Bible as the inspired Word of Jehovah.

Practical Application: Case Studies and Examples

Having delineated the underlying principles of liberal-moderate subjective historical-critical interpretation, we will now examine practical case studies that highlight how these methods are applied to biblical texts. We will also discuss how these applications often deviate from a conservative, objective understanding of the Scriptures.

Case Study 1: The Creation Account in Genesis

The subjective historical-critical approach often interprets the Creation account in Genesis as a myth or allegory rather than a historical record. However, Paul affirms the historical Adam in Romans 5:12-21. By turning the Creation account into a myth, this method undermines essential doctrines like original sin.

Case Study 2: Isaiah's Servant Songs

The Servant Songs in Isaiah are traditionally understood to prophesy about the Messiah. Yet, subjective historical-critical methods might suggest that the "servant" merely refers to Israel as a nation or another historical figure. This ignores the New Testament confirmation of these prophecies pointing to Christ (Acts 8:30-35).

Case Study 3: The Authorship and Date of Daniel

Liberal-moderate scholars often date Daniel to the Maccabean period, casting doubt on its prophetic authenticity. However, this contradicts Jesus' affirmation of Daniel as a prophet (Matthew 24:15). The book's detailed prophecies about subsequent empires are also overlooked.

Case Study 4: The Bread of Life Discourse in John 6

John 6:35-58 is often understood in symbolic terms, even though Jesus repeatedly emphasized the literal necessity of eating His flesh and drinking His blood for eternal life. This has significant implications for doctrines like the atonement and communion.

Case Study 5: Paul's Letters and Pseudonymity

The authorship of Pauline epistles like Ephesians and Colossians is often questioned, arguing that they might be pseudonymous works from a later period. This casts a shadow over their canonical authority and denies early Church tradition.

Case Study 6: The Resurrection Narratives

As previously mentioned, the resurrection accounts in the Gospels are often seen as conflicting and therefore unreliable. By questioning the literal resurrection, the cornerstone of Christian faith is undermined (1 Corinthians 15:17).

Consequences and Implications for the Church

1. **Theological Drift**: The application of subjective methods can lead to theological drift, destabilizing core beliefs and causing division within the Body of Christ.
2. **Reduced Reliability**: These interpretations often render the Bible less reliable, which in turn undermines its role as the authoritative Word of Jehovah in the life of the believer (2 Timothy 3:16-17).
3. **Syncretism and Compromise**: The blending of secular ideologies within biblical interpretation leads to syncretism and compromise, diluting the transformative power of the Gospel.

The Need for an Objective Approach: The Historical-Grammatical Method

The Historical-Grammatical method is an objective alternative that prioritizes the original intent of the biblical authors, both human and Divine. By focusing on the historical and grammatical context of the text, it aims to uncover the intended meaning, respecting the authority and inerrancy of the Scriptures.

The practical applications of liberal-moderate subjective historical-critical methods reveal how they often depart from a conservative, objective understanding of the Bible. These applications frequently undermine foundational doctrines and create unnecessary confusion among believers. Given these limitations, it is crucial to employ a method of interpretation that respects the authority and inerrancy of the Bible as Jehovah's inspired Word. The historical-grammatical method offers such an approach, aligning more closely with the conservative principles that prioritize the Word of Jehovah as the ultimate authority for life and faith.

CHAPTER 3 The Basics of Conservative Biblical Exegesis

Foundations of Conservative Exegesis

As we embark on this exploration of conservative biblical exegesis, it's crucial to underline that the primary goal is to uphold the authority, reliability, and inerrancy of Scripture. Unlike liberal-moderate approaches, conservative biblical exegesis is grounded in the conviction that the Bible is Jehovah's inspired Word and thus completely trustworthy (2 Timothy 3:16).

Fundamental Tenets

1. **Inerrancy and Inspiration**: A conservative approach starts with the belief that the Bible is inerrant and inspired by Jehovah (2 Peter 1:20-21).
2. **Literal Interpretation**: Conservatives aim for a straightforward reading of the text, as indicated by the historical-grammatical method. For example, the Creation account in Genesis is taken to be a historical event, considering corroborative statements like Exodus 20:11.
3. **Historical Context**: The Scriptures must be interpreted within their original historical context. Paul's letters, for instance, are understood as specific addresses to particular congregations with unique challenges, yet carrying timeless principles (1 Corinthians 10:11).
4. **Grammatical Rules**: Grammar, syntax, and linguistic elements guide the interpretation. This anchors the text to its original meaning and safeguards against unwarranted theological extrapolations.

The Historical-Grammatical Method

As the name implies, the historical-grammatical method employs two key elements—historical context and grammatical structure. The method aligns with Paul's instruction to Timothy to rightly handle the Word of Truth (2 Timothy 2:15).

1. **Historical Context**: Whether it's the Babylonian captivity, the Roman occupation, or the Greek influence on early Christianity, the historical backdrop aids in interpreting the text. For instance, understanding the

Jewish concept of the Kingdom of God enriches the reading of Jesus' parables.

2. **Grammatical Analysis**: This involves dissecting sentence structure, word choices, and language rules. A classic example is the careful study of Greek words like "agape" and "phileo," both translated as "love" but with nuanced meanings, as seen in John 21:15-17.

Application of the Historical-Grammatical Method

1. **The Law and Grace**: Understanding the historical shift from the Mosaic Law to the New Covenant of grace clarifies seemingly contradictory statements in the Old and New Testaments (Romans 6:14; Galatians 3:23-25).
2. **Eschatological Passages**: The apocalyptic language in books like Revelation is evaluated in light of its first-century context and the Old Testament imagery it often employs, rather than superimposing modern events.
3. **Parables and Literary Forms**: While allegory is to be avoided, the parables of Jesus are understood as illustrative stories meant to communicate spiritual truths. Their interpretation aligns with the broader context of Jesus' teachings (Luke 15:1-7).

Avoiding Subjective Pitfalls

1. **Allegorical Interpretation**: Allegorical methods inject subjectivity and vagueness, and they often deviate from the text's clear message.
2. **Typological Interpretation**: While the New Testament occasionally employs typology, it's not a license for free-wheeling connections between Old and New Testament figures or events unless such patterns are explicitly stated in Scripture.

Conservative exegesis champions the authority and inerrancy of Scripture by employing the historical-grammatical method. This approach respects the text's original historical and grammatical context, providing a stable platform for interpretation. By adhering to these principles, readers can unearth the text's intended meaning, fortifying their faith in Jehovah's inspired Word and safeguarding against the pitfalls of subjective interpretation. With this foundation, the believer is well-equipped to navigate complex theological discussions and arrive at conclusions that are not only biblically sound but also intellectually satisfying. Therefore, the conservative exegetical method is not just an academic exercise; it is a spiritual discipline that enriches one's relationship with Jehovah and His revealed Word.

Contextual Analysis in Conservative Exegesis

In the quest to uphold the authority, reliability, and inerrancy of Scripture, Contextual Analysis becomes a crucial component of conservative exegesis. Employing the objective Historical-Grammatical method of interpretation, Contextual Analysis assists us in navigating the layers of historical, cultural, linguistic, and theological elements that reside within the biblical texts. Through this lens, the Bible stands not merely as an ancient manuscript but as Jehovah's enduring and infallible Word (Isaiah 40:8).

Layers of Context

1. **Historical Context**: Information about the cultural, social, and historical circumstances in which a text was written or received. For example, understanding the temple worship system of ancient Israel offers invaluable insights into the Book of Hebrews.

2. **Literary Context**: This concerns the type of literature (genre), structure, and flow of thought in a passage or book. Recognizing that the Book of Psalms consists largely of poetic expressions allows us to distinguish between literal and poetic language.

3. **Theological Context**: This is the doctrine or teaching conveyed through a text. For example, Paul's discussion on justification by faith in Romans shapes the soteriology (doctrine of salvation) in the New Testament (Romans 3:21-26).

4. **Canonical Context**: This refers to a text's relationship with other parts of the Bible. An example is how Daniel's prophetic visions correlate with John's visions in Revelation, providing a comprehensive eschatological narrative.

Historical Context

The historical backdrop can be crucial in interpreting the text properly. For instance, Jesus' Sermon on the Mount (Matthew 5-7) can be better appreciated when understood within the context of Jewish legalism and Roman oppression.

Scriptural Example: The Book of Galatians cannot be adequately understood without recognizing the influence of Judaizers, who attempted to impose Mosaic Law upon Gentile believers (Galatians 2:11-16).

Literary Context

Identifying the genre and rhetorical devices can help distinguish between literal and metaphorical language.

Scriptural Example: When Jesus says, "I am the door" (John 10:9), recognizing the metaphorical nature prevents us from taking this claim as a literal description.

Theological Context

Theological context helps to bridge the immediate text with larger biblical doctrines.

Scriptural Example: In Isaiah 53, the concept of the suffering servant is introduced. When we read the Gospels, it becomes clear that Jesus is the fulfillment of this prophetic role, explicitly confirming in passages like Acts 8:30-35.

Canonical Context

Understanding how a text fits within the whole canon of Scripture allows for a more harmonious interpretation.

Scriptural Example: The concept of the "new heavens and new earth" appears in Isaiah 65:17 and is revisited in 2 Peter 3:13 and Revelation 21:1, showing a continuous theological thread.

Tools for Contextual Analysis

1. **Concordances**: Useful for tracking the usage of specific words throughout Scripture.

2. **Bible Dictionaries**: Provide historical and cultural background.

3. **Commentaries**: While these are human works and thus fallible, conservative commentaries often offer valuable insights while adhering to a high view of Scripture.

Pitfalls to Avoid

1. **Proof-texting**: This involves taking a verse out of its context to support a particular view, which is misleading and counterproductive.

2. **Over-Spiritualizing**: The tendency to find a "deeper" spiritual meaning, often through allegorical or typological interpretation, should be avoided in favor of a more straightforward reading of the text.

Conclusion

Contextual Analysis is a vital component in conservative biblical exegesis. By giving due attention to the various layers of context—historical, literary, theological, and canonical—readers are equipped to delve deeper into the rich tapestry of Jehovah's Word. Employing the Historical-Grammatical method ensures that interpretations remain anchored in the objective reality of the text, thereby maintaining the Bible's integrity. In doing so, we honor Jehovah, the author of Scripture, by engaging with His Word in a manner that seeks to understand it as He intended. Thus, Contextual Analysis is not merely an academic exercise but a devout act of worship, providing the believer with both intellectual satisfaction and spiritual enrichment.

Principles of Literal Interpretation

Literal interpretation is the bedrock of conservative biblical exegesis, ensuring that the authority and inerrancy of Scripture are upheld. The essence of literal interpretation lies in taking the words of the Bible in their most straightforward and obvious meaning, within the context in which they are found. By adhering to the principles of literal interpretation, we can arrive at conclusions that respect both the integrity of the Bible and the intent of its divine and human authors.

Key Principles of Literal Interpretation

1. **Grammatical Principle**: One must understand the rules of the language in which the text was written—Hebrew, Aramaic, or Greek—to ensure that the words are interpreted as they were originally intended.

Scriptural Example: The Greek word "hamartia," commonly translated as "sin," carries the connotation of "missing the mark." Understanding this nuance aids in interpreting passages like Romans 3:23, "For all have sinned and fall short of the glory of God."

2. **Contextual Principle**: This involves interpreting a word or passage within the surrounding verses, chapters, and books. Isolated verses should not be employed to build doctrine.

Scriptural Example: Philippians 4:13, "I can do all things through him who strengthens me," is often taken out of context to imply a universal capability, while Paul is specifically referring to contentment in every situation.

3. **Historical Principle**: Interpretation should consider the historical setting and cultural norms of the text.

Scriptural Example: The prohibition against eating pork in Leviticus 11 had specific historical and cultural applications for the Israelites.

4. **Unity Principle**: Scripture interprets Scripture. Clearer passages can illuminate more ambiguous ones.

Scriptural Example: The creation account in Genesis is clarified by other Scriptures, such as Exodus 20:11, which reaffirms a literal six-day creation.

5. **Progressive Revelation Principle**: God's revelation is progressive, meaning earlier texts may be clarified or expanded upon in later books.

Scriptural Example: The concept of the Messiah is progressively revealed from Genesis to Revelation, culminating in the full revelation of Jesus Christ.

6. **Sensus Literalis Principle**: The words should be understood in their literal sense unless the text clearly indicates otherwise.

Scriptural Example: When Jesus declares, "This is my body" (Matthew 26:26), the immediate and broader context shows he was employing metaphorical language.

Tools for Literal Interpretation

1. **Concordances**: Help trace the occurrence and translation of specific words.
2. **Lexicons and Dictionaries**: Provide the meanings, derivations, and usage of biblical words.
3. **Interlinear Bible**: Displays the original languages alongside the English translation, aiding in direct study.
4. **Conservative Commentaries**: These can offer additional insights into the text, although they should not replace direct interaction with Scripture.

Pitfalls to Avoid

1. **Eisegesis**: Reading one's own ideas into the text, rather than extracting the text's actual meaning (exegesis).
2. **Selective Interpretation**: Picking and choosing verses to support a preconceived idea, thereby violating the Unity Principle.
3. **Over-Spiritualizing**: While the Bible contains supernatural elements, not every text has a hidden, spiritual meaning. Attempts to over-spiritualize can distort the intended message.

Literal interpretation serves as a bulwark against the subjective and often misleading methodologies that have marred the field of biblical studies. Adhering to the principles of literal interpretation ensures that the exegete remains anchored to the text, honoring both its human authors and its ultimate divine Author, Jehovah. In turn, this fosters a more profound understanding and application of the Scriptures, enriching both our intellectual grasp and our spiritual lives.

Through this rigorous approach, the objective truth of the Bible is unveiled, allowing believers to stand firm in an age where skepticism and relativism seek to undermine the inerrancy and authority of the Scriptures. It is through such unwavering commitment to the literal interpretation of the Bible that its transformative power is most fully realized, both in individual lives and within the broader community of faith.

YOUR GUIDE FOR DEFENDING THE BIBLE

Case Studies in Conservative Exegesis

Understanding conservative biblical exegesis isn't just about principles; it becomes clearer through concrete examples. This chapter will dissect various passages from the Bible to demonstrate how a conservative, literal interpretation unfolds in practice. These case studies will affirm the authority and inerrancy of Scripture, highlighting the value of the objective historical-grammatical method.

Case Study 1: Creation Account in Genesis

Exegetical Focus: Genesis 1:1 - "In the beginning, God created the heavens and the earth."

Literal Interpretation: This passage does not accommodate the idea of a pre-existing universe or theistic evolution. It affirms that God, referred to as Jehovah in other parts of the Old Testament, is the sole Creator of the heavens and the earth.

Historical Context: The Israelites would have understood this as a direct challenge to the polytheistic creation myths of surrounding cultures.

Grammatical Considerations: The Hebrew verb "bara" (create) is exclusively used with God as the subject, implying an act only He can perform.

Case Study 2: Paul's Statement on Women in Church

Exegetical Focus: 1 Corinthians 14:34 - "The women should keep silent in the churches."

Literal Interpretation: A cursory reading might suggest a universal prohibition against women speaking in church. However, context indicates Paul was addressing a specific issue of disruptive speaking, not creating a general rule for all time.

Historical Context: In first-century Corinth, women were not as educated as men in religious matters, which could have contributed to disorder during church meetings.

Grammatical Considerations: Paul uses a specific Greek word, "sigao," which indicates a kind of silence intended to maintain order.

Case Study 3: The Resurrection Accounts

Exegetical Focus: Matthew 28:1-10, Mark 16:1-8, Luke 24:1-12, and John 20:1-18

Literal Interpretation: These accounts affirm the bodily resurrection of Jesus Christ. Any discrepancies in detail are better understood as complementary, not contradictory.

Historical Context: The resurrection was a direct rebuttal to the Jewish Sanhedrin and Roman authorities, validating Jesus as the Messiah.

Grammatical Considerations: The Greek word "anastasis" is used, signifying a bodily resurrection, not a spiritual or symbolic one.

Case Study 4: The Role of Faith and Works

Exegetical Focus: James 2:17 - "So also faith by itself, if it does not have works, is dead."

Literal Interpretation: James is not contradicting Paul's teachings on faith. Rather, he emphasizes that true faith naturally produces works.

Historical Context: James likely wrote to Jewish Christians who were overemphasizing the role of faith to the neglect of good works.

Grammatical Considerations: The Greek word "nekra," translated as "dead," serves to emphasize the incomplete and ineffective nature of faith without works.

Pitfalls to Avoid in Conservative Exegesis

1. **Cherry-Picking**: Using isolated verses to support a doctrine while ignoring context.
2. **Anachronism**: Inserting modern-day ideas or interpretations into ancient texts.
3. **Cultural Imposition**: Failing to understand the cultural and historical setting in which the text was written, thereby potentially distorting its intended message.

The case studies above are illustrative of how conservative biblical exegesis, anchored in a literal interpretation, is not only faithful to the text but intellectually rigorous. By respecting the grammatical nuances, historical context, and the unity of Scripture, we honor both the human and divine elements of this sacred text.

Conservative exegesis is an antidote to the ideological biases that have infiltrated biblical studies, distorting the message of the Scriptures. It offers a methodological framework grounded in the belief that the Bible is the authoritative, inerrant Word of God, providing a robust defense against the challenges posed by modern skepticism and liberal-moderate biblical criticism.

In an age where the reliability and relevance of the Bible are continually questioned, conservative exegetical methods serve as an indispensable tool for both apologetics and faithful Christian living. These principles and case studies are not merely academic exercises but form the bedrock of a Christian worldview that is rooted in the infallible Word of God.

CHAPTER 4 The History of Higher Criticism—Its Assault on the Bible?

Early Skepticism: Thomas Hobbes (1588-1679)

Thomas Hobbes, a 17th-century English philosopher, is an important figure in the early development of higher criticism, a stream of biblical analysis that has been often critiqued for its liberal-moderate stance and speculative methodologies. His work marked a departure from traditional reverence for the Bible's authority and inerrancy, providing a foundational layer for subsequent scholars who have adopted a skeptical view toward Scripture.

The Intellectual Landscape: From Reformation to Enlightenment

Before delving into Hobbes' contribution to higher criticism, it's crucial to understand the intellectual currents of his time. The Reformation had fractured Christendom, spawning a myriad of interpretations and religious sects. The Enlightenment was in its nascency, emphasizing reason and empirical inquiry. It was against this backdrop that Hobbes propounded his ideas, as outlined primarily in his seminal work "Leviathan."

Hobbes on Scripture: Undermining Authority and Inerrancy

Hobbes questioned the traditional understanding of the Bible in several ways:

1. **Authorship**: He doubted Mosaic authorship of the Pentateuch, for example, a significant departure from both Jewish and Christian tradition. In doing so, he implicitly questioned the reliability of other traditionally attributed biblical authors.

2. **Miracles**: Hobbes was skeptical of supernatural events, considering them incompatible with the natural laws. This is a problematic stance given that miracles like the parting of the Red Sea (Exodus 14:21-22) or Christ's resurrection (Matthew 28:5-6) are integral to the biblical narrative and theological understanding.

3. **Interpretation**: While he did not reject religion outright, Hobbes believed that interpretation should rest with the civil authority. This undermines the personal and communal aspect of studying Scripture, as shown in Acts 17:11, where the Bereans were praised for examining the Scriptures themselves.

Hobbes and Historical Criticism

Though Hobbes was not a biblical scholar, his skeptical approach laid the groundwork for what would eventually evolve into historical criticism, which employs a range of methodologies, including literary criticism, form criticism, and redaction criticism among others. Each of these is deeply flawed for multiple reasons:

1. **Speculative Nature**: These methods are not empirically verifiable and rely heavily on the presuppositions of the scholar.
2. **Devaluation of Scripture**: Higher criticism often discounts the divine element in Scripture, viewing it merely as another piece of ancient literature, thus distancing it from its true, inerrant nature (2 Timothy 3:16).
3. **Subjectivity**: Techniques like form criticism and redaction criticism allow for extreme subjectivity, as interpretations are often filtered through contemporary philosophical or ideological frameworks.

The Fallout: A Warning

Hobbes' influence was a precursor to the undermining of the Bible's authority that escalated in subsequent centuries. With the advent of German higher criticism and the post-Enlightenment skepticism, the field has been inundated with pseudo-scholarly works that have eroded people's confidence in the Bible.

A Conservative Counterpoint

As proponents of the historical-grammatical method, we assert that the most reliable way to understand the Bible is through a literal, context-sensitive approach. We respect both the human and divine elements of the text. Where Hobbes and his intellectual descendants drift into subjectivity and skepticism, the historical-grammatical method seeks objectivity and faithfulness to the text.

Thomas Hobbes, in questioning the traditional views on biblical authorship, miracles, and interpretation, set a precedent that has had far-reaching implications. The methodology he helped to seed—historical criticism—is flawed in its approach and diverges from an understanding of the Bible as the authoritative, inerrant Word of God. It's crucial for Christians today to be aware of these issues as they navigate their own understanding of the Bible, ensuring that they employ methods of interpretation that are both intellectually rigorous and spiritually faithful.

In a world increasingly influenced by skeptical and subjective perspectives on Scripture, it's paramount that believers equip themselves with robust, conservative exegetical methods. Such an approach serves as both an antidote to and a defense against the kinds of critical methods that have led many away from the true understanding of God's Word. By remaining anchored in the historical-grammatical method, we honor the text's inherent complexity while upholding its divine authority.

Rationalism Emerges: Benedict Spinoza (1632-1677)

Benedict Spinoza, a 17th-century Dutch philosopher, was one of the early figures in the evolution of higher criticism and biblical interpretation. He was a rationalist who sought to apply reason to all areas of human life, including religious texts. His work laid some of the intellectual groundwork for the methodologies that would later be grouped under higher criticism.

Background: From Reformation to Enlightenment

The 17th century was a tumultuous period in Europe, with religious, scientific, and philosophical upheavals. The Reformation had challenged the Catholic Church's monopoly on religious interpretation, and the Enlightenment was ushering in a new era of reason and scientific inquiry. Spinoza's life and work should be understood against this backdrop.

Spinoza's Treatise: "Theological-Political Treatise"

In his "Theological-Political Treatise," Spinoza questioned the divine origin and authority of the Bible. This was a radical departure from the views that had been prevalent among Christians, Jews, and Muslims for centuries. Let's examine some of his critiques:

1. **Questioning Authorship**: Spinoza was among the first to challenge the Mosaic authorship of the Pentateuch, long before the emergence of documentary hypothesis. This is problematic because it undermines the textual authority, which is rooted in its divine inspiration (2 Timothy 3:16).

2. **Miracles as Natural Phenomena**: Spinoza believed that what are considered miracles in the Bible are actually natural events that were misunderstood. This directly contradicts Scripture, where miracles serve as signs from God, such as Jesus turning water into wine (John 2:1-11).

3. **Rationalistic Interpretation**: Spinoza applied a rationalistic lens to Scripture, considering anything that didn't conform to reason as

metaphorical or symbolic. This is inconsistent with a historical-grammatical approach, which treats the text as historically accurate and reliable.

The Flaws of Spinoza's Approach

Spinoza's rationalistic approach is deeply problematic for several reasons:

1. **Selective Skepticism**: While applying reason to religious texts, he did not equally scrutinize the assumptions undergirding his own rationalistic philosophy.
2. **Subjective Foundation**: His approach inherently assumes that human reason is the ultimate arbiter of truth, which is inconsistent with the Scriptural claim that God is the ultimate source of all wisdom and knowledge (Proverbs 1:7).
3. **Disrupts Cohesion**: By casting doubt on traditional understandings of the Bible, Spinoza's critique serves to fragment the unity of Scripture. The Bible presents itself as a unified narrative from Genesis to Revelation, each part serving to illuminate the others.

The Legacy of Spinoza and Its Warning

Spinoza's influence was profound and paved the way for future scholars who would employ even more elaborate forms of criticism that deviated further from a conservative, historical-grammatical interpretation of Scripture. His work is part of a larger trend in higher criticism that reduces the Bible to another human document, thereby undermining its unique authority and role in revealing God's will to mankind.

A Conservative Counterpoint

The historical-grammatical method stands in stark contrast to the rationalism of Spinoza and subsequent higher critics. This method preserves the Bible's inherent divine authority, treating it as both historically reliable and theologically relevant. We acknowledge the dual human and divine authorship of the Bible, considering the historical and grammatical context to interpret it responsibly.

Benedict Spinoza was a pivotal figure in the trajectory that led to modern higher criticism. His rationalistic approach to Scripture introduced assumptions that are fundamentally at odds with a conservative, historical-grammatical method of interpretation. His work serves as a cautionary example of how one's presuppositions can significantly influence biblical interpretation.

In a world that increasingly leans toward skepticism and subjectivity in treating Scripture, it is imperative for believers to ground themselves in conservative exegetical methods. These methods are not merely academic exercises but are crucial for maintaining the authority and inerrancy of Scripture as the Word of God. The historical-grammatical approach allows us to engage the Bible in a manner that honors its complexity, cultural background, and divine inspiration, enabling us to glean the truths God has intended for us.

The Birth of Source Criticism: Jean Astruc (1684-1766)

Jean Astruc, a French physician and professor, is often credited with laying the foundation of modern Source Criticism of the Bible, particularly the Pentateuch. Although he intended to defend the Mosaic authorship of the Pentateuch, his work would later be used to undermine it.

Intellectual Climate of the 18th Century

The Enlightenment era was marked by a shift from reliance on faith and tradition to the prioritization of reason and empirical observation. During this period, scholars, influenced by the scientific revolution, began to employ a more critical approach to texts, including religious texts. This context makes the emergence of Astruc's ideas less surprising.

Astruc's Contribution: Conjectures sur les mémoires originaux

In his 1753 work "Conjectures sur les mémoires originaux, dont il parait que Moyse s'est servi pour composer le livre de la Genèse" (Conjectures on the Original Documents that Moses Appears to Have Used in Composing the Book of Genesis), Astruc sought to explain variations in the Pentateuch. He divided the text into columns based on the use of divine names—Jehovah and Elohim. He surmised that Moses used two distinct sources, which he combined to produce the Pentateuch.

Flaws and Problematic Implications

1. **Shifting Focus from Divine Inspiration**: By focusing on "sources," Astruc inadvertently moved the conversation away from the traditional belief that the Pentateuch was divinely inspired. This contradicts Scriptures like 2 Peter 1:21, which states, "For no prophecy was ever produced by the will of man, but men spoke from God as they were carried along by the Holy Spirit."

2. **Undermining Scriptural Cohesion**: Astruc's theories encourage viewing the Bible as a composite document stitched together from various sources, rather than a cohesive revelation. This counters the holistic nature of Scripture where "All Scripture is breathed out by God and profitable for

teaching, for reproof, for correction, and for training in righteousness" (2 Timothy 3:16).

3. **Leeway for Further Speculations**: Astruc's foundational work opened the floodgates for later, more radical scholars to speculate wildly about Biblical origins. This led to the Documentary Hypothesis and its successors, which question the Bible's historical accuracy and integrity.

4. **Subjective Interpretations**: Astruc's method does not employ a conservative historical-grammatical method, and thus becomes a tool for subjective interpretations, contrary to a conservative viewpoint that views the Scripture as the inerrant word of God.

Counterpoint: The Historical-Grammatical Method

The historical-grammatical method, as a conservative approach to biblical interpretation, rejects speculative theories that divert from treating the Bible as a divinely inspired text. By focusing on the language, culture, and historical context in which the Bible was written, this method allows for a more faithful interpretation of the Scriptures. A textual phenomenon, like the use of different names for God, can be understood as a stylistic choice, without necessitating a fractured view of Scriptural authorship or inspiration.

Legacy of Astruc: A Cautionary Tale

Though Astruc may not have intended to undermine the Bible, his methodology paved the way for critical scholars to cast doubt on the Bible's historical and divine authority. Source Criticism has led many to a fragmented and skeptical view of the Bible, and by extension, has eroded faith in its Divine message.

Jean Astruc's influence is monumental, not because he solved any particular puzzle about the Bible, but because he popularized a method that led to sweeping changes in how the Bible was studied. His methods stand in stark contrast to the historical-grammatical method, which focuses on historical context and grammar to understand the Scriptures faithfully. The pitfalls of Astruc's approach serve as a warning for scholars and believers alike, emphasizing the need for a methodologically sound and faithful approach to studying the Bible. It underscores the importance of adhering to exegetical methods that honor the integrity, cohesion, and divine inspiration of Scripture. In doing so, we preserve the authority and reliability of the Bible as God's inerrant Word.

Reformed Opposition: Jean Alphonse Turretin (1671-1737)

Jean Alphonse Turretin, a Swiss-Italian Reformed scholastic theologian, represents a beacon of orthodoxy during an era increasingly enthralled by Enlightenment ideals. At a time when figures like Jean Astruc began to delve into Source Criticism, Turretin staunchly defended the integrity, inerrancy, and unity of Scripture.

Background and Context

Turretin hailed from a family well-entrenched in the world of Reformed Protestant theology. His father, Francis Turretin, was also a renowned theologian. Coming of age during the Enlightenment, Turretin found himself amidst a sweeping intellectual climate that challenged the foundations of Christian orthodoxy. The Enlightenment's emphasis on human reason over divine revelation presented a particular challenge to the authority of Scripture.

Theological Positions

Turretin's approach could be best described as scholastic, focused on structured theological arguments grounded in Scripture. His work defended the unity of Scripture against attacks that portrayed it as a disparate compilation of texts. Turretin maintained that the Bible's consistency is a testimony to its divine origin. He emphasized that "all Scripture is breathed out by God and profitable for teaching, for reproof, for correction, and for training in righteousness" (2 Timothy 3:16, ESV).

Response to Higher Criticism

1. **Defense of Mosaic Authorship**: Turretin defended the traditional view that Moses was the author of the Pentateuch. He argued that the linguistic and stylistic unity of these books pointed towards a single author rather than a compilation of sources. This approach aligns with the historical-grammatical method, which emphasizes the original languages, history, and literary forms.

2. **Rejection of Subjectivity**: Turretin criticized approaches that subordinated Scripture to human reason, rejecting the speculation and subjectivity that characterized Higher Criticism. He viewed the rise of such methods as harmful, being inconsistent with a biblically rooted worldview.

3. **Scriptural Integrity**: Turretin argued that the Bible should be read as a unified, coherent text, divinely inspired and preserved across centuries. He emphasized the divine qualities of Scripture, as echoed in passages like 2

Peter 1:21, which states, "For no prophecy was ever produced by the will of man, but men spoke from God as they were carried along by the Holy Spirit."

Influence on Reformed Thought

Turretin's work was highly influential among Reformed theologians and continues to be studied today as a seminal text on Reformed dogmatics. His theological stances offer a robust counter-argument to the emergent critical approaches of his time.

Legacy: The Necessity of Guarding Orthodoxy

Turretin's life and work serve as a poignant reminder of the ongoing necessity to defend the inerrancy and integrity of Scripture. He showcases the viability of an exegetical method that does not compromise on these essential aspects of biblical theology. In doing so, he stood against the tide of Enlightenment skepticism that questioned the divine origins of the Bible.

The emergence of figures like Jean Alphonse Turretin serves as a reminder that opposition to Higher Criticism and its associated methods is not a modern phenomenon but has historical roots. Turretin set a benchmark for how to engage critically yet faithfully with the Bible. His staunch defense of the divine authority, unity, and inerrancy of Scripture provides a robust framework for modern Christians to understand and engage the Bible. He remains a pertinent voice in discussions surrounding the Bible's integrity, emphasizing that Scripture, when approached from a position of faith, retains its unity and coherence. In a climate increasingly skeptical of the Bible's divine origin, Turretin serves as a valuable reference point for defending the traditional, conservative understanding of Scripture. His work stands as an enduring example of the importance of upholding exegetical and theological standards grounded in a commitment to the authority of God's Word.

Rational Interpretation: Heinrich Paulus (1761-1851)

Heinrich Paulus, a German theologian and orientalist, is a significant figure in the development of Higher Criticism, particularly for his attempts to harmonize biblical narratives with rational explanations. While he claimed to uphold the truth of Scripture, his approach significantly altered the fabric of traditional exegesis, veering into rationalism.

Background and Context

Paulus emerged at the intersection of Enlightenment rationalism and burgeoning biblical criticism. He was a professor at multiple institutions and gained notoriety for his controversial views on miracles, which he sought to explain using natural phenomena.

Theological Orientation

Paulus did not deny the occurrence of miracles per se but argued that they could be rationalized. For instance, he suggested that Jesus walking on water (Matthew 14:22-33) might have involved shallow terrain. Such a stance effectively nullifies the supernatural elements of the biblical accounts, undermining their purpose and meaning.

Rational Interpretation vs. Historical-Grammatical Method

1. **Miracles and Rational Explanations**: Paulus' attempt to rationalize miracles infringes on the notion of divine intervention. In contrast, the historical-grammatical method upholds that miracles are real acts of God, with no need for rational explanation. They serve a purpose, whether it's to affirm the authority of Christ or to fulfill God's promises (John 20:30-31).

2. **Cherry-picking Scripture**: Paulus' rational interpretation often resorted to selective readings of biblical texts. This undermines the holistic understanding of Scripture as divinely inspired and interconnected, as highlighted in 2 Timothy 3:16.

3. **Subverting Authorial Intent**: By focusing on rational explanations, Paulus' method disrespects the original authors' intent and context. The historical-grammatical method emphasizes understanding the original languages, culture, and circumstances surrounding a text, as evidenced in Acts 17:11, where the Bereans examined the Scriptures to confirm Paul's teachings.

4. **Impact on Christology**: Rationalizing miracles poses critical threats to the doctrines concerning the person and work of Christ. The historical-grammatical method maintains the dual nature of Christ as both fully human and fully divine (Colossians 2:9).

Impact on Biblical Studies and Repercussions

1. **Erosion of Supernatural Elements**: Paulus' approach led many to doubt the supernatural aspects of Scripture, thus weakening the perception of its divine origins.

2. **Undermining Inerrancy**: The rationalistic approach fosters an environment where Scripture's inerrancy can be easily challenged. This is contrary to Proverbs 30:5, which declares that "Every word of God proves true."

3. **Diverting from Faith**: Rational interpretations deter readers from approaching Scripture in a posture of faith. Hebrews 11:1 defines faith as "the assurance of things hoped for, the conviction of things not seen," a concept that becomes irrelevant if miracles are rationalized.

Heinrich Paulus stands as a cautionary figure. His methods, built on rationalism and speculation, have long-lasting implications that still reverberate in theological circles. While he did not deny the importance of Scripture, his approach dangerously blurred the lines between human reason and divine revelation. The rational interpretation method effectively diminishes the authority, inerrancy, and supernatural elements of the Bible, thereby distancing it from its original, divine intention.

In contrast, the historical-grammatical method upholds the integrity and divinely inspired nature of Scripture. It strives to understand the Bible within its historical and grammatical context, respecting the authorial intent and the overarching narrative of God's revelation to humanity. This method aligns with the principle that Scripture is God-breathed and serves to equip the believer for every good work (2 Timothy 3:17). As such, the historical-grammatical approach not only preserves the doctrinal integrity of the Bible but also fortifies the believer's faith in its divine authority. It is imperative, therefore, that scholars and believers alike remain vigilant against methodologies that compromise these foundational truths.

The Historical-Critical Method: Johann Salomo Semler (1725-1791)

Johann Salomo Semler is a seminal figure in the history of biblical criticism, particularly known for his development and promotion of the historical-critical method. Born in Germany during the Enlightenment, Semler's work represented a departure from traditional biblical exegesis and paved the way for modern critical scholarship. Although Semler considered himself a defender of Christianity, his methodology has been seen as corrosive to the foundational tenets of Scripture.

Semler's Contributions and Methodology

Semler advocated for the demarcation of "canon within the canon," essentially arguing that some books of the Bible hold greater doctrinal authority than others. His historical-critical method aimed to study Scripture through the lens of history, focusing on the text's origins, the historical context, and the intent of the authors.

Problems and Critique

1. **Canon Within a Canon**: Semler's notion of a "canon within the canon" contradicts the traditional Christian belief that all Scripture is divinely inspired and useful for teaching, rebuking, correcting, and training in righteousness (2 Timothy 3:16).

2. **Neglect of Divine Inspiration**: By prioritizing historical context over divine inspiration, Semler undermines the authoritative nature of Scripture. This is at odds with passages like 2 Peter 1:21, which states, "For no prophecy was ever produced by the will of man, but men spoke from God as they were carried along by the Holy Spirit."

3. **Historical Reconstruction Over Authorial Intent**: Semler's methodology often sacrifices the original meaning of the text in favor of reconstructing the historical context. This is misaligned with the objective historical-grammatical approach, which takes into account the historical setting but upholds the author's intent as a guiding principle.

4. **Speculative Interpretation**: The historical-critical method is prone to speculative conclusions, often lacking concrete evidence. This has the dangerous potential of leading scholars away from the truth. The Bereans, as cited in Acts 17:11, are exemplars of scrutinizing Scripture to discern truth.

5. **Erosion of Faith**: The historical-critical method can lead to an erosion of faith, as it often questions the veracity and inerrancy of the Bible. Hebrews 11:1 defines faith as "the assurance of things hoped for, the conviction of things not seen," a concept difficult to maintain when the Bible's authority is undermined.

The Historical-Critical Method vs. the Historical-Grammatical Method

1. **Objective vs. Subjective**: While the historical-critical method often involves a subjective reinterpretation of the text, the historical-grammatical method relies on objective facts and aims for a straightforward interpretation of the text based on its grammatical and historical context.

2. **Authority of Scripture**: The historical-grammatical method upholds the divine inspiration and inerrancy of the Bible, consistent with the conviction that every word of God is flawless (Proverbs 30:5).

3. **Sola Scriptura**: The historical-grammatical method aligns with the Reformation principle of *Sola Scriptura*, affirming Scripture alone as the ultimate authority for faith and practice. This stands in stark contrast to the

historical-critical method's tendency to give equal or greater weight to extra-biblical sources and human reasoning.

Johann Salomo Semler, despite his intentions, played a significant role in steering biblical interpretation down a path that has been damaging to the authority and integrity of Scripture. The historical-critical method, although presented as an academic and objective approach, is deeply flawed, tending to inject human bias and speculative thinking into the exegesis of the Bible. By contrast, the historical-grammatical method seeks to honor the divine inspiration of the text, respecting its historical and grammatical context while avoiding speculative conclusions. This method is crucial for preserving the Bible's integrity, serving as a bulwark against the ideological trends that have infiltrated modern biblical scholarship.

The Challenge of Deism: Matthew Tindal (1657-1733)

Matthew Tindal, a prominent English deist, made a significant impact on the realm of biblical criticism during the Enlightenment period. His work, primarily his controversial book *Christianity as Old as the Creation*, aimed to show that natural religion was sufficient for man's moral and spiritual needs. This represented an ideological shift away from recognizing the authority and divine inspiration of Scripture, thereby posing a considerable challenge to orthodox Christianity.

Tindal's Deistic Views

Deism argues that God can be known through reason and the natural world, making divine revelation through Scripture unnecessary. Tindal was a significant proponent of this view. He asserted that natural religion, discerned through reason, was in essence the "religion of mankind," making the Bible secondary, if not irrelevant.

Theological and Scriptural Implications

1. **Denial of Special Revelation**: Tindal's deistic philosophy implicitly denies the importance of special revelation. This is problematic as the Bible itself claims to be divinely inspired and useful for "teaching, for reproof, for correction, and for training in righteousness" (2 Timothy 3:16, ESV).
2. **Dismissal of Christ's Unique Role**: The New Testament emphasizes the unique and exclusive role of Christ in redemption (Acts 4:12; John 14:6). Deism, including Tindal's version, negates this, suggesting that man can attain morality and possibly salvation through reason alone.

3. **Erosion of Biblical Authority**: By elevating natural religion and reason over the Bible, Tindal's deistic views undermine the authority of Scripture, which contradicts biblical assertions like, "The fear of Jehovah is the beginning of knowledge" (Proverbs 1:7).

Critique and Problems with Tindal's Approach

1. **Subjectivity of Human Reason**: Deism places immense trust in human reason, but the Bible warns that "the heart is deceitful above all things" (Jeremiah 17:9). Human reason is flawed and cannot replace divine wisdom.
2. **Disregard for the Fall**: Tindal's deistic view does not account for the Fall of man in Genesis 3, which led to a broken relationship with God. This relationship can only be restored through divine intervention, as illustrated through Christ's atoning sacrifice (Romans 5:8).
3. **Selective Reading of Scripture**: By picking and choosing portions of the Bible that seem to align with his deistic views, Tindal engaged in a sort of "canon within a canon," undermining the integrity of the entire biblical narrative.

The Historical-Grammatical Method as a Response

1. **Scriptural Primacy**: This method upholds the primacy of the Bible as divinely inspired, authoritative, and inerrant, in contrast to Tindal's undermining of Scriptural importance.
2. **Objective Analysis**: The historical-grammatical method provides a balanced and objective approach to interpreting Scripture. Unlike deism, which is influenced by the subjectivity of human reason, this method remains grounded in the text.
3. **Preservation of Biblical Theology**: An objective historical-grammatical approach preserves key theological tenets such as the necessity of grace, the unique role of Christ, and the significance of faith, all of which are diluted or dismissed in Tindal's deistic framework.

Matthew Tindal's deistic approach to religion has contributed to the erosion of biblical authority, placing human reason above divine revelation. While Tindal claims to uphold morality and reason, his approach contradicts vital aspects of the biblical worldview, notably the need for special revelation and the unique role of Christ in redemption. The historical-grammatical method of interpretation, on the other hand, safeguards against such erosion by upholding the primacy, integrity, and inerrancy of Scripture. By doing so, it offers a robust response to the challenges posed by deistic thought, championing the Bible's unique role in providing comprehensive moral and spiritual guidance.

The Quest for the Historical Jesus: Hermann Samuel Reimarus (1694-1768)

Hermann Samuel Reimarus, a German philosopher and writer, made significant contributions to the field of biblical criticism through his posthumously published work known as the "Wolfenbüttel Fragments." He is renowned for his "Quest for the Historical Jesus," a movement aiming to separate the "historical Jesus" from the "Christ of faith." His approach, deeply rooted in Enlightenment skepticism, sought to extract a historical figure from the New Testament apart from any divine attributes or miraculous events. This chapter critically evaluates Reimarus's methodology and its subsequent implications for biblical interpretation and theology.

Reimarus's Position on Jesus

Reimarus contended that the Jesus found in the Gospels is largely a creation of his disciples. According to him, Jesus was a Jewish revolutionary, not the divine Messiah. His disciples, dismayed by his crucifixion, allegedly created a theological construct to continue their movement.

Theological and Scriptural Implications

1. **Denial of Divine Christology**: Reimarus's work stands in stark contrast to clear New Testament affirmations of Jesus's divinity (John 1:1, Philippians 2:5-11).

2. **Undermining the Resurrection**: If Jesus was merely a political revolutionary, the cornerstone of Christian faith—the resurrection—loses all validity (1 Corinthians 15:14).

3. **Questioning Scriptural Inerrancy**: Reimarus's work implies that the Gospel writers were not reliable witnesses but rather constructors of a myth. This contradicts claims like Peter's in 2 Peter 1:16, which affirm that the apostolic witness is not "cleverly devised myths."

Critique and Problems with Reimarus's Approach

1. **Ignoring Historical Context**: Reimarus neglected the historical context in which the Gospels were written. The willingness of the disciples to die for their belief in the resurrected Jesus strongly argues against the notion that they fabricated these events (Acts 7:59-60; 12:2).

2. **Presuppositional Bias**: Reimarus started his inquiry with a naturalistic bias, excluding any possibility of the miraculous, a priori. This is inconsistent with an open and balanced approach to historical inquiry.
3. **Selective Skepticism**: He accepted some historical elements of the New Testament while rejecting others, without a consistent method for these choices.

The Historical-Grammatical Method as a Response

1. **Scriptural Integrity**: By respecting the coherence and unity of Scripture, the historical-grammatical method opposes Reimarus's fragmented approach. It asserts that Scripture is not a collection of myths but is divinely inspired and inerrant (2 Timothy 3:16).
2. **Objective Criteria**: This method relies on historical and grammatical criteria for interpretation, rather than personal or ideological biases. It insists on interpreting the text within its original linguistic, historical, and literary context.
3. **Consistency with Apostolic Teaching**: An objective exegesis guided by the historical-grammatical method aligns with apostolic teachings about Christ's life, death, and resurrection (1 Corinthians 15:3-8).

Hermann Samuel Reimarus's quest for the historical Jesus constitutes a significant episode in the history of higher criticism, one that has left an enduring impact. However, his methodology is marred by ideological bias, inconsistent application, and a disregard for the integrity of the New Testament. The historical-grammatical method, by contrast, offers an exegetical approach that upholds the authority, unity, and inerrancy of Scripture. This method affirms the Jesus of history as the Christ of faith, countering Reimarus's skeptical assertions. By adhering to sound exegetical principles, we can confidently reject the speculative approaches that have led many astray, reaffirming our trust in the coherent and divinely inspired account of Jesus Christ as presented in the New Testament.

Old Testament Criticism: Johann David Michaelis (1717-1791)

Johann David Michaelis, a German biblical scholar of the 18th century, is known for his application of critical methodologies to the Old Testament. Although he was a skilled Hebraist, Michaelis introduced a form of higher criticism into Old Testament studies that challenges the traditional understanding of the text. This chapter aims to scrutinize his approach and its implications for Scriptural interpretation.

Michaelis's Methodology and Theories

Michaelis was heavily influenced by the Enlightenment's rationalistic and humanistic tendencies. His work, "Introduction to the New Testament," ironically focused heavily on the Old Testament as well. He approached the Old Testament with a presupposition of questioning the Mosaic authorship of the Pentateuch and probing the historicity of the Hebrew Bible. This method of higher criticism seeks to dissect the text, searching for inconsistencies and redactions to formulate theories about its origins.

Theological and Scriptural Implications

1. **Questioning Mosaic Authorship**: Michaelis was skeptical of the traditional belief that Moses wrote the Pentateuch. This clashes with the testimony of Scripture itself, where Moses is often cited as the lawgiver and author (Exodus 17:14, Deuteronomy 31:9-11).

2. **Challenging Prophecy and Historicity**: He questioned the prophetic elements and historical details in the Old Testament, negating claims like those found in Isaiah 53 about the coming Messiah.

3. **Indirect Challenge to New Testament**: By undermining the Old Testament, Michaelis indirectly challenged the New Testament authors who quote and rely on it, including Jesus Christ Himself (Matthew 5:17-18).

Critique and Problems with Michaelis's Approach

1. **Ignoring Apostolic Testimony**: Apostles like Peter affirmed the prophetic origin of the Old Testament (2 Peter 1:20-21). Ignoring this amounts to an affront to apostolic authority.

2. **Presuppositional Bias**: Michaelis employed Enlightenment rationalism as his starting point, dismissing the possibility of the supernatural or divine inspiration (2 Timothy 3:16).

3. **Selective Use of Data**: Michaelis's approach often involved picking and choosing which data to consider, a method that is inherently subjective and inconsistent.

4. **Undermining Unity of Scripture**: His methodology risks fracturing the Old and New Testaments, despite the fact that both Testaments are parts of one cohesive revelation (Luke 24:27).

The Historical-Grammatical Method as a Response

1. **Commitment to Authorial Intent**: By focusing on what the original authors, inspired by God, intended to convey, this method ensures a more faithful interpretation (2 Peter 1:20-21).

2. **Contextual Analysis**: This method insists that passages should be interpreted in their immediate, book, and even biblical context, offering a more robust understanding of Scripture.

3. **Apologetic Value**: This method can defend the reliability and inerrancy of Scripture, serving as an antidote to the skepticism fostered by higher criticism.

Johann David Michaelis's contributions to higher criticism have lasting implications for how the Old Testament is viewed and studied. However, his approach is fraught with inconsistencies, subjective choices, and presuppositions that are foreign to the text. The historical-grammatical method, grounded in an unwavering commitment to the authority and inerrancy of Scripture, offers a more reliable alternative for interpreting the Old Testament. It respects the text's original context, upholds its divine origin, and maintains the unity and coherence of Scripture. By adhering to this method, we can better appreciate the richness of the Old Testament and its consistent testimony to the same God revealed in the New Testament. This commitment to a more objective form of analysis serves as a safeguard against the pitfalls of higher criticism and helps to restore confidence in the Scriptures as the inspired Word of God.

Broadening Scope: Johann Gottfried Eichhorn (1752-1827)

Johann Gottfried Eichhorn stands as a significant figure in the history of higher criticism of the Bible, building upon the work of predecessors like Johann David Michaelis. A product of his time, Eichhorn was heavily influenced by the Enlightenment period's rationalism and skepticism, which left a lasting imprint on biblical studies. This chapter aims to elucidate Eichhorn's methodologies, theories, and their impact on the study of the Bible.

Eichhorn's Methodology and Theories

Eichhorn was one of the first scholars to systematically apply historical criticism to both the Old and New Testaments. His work is often seen as a precursor to more liberal forms of criticism, including source criticism and form criticism.

1. **Divisive Authorship**: Eichhorn was instrumental in popularizing the Documentary Hypothesis, questioning the traditional understanding that

Moses authored the Pentateuch. This directly contradicts passages like Deuteronomy 31:24-26, where Moses is explicitly credited with writing the Law.

2. **Mythologizing Miracles**: He also scrutinized the miraculous events described in the Bible, such as the parting of the Red Sea, effectively relegating them to the realm of myths. This stance undermines texts like Exodus 14:21-31, where the parting of the sea is clearly attributed to God's intervention.

Theological and Scriptural Implications

1. **Undermining Prophetic Fulfillment**: Eichhorn's critical approach disrupts the concept of prophetic fulfillment. Passages like Isaiah 53, cited in the New Testament as prophecies fulfilled by Christ (Acts 8:30-35), are delegitimized by his methodology.
2. **Straining New Testament Credibility**: By casting doubt on Old Testament texts, Eichhorn indirectly questions the authority and reliability of the New Testament authors who often cited them (e.g., Matthew 22:29-32).

Critique and Shortcomings of Eichhorn's Approach

1. **Presuppositions**: One of the most glaring issues with Eichhorn's methodology is his a priori rejection of divine intervention or inspiration (2 Timothy 3:16-17). His perspective starts with human reasoning and does not leave room for the supernatural.
2. **Bias Toward Rationalism**: Eichhorn's approach is strongly rooted in Enlightenment rationalism, ignoring the nuances and spiritual dimensions of the texts. This leads to a reductionist and human-centric interpretation of the Bible.
3. **Loss of Coherence**: By dissecting the Bible into various sources and redactions, the sense of a unified, divinely-inspired message becomes fragmented (2 Peter 1:20-21).
4. **Lack of Objectivity**: Despite claims of scientific rigor, Eichhorn's methodology is plagued by subjectivity, rooted more in the Zeitgeist of his era than in the text itself.

Historical-Grammatical Method as an Alternative

1. **Textual Integrity**: The historical-grammatical method upholds the integrity of the Bible as a unified, coherent work. This stands in contrast to Eichhorn's fragmented perspective.

2. **Respect for Inspiration**: While Eichhorn dismisses the idea of divine inspiration, the historical-grammatical method maintains it as a central tenet (2 Timothy 3:16-17).

3. **Objective Exegesis**: By focusing on the literal, historical, and grammatical aspects of the text, this method avoids the pitfalls of subjectivity inherent in higher criticism.

4. **Cohesion with New Testament**: This method allows for a seamless integration of Old and New Testament texts, appreciating the way the New Testament builds upon and fulfills the Old (Matthew 5:17-18).

Johann Gottfried Eichhorn's work represents a significant landmark in the field of higher criticism, one that broadened its scope and deepened its skepticism. While intellectually rigorous, his approach suffers from a range of deficiencies, including unexamined presuppositions, inherent subjectivity, and an undermining of Scriptural unity and authority. In contrast, the historical-grammatical method provides a more faithful and consistent approach to biblical interpretation. It takes into account the text's historical and grammatical contexts while recognizing its divine inspiration, thereby upholding the integrity and authority of the Bible. Consequently, it serves as a reliable counterpoint to the speculative and divisive methodologies introduced by Eichhorn and his successors.

Methodological Foundations: Johann Philipp Gabler (1753-1826)

Johann Philipp Gabler, a German Protestant theologian, was an influential figure in the field of higher criticism. He is best known for his bifurcation between "biblical theology" and "dogmatic theology," which laid the groundwork for the development of the historical-critical method. While Gabler's ideas were innovative and captured the zeitgeist of his era, they have led to a range of interpretive problems and have contributed to undermining the authority and integrity of Scripture.

Gabler's Methodology and Theories

Gabler sought to differentiate between what the Bible said in its historical context ("biblical theology") and the Church's interpretive or confessional stances ("dogmatic theology"). This separation was ostensibly aimed at purifying each area of study from the influence of the other. However, in effect, it led to several problematic outcomes:

1. **Introduction of Subjectivity**: Gabler's division opened the door to subjective approaches that emphasize the Bible as a mere product of human history. This stands in stark contrast to the view that "all Scripture is breathed out by God and profitable for teaching, for reproof, for correction, and for training in righteousness" (2 Timothy 3:16, ESV).

2. **Relativization of Doctrine**: By separating "biblical theology" from "dogmatic theology," Gabler paved the way for the idea that doctrines are not absolute but are subject to historical and cultural contexts.

Theological and Scriptural Implications

1. **Dissolution of Unity**: Gabler's methodology risks diluting the unified message of Scripture. The Bible asserts its own unity, as seen in passages like 2 Peter 1:20-21, which emphasizes that no prophecy of Scripture comes from someone's own interpretation.

2. **Erosion of Authority**: If biblical statements are merely culturally or historically conditioned, then their normative or authoritative role for the Church today becomes questioned. This runs contrary to Christ's assertion that "Scripture cannot be broken" (John 10:35, ESV).

Critique and Shortcomings of Gabler's Approach

1. **Historical Disconnect**: Gabler's bifurcation ignores the historical reality that dogmatic theology has often been rooted in biblical theology. The early Church Fathers and Reformers did not treat these as isolated fields but saw them as integrally connected.

2. **Suppression of Divine Inspiration**: Gabler's method does not adequately account for divine inspiration, a central tenet of the Bible. He marginalizes the work of the Holy Spirit in the development of both the Old and New Testaments.

3. **Intellectual Hubris**: There is a certain arrogance in believing that one can wholly separate the 'historical' from the 'theological' given that the Bible itself never makes this division. This directly challenges Paul's admonition to "rightly handle the word of truth" (2 Timothy 2:15, ESV).

4. **Selective Skepticism**: Gabler's methodology is suspicious of religious or doctrinal constructs but often fails to scrutinize its own philosophical underpinnings, such as Enlightenment rationalism or German Idealism.

The Historical-Grammatical Method as an Alternative

1. **Preservation of Unity**: This method sees the Bible as a unified, coherent narrative that includes historical events, laws, poetry, and prophecies, all contributing to a single divine plan.
2. **Acknowledgment of Divine Agency**: Unlike Gabler's approach, the historical-grammatical method acknowledges the role of divine inspiration in the text, holding to the Pauline affirmation that "all Scripture is breathed out by God" (2 Timothy 3:16, ESV).
3. **Objective Exegesis**: The historical-grammatical method aims for an objective interpretation based on the historical and grammatical context, thereby avoiding the pitfalls of subjectivity.
4. **Safeguarding Doctrine**: This method allows for the development of sound doctrine based on a reliable understanding of Scripture, conforming to the biblical admonition to hold "the pattern of sound words" (2 Timothy 1:13, ESV).

Johann Philipp Gabler played a pivotal role in shaping the terrain of modern biblical studies, but his methodology has led to a fragmentation and relativization of Scriptural interpretation. As a result, it has fostered skepticism and subjectivity, undermining the authority, unity, and divine inspiration of the Bible. In contrast, the historical-grammatical method seeks to respect the Bible's own self-claims and its historic doctrinal formulations, thereby upholding its integrity and authority. This method serves as a corrective lens, refocusing our attention on the objective truths that Scripture conveys, unmuddied by the subjective biases that have infiltrated biblical studies through methodologies like Gabler's.

Grammatical-Historical Method: Georg Lorenz Bauer (1755-1806)

Georg Lorenz Bauer was an 18th-century German scholar who significantly contributed to the development of the grammatical-historical method of biblical exegesis. This method stands in contrast to the subjective and often speculative methodologies found in higher criticism, advocating for a more objective approach grounded in the text's historical and grammatical context. While Bauer's contributions have been lesser-known compared to others like Johann Philipp Gabler, his methodology aligns more closely with conservative approaches to biblical interpretation.

Bauer's Methodological Contributions

1. **Emphasis on Language**: Bauer stressed the importance of understanding the original languages of Scripture. He believed that a strong grasp of Hebrew and Greek was essential for interpreting the Bible. This insistence aligns with the Apostle Paul's exhortation to Timothy to "rightly handle the word of truth" (2 Timothy 2:15, ESV).
2. **Contextual Analysis**: Bauer encouraged studying the historical and cultural contexts in which the biblical texts were written. This harmonizes with the historical narratives and epistles in Scripture, which were penned within specific cultural and historical frameworks.
3. **Importance of Grammar**: Bauer argued that understanding the syntax and grammar of the original texts is crucial for accurate interpretation. This is consistent with the fact that the Bible itself employs various literary forms such as poetry, narrative, and apocalyptic literature, each with its unique grammatical rules.

Theological and Scriptural Implications

1. **Upholding Inerrancy and Authority**: Bauer's method lends itself to a high view of Scripture, affirming Paul's statement that "all Scripture is breathed out by God and profitable for teaching, for reproof, for correction, and for training in righteousness" (2 Timothy 3:16, ESV).
2. **Objectivity**: Unlike the subjective interpretations often found in higher criticism, the grammatical-historical method emphasizes objectivity. This aligns with the biblical ideal of "letting Scripture interpret Scripture," thereby removing personal biases from the interpretation.
3. **Unity of Scripture**: Bauer's methodology contributes to understanding the Bible as a unified whole. For instance, the New Testament often quotes and interprets the Old Testament, showing that both Testaments are part of a single, divine narrative.

Advantages and Strengths of Bauer's Approach

1. **Avoidance of Eisegesis**: Bauer's method discourages reading one's own ideas into the text, thus avoiding eisegesis. For example, when Jesus states, "It is written, 'Man shall not live by bread alone, but by every word that comes from the mouth of God'" (Matthew 4:4, ESV), the grammatical-historical method insists on understanding this in its broader biblical and historical context.

2. **Honoring the Author's Intent**: By focusing on the text's original meaning within its historical and grammatical context, this method honors the intent of the human and Divine Author.
3. **Accessible to the Layperson**: While understanding the original languages is beneficial, the grammatical-historical method also enables those without such expertise to engage deeply with Scripture.

Critique and Limitations

1. **Potential for Over-Literalism**: While the method emphasizes a literal interpretation, care must be taken not to ignore idiomatic expressions or figures of speech present in the original languages.
2. **Limited Cultural Insight**: Even though Bauer emphasized historical context, his own cultural and historical setting could have potentially influenced his methodology. However, this is a minor point and does not significantly undermine the approach.

Georg Lorenz Bauer stands as an important figure in the development of the grammatical-historical method, an approach that aligns with conservative principles of biblical interpretation. By emphasizing the importance of language, context, and grammar, Bauer's methodology encourages a more disciplined and objective approach to biblical exegesis. This allows for the authority and inerrancy of Scripture to be upheld while enabling a deep and rich understanding of the text. In a landscape often dominated by subjective and speculative methodologies, the grammatical-historical method serves as a robust alternative, one deeply grounded in the objective realities of the biblical text. It is, therefore, an invaluable tool for those committed to upholding the integrity, unity, and divine inspiration of Scripture.

Tubingen School: Ferdinand Christian Baur (1792-1860)

Ferdinand Christian Baur, a key figure in the Tübingen School of theology in Germany, was instrumental in the development of the historical-critical method of biblical interpretation. Unlike the grammatical-historical method, which seeks to uphold the authority and inerrancy of the Bible, Baur's approach has been identified as a facet of Higher Criticism, which is known for its speculative and often subjective methodologies. His work, therefore, provides an important backdrop for understanding the historical evolution of biblical criticism that diverges from conservative approaches to Scripture.

Baur's Methodological Assumptions

1. **Dialectical Development**: Baur applied Hegelian dialectics to his study of early Christianity. He posited that Pauline and Petrine schools of thought represented the thesis and antithesis, with early Catholicism as the synthesis. This speculative method is inconsistent with the New Testament's portrayal of unity among the apostles (Ephesians 4:1–6; Acts 15).

2. **Late Dating**: Baur proposed late dating for many New Testament books, questioning their apostolic authorship. This undermines Paul's warning about the importance of apostolic tradition (2 Thessalonians 2:15).

3. **Historical Skepticism**: Baur doubted the historical reliability of several biblical books. This conflicts with Luke's emphasis on the historical accuracy of his Gospel (Luke 1:1–4).

Theological and Scriptural Implications

1. **Questioning Inerrancy and Authority**: Baur's methodology necessarily calls into question the Bible's inerrancy and authority. This contradicts the principle that "all Scripture is breathed out by God and profitable for teaching, for reproof, for correction, and for training in righteousness" (2 Timothy 3:16, ESV).

2. **Divisiveness**: By pitting Pauline and Petrine traditions against each other, Baur's method encourages divisiveness, contrary to the biblical calls for unity (1 Corinthians 1:10).

3. **Subjectivity**: The subjective nature of Baur's historical-critical method diverges from the biblical ideal of objective truth (John 17:17).

Critique of Baur's Approach

1. **Historical Anachronism**: Baur imposes 19th-century Hegelian dialectics onto the 1st-century Christian community, which distorts the historical context of the biblical text.

2. **Selective Evidence**: Baur cherry-picks textual evidence to support his theories, often disregarding material that contradicts them.

3. **Lack of Internal Consistency**: His theories require ignoring or reinterpreting clear scriptural passages that show unity among the apostles or that affirm the early dating and authorship of New Testament books.

4. **Neglect of Manuscript Evidence**: The abundant manuscript evidence supporting the New Testament's reliability stands in contrast to Baur's skepticism.

Response: Upholding the Grammatical-Historical Method

1. **Commitment to Authorial Intent**: The grammatical-historical method, unlike Baur's approach, seeks to understand the original meaning intended by the human and Divine Author of Scripture.

2. **Contextual Analysis**: This method insists on examining a text within its original historical and cultural context, allowing the Bible to speak for itself.

3. **Honoring the Unity of Scripture**: By interpreting Scripture with Scripture, the grammatical-historical method recognizes the Bible as a harmonious and unified revelation from God.

Ferdinand Christian Baur's influence through the Tübingen School has had a lasting impact on the field of biblical criticism. However, his approach fundamentally diverges from a conservative, grammatical-historical method of biblical interpretation, which upholds the authority, inerrancy, and unity of Scripture. Baur's methodology, imbued with subjective assumptions and speculative theories, exemplifies the pitfalls of Higher Criticism. It's vital for those committed to the integrity of the Bible to discern the inherent weaknesses in such an approach and to adopt a methodology that is grounded in the objective realities of the biblical text. In this way, we can adhere to an exegesis that respects the God-breathed nature of Scripture and guards against the undermining of its divine authority.

The Life of Jesus: David Strauss (1808-1874)

David Friedrich Strauss was a German theologian and philosopher best known for his work "Das Leben Jesu" ("The Life of Jesus, Critically Examined"). His work serves as an early, pivotal exercise in Higher Criticism, a method that frequently prioritizes human reason over divine revelation. For conservative scholars who take a high view of Scripture, Strauss's work stands as an example of how skepticism can undermine the faith and lead one away from the historical, grammatical interpretation of the text.

Strauss's Main Contentions

1. **Mythical Interpretation**: Strauss argued that the Gospel accounts are largely mythical, developed by the early Christian community to express theological truths rather than historical facts. This runs counter to passages like John 20:30–31, which assert the historical events as "signs" meant to lead to belief in Jesus.

2. **Rejecting Miracles**: He also categorically rejected miracles, including the Virgin Birth and the Resurrection. However, miracles are integral to the Gospels, validated even by the enemies of Jesus (John 11:47).

3. **Reduced Christology**: Strauss's method effectively strips Jesus Christ of His divinity, contradicting explicit Scriptural declarations, such as John 1:1, which states, "In the beginning was the Word, and the Word was with God, and the Word was God."

Theological and Scriptural Implications

1. **Authority and Inerrancy**: As with other forms of Higher Criticism, Strauss's methodology seriously undermines the doctrines of Scriptural authority and inerrancy. This is contrary to Paul's assertion in 2 Timothy 3:16 that all Scripture is "breathed out by God."

2. **Faith and Salvation**: By denying Christ's divinity and the truth of His miraculous works, Strauss jeopardizes the very foundation of Christian faith and salvation, which rely on the uniqueness and divinity of Jesus (Acts 4:12).

3. **Objective Truth**: The mythical interpretation posited by Strauss effectively turns objective biblical truths into mere subjective narratives, thus negating Jesus's statement that God's word is truth (John 17:17).

Critique of Strauss's Approach

1. **Textual Disrespect**: Strauss's method ignores the genre and literary styles within the New Testament, dismissing eye-witness accounts and well-preserved traditions as myths.

2. **Historical Flaws**: Strauss's interpretation is heavily influenced by the philosophical and theological debates of his own time, rendering his work anachronistic when applied to first-century documents.

3. **Cherry-Picking**: His method relies on selective readings of the texts, omitting portions that contradict his thesis. This stands in stark contrast to the balanced and comprehensive approach encouraged by grammatical-historical interpretation.

4. **Moral and Doctrinal Consequences**: By interpreting the life of Jesus as myth, Strauss inevitably erodes the moral and doctrinal teachings that stem from a historical understanding of Jesus's life and ministry.

Upholding the Grammatical-Historical Method

1. **Respect for Genre**: Unlike Strauss, the grammatical-historical method considers the literary genre of each biblical book and aims to interpret it within its original context.
2. **Historical Credibility**: This method takes seriously the eye-witness accounts and external evidences that validate the New Testament's historical claims.
3. **Unity and Coherence**: Viewing Scripture as a coherent, unified revelation from God allows for an integrated theology that stands in opposition to the fragmented and contradictory views arising from Higher Criticism.

The work of David Friedrich Strauss had a substantial impact on subsequent biblical scholarship but is fraught with methodological and theological problems. For those committed to the inerrancy and authority of Scripture, Strauss's work serves as a cautionary tale. It underscores the need for a conservative, grammatical-historical method of interpretation that respects the text's original context, honors its claims to historical accuracy, and upholds the truth and authority of Scripture. Such an approach provides a robust defense against the skeptics and equips believers to discern truth from error, thus maintaining the integrity of the Christian faith.

The History of Religions School: Albrecht Ritschl (1822-1889)

Albrecht Ritschl was a German theologian whose work laid the foundation for the "History of Religions School," which aimed to place Christianity within the broader context of world religions. Although not directly engaging in Higher Criticism per se, his approach laid fertile ground for such criticism by detaching Christian beliefs from their historical roots in revelation.

Ritschl's Main Tenets

1. **Ethical View of Religion**: Ritschl proposed that religion should be primarily understood in ethical terms rather than metaphysical ones. This downplays passages like Romans 3:22-24, which describe justification as a gift from God, and not just an ethical accomplishment.
2. **Rejection of Orthodox Doctrines**: Ritschl was known for dismissing orthodox Christian doctrines like the Trinity and Original Sin. He challenged these beliefs as non-essential to the practical objectives of Christianity.
3. **Kingdom of God**: He focused on the "Kingdom of God" as a moral community, downplaying the eschatological and divine elements associated with it in Scriptures like Matthew 24:30-31.

Theological and Scriptural Implications

1. **Relativizing the Divine**: By focusing on the ethical, Ritschl reduced the divine to moral ideals. This contradicts Scriptures like 1 Timothy 3:16, which emphasizes the mystery of godliness and the divine nature of Jesus Christ.
2. **Selective Reading**: Ritschl's approach can encourage a selective reading of the Scriptures, focusing on texts that support ethical values while ignoring those that stress divine action, judgment, or grace, such as Romans 6:23.
3. **Reductionist**: His methodology tends to reduce complex theological ideas to simpler ethical categories. This oversimplification fails to capture the comprehensive theology of the Bible, as seen in passages like Ephesians 1:3-14.

Critique of Ritschl's Approach

1. **Oversimplification**: By reducing religion to ethics, Ritschl overlooks the multifaceted nature of faith, which involves doctrine, ethics, and the transformative power of grace (Titus 2:11-14).
2. **Denial of Essential Doctrine**: His denial of key Christian doctrines undermines the authority of the New Testament writers who were moved by the Holy Spirit to declare these truths (2 Peter 1:20-21).
3. **Rationalization Over Revelation**: Ritschl relies more on human rationalization rather than divine revelation. This conflicts with 2 Timothy 3:16-17, where Scripture is said to be "God-breathed" and beneficial for correction and training in righteousness.

Upholding the Grammatical-Historical Method

1. **Clarity and Authority**: Using a grammatical-historical interpretation places the text within its original context, capturing both the ethical and divine elements that are inherent in Scripture (1 Thessalonians 2:13).
2. **Objective Exegesis**: This method aims for an objective interpretation of the text, which gives due respect to the original author's intent and allows for a fuller understanding of the Scripture (John 17:17).
3. **Integrated Theology**: The grammatical-historical approach allows for an integrated theology that accounts for the full spectrum of Scriptural teaching, from moral commands to deep doctrinal truths (2 Timothy 2:15).

The work of Albrecht Ritschl has far-reaching implications that can be seen as detrimental from a conservative perspective that values the authority, inerrancy, and holistic interpretation of Scripture. By promoting an ethical view of religion, Ritschl managed to detract from the full richness of Christian doctrine and faith. This has subsequently opened doors for other methods that further undermine the reliability of the Bible. Those committed to the inerrancy and authority of Scripture must be cautious in navigating such approaches, ever adhering to exegetical methods that respect the text's historical and grammatical context, to guard against dilution or distortion of Biblical truth.

The Synoptic Problem: Heinrich Julius Holtzmann (1832-1910)

The Synoptic Problem and its underlying theories, including the hypothetical source "Q" and the priority of Mark, represent a confluence of modern critical methodologies that challenge the traditional understanding of the Gospels. The Historical-Grammatical method of interpretation, to which I subscribe, differs fundamentally from these modern approaches in both intent and methodology. While higher criticism delves into speculative territory, the Historical-Grammatical method seeks to understand the text based on its historical and grammatical context, thereby upholding the authority and inerrancy of Scripture.

Heinrich Julius Holtzmann and His Impact

Heinrich Julius Holtzmann was a German theologian and New Testament scholar who lived from 1832 to 1910. He was a prominent figure in the development of the Two-Source Hypothesis, which posits that Matthew and Luke used Mark and a hypothetical document, usually referred to as "Q," as their sources. Holtzmann's influence reached far and wide and set the stage for modern critical scholarship. However, from the standpoint of conservative scholarship, his theories are fraught with difficulties.

Were the Gospel Writers Plagiarists?

Firstly, the idea that Matthew and Luke copied from Mark and "Q" essentially demotes the Gospel writers to mere compilers or editors. This stance undermines the principle of inspiration outlined in 2 Timothy 3:16: "All Scripture is breathed out by God and profitable for teaching, for reproof, for correction, and for training in righteousness." Each Gospel presents a unique perspective on the life and teachings of Jesus Christ, fulfilling different purposes and speaking to different audiences.

The similarities among the Synoptic Gospels can be explained without invoking the Two-Source Hypothesis. Jesus himself promised that the Holy Spirit would remind his disciples of his teachings (John 14:26). Such divine aid could ensure that the apostles remembered the same events and teachings when they wrote their accounts.

Questions About Markan Priority

The theory of Markan priority—that Mark wrote first—isn't built on definitive evidence. If we assume that Mark was written first simply because it is shorter, then we risk falling into the logical fallacy of argumentum ad ignorantiam, arguing from ignorance. The premise itself is problematic. While Mark's account is shorter, it contains unique elements and a fast-paced narrative that contribute valuable insights into the life of Jesus.

The Mysterious "Q"

Another troubling aspect is the conjectural "Q" source. No such document has ever been found, nor is it mentioned by early Church Fathers. The idea of a "Q" source serves as a foundational pillar for modern critical theories but lacks empirical evidence. The absence of "Q" in any early Christian writings or citations raises serious questions about its very existence.

The Gospel's Credibility

The early Church Fathers overwhelmingly attested to the authenticity and reliability of the Gospel accounts. Luke, for instance, opens his Gospel by stating that he had "followed all things closely for some time past" and chose to "write an orderly account" (Luke 1:3). Such statements indicate meticulous research rather than mere compilation.

The Dangers of Higher Criticism

When we apply higher criticism to the Bible, we are imposing an external framework onto the text. This approach is closely aligned with broader ideological systems like Enlightenment rationalism, which inherently question the supernatural elements in the text. In doing so, the method carries the risk of devaluing the text's divine origin and inspiration.

In summary, higher criticism, epitomized by figures like Heinrich Julius Holtzmann, often compromises the text's divinity and inerrancy, which conservative scholars, using the Historical-Grammatical method, strive to preserve. We are reminded of Paul's counsel to Timothy: to stay away from irreverent babble and contradictions of what is falsely called "knowledge" (1 Timothy 6:20). The speculative theories revolving around the Synoptic Problem, including the priority of Mark and the hypothetical "Q," have arguably led many to question the divine inspiration of the Scriptures, which is not the approach or attitude commended in the Bible itself. Therefore, a conservative approach grounded in the Historical-Grammatical method remains critical for those committed to upholding the authority and inerrancy of Scripture.

Documentary Hypothesis: Julius Wellhausen (1844-1918)

The Documentary Hypothesis, particularly as popularized by German scholar Julius Wellhausen in the late 19th century, posits that the Pentateuch—the first five books of the Old Testament—is not a unified work penned by Moses, but rather a compilation from various sources, stitched together by a series of editors. This hypothesis mainly identifies four sources: J (Jehovist), E (Elohist), P (Priestly), and D (Deuteronomist).

This hypothesis has been a significant tenet of higher criticism, a method that employs secular academic tools to dissect and interpret biblical texts, frequently separating them from their historical, doctrinal, and spiritual context. Higher criticism often regards the Bible as merely a human product, disassembling the traditional conservative understanding that regards the text as divinely inspired and inerrant.

Let's first consider the Historical-Grammatical Method as a contrast. The Historical-Grammatical Method seeks to understand a text in its original context, considering the language, culture, and background information, without imposing modern or foreign concepts onto the text. This method is fundamentally objective and is committed to the authority of the Scripture. Higher criticism, on the other hand, has shown tendencies to intermingle subjective ideologies into its methodology. It has roots in the Enlightenment era, incorporating elements of secular humanism and German idealism, thus often coming across as an "assault" on the traditional understanding of the Bible.

The Documentary Hypothesis and higher criticism at large encounter several issues when scrutinized carefully. For example, Wellhausen's theory heavily relied on the notion that the use of different names for God (Elohim and Jehovah) indicates different sources. However, throughout Scripture, it's common for the names of God to vary depending on the context. Psalm 19, for instance, uses both Elohim and Jehovah to describe God's revelation and law. Similarly, Exodus 3:14-15 unifies the usage of both Elohim and Jehovah in a single conversation between God and Moses. This is not evidence of dual authorship, but of a theological point being made about the character and attributes of God.

The Documentary Hypothesis also struggles to account for the internal coherence within the Pentateuch. For instance, the theme of the Abrahamic covenant (Genesis 12, 15, 17) pervades through all the five books, showing a level of unity and purpose that is hard to reconcile with the idea of multiple, disconnected sources. Furthermore, Jesus Christ Himself attributed the Torah to Moses (John 5:46-47). The same goes for the apostle Paul, who recognized Moses as the author of the Law (Romans 10:5).

The notion that Moses couldn't have written the Pentateuch because the style varies or because it contains rituals and laws also raises questions. These arguments overlook the rich literary devices and techniques used in ancient Semitic languages and literature. They assume a static form of religious development, ignoring the dynamic nature of language and ritual practices that can occur within a single authorship. Even today, a single author can employ various styles depending on the purpose of their writing.

One of the primary reasons higher criticism has gained traction in the scholarly world is because it suits the presuppositions of secular academia, which often seeks to de-divinize religious texts and fit them within a naturalistic framework. This approach undermines the divine inspiration of the Bible and, therefore, its doctrinal and moral authority.

Archaeological discoveries have also not been particularly kind to higher criticism's hypotheses. Archaeology, more often than not, has substantiated the historical reliability of the Bible, even regarding its oldest accounts. Places like Jericho, once considered a biblical "myth," have been unearthed, fitting well with the biblical narrative. This gives credence to the notion that the accounts in the Old Testament are not late compositions but have a historical basis.

In conclusion, the Documentary Hypothesis, as a part of higher criticism, is fraught with issues, both methodologically and evidentially. It often starts with presuppositions that undermine the authority and inspiration of Scripture, leading to conclusions that further distance the Bible from its rightful place as the divinely inspired Word of God. While it may have been popularized in academic circles, its methodologies and conclusions conflict with an objective Historical-Grammatical approach, which remains committed to the authority, coherence, and divine inspiration of Scripture. Therefore, for those committed to a conservative understanding of the Bible, higher criticism's methods and conclusions are to be approached with extreme caution.

Quest for the Historical Jesus: Albert Schweitzer (1875-1965)

In academic circles, the study of the Bible underwent a dramatic shift with the advent of Higher Criticism. This form of scrutiny subjects the biblical texts to literary and historical analysis, aiming to discern matters like authorship, date of writing, and historical context. However, this has often led to speculative theories that challenge the Bible's integrity, authority, and inerrancy. Among the figures that loom large in this field is Albert Schweitzer, known for his "Quest for the Historical Jesus."

Quest for the Historical Jesus: Albert Schweitzer (1875-1965)

Albert Schweitzer approached the life of Jesus through a historical lens, setting aside doctrinal beliefs to uncover what he considered to be the "real" Jesus. While this might sound like an innocuous endeavor, Schweitzer's method involved critically analyzing and dismissing much of what the Gospels claim about Jesus. His conclusion was that Jesus was essentially an apocalyptic prophet who mistakenly believed that the end of the world was imminent.

The primary issue here is the way Schweitzer employed Higher Criticism to reach his conclusions. He disregarded any element in the Gospels that did not fit into his predetermined framework, dismissing miraculous events, such as Jesus' resurrection, as later theological additions. This approach reflects the naturalistic assumptions of Higher Criticism, which precludes any supernatural intervention.

The Assault on Scripture

Higher Criticism often prides itself on being an objective, scientific methodology. However, its basis in Enlightenment rationalism and secular humanism means that it inherently carries an ideological bias against the supernatural. While claiming to reveal the text's "real" meaning, Higher Criticism often distorts and undermines the very essence of the Bible. For example, it calls into question the Mosaic authorship of the Pentateuch or the Pauline authorship of the pastoral epistles, challenging foundational beliefs that have been held by the faithful for millennia. In essence, it replaces the authority of Scripture with the authority of human scholarship.

The Importance of the Historical-Grammatical Method

Contrary to Higher Criticism, the Historical-Grammatical method of interpretation endeavors to understand the text in its original context, taking into account the language, grammar, and historical backdrop. The goal is to discover the author's intended meaning rather than imposing external ideas or ideologies onto the text. This method aligns with 2 Timothy 2:15, which encourages believers to rightly handle the word of truth.

Subjective Vs. Objective Methods

While Higher Criticism often claims scientific objectivity, it frequently ends up being subjective, influenced by the ideological leanings and biases of the scholars employing it. It can interpret texts in ways that are far removed from their intended meaning, thus diminishing the Bible's value and authority. Conversely, the Historical-Grammatical method seeks to understand the Bible in its original setting, thereby safeguarding its authority. Psalm 119:160 states, "The sum of your word is truth, and every one of your righteous rules endures forever," underscoring the timeless authority of Scripture.

A Warning

It's crucial to approach the Bible with the reverence and humility it deserves, recognizing it as the inspired word of God. We are reminded in Hebrews 4:12 that the word of God is "living and active, sharper than any two-edged sword." As such, attempts to dissect it through flawed human reasoning risk undermining the power it has to transform lives. Schweitzer's work, while scholarly, carried with it assumptions that distanced his conclusions from the divinely revealed truth of Scripture.

The advent of Higher Criticism and figures like Albert Schweitzer have had a profound impact on the study of the Bible, but not without considerable flaws and risks. These approaches often replace divinely inspired wisdom with human conjecture, steering people away from the transformative power of God's word. Therefore, it's imperative that one approaches the Bible with a method that respects its divine inspiration and inerrancy, such as the Historical-Grammatical method, which seeks to understand Scripture on its own terms rather than imposing foreign ideologies upon it. Only then can one truly understand the depth, richness, and eternal relevance of God's inspired Word.

Dialectical Theology: Karl Barth (1886-1968)

Karl Barth, a Swiss Reformed theologian, stands as one of the most influential figures of the 20th century in theological circles. His work laid the groundwork for Dialectical Theology, a movement that sought to overcome the perceived inadequacies of both liberal and orthodox theologies by focusing on the dialectic or tension between God and humanity. Barth's most famous work, "Church Dogmatics," reflects this dialectical approach and has had far-reaching implications for theology and biblical interpretation.

Dialectical Theology and Higher Criticism

While Barth initially adopted liberal theology, he soon moved away from its reliance on human experience and reason. However, his departure did not mean he reverted to a conservative stance that upheld the inerrancy and authority of Scripture. Barth viewed the Bible not as the direct Word of God but as a human witness to the divine revelation in Jesus Christ. While this seems like a nuanced distinction, it had significant implications. It effectively sidelined traditional views of inspiration, which saw the Scriptures as "God-breathed" (2 Timothy 3:16). Instead, for Barth, the Bible became a subordinate authority that could err and needed to be questioned, thus opening the door to Higher Criticism.

Ideological Underpinnings

Dialectical Theology still carries remnants of Enlightenment rationalism and modernist skepticism. This skepticism tends to obscure or even deny the clarity and sufficiency of Scripture. It's worth noting that Scripture itself claims that God's words are "a lamp to my feet and a light to my path" (Psalm 119:105), emphasizing its sufficiency for guidance in all matters of life and doctrine. The ideological roots of Barth's method, consciously or not, deviate from this claim and introduce human reason as a significant authority in interpreting Scripture.

The Importance of Objective Interpretation: The Historical-Grammatical Method

An interpretation methodology that respects the inerrancy and divine origin of the Scriptures is the Historical-Grammatical method. Unlike Barth's approach, which complicates the plain message of the Bible by introducing a dialectical tension, the Historical-Grammatical method seeks to understand the author's intended meaning based on the historical context, language, and grammar. The apostle Peter emphasizes the divine origin of Scripture when he says, "For no prophecy was ever produced by the will of man, but men spoke from God as they were carried along by the Holy Spirit" (2 Peter 1:21).

Dialectical Theology's Effect on Biblical Authority

The approach Barth and his followers adopted doesn't merely offer a different viewpoint. It signifies a paradigm shift that affects the believer's confidence in the Bible. It relativizes the Scripture's authority by making its interpretation flexible and susceptible to subjective human reasoning. This is contrary to the apostle Paul's exhortation to Timothy to "preach the word; be ready in season and out of season; reprove, rebuke, and exhort, with complete patience and teaching" (2 Timothy 4:2), a call that presupposes the authority and clarity of the Scriptures.

A Warning on Higher Criticism

It's critical to be aware that the methodologies adopted in Higher Criticism, whether directly or indirectly through frameworks like Dialectical Theology, often serve as subtle assaults on the Bible's authority. They can lead to a significant loss of confidence in the Bible as the inerrant word of God, making room for speculative and subjective interpretations that have no grounding in the text itself.

While Karl Barth's Dialectical Theology sought to find a middle ground between liberal and orthodox theologies, its reliance on dialectic reasoning and its openness to Higher Criticism posed serious challenges to the traditional understanding of the Bible's inerrancy and authority. In doing so, it effectively dislodged the Scripture from its role as the ultimate, sufficient guide for faith and practice.

In contrast, a conservative approach that employs the Historical-Grammatical method aims to understand the Bible based on its original context, treating it as the inerrant and sufficient Word of God. It adheres to the belief that "All Scripture is breathed out by God and profitable for teaching, for reproof, for correction, and for training in righteousness" (2 Timothy 3:16).

Thus, while Dialectical Theology may present itself as an advanced, nuanced method of understanding Scripture, it introduces problematic elements that undercut the authority and sufficiency of God's Word. Therefore, scholars and believers alike must approach such methodologies with caution, holding fast to methods of interpretation that respect the divine inspiration and authority of the Scriptures.

Existential Interpretation: Rudolf Bultmann (1884-1976)

Rudolf Bultmann, a German Lutheran theologian, is most notably associated with the concept of "demythologization," a term which essentially means to remove the mythical or supernatural elements from the Bible in order to make it palatable to modern audiences. This is part of his broader program of existential interpretation of Scripture, rooted deeply in existentialist philosophy, notably the works of Martin Heidegger.

The Core Tenets of Bultmann's Existential Interpretation

Bultmann argued that many of the events in the Bible, including miracles and other supernatural occurrences, were not historically accurate but were myths that needed to be interpreted existentially. According to him, this mythical language is just a cloak for deeper existential truths about the human condition. His aim was not to discard these stories but to interpret them in a way that modern man could find meaningful.

Critique from a Conservative Perspective

From a conservative viewpoint, Bultmann's approach is fraught with issues. Firstly, his methodology contradicts the biblical narrative, which presents events like miracles as historical facts, not as myths. When the apostle Peter recounts the life and works of Jesus in Acts 2:22, he insists these were "attested to you by God with mighty works and wonders and signs that God did through him in your midst, as you yourselves know." Peter's argument relies on the historicity of these events. Bultmann's method, therefore, not only denies the historicity of such events but also detracts from their significance and the significance of the Scripture that records them.

Implications for Biblical Authority

The gravest implication of existential interpretation is the eroding of biblical authority. When we demythologize the Bible, we subject it to human reason and skepticism, failing to treat it as the inspired Word of God. This is in stark contrast to 2 Timothy 3:16, which affirms that "All Scripture is breathed out by God and profitable for teaching, for reproof, for correction, and for training in righteousness."

Higher Criticism and Existential Interpretation

Bultmann's existential interpretation falls under the broader umbrella of Higher Criticism, which often seeks to deconstruct the Bible rather than to understand it as it is. Existential interpretation can be perceived as a sophisticated form of Higher Criticism, often employed in tandem with form criticism and redaction criticism. Like other forms of Higher Criticism, existential interpretation also embodies elements from broader ideological systems like existentialism and secular humanism.

Objective vs. Subjective Methods

One of the main issues with existential interpretation is its inherent subjectivity. Bultmann prioritized the reader's existential situation over the author's original intent, which undermines the objective truth that Scripture seeks to convey. A more reliable method is the Historical-Grammatical approach, which seeks to understand the original intent of the author by considering the historical and cultural context, as well as the grammar and structure of the text. This method aligns more closely with the biblical view that the Scriptures are divinely inspired and objectively true.

A Warning Against Higher Criticism

The need for caution when encountering existential interpretation or any form of Higher Criticism is paramount. These methodologies often employ subjective reasoning and presuppositions that stand in contrast to the divine inspiration and inerrancy of Scripture. Paul's admonition to Timothy in 2 Timothy 4:2–3 is ever pertinent here: "For the time is coming when people will not endure sound teaching, but having itching ears they will accumulate for themselves teachers to suit their own passions."

Rudolf Bultmann's existential interpretation, rooted in existential philosophy and skepticism, deviates substantially from a conservative, literal understanding of Scripture. It undermines the historical events of the Bible, challenges the authority of Scripture, and introduces unwarranted subjectivity into biblical interpretation. While Bultmann's work has been influential, it has also led many to question the credibility and authority of the Bible.

In contrast, the Historical-Grammatical method of interpretation seeks to be objective, grounding its understanding in the original context and meaning of the text. It respects the inerrancy of Scripture and considers it to be the authoritative Word of God, suitable for "teaching, for reproof, for correction, and for training in righteousness" (2 Timothy 3:16).

As scholars and believers who hold to the authority and inerrancy of Scripture, we must exercise discernment when encountering methodologies like existential interpretation that undermine these fundamental truths. Our faith is rooted in the historical events of the Bible and the doctrinal truths they convey, and it is these that we must defend against the skeptical claims of Higher Criticism and its variants.

Philosophy and Theology: Martin Heidegger (1889-1976)

Martin Heidegger, a seminal figure in 20th-century philosophy, although not explicitly a theologian or biblical scholar, has had a considerable impact on modern theological discourse. Primarily associated with existentialism, Heidegger's philosophy can be summed up by the term "Being and Time," which is also the title of his magnum opus. His philosophy has seeped into theological approaches, impacting the way people understand the Bible, notably through existential interpretation.

Heidegger's Core Philosophy and its Theological Applications

Heidegger's principal concern was with the nature of "Being" — what it means to "be" and how individuals exist authentically. Although he did not develop a theology, his thought has deeply influenced existential theology. His philosophical vocabulary has found its way into some theological circles, affecting the way Scripture is interpreted.

Critique from a Conservative Perspective

From a conservative perspective, the problems with adopting Heidegger's philosophical framework into biblical studies are multiple. His views inherently inject subjectivity into the understanding of Scripture, allowing for interpretative flexibility that can distort the original meaning of the text. This flies in the face of 2 Timothy

3:16-17, where Paul stresses that "All Scripture is breathed out by God and profitable for teaching, for reproof, for correction, and for training in righteousness."

Impact on Biblical Authority

The crux of the problem lies in the undermining of the authority and inerrancy of Scripture. When philosophical existentialism replaces a biblically grounded worldview, it no longer serves as the ultimate authority for faith and practice. The Bible itself warns against this in Colossians 2:8: "See to it that no one takes you captive by philosophy and empty deceit, according to human tradition, according to the elemental spirits of the world, and not according to Christ."

Philosophical Existentialism vs. Biblical Existence

Heidegger's existentialism often focuses on creating an "authentic existence" defined by the individual, yet this is incongruent with the biblical concept of existence, where the focus is on being reconciled with God through Christ. For instance, Ephesians 2:8-10 speaks of the believer's identity as God's workmanship, created in Christ Jesus for good works — a far cry from an individually defined "authentic existence."

Heidegger and Higher Criticism

Although Heidegger was not a biblical scholar per se, his influence falls in line with the tendencies of Higher Criticism to lean on extra-biblical theories and ideologies. Like other forms of Higher Criticism, his philosophy also resonates with broader ideological systems such as existentialism, which is often at odds with a conservative, historical-grammatical interpretation of the Bible. His work, while not directly a form of biblical criticism, parallels its subjective tendencies, making it equally problematic for those committed to the authority of Scripture.

The Historical-Grammatical Method

In contrast to the existential leanings promoted by Heidegger's philosophy, the Historical-Grammatical method is rooted in the belief that the Bible is the inspired Word of God. It aims to understand the text as it was originally intended by its human authors, inspired by the Holy Spirit. This approach is supported by passages such as 1 Corinthians 2:13, which states, "And we impart this in words not taught by human wisdom but taught by the Spirit, interpreting spiritual truths to those who are spiritual."

A Cautionary Note on Philosophical Intrusions into Theology

Heidegger's philosophy serves as a cautionary tale against the uncritical integration of secular philosophies into biblical interpretation. 1 Timothy 6:20 warns us, "O Timothy, guard the deposit entrusted to you. Avoid the irreverent babble and contradictions of what is falsely called 'knowledge.'"

While Martin Heidegger's philosophical work is undeniably influential in the realms of philosophy and existential theology, its utility in biblical studies is deeply problematic. The existentialism that Heidegger espouses allows for an undue level of subjectivity that contradicts the objective truth claims presented in Scripture. Heidegger's philosophy, though not directly associated with Higher Criticism, dovetails with its tendencies to prioritize human reasoning over divine revelation. Such an approach undermines the authority and inerrancy of Scripture, leading one away from a proper understanding of the text.

For those committed to a conservative understanding of the Bible, the risks involved in integrating Heidegger's philosophy into biblical interpretation are far too great. We are advised to heed the apostolic warning to not be taken "captive by philosophy and empty deceit," but to root our understanding of the Bible in the solid foundation of its own claims to authority and the historical-grammatical approach that best honors those claims. The aim should always be to handle the Word of God rightly, as a reliable guide for faith and practice, and not to subject it to philosophical frameworks that are inherently at odds with it.

American Schools: Emil G. Kraeling (1897-1966)

Emil G. Kraeling was a scholar whose works in American biblical academia cast a long shadow. Kraeling was trained in the tradition of the historical-critical method, a tradition grounded in the Enlightenment's skepticism and rationalism. He was particularly known for his works on the Old Testament, including the religious context of the ancient Near East. His ideas have permeated theological seminaries and religious studies departments in the United States, influencing the way the Old Testament is taught and understood.

Kraeling's Approach and Its Implications

Kraeling was part of the wave of scholars who treated the Bible as a historical document that could be dissected using the tools of literary criticism. This approach presumes that the Bible is not necessarily a sacred or divinely inspired text but is a cultural artifact that reflects the ideas, stories, and biases of its human authors.

In this light, the infallibility of the Scriptures is called into question. The issue here lies fundamentally against the essence of 2 Timothy 3:16, which states, "All Scripture is breathed out by God and profitable for teaching, for reproof, for correction, and for training in righteousness." The authority of the Bible is devalued when seen through the lens of historical-critical analysis.

The Assault on Scriptural Inerrancy

One significant consequence of Kraeling's approach is the undermining of the inerrancy of the Scriptures. The problem here isn't just academic; it's spiritual. When the Bible is stripped of its divine origin, it ceases to be the authoritative guide for life and doctrine. The Apostle Peter warns against such private interpretations in 2 Peter 1:20–21: "Knowing this first of all, that no prophecy of Scripture comes from someone's own interpretation. For no prophecy was ever produced by the will of man, but men spoke from God as they were carried along by the Holy Spirit."

Problems with Subjectivity

The historical-critical approach that Kraeling adopted relies heavily on subjective analysis. This methodology allows scholars to impose their ideologies on the text, leading to interpretations that are far removed from the intended meaning. One can cite Proverbs 30:5-6 in this regard, "Every word of God proves true; he is a shield to those who take refuge in him. Do not add to his words, lest he rebuke you and you be found a liar."

Kraeling's Influence and the Pervasiveness of Higher Criticism in American Theological Schools

Kraeling's methods have infiltrated American seminaries and theological institutions, often displacing conservative, historical-grammatical approaches to biblical interpretation. This methodological shift has contributed to a more liberal understanding of the Scriptures, diminishing the confidence of believers and seminary students in the inerrancy and reliability of the Bible.

Alternative: The Historical-Grammatical Method

The historical-grammatical method is fundamentally different from the historical-critical method. It seeks to understand the Scriptures within their original historical context while acknowledging their divine origin. This methodology stands on the conviction of the Bible's divine inspiration and authority, aligning with Paul's assertion in 1 Corinthians 2:13: "And we impart this in words not taught by human wisdom but taught by the Spirit, interpreting spiritual truths to those who are spiritual."

Disintegration of Biblical Authority: A Cautionary Tale

The influence of Kraeling and like-minded scholars serves as a cautionary tale for modern-day believers. The Apostle Paul warns Timothy in 1 Timothy 6:20, "O Timothy, guard the deposit entrusted to you. Avoid the irreverent babble and contradictions of what is falsely called 'knowledge.'" The challenge for us today is to be vigilant in maintaining the integrity of the Scriptures, ensuring that they remain the cornerstone of our faith and practice.

The influence of Emil G. Kraeling and the school of higher criticism that he represents casts a long shadow over American biblical academia. His historical-critical approach has had a profound impact on how the Bible is studied, understood, and taught. While Kraeling's scholarship may have contributed to our understanding of the cultural and historical backdrop of the Scriptures, the methodology he used threatens the inerrancy and authority of the Bible. Those committed to a conservative, historical-grammatical understanding of the Bible must remain vigilant in defending the Scriptures from methods that undermine their divinity and authority.

By recognizing the biases and assumptions that underpin higher criticism, we can better appreciate the robust, conservative alternatives that do justice to the Bible as the divinely inspired Word of God. Those who adhere to the historical-grammatical method of interpretation continue to uphold the inerrancy and authority of the Scriptures, presenting a far more trustworthy approach to the eternal truths contained within the Bible.

The Parables: Joachim Jeremias (1900-1979)

Joachim Jeremias was a prominent New Testament scholar known for his work on the parables of Jesus. His research emerged from the realm of higher criticism, applying various forms of literary criticism to the study of biblical texts. Although his work was scholarly and influential, it raises questions about the efficacy and faithfulness of the methodologies he employed in approaching the divinely inspired Scriptures.

Jeremias' Approach to the Parables

Jeremias employed a methodology that attempted to reconstruct the original form of the parables, purportedly as they were spoken by Jesus. In doing so, he drew from form criticism, a branch of higher criticism. Jeremias was of the opinion that the parables had been significantly altered during the transmission through the early Christian communities.

The issue with this view lies in its inherent undermining of the doctrine of Scriptural inerrancy. According to 2 Timothy 3:16, "All Scripture is breathed out by God and profitable for teaching, for reproof, for correction, and for training in righteousness." In contrast, Jeremias' approach casts doubt upon the authoritative nature of the parables as recorded in the Bible.

Stripping the Divine Element

By seeking to reconstruct the original words of Jesus, Jeremias implicitly questioned the inspiration of the evangelists who recorded these parables. This approach reduces the divine aspect of the Bible, thereby denying the inspiration expressed in 2 Peter 1:20-21: "Knowing this first of all, that no prophecy of Scripture comes from someone's own interpretation. For no prophecy was ever produced by the will of man, but men spoke from God as they were carried along by the Holy Spirit."

Subjectivity and Bias

One major problem with Jeremias' approach to the parables is the subjectivity it introduces. Critics who adopt this form-critical approach are left with the freedom to interpret parables in a way that conforms to their pre-existing assumptions. This conflicts with Proverbs 30:5-6, which warns, "Every word of God proves true; he is a shield to those who take refuge in him. Do not add to his words, lest he rebuke you and you be found a liar."

Influence and Impact

The impact of Jeremias' work has been widespread, especially in academic circles where higher criticism is accepted as a scholarly pursuit. While his contributions have enriched our understanding of the cultural and historical context of the parables, the methodology threatens the integrity of the Scriptures. His influence echoes in the halls of theological institutions, casting a long shadow over the interpretation of the parables, arguably one of the most essential aspects of Jesus' teaching ministry.

An Alternative: The Historical-Grammatical Method

The historical-grammatical method offers a conservative alternative to Jeremias' form-critical approach. This method focuses on understanding the Scriptures in their original historical and grammatical context, while also acknowledging their divine inspiration. It aligns with the teachings of Paul in 1 Corinthians 2:13, where he says, "And we impart this in words not taught by human wisdom but taught by the Spirit, interpreting spiritual truths to those who are spiritual."

Dangers to Faith and Doctrine

Jeremias' form-critical approach could potentially lead to a loss of confidence in the reliability and authority of the Scriptures. This is a precarious situation, especially given the Apostle Paul's warning in 1 Timothy 6:20: "O Timothy, guard the deposit entrusted to you. Avoid the irreverent babble and contradictions of what is falsely called 'knowledge.'"

Joachim Jeremias' work on the parables has left an indelible impact on biblical scholarship, but it is not without its problems. While Jeremias and scholars of his ilk offer valuable cultural and historical insights, the methodologies they employ are fraught with assumptions and biases that erode the authority of the Scriptures. For those who seek a more conservative approach to biblical interpretation, the historical-grammatical method offers a robust alternative. It respects both the divine inspiration and the human elements in Scripture, allowing for a more balanced, accurate, and reverent approach to the Bible. By recognizing the limitations and potential dangers of higher criticism, one can more fully appreciate the eternally reliable nature of God's Word, affirming its role as the ultimate guide for faith and practice.

Old Testament Theology: Gerhard von Rad (1901-1971)

Gerhard von Rad, a German Old Testament scholar, was a prominent figure in 20th-century biblical studies. He is best known for his Old Testament theology, notably his concept of "Heilsgeschichte" (salvation history). While his contributions have shaped much of contemporary Old Testament studies, there are several concerns when evaluated from a conservative Christian viewpoint.

Salvation History According to von Rad

Von Rad introduced the idea of "Heilsgeschichte" to describe how God's interactions with His people serve as the backbone of Old Testament theology. This term emphasizes the acts of God in history, particularly those of deliverance and covenant formation. However, von Rad's understanding of "Heilsgeschichte" divorces the historical accounts in the Bible from their broader theological implications, something that seems at odds with passages like Psalm 105:5-7, which affirm both the acts and the commands of Jehovah as integral to Israel's understanding of their God.

Methodology and Its Flaws

Von Rad heavily relied on form criticism and historical criticism to dissect the Old Testament. These methods assume the fluidity of the text and that it underwent significant alteration over time, an assumption that contradicts the view of Scripture as inerrant and divinely inspired (2 Timothy 3:16-17).

Subverting Scriptural Authority

By applying form and historical criticism to Old Testament texts, von Rad subtly questions the divine authority behind these texts. This is concerning, especially considering Peter's acknowledgment that people spoke from God as they were carried along by the Holy Spirit (2 Peter 1:21).

Subjectivity and Ideological Biases

Von Rad's approach is imbued with subjectivity. The use of form criticism and historical criticism allows for speculative reconstructions of the text, governed more by modern assumptions than by the objective facts presented in the Scriptures. The danger here is the potential for skewing or even negating the original message, a serious issue when the Bible itself warns against adding or taking away from its words (Proverbs 30:5-6).

Influence and Contemporary Relevance

Von Rad's theology and methodology have deeply influenced contemporary biblical scholarship. This legacy is problematic when we consider how these methods distance people from understanding the Bible as the authoritative Word of God. It's a disservice, particularly when Paul in 1 Corinthians 2:13 emphasizes that true spiritual understanding comes through words taught by the Spirit, not human wisdom.

An Alternative Approach: Historical-Grammatical Method

A better approach would be the historical-grammatical method, which seeks to understand the text within its original historical and cultural context, preserving its divinely inspired integrity. This method aligns closely with Paul's advice to Timothy to rightly handle the Word of truth (2 Timothy 2:15).

Implications for Faith and Doctrine

The methodologies employed by von Rad can erode the foundational doctrines of biblical authority and inspiration. Such erosion is a slippery slope that may lead to theological heterodoxy, undermining the call to preserve sound doctrine (Titus 1:9).

Counteracting the Impact

To counteract the impact of higher criticism, scholars and believers should acquaint themselves with conservative hermeneutical principles that respect both the divine and human elements of Scripture. Such a methodology would serve as a more reliable guide to interpreting the Old Testament, in line with the Apostle Paul's advice to Timothy to cling to the Scriptures, which are able to make one wise for salvation through faith in Christ Jesus (2 Timothy 3:15).

Gerhard von Rad was a towering figure in Old Testament scholarship whose work continues to influence the field. However, from a conservative standpoint, the methods and theories he advanced raise significant concerns. The most pressing of these relate to the authority and inerrancy of the Scriptures. While von Rad brought many valuable insights into Old Testament studies, it is crucial for the Christian community to evaluate his work critically and cautiously. By doing so, one can better uphold the integrity of the Scriptures, ensuring that the Word of God remains the ultimate and authoritative source for doctrine, reproof, correction, and training in righteousness.

Marxist Interpretation: Norman Gottwald (1922-2015)

Norman Gottwald was a biblical scholar and social historian who utilized a Marxist approach to interpret the Hebrew Bible. His most prominent work, "The Tribes of Yahweh," contended that the formation of ancient Israel was a social revolution of disenfranchised Canaanite peasants. While Gottwald's methodology and analyses have attracted academic attention, they present multiple issues, especially when evaluated from a conservative, Scripture-centered perspective.

Marxist Lens and Its Implications

Gottwald's Marxist lens prioritizes socio-economic factors over divine intervention and the inerrancy of Scripture. This approach fundamentally challenges the biblical narrative, which asserts the direct involvement of Jehovah in the formation and preservation of Israel (Exodus 6:2-8; Deuteronomy 7:6-8). By focusing on class struggle, it relegates divine influence to the margins, ignoring the central role that God plays in the story of His people.

The Reinterpretation of Israel's Origin

In "The Tribes of Yahweh," Gottwald posited that Israel originated from a peasant revolution within Canaan, rather than from an exodus and conquest. This theory conflicts with the biblical account, which clearly describes Israel's enslavement in Egypt, the exodus led by Moses, and the conquest of Canaan (Exodus 12:31-42; Joshua 6:1-27). To dismiss these as merely ideological constructions not only challenges the reliability of the biblical text but also compromises the authority of Scripture (2 Timothy 3:16-17).

Methodology and Biases

Marxist interpretation relies heavily on socio-economic analysis and often employs higher criticism techniques like historical criticism and redaction criticism. This approach is replete with subjectivity and speculative reconstructions, disregarding the objective, historical-grammatical interpretation that prioritizes the text's original meaning, context, and divine inspiration (2 Peter 1:20-21).

Socio-Economic Overemphasis

While the Bible does speak to issues of social justice and economics (e.g., Proverbs 31:8-9; Isaiah 1:17), Gottwald's approach diminishes the spiritual and moral teachings of Scripture. By treating the Bible as a mere historical artifact reflecting economic conditions, he neglects its role as the divinely inspired guide for faith and practice (Psalm 19:7-11).

Undermining Biblical Authority

Gottwald's methods contribute to undermining the biblical text's inherent authority by interpreting it through an extra-biblical ideological framework. For instance, attributing Israel's formation to a socio-economic revolution rather than divine initiative undermines passages that assert Jehovah's sovereignty over the affairs of nations (Daniel 4:17).

Misalignment with Christian Doctrine

Gottwald's Marxist approach conflicts with foundational Christian doctrines. It destabilizes the doctrines of divine providence, revelation, and biblical inerrancy. By ascribing the events of Scripture primarily to human socio-economic activities, the Marxist perspective contradicts Paul's affirmation that Scripture is "God-breathed" and serves to equip the believer for good works (2 Timothy 3:16-17).

Contemporary Influence and Consequences

The impact of Gottwald's work extends to modern biblical scholarship, particularly among those who prioritize socio-political factors in biblical interpretation. While socio-economic considerations aren't entirely irrelevant to biblical studies, they should be understood within the greater theological framework of Scripture.

The Need for Objective Biblical Interpretation

To counter the influence of Marxist interpretation, a more objective, historical-grammatical method should be pursued. This approach respects the text's historical and cultural background while upholding its divine inspiration. It allows us to better align our interpretive frameworks with the intentions of the biblical authors, rather than with 20th or 21st-century ideologies.

Norman Gottwald made significant contributions to biblical studies from a socio-historical perspective. However, when his work is evaluated from a conservative, Scripture-centered standpoint, it presents critical issues. Most notably, it downplays the divine initiatives described in the Bible, reduces the complex phenomena of Israel's formation to mere socio-economic factors, and employs speculative methodologies that diverge from an objective, historical-grammatical approach. Consequently, Gottwald's Marxist interpretation poses significant challenges to the conservative Christian belief in the authority and inerrancy of Scripture, urging us to approach his work and its intellectual offspring with caution. As believers committed to the authority of Scripture, we are called to "test everything; hold fast what is good" (1 Thessalonians 5:21), particularly in matters of biblical interpretation.

The Jesus Seminar: John Dominic Crossan (born 1934)

John Dominic Crossan, a notable figure within the Jesus Seminar, is a controversial biblical scholar who has gained recognition for his critical examinations of the historical Jesus. The Jesus Seminar itself is a collective of scholars applying higher criticism techniques to the Gospels, seeking to separate the "authentic" words of Jesus from later additions. Crossan's work stands out for its heavy reliance on historical-critical methods, socio-political considerations, and form criticism. Though intriguing to some, his methodologies and conclusions raise substantial issues, particularly when scrutinized from a conservative, Scripture-centered vantage point.

The Historical-Critical Method and Crossan

Crossan employs the historical-critical method, a technique that attempts to deconstruct biblical texts by disassembling them into distinct layers based on their perceived historical development. This approach, however, is fraught with subjectivity and speculative assumptions. By prioritizing skepticism and human reasoning over divine inspiration, this methodology contradicts Paul's assertion that "All Scripture is breathed out by God and profitable for teaching, for reproof, for correction, and for training in righteousness" (2 Timothy 3:16, ESV).

The Quest for the "Real" Jesus

One of the major efforts of Crossan and the Jesus Seminar is to discover the "real" historical Jesus, separate from what they consider to be later doctrinal or mythological embellishments. This endeavor fundamentally challenges the integrity of the Gospel accounts, which present a divinely inspired record of Jesus' life, teachings, crucifixion, and resurrection (John 20:31).

Form Criticism and its Limitations

Crossan often employs form criticism, a method aimed at identifying the literary forms and traditions behind biblical texts. This approach assumes that much of the Gospel material originated from communal settings rather than eyewitness accounts or divine inspiration. However, the apostle Peter emphasizes that the apostolic testimony is not "devised myths" but stems from "eyewitnesses of his [Jesus'] majesty" (2 Peter 1:16, ESV).

Social and Political Undertones

Crossan often infuses his biblical interpretation with social and political considerations, such as the socio-economic conditions of first-century Palestine. While understanding historical context is important, it should not lead us to dismiss or reinterpret the miraculous or divine elements presented in Scripture (e.g., Matthew 14:22-33; John 11:1-44).

Selective Use of Extra-Biblical Texts

Crossan frequently relies on apocryphal and Gnostic texts to supplement the biblical narrative. This is problematic because these texts lack the canonical authority and divine inspiration that are central to a conservative understanding of Scripture (Revelation 22:18-19).

The Resurrection Controversy

One of the most contentious aspects of Crossan's work is his rejection of Jesus' bodily resurrection, which he sees as a metaphorical or spiritual event. This view directly contradicts the foundational Christian doctrine of the resurrection (1 Corinthians 15:12-22), a doctrine vital for Christian hope and soteriology.

Ideological Biases and Scriptural Authority

Crossan's methodologies and conclusions can be seen as symptomatic of broader ideological influences, such as Enlightenment rationalism and postmodern relativism. These influences have infiltrated biblical scholarship and have the potential to distance biblical interpretation from the actual truth, undermining people's confidence in the Bible.

Implications for Christian Doctrine

Crossan's approach significantly undermines key Christian doctrines, including the divine inspiration of Scripture, the virgin birth, the miracles, the atonement, and the resurrection. These are not merely peripheral issues but are foundational to Christian faith and practice.

Counteracting the Influence

For those committed to the authority and inerrancy of Scripture, an objective, historical-grammatical method is crucial. This method relies on a careful consideration of the text's original languages, historical background, and grammatical constructs while upholding its divine inspiration.

John Dominic Crossan and the Jesus Seminar have made significant contributions to biblical studies, but from a deeply flawed methodological basis. Their work poses a direct challenge to the conservative, Scripture-centered approach to biblical interpretation. Crossan's skeptical methodologies and liberal theological presuppositions offer a striking example of how higher criticism can erode biblical authority and lead people away from the foundational truths of the Christian faith. It is incumbent upon those who hold to the inerrancy and divine inspiration of Scripture to carefully scrutinize such methodologies and to steadfastly affirm the Bible as the authoritative Word of God. "But test everything; hold fast what is good" (1 Thessalonians 5:21, ESV) remains a relevant exhortation, particularly in the realm of biblical interpretation.

Gnostic Influence: Elaine Pagels (born 1943)

Elaine Pagels is a well-known scholar whose work largely focuses on early Christian history and Gnostic texts. She gained widespread recognition with her book "The Gnostic Gospels," which explored early Christian texts excluded from the canonical New Testament. While her work has been academically praised, it's essential to scrutinize her methodology and conclusions, especially from a conservative Christian perspective that emphasizes the authority, inerrancy, and inspiration of Scripture.

The Gnostic Texts and Their Problems

Pagels explores Gnostic texts like the Gospel of Thomas and the Gospel of Mary to posit alternative narratives about early Christianity. These Gnostic texts were not included in the biblical canon, and for good reason. The New Testament canon was developed under a stringent set of criteria, including apostolic authority and doctrinal consistency with the Old Testament and the teachings of Jesus and His apostles. For instance, the Apostle Paul warns against different gospels or teachings (Galatians 1:6-9), emphasizing the need for doctrinal consistency.

Historical-Critical Method

Like many scholars influenced by higher criticism, Pagels applies the historical-critical method to assess both the canonical and Gnostic texts. This approach's inherent subjectivity and speculative nature raise concerns. It fundamentally contradicts the conservative Christian understanding that Scripture is "breathed out by God" and is reliable for teaching and doctrine (2 Timothy 3:16).

The Issue of Authority and Inerrancy

Pagels often suggests that the exclusion of Gnostic texts from the canon was politically motivated. However, the concept of canon is rooted in recognizing the authority and inerrancy of the divinely inspired writings. These were not arbitrary decisions but followed the community's recognition of the texts' divine qualities, as affirmed by Peter when he compares Paul's writings to the "other Scriptures" (2 Peter 3:16).

Ideological Frameworks

Elaine Pagels' scholarship is deeply influenced by ideologies originating from secular humanism and Enlightenment rationalism. These perspectives often undermine the divinely inspired nature of Scripture, opting instead for a human-centered understanding that dilutes the text's spiritual and doctrinal integrity. Such ideologies often make higher criticism not just a method but a lens that colors all interpretations, thus veering away from the truth that Scripture aims to convey.

The Infiltration of Gnosticism in Modern Scholarship

Gnosticism often teaches dualism and a radical separation between the material and spiritual worlds. These views are contrary to the biblical narrative, which holds that Jehovah created the material world with a purpose (Isaiah 45:18). The Bible also maintains that Jesus Christ was both fully human and fully divine (John 1:14; Colossians 2:9), contrary to some Gnostic texts that deny His human aspects. Gnostic teachings, therefore, can undermine key doctrines of Christian theology, such as creation, the nature of God, and the Incarnation.

Doctrinal Implications

Pagels' work often challenges key tenets of orthodox Christianity, including the authority of apostolic teaching, the nature of God, and the understanding of salvation. For example, Gnostic texts frequently advance a works-based salvation, contrary to the New Testament, which states salvation is by faith, not works (Ephesians 2:8-9).

The Loss of Historical Context

Gnostic texts are often dated much later than the canonical Gospels and are not grounded in the historical context of first-century Palestine. They lack the apostolic authority that gives weight to the New Testament documents. Furthermore, Gnostic texts frequently reflect the syncretistic tendencies of their time, merging Christian themes with various mystical and philosophical ideas, contrary to the New Testament's clear monotheistic focus.

While Elaine Pagels has made substantial contributions to the study of early Christianity, the methodological and ideological foundations of her work present significant concerns. From a conservative Christian perspective, her approach fails to uphold the authority, inspiration, and inerrancy of Scripture. Furthermore, her inclusion of Gnostic texts and teachings into the discussion serves to dilute the foundational doctrines and beliefs that have sustained Christianity for centuries. For those committed to the reliability and authority of the Bible, it is vital to approach Pagels' work—and similar scholarship—with discernment and caution. Christians must be like the Bereans, who "received the word with all eagerness, examining the Scriptures daily to see if these things were so" (Acts 17:11, ESV). By adhering to a historical-grammatical method of interpretation, believers can better defend their faith against the influence of higher criticism and its associated ideologies.

British Scholarship: John Barton (born 1948)

John Barton, a prominent British theologian and biblical scholar, has left a considerable imprint on the landscape of biblical studies, particularly in the area of Old Testament interpretation. However, his work has not been without controversy, especially when examined through a conservative Christian lens that upholds the inerrancy, inspiration, and authority of Scripture. The following critique aims to elucidate key aspects of Barton's scholarship, highlighting where it diverges from conservative Christian principles.

Methodological Underpinnings: Historical-Critical Method

Barton has been a proponent of the historical-critical method of biblical interpretation, which seeks to understand the Bible within its historical context but often disregards the idea of divine inspiration. This approach stands in sharp contrast to the historical-grammatical method, which takes into account both the historical context and the inspired nature of the text. The Apostle Paul emphasizes the inspired nature of Scripture, stating, "All Scripture is breathed out by God and profitable for teaching, for reproof, for correction, and for training in righteousness" (2 Timothy 3:16, ESV).

Ideological Influences

Much like other scholars who employ higher criticism, Barton's work often reflects broader ideological trends like secular humanism and Enlightenment thinking. This ideological stance can be particularly problematic because it tends to subordinate Scripture to human reason. The Prophet Isaiah warns against relying solely on human understanding: "For my thoughts are not your thoughts, neither are your ways my ways, declares Jehovah" (Isaiah 55:8, ESV).

Old Testament Interpretation

Barton's treatment of the Old Testament often hinges on source criticism and redaction criticism. Such methods, while potentially useful for historical analysis, introduce a level of speculation not warranted by the text itself. For example, he dissects the Pentateuch into various sources (J, E, D, P), casting doubt on Mosaic authorship. This undermines the New Testament witness to Moses as a lawgiver and prophet (e.g., Matthew 19:7-8).

Canon Formation

Another area where Barton's work diverges from conservative understanding is his interpretation of how the biblical canon was formed. He often describes it as a more fluid and politically influenced process, in contrast to conservative views that see the canon's formation as a recognition of inspired texts. Peter's second letter, which equates Paul's letters with "other Scriptures" (2 Peter 3:16, ESV), suggests a recognition of canonical authority that was based not on politics but on apostolic authority and doctrinal consistency.

On Ethics and Morality

Barton has also written on biblical ethics, arguing that the Bible offers multiple ethical perspectives and is not always consistent. This viewpoint raises concerns, as it undermines the concept that Scripture provides a unified, divinely inspired ethical framework. This goes against passages like Psalm 119:160, which states, "The sum of your word is truth, and every one of your righteous rules endures forever" (ESV).

Deconstruction of Traditional Beliefs

While Barton's work may appeal to academic circles interested in deconstructing traditional views, it presents a challenge for those who uphold the Bible as the infallible Word of God. His interpretive strategies often have the effect of diminishing key doctrines such as the Fall, the Covenant, and even the nature of God as revealed in the Old Testament.

Unwarranted Skepticism

One of the most troubling aspects of Barton's work is the skepticism it fosters towards the Bible. His methodologies often leave the lay reader with more questions than answers, undermining the confidence that believers should have in the Scriptures. This is in stark contrast to the Bereans, who were commended for their eagerness in examining the Scriptures to ascertain the truth (Acts 17:11, ESV).

Conclusion

John Barton's contributions to biblical scholarship cannot be denied. However, when his work is scrutinized under a conservative lens that upholds the authority, inerrancy, and inspiration of Scripture, numerous problems come to light. His methodological and ideological choices often distance the interpretation from the truths that Scripture aims to convey, thereby eroding the foundational doctrines and beliefs that have been the bedrock of Christianity for millennia.

The goal of any serious Bible student should be, like the Apostle Paul suggests, to "rightly handle the word of truth" (2 Timothy 2:15, ESV). It is crucial to remain vigilant and discerning when encountering works that employ higher criticism and its associated methods. These methodologies, often portrayed as scientifically rigorous and objective, are in fact embedded in larger ideological frameworks that can seriously compromise the integrity of biblical interpretation. Hence, it is imperative to approach such works with caution, always measuring them against the unfailing standard of the inspired, inerrant Word of God.

Textual Criticism in Modernity: Bart Ehrman (born 1955)

Bart D. Ehrman is a widely known biblical scholar whose works have had a significant impact on the study of the New Testament. Although he began his academic career within the Evangelical tradition, Ehrman eventually distanced himself from these roots, becoming an agnostic. His body of work has delved into textual criticism, focusing on the inconsistencies and alleged contradictions in the New Testament manuscripts. Here, we critically assess Ehrman's approach and its implications for conservative biblical scholarship.

Ehrman's Textual Criticism and Its Foundation

Ehrman's work predominantly revolves around textual criticism, a scholarly discipline aimed at understanding the most authentic version of a text. While textual criticism is a legitimate tool, Ehrman employs it in a way that brings the reliability of the New Testament into question. He argues that the variations across manuscripts compromise the integrity of the text, a claim at odds with the New Testament's self-affirmation as inspired by God. As Paul writes, "All Scripture is breathed out by God" (2 Timothy 3:16, ESV).

Ideological Underpinnings

Ehrman's shift from Evangelical Christianity to agnosticism is not just a personal transition but also a methodological one. His agnostic viewpoint underlies much of his scholarship and influences his readings of the text. Such a stance does not seek to uphold the integrity and authority of Scripture. Instead, it attempts to analyze the Bible through a lens that allows for, and even expects, errors and inconsistencies.

Manuscript Variations: A Distorted Perspective

One of Ehrman's key arguments focuses on the variations among New Testament manuscripts. While it is true that manuscripts have differences, Ehrman's emphasis on these differences is overstated and often taken out of context. Many of the variations are inconsequential and do not affect core doctrinal issues. In fact, the sheer number of available manuscripts should be seen as a strength, offering us a wealth of material to arrive at a text that closely resembles the original. Jesus affirmed the enduring nature of Scripture when He said, "Heaven and earth will pass away, but my words will not pass away" (Matthew 24:35, ESV).

The Question of Contradictions

Ehrman also discusses what he views as contradictions in the Bible, especially in the New Testament. However, many of these so-called contradictions arise from an inadequate understanding of the cultural, historical, and linguistic context within which the Bible was written. The historical-grammatical method helps in resolving these issues by taking into account the text's original setting and intended meaning.

Discrediting Apostolic Authorship

Ehrman further erodes confidence in the New Testament by questioning the apostolic authorship of various books, including the letters traditionally attributed to Paul. This is problematic because it undermines the apostolic foundation of the New Testament, which is a key criterion for canonicity and authority. As Peter writes, Paul's letters contain "some things hard to understand, which the ignorant and unstable twist to their own destruction, as they do the other Scriptures" (2 Peter 3:16, ESV).

Ehrman's Influence and the Popular Mindset

Ehrman's work is not limited to academic circles; it has permeated popular culture and media, often being cited as proof against the reliability of the New Testament. This has the dangerous potential of swaying uninformed readers away from faith in Scripture. It directly contradicts the Bible's own exhortation to equip oneself with the "sword of the Spirit, which is the word of God" (Ephesians 6:17, ESV).

Bart Ehrman's scholarship, particularly his work in textual criticism, presents a significant challenge to those who affirm the authority, inspiration, and inerrancy of the Bible but are not familiar with the basics of textual criticism. His approach, however, is marred by an agnostic presupposition that does not accord the Bible the respect it demands as an inspired text. Moreover, his methodological choices often employ a form of higher criticism that veers into speculation and subjectivity, clouding the objective analysis of the biblical text. The impact of his work extends beyond academia, affecting popular perceptions of the Bible's reliability. As believers committed to the authority of Scripture, it is imperative to approach such scholarship with discernment and caution, weighing it against the clear witness of the Bible itself. It's important to remember the Apostle Paul's counsel to Timothy: "O Timothy, guard the deposit entrusted to you. Avoid the irreverent babble and contradictions of what is falsely called 'knowledge'" (1 Timothy 6:20, ESV).

CHAPTER 5 Interpreting Different Genres

Rules for Interpreting Parables

Parables are a prominent feature in the teaching ministry of Jesus Christ. The Gospels record numerous parables that Jesus used to impart spiritual truths, ethical guidelines, and insights into the kingdom of God. Given their importance, it is crucial to interpret parables in a manner consistent with sound exegetical principles. This chapter outlines rules for interpreting parables, relying heavily on the objective historical-grammatical method.

Understanding the Nature of Parables

Parables are simple stories used to illustrate a moral or spiritual lesson. They are not allegories where every element of the story has a symbolic meaning; rather, they usually have one main point or central truth they aim to communicate. Understanding this is essential because it guards against unwarranted extrapolations and ensures the primary message is not obscured.

Context is King

The first rule for interpreting parables is to consider the context. The parable should be understood within the larger narrative or discourse in which it appears. For example, the Parable of the Sower in Matthew 13 is situated in a context where Jesus is explaining the different responses to the message of the kingdom of God. Context helps to identify the primary audience and the pressing issues or questions that the parable addresses.

Identify the Main Point

Jesus often interpreted His own parables, providing a definitive meaning. In the case of the Parable of the Sower, He explained that the different types of soil represent various responses to the word of God (Matthew 13:18-23). The focus should always be on the main point that the parable is intended to make.

Historical and Cultural Background

Understanding the historical and cultural background can add depth to our interpretation. The Parable of the Good Samaritan (Luke 10:25-37), for example, gains additional layers of meaning when one understands the social dynamics and hostilities between Jews and Samaritans in the first-century Judean context.

Be Cautious with Details

While the details in a parable can be colorful and engaging, they are usually intended to support the main point. For example, in the Parable of the Prodigal Son (Luke 15:11-32), the details about the younger son's riotous living are not meant to be interpreted in a hyper-literal sense but serve to amplify the central theme of repentance and divine forgiveness.

Consult the Rest of Scripture

Parables should never be interpreted in isolation but should be understood in light of the broader teachings of Scripture. For example, the Parable of the Ten Virgins (Matthew 25:1-13) echoes themes found in other teachings of Jesus, like the necessity of watchfulness and preparation for His return.

Avoiding Common Pitfalls

- **Speculation**: Always keep interpretations grounded in the text. Speculating beyond the information given can lead to erroneous conclusions.
- **Isolation**: Interpretation should always be in harmony with the general teachings of the Bible. It is erroneous to build an entire doctrine solely on the basis of a parable.
- **Modernization**: While it's tempting to read parables in light of contemporary issues, we should avoid such anachronistic readings.

Parables are a potent tool that Jesus used to teach profound spiritual truths. However, their interpretation needs to be handled with care. Using the historical-grammatical method, focusing on context, and being cautious with details can prevent the abuse of these texts and help to convey their intended message faithfully. In doing so, we adhere to Paul's exhortation to Timothy: "Do your best to present yourself to God as one approved, a worker who has no need to be ashamed, rightly handling the word of truth" (2 Timothy 2:15, ESV). This approach not only honors the divine inspiration behind these teachings but also safeguards the church from the pitfalls of subjective interpretations and speculative doctrines.

Rules for Interpreting Figurative Language

Figurative language is a literary device that uses words or expressions in a way that differs from their literal interpretation. While the Bible contains a great deal of straightforward, literal language, it also employs various forms of figurative language, such as metaphors, similes, hyperboles, and personification. Misinterpreting figurative expressions can lead to false doctrines or misconceptions about Scriptural teachings. Therefore, rules for interpreting figurative language are vital for a robust biblical exegesis.

Recognizing Figurative Language

The first step in interpreting figurative language is to recognize it. The context is often the best guide for this. For example, when Jesus says, "I am the door" (John 10:9, ESV), it's evident from the context that He is using metaphorical language to express that He is the way to salvation.

Context is Key

Understanding the immediate and broader context of a passage is crucial for accurate interpretation. Just as you wouldn't pluck a verse out of context to build an entire doctrine, you shouldn't do so with a piece of figurative language. For instance, in Isaiah 55:12, where it says, "the mountains and the hills before you shall break forth into singing," it's clear from the surrounding verses that the prophet is speaking about the joy that will come with God's redemption, rather than literal mountains singing.

Identifying the Literal Truth Behind the Figure

Every piece of figurative language aims to convey a literal truth. For example, when Jesus says, "I am the bread of life" (John 6:35, ESV), He is not saying that He is literally made of bread; rather, He is the source of spiritual nourishment and life. The objective is to understand this underlying truth accurately.

The Role of Cultural and Historical Background

Understanding the historical and cultural backdrop of the biblical text can shed light on its figurative language. For instance, in Revelation 3:16, the message to the Laodicean church about being "neither cold nor hot" makes more sense when we understand that Laodicea had a supply of lukewarm water, unlike the cold, refreshing water in nearby Colossae or the hot medicinal springs in Hierapolis.

Correlation with Other Scripture

Scripture interprets Scripture. If a piece of figurative language is difficult to understand, other passages can often clarify its meaning. For example, the phrase "Lamb of God" used to describe Jesus in John 1:29 is illuminated by passages from the Old Testament, particularly the sacrificial system described in Leviticus, as well as Isaiah's Suffering Servant prophecy (Isaiah 53).

Guarding Against Common Pitfalls

- **Over-literalizing**: Taking figurative language too literally can lead to bizarre and incorrect interpretations. For example, interpreting the "four corners of the earth" in Revelation 7:1 as evidence for a flat earth.

- **Over-allegorizing**: While allegorical interpretations can be tempting, they often lead to subjective and incorrect understandings. Therefore, allegorical methods should be avoided in favor of the more objective historical-grammatical method.

- **Isolated Interpretation**: Figurative language should never be interpreted in isolation but must be understood in harmony with the overall teaching of Scripture.

Examples to Consider

- "Our God is a consuming fire" (Hebrews 12:29, ESV). This metaphor is not implying that God is literally a fire but aims to convey His holiness and judgment against sin.

- "You are the salt of the earth" (Matthew 5:13, ESV). Here, Jesus employs a metaphor to describe the preserving and flavoring influence Christians should have in the world.

Interpreting figurative language in the Bible is a task that requires careful attention to context, a grasp of historical and cultural backgrounds, and a commitment to correlate the interpretation with the rest of Scripture. By adhering to these principles grounded in the historical-grammatical method, one can arrive at an understanding of the Bible that is both intellectually rigorous and spiritually enriching. This approach aligns with Paul's directive in 2 Timothy 2:15, "Do your best to present yourself to God as one approved, a worker who has no need to be ashamed, rightly handling the word of truth" (ESV). Thus, by cautiously interpreting figurative language in the Bible, we respect its divine origin, honor its inerrancy, and safeguard the integrity of its message.

Rules for Interpreting Similes and Metaphors

Similes and metaphors are among the most prevalent forms of figurative language in the Bible. While they serve to enrich the text and facilitate understanding, they also pose challenges in interpretation. This chapter aims to lay down rules and guidelines for interpreting these forms of figurative language within the bounds of a conservative approach to biblical interpretation, grounded in the Historical-Grammatical method.

Definition and Identification

- **Simile**: A figure of speech that compares one thing to another using the words "like" or "as." For example, "He will be like a tree planted by streams of water" (Psalm 1:3, ESV).

- **Metaphor**: A figure of speech in which a word or phrase is applied to an object or action to which it is not literally applicable. For example, "I am the bread of life" (John 6:35, ESV).

Importance of Context

Understanding the context of the Scripture in which a simile or metaphor appears is vital for correct interpretation. The context will usually make it clear that the language is not meant to be taken literally.

Examples in Scripture

1. **Simile**: "He is like a lion eager to tear, as a young lion lurking in ambush" (Psalm 17:12, ESV). Here, the wicked are not literally lions but share attributes of predatory behavior.
2. **Metaphor**: "You are the salt of the earth" (Matthew 5:13, ESV). Jesus is not suggesting that His disciples are made of salt but that they play a crucial, preserving role in the world.

Rules for Interpretation

1. **Immediate Context**: Always consider the immediate verses or chapters around the simile or metaphor. For example, in interpreting "I am the vine; you are the branches" (John 15:5, ESV), the surrounding text talks about remaining in Christ and bearing fruit, helping us understand that the metaphor is about spiritual connectedness and fruitfulness.

2. **Broader Context**: Sometimes a simile or metaphor is a motif that appears throughout a book or even across several books of the Bible. For instance, the metaphor of Jehovah as a shepherd is found in both the Old and New Testaments, providing a consistent portrayal of His care and guidance.

3. **Cultural and Historical Background**: Understanding the life and times of the original audience can be extremely helpful. In the case of the metaphor "I am the bread of life," familiarity with the importance of bread in ancient Near Eastern society can provide deeper insights.

4. **Literal Truth Behind the Figure**: Every simile and metaphor intends to convey a literal truth. For example, when Paul states, "For we are the aroma of Christ to God" (2 Corinthians 2:15, ESV), he is emphasizing that Christians have a defining quality that sets them apart for a holy purpose.

5. **Correlation with Other Scriptures**: Always allow Scripture to interpret Scripture. If a metaphor or simile is challenging to understand, look for other places in the Bible where similar language is used.

Common Pitfalls and How to Avoid Them

- **Over-Literalizing**: It's essential to recognize when language is figurative. For example, when the Bible says that God "covers you with His feathers" (Psalm 91:4, ESV), it is not suggesting that God is a bird but is using metaphorical language to express His protective nature.

- **Ignoring the Complexity**: Sometimes a metaphor or simile carries more than one aspect of meaning. It is crucial to explore these multiple layers carefully.

- **Subjective Interpretation**: Since the objective is to determine what the author intended to convey, one's personal opinions or experiences should not dictate the interpretation.

Similes and metaphors are powerful literary tools used by biblical writers to convey deep spiritual truths. By adhering to conservative principles of interpretation and relying on the historical-grammatical method, one can draw out these truths faithfully. This meticulous approach is essential for understanding the Word of God accurately, thereby ensuring that the message of Scripture remains as pure as its divine Author intended. In this endeavor, we are guided by Paul's exhortation to Timothy: "Do your best to present yourself to God as one approved, a worker who has no need to be ashamed, rightly handling the word of truth" (2 Timothy 2:15, ESV). Through faithful interpretation, we not only enrich our own understanding but also honor the sacred text that has been given to guide us in all truth.

Rules for Interpreting Idioms

Idiomatic expressions can often be stumbling blocks in the path of a clear understanding of Scripture. An idiom is a phrase or an expression that has a meaning that cannot be deduced solely from the individual words used. To get the most from the Bible, a conservative method of interpretation, underpinned by the Historical-Grammatical approach, is indispensable. This chapter will elaborate on the rules to interpret idioms found in the Bible faithfully.

Definition and Identification

- **Idiom**: A set expression of two or more words that means something other than the literal meanings of its individual words.

Importance of Context

Grasping the cultural and historical context is crucial. The first readers or listeners of a biblical text understood these idiomatic expressions based on their common usage, so understanding that usage can reveal the author's original intent.

Examples in Scripture

1. **Eye of a Needle**: In Matthew 19:24, Jesus states, "Again I tell you, it is easier for a camel to go through the eye of a needle than for a rich person to enter the kingdom of God" (ESV). The idiom here illustrates the impossibility and challenges of a specific action.
2. **Broken Heart**: Psalm 34:18 reads, "Jehovah is near to the brokenhearted and saves the crushed in spirit" (ESV). The term "brokenhearted" doesn't refer to a literal heart broken into pieces but to a state of deep emotional distress.

Rules for Interpretation

1. **Immediate Context**: The verses immediately surrounding the idiomatic expression can provide clues for interpretation.
2. **Historical Context**: Understanding the social, cultural, and historical background can offer invaluable insights into the meaning of an idiom.
3. **Scripture Interprets Scripture**: Before arriving at an interpretation of an idiom, see how that phrase or similar phrases are used elsewhere in the Bible.

4. **Literal Sense Behind the Idiom**: Idioms generally express literal truths in a non-literal manner. Extracting this literal sense is vital for proper understanding.
5. **Consult Reliable Resources**: When in doubt, consult dictionaries of biblical idioms, lexicons, and commentaries that adhere to a conservative, historical-grammatical approach to Scripture.

Common Pitfalls and How to Avoid Them

1. **Over-Literal Interpretation**: Taking idioms literally can lead to significant misunderstandings. For example, interpreting the "arm of the Lord" as Jehovah's physical arm would be a mistake; it's an idiom describing His power and authority.
2. **Ignoring Cultural Relevance**: Idioms are often grounded in specific cultural practices or understandings. Ignorance of these can lead to erroneous interpretations.
3. **Subjectivity**: It is crucial to avoid applying one's own cultural understanding of an idiom when interpreting Scripture. The objective is to ascertain the original intended meaning.
4. **Isolated Interpretation**: Ignoring how an idiom is used elsewhere in Scripture can lead to inconsistencies in understanding and application.

Idioms present unique challenges in biblical interpretation but are not insurmountable obstacles. By applying a disciplined, historical-grammatical method of interpretation, one can grasp the intended meaning behind these phrases. The aim is not merely academic but spiritual, as Paul exhorts in 2 Timothy 2:15 (ESV): "Do your best to present yourself to God as one approved, a worker who has no need to be ashamed, rightly handling the word of truth." Properly understanding idioms in Scripture allows us to comply with this directive, deepening both our knowledge and our relationship with Jehovah, the author of the Bible. We strive for an unadulterated understanding of the text to preserve the sanctity and the authority of the Scriptures. In this endeavor, conservative exegetical methods, grounded in the reverence for the inerrancy and authority of Scripture, prove to be indispensable. Thus, by carefully navigating the idiomatic expressions in the Bible, we can fully engage with its timeless message, as originally intended by its divine and human authors.

Rules for Interpreting Hyperbole

Hyperbole is another literary device employed in Scripture that, if misunderstood, can lead to problematic interpretations. Hyperbole is intentional exaggeration or overstatement used for effect, often to emphasize a particular point. Understanding hyperbole is critical for a balanced and accurate application of the historical-grammatical method, which emphasizes the importance of context, both historical and grammatical, in interpreting the Bible.

Defining Hyperbole

- **Hyperbole**: A figure of speech in which exaggeration is used for emphasis or effect; it is an extravagant statement that is not to be taken literally.

Recognizing Hyperbole

Determining whether a statement in the Bible is hyperbolic involves examining the context, the author's intent, and the general norms of language and literature of the time. The historical-grammatical approach allows us to discern the intent behind such expressions.

Scriptural Examples

1. **Plucking Out Your Eye**: In Matthew 5:29, Jesus says, "If your right eye causes you to sin, tear it out and throw it away" (ESV). This is a hyperbolic statement made to emphasize the severe measures one should consider to avoid sin. It is not an instruction to mutilate oneself but to take drastic action against the causes of sin.

2. **Camel Through the Eye of a Needle**: In Matthew 19:24, Jesus again uses hyperbole by stating that "it is easier for a camel to go through the eye of a needle than for a rich person to enter the kingdom of God" (ESV). The aim is to stress the enormous difficulty, yet not the impossibility, of a rich man entering heaven if he puts his trust in wealth.

Rules for Interpretation

1. **Examine the Context**: Like idioms, hyperboles are best understood within their immediate context. Assess the surrounding verses and the overarching message of the passage.

2. **Understand the Intention**: Hyperboles aim to emphasize a point, not to be taken literally. Identifying what is being emphasized helps to unlock the intended meaning.

3. **Refer to Other Scriptures**: The principle of "Scripture interprets Scripture" applies here as well. Does the exaggerated statement align with the broader teaching of the Bible?

4. **Consult Conservative Scholarship**: Utilize resources that align with the historical-grammatical method to gain insights into particular hyperbolic statements in Scripture.

Common Pitfalls and How to Avoid Them

1. **Literalism**: The most apparent risk is taking hyperbolic statements literally. The historical-grammatical approach helps prevent this error by emphasizing context and authorial intent.
2. **Ignoring Original Audience Understanding**: Remember, the original readers or hearers in the biblical setting would have recognized these as exaggerations meant for emphasis.
3. **Isolating Text**: Using a hyperbole to construct an entire doctrine can lead to significant error. Each statement, even hyperbolic ones, should be considered part of a larger biblical narrative.
4. **Personal Bias**: Interpreters must avoid projecting their biases or contemporary understandings of hyperbole onto the biblical text.

Hyperbole in Scripture is not a mark of inaccuracy or imprecision; rather, it serves a clear, focused pedagogical purpose. As with any form of biblical literature, the key to accurate interpretation lies in the conservative, historical-grammatical method, guided by an unflinching commitment to the authority and inerrancy of Scripture. We interpret hyperbole with the same level of respect and caution we apply to every other genre or rhetorical device in the Bible, understanding that each serves to convey the multifaceted revelation of Jehovah to His creation.

Hyperbolic language, when correctly interpreted, enriches our understanding of the biblical message. Like all other figures of speech, it's a tool in the hands of divinely inspired writers to drive home essential truths about our relationship with God, ethical conduct, and the unfolding of His plan for humanity.

We also bear in mind Paul's exhortation in 2 Corinthians 4:2 (ESV), "But we have renounced disgraceful, underhanded ways. We refuse to practice cunning or to tamper with God's word, but by the open statement of the truth we would commend ourselves to everyone's conscience in the sight of God." This means that we do not twist or distort the Bible to fit our own agenda. We are committed to presenting the truth of God's word in a clear and honest way. We have the utmost respect for the inerrant Word. We believe that the truth of God's word is ultimately persuasive. We trust that if we present the truth clearly and honestly, it will win over the hearts and minds of people.

In other words, 2 Corinthians 4:2 is a statement of the apostle Paul's commitment to truthfulness and integrity in his communication. He refuses to use any methods that are dishonest or deceptive, and he is confident that the truth of God's word will ultimately win out. This passage is a reminder to all of us that we should be careful about how we communicate. We should be honest and truthful in our words and actions, and we should avoid any methods that are manipulative or deceptive. If we do this, we can be confident that the truth will ultimately prevail.

Rules for Interpreting Riddles

The Bible, a complex and rich text, encompasses a variety of literary forms, one of which is the riddle. Although not as prevalent as other genres, riddles do make an appearance in the biblical text. Their existence compels us to consider the rules for their interpretation, especially when employing the historical-grammatical method, which insists on strict adherence to the text's historical and grammatical context.

Defining Riddles

- **Riddle**: A statement or question that requires creative thinking to solve. It is often designed to engage the mind and present a challenge, sometimes to illustrate a deeper truth or principle.

Recognizing Riddles

Riddles in the Bible aren't always presented explicitly as such; you often have to discern them from the context. Sometimes, they appear in the form of parables or complex metaphors that require solving.

Scriptural Examples

1. **Samson's Riddle**: Perhaps the most well-known biblical riddle is found in Judges 14:14, where Samson poses a riddle to the Philistines during his wedding feast. He says, "Out of the eater came something to eat. Out of the strong came something sweet" (ESV). Here, the riddle serves as a test of wit and also serves to advance the narrative.
2. **Riddles in Proverbs**: While not explicitly labeled as riddles, some proverbs require thoughtful contemplation to understand. For example, Proverbs 30:4 asks several questions that serve as a riddle pointing to Jehovah as the Creator.
3. **Ezekiel's Riddles**: Ezekiel 17 presents a riddle about two eagles and a vine, serving as an allegory for Israel's political alliances. This is more complex and serves a prophetic function.

Rules for Interpretation

1. **Examine the Context**: As always, context is crucial. What precedes and follows the riddle? Who are the primary audiences, and what circumstances surround its telling?

2. **Identify the Elements**: Break down the riddle into its component parts. This often involves recognizing metaphors or symbols and their referents.
3. **Refer to Other Scriptures**: Sometimes the Bible itself provides the key to unlock a riddle. Thus, we apply the principle that Scripture interprets Scripture.
4. **Consider the Historical-Cultural Background**: Understanding the norms of ancient Near Eastern riddles, for example, might provide insights into why a riddle was posed in a particular way.
5. **Consult Conservative Scholarship**: Resources committed to a historical-grammatical methodology often provide valuable insights into riddles and their intended meanings.

Common Pitfalls and How to Avoid Them

1. **Over-Spiritualizing**: Some may be tempted to attribute deeply spiritual meanings to riddles that were not intended by the original author. This is to be avoided.
2. **Ignoring the Historical Setting**: Without understanding the historical context, we can misinterpret a riddle's meaning. For example, understanding the Philistine culture can shed light on why Samson's riddle was significant.
3. **Selective Reading**: Picking and choosing elements of a riddle while ignoring others can lead to skewed interpretations. Every aspect of a riddle usually contributes to its overall meaning.
4. **Confirmation Bias**: When interpreting riddles, one must be cautious not to impose one's theological or doctrinal biases onto the text, but let the text speak for itself.

Numbers 12:8 Updated American Standard Version (UASV)

8 With him I speak mouth to mouth,[1] clearly, and not in riddles, and he beholds the form of Jehovah. Why then were you not afraid to speak against my servant Moses?"

God told the Israelites that he speaks with Moses plainly, not in confusing riddles or ambiguous sayings, so that he will be understood.

Daniel 8:23 Updated American Standard Version (UASV)

23 And at the latter end of their kingdom, as the transgressors act to a completion, a fierce-looking king who is skilled in intrigue shall stand up.

---

[1] That is, *face to face*; an expression that is referring to the manner of the communication.

Scholars agree that Daniel 8:23 is speaking of the wicked king, Antiochus IV, who certainly was "a master of intrigue." (Slotki, *Daniel*, 70)

Psalm 49:4 Updated American Standard Version (UASV)

⁴ I will incline my ear to a proverb;
I will expound my riddle with the harp.

The Hebrew word, *chidah*, is used as an expression corresponding to "a proverb" because a riddle can very much be a statement that possess much meaning but is used with ambiguous language.

Proverbs 30:18-19 Updated American Standard Version (UASV)

¹⁸ Three things are too wonderful for me;
four I do not understand:
¹⁹ the way of an eagle in the sky,
the way of a serpent on a rock,
the way of a ship on the high seas,
and the way of a man with a young woman.

There is a similarity to the above list. An eagle soars through the sky; the way of a serpent on a rock is that it crosses the rock, the way of a ship on the high seas as it cuts through the waves. The similarity is that none of these three leaves a trail, which does not allow anyone to follow their path. This now helps us establish the similarity of number four, where the proverb was leading us, "the way of a man with a virgin."

A man may engage in cunning ways of using insincere flattery and pleasantness, especially in order to persuade somebody to do something, to capitalize upon the friendliness of an innocent virgin. She is innocent and untested; she would not be able to discover his charms. It is nearly impossible for her to see the trail or path of a seductive man, yet he has a goal just as "the way of an eagle in the sky, the way of a serpent on a rock, the way of a ship on the high seas." The seductive man has the objective of exploiting her for sex.

Proverbs 1:5-6 Updated American Standard Version (UASV)

⁵ Let the wise hear and increase in learning,
and a man of understanding will acquire wise guidance,
⁶ to understand a proverb and a saying,
the words of the wise and their riddles.

Framing a riddle, which frequently comprises an ambiguous but accurate analogy, involves a powerful and deep mind, and cracking such a riddle calls for the facility to see how things relate to one another; accordingly, the Bible speaks of riddles as belonging to wise persons, and as something, a man of understanding comprehends. This same Hebrew word, which is rendered as "riddles" many times throughout the Hebrew Old Testament, is also rendered "difficult questions" in a different context. – 2 Chronicles 9:1

God himself inspired writers to use riddles or ambiguous sayings or words when speaking of his will and purposes. These are statements that at first seem quite perplexing (because the answer is obscured), but after the time of the original writer, they are understood, making perfect sense.

Zechariah 3:8 Updated American Standard Version (USV)

8 Hear now, O Joshua the high priest, you and your friends who sit before you, for they are men who are a sign: behold, I will bring my servant the sprout.

In the above text, Zechariah and those he spoke to would not have known whom God was referring to when he spoke of "my servant the sprout." They do not know that he is the offspring of the royal line of David, the Son of God, who would be born of a virgin, herself a descendant of King David.

Revelation 13:18 Updated American Standard Version (USV)

18 Here is wisdom. Let the one who has understanding calculate the number of the beast, for it is the number of a man, and his number is six hundred and sixty-six.

Notice first, we are not told the significance of the number six hundred and sixty-six. However, we are told here who will ascertain the significance of that number, the "one who has understanding." We do know some things. We know that "man" (Gk., *anthrōpos*), often signifies the whole of mankind, i.e., humanity. We also know that the number six in the Bible, one less than seven (perfect), can denote imperfection. We also know that when something is mentioned three times, it intensifies what is being said. Therefore, six hundred and sixty-six (666) could be signifying gross human imperfection.

Riddles are designed to confuse and puzzle the hearer. The objective of the riddle is to obscure the significance of everyone except those who have an understanding. The reason the King James Version rendered Hebrew term five times as "dark sentences" is because "the Hebrew word for riddle (*chidah*) is from a root which means to twist, or tie a knot, and is used of any dark and intricate saying, which requires peculiar skill and insight to unravel." (Terry 1883, 268) While what is said is true, the reader should see the root fallacy section below in chapter 7.

A Riddle with a Reassuring Response

Throughout history, many have been jealous of or even confounded by the man who lives outside of the law. The dishonest and corrupt man will often gain a position of great authority. After that, he will take advantage of dominating the poor and the troubled. Should we live in fear of the wicked man? This very question a component of the riddle, is answered in Psalm 49,[2] a psalm of the sons of Korah. It begins,

---

[2] **49:1 all peoples . . . all inhabitants**. The scope of his message is geographically universal. 49:2 low and high, rich and poor. Note the chiastic order (i.e., A-B; B-A) of these

Psalm 49:1-4 Updated American Standard Version (UASV)

49 Hear this, all peoples!
Give ear, all inhabitants of the world,
² both low and high,
rich and poor together.
³ My mouth will speak wisdom,
the meditation of my heart will be understanding.
⁴ I will incline my ear to a proverb;
I will expound my riddle with the harp.

Anders and Lawson write, "The psalmist called upon **all** the **peoples** of the world, both those in low and high positions of society. He requested that they **hear** what his mouth would speak. This was a man who had to be heard. He conveyed **words of wisdom** (Heb. *hokma*, 'skill in successful living') which would give **understanding** (Heb. *tebuna*, 'prudence, insight, discretion'). In words similar to Solomon, the psalmist declared, I will turn my ear to a proverb to teach it. Others would hear this psalm sung accompanied by the harp."[3]

Psalm 49:5-6 Updated American Standard Version (UASV)

⁵ Why should I fear in times of trouble,
when the very error of my persecutors surrounds me,
⁶ those who trust in their wealth
and boast of the abundance of their riches?

Anders and Lawson write go on saying, "The psalmist was perplexed about why he should **fear when evil days** came—evil days caused by **wicked deceivers**. He knew that the success of those who trusted in their wealth and boasted of their great riches was short-lived. Although they strutted about in pride, God would bring them down in judgment."[4]

Psalm 49:7-9 Updated American Standard Version (UASV)

⁷ Surely no man can redeem a brother,
Or give to God a ransom for him,
⁸ (for the redemption of their soul is costly,
and it always fails),
⁹ that he should live on forever
and not see the pit.

---

descriptives. The scope of his message is also socially universal.—MacArthur, John. The MacArthur Bible Commentary (Kindle Locations 22116-22117). Thomas Nelson. Kindle Edition.

[3] Anders, Max; Lawson, Steven. Holman Old Testament Commentary - Psalms: 11 (pp. 257-258). B&H Publishing. Kindle Edition.

[4] Ibid., p. 258

Anders and Lawson write, "Wealth cannot **redeem** (Heb. ***pada***, 'to ransom, purchase') **the life of another** and provide escape from death. **Life** is such a **costly** commodity that it may not be purchased. **No payment**, even from the wealthiest man, is **ever enough** to deliver from the certain destiny of death and decay."[5]

Psalm 49:10-12 Updated American Standard Version (UASV)

[10] For he sees that even wise men die;
the fool and the senseless alike must perish
and leave their wealth to others.
[11] Their inner wish is that their houses will last forever,
their dwelling places from generation to generation,
they have called their lands after their own names.
[12] Man in his pomp will not remain;
he is like the beasts that perish.

Anders and Lawson write, "It is obvious to any observer of life that wise men die just like **the foolish and the senseless**. Death is no respecter of persons. All will leave **their wealth to others** when they die (Eccl. 2:19–21). **Their tombs** will become their new houses, even though their names are attached to large estates that remain. No matter how much money a person may have, he cannot escape death for he will **not endure**. He will die like **the beasts that perish** (Eccl. 3:19)."[6]

Psalm 49:13-15 Updated American Standard Version (UASV)

[13] This is the path of those who have foolish confidence;
and those after them who accept their words. *Sela*
[14] Like sheep they are appointed for Sheol;
death shall be their shepherd,
and the upright shall rule over them in the morning,
and their form shall be for Sheol to consume, so that they have no habitation.
[15] But God will ransom my soul from the hand of Sheol,
for he will receive me. *Selah*!

Anders and Lawson write, "The phrase **those who trust in themselves** refers to the proud rich. Their fate will be like that of **sheep** being led to **the grave**. **The upright will** ultimately triumph over the wicked, whether in this life or in the life beyond **the grave**. Regarding the righteous, the psalmist knew God would **redeem** their lives **from the grave**, paying the ransom himself. This is a payment that no man could pay (vv. 7–8). Thus, the psalmist knew that God would take him **to himself** after death (Ps. 73:24), a fate unlike that of those who trusted in themselves."[7]

---

[5] Ibid., p. 258
[6] Ibid., p. 258
[7] Ibid., p. 258

Psalm 49:16-19 Updated American Standard Version (UASV)

¹⁶ Be not afraid when a man becomes rich,
when the glory of his house increases.
¹⁷ For when he dies he will carry nothing away;
his glory will not go down after him.
¹⁸ For during his lifetime he kept blessing his own soul
(men praise you when you do well for yourself)
¹⁹ his soul will go to the generation of his fathers,
who will never again see light.

Anders and Lawson write, "Because the wicked would perish in spite of their wealth (vv. 6–14), the godly must not let the prosperity of the rich captivate their hearts. **Do not be overawed when a man grows rich**, the psalmist warned. The rich who die would **take nothing with** them (cp. Eccl. 5:15). Why envy the temporal trappings of a meaningless life? After death the wealthy who trusted in their riches would never **see the light of life**."[8]

Psalm 49:20 Updated American Standard Version (UASV)

²⁰ Man in his pomp yet without understanding is like the beasts that perish.

Anders and Lawson write, "Ending this psalm with dramatic bluntness, the psalmist described a person **who has riches** in this world yet does not understand spiritual truths about God, eternity, and redemption. Such a person is **like the beasts that perish**. They have fleeting riches that will soon be taken away by death. It is far better to fear God."[9]

With these words of 49:1, we see that both the rich and the poor could benefit from what was to follow. We see in Psalm 49:3-4 that what the Psalmist expressed came about through the meditation under the guidance of God's Holy Spirit. This is no mere wisdom from man. Under inspiration, he would present his riddle or perplexing problem. In Psalm 49:5, we learn the question, "Why should I fear in times of trouble, when the very error of my persecutors surrounds me"? Yes, should he give way to fear when times of trouble and difficulty come a calling because persecutors, wicked men wish to deprive him of his God given rights? These persecutors were wealthy men. These wealthy persecutors used their power to make even more profits unjustly as they took advantage of the poor. We should not fear such ones, nor envy the wealth and power that they might enjoy. The only possession that they have is their wealth. They have no friends, no loved ones, just those who obey them through fear and persecution. The only life they have is one of boasting own instead of looking to the Creator, who brought these things into existence. Their trust lays in their wealth, not the Almighty God. These wicked ones will not live forever, and their riches are but for a mere moment of time.

---

[8] Ibid, p. 258
[9] Ibid., p. 258

As the psalmist points out at 49:6-10, riches cannot save your brother from death. We could accumulate all of the wealth on the planet, and that is not enough to cover the ransom of one human life. Human imperfection and death are inevitable. Being ransomed from sin and death is beyond all humans. There is no amount of money or any technology, which will cover the price and prevent any man from suffering the penalty of death, allowing him to continue living. "Even wise men die; the fool and the senseless alike must perish and leave their wealth to others." (49:10) The wealthy wicked one would like it to be otherwise. Thus, in compensation, they believe that they can at least keep the family name alive from generation to generation.

Since these wicked ones have used their family name, they believe they are perpetuating their memory. (49:11-14) However, they do not understand that they are mere dust. Even though their wealth and power gave them a name for a very brief time, it will not last forever. They may attempt to sear their family name in the minds of humans for generations to come but that will only be short-lived. Even ancient names like Alexander the Great, Roman Emperor Nero and Caligula, Attila the Hun, Genghis Khan, and more recently, Adolf Hitler, will live on in this brief time of imperfection. However, after Armageddon and the millennium, once perfect humanity is hundreds of millions of years removed from this era, who will be thinking of them? The will be no more remembered than unreasoning animals that perish.

In 49:15-20, the Psalmist contrasts his life with that of the wealthy, powerful persecutor. Like the Psalmist, we need to focus our lives on the doing of the Father's will (Matt. 7:21-23) and not be sidetracked. The apostle John writes, "Do not love the world or the things in the world. If anyone loves the world, the love of the Father is not in him. For all that is in the world, the lust of the flesh, the lust of the eyes, and the boastful pride of life is not from the Father but from the world. The world is passing away, and its lusts, but the one who does the will of God remains forever." (1 John 2:15-17) If we do the will of the Father, he will rescue us from Sheol, not allowing us to suffer an everlasting death that the wicked faces. Thus, his life will be given not to Sheol but into the hands of God. When we have God, there is no reason to give into the fear of man, not envy his wealth. Death is the only thing the wicked man will inherit from his forefathers and pass onto his offspring. Hence, the wicked one has only a world of darkness, not light. Therefore, the wealthy, self-seeking wicked man will live and perish like a beast.

Riddles in Scripture serve various purposes: some test wit, some illuminate wisdom, and others convey prophetic messages. While they are not a dominant genre in the Bible, they offer unique challenges for interpretation. As stewards of God's Word, it's our responsibility to handle these complexities carefully and accurately, adhering to the principles of historical-grammatical interpretation.

We must exercise due diligence in interpreting biblical riddles, knowing that each one is a piece of a much larger puzzle that reveals Jehovah's character, will, and divine plan. As we unpack these challenging texts, we gain not only cognitive knowledge but spiritual wisdom, understanding more profoundly the nature of God and His redemptive work in history. By remaining committed to conservative exegetical principles, we can solve these riddles in a way that honors God and aligns with the overall narrative of Scripture. Note that we cannot do this in depth on every genre, as space does not allow it, so we chose this one to demonstrate the benefits of having knowledge of how to interpret the Bible correctly.

Rules for Interpreting Prophecy

Prophecy is one of the most complex genres in the Bible, carrying with it theological weight and potentially impactful ramifications on one's understanding of God's purposes. Correct interpretation is crucial to preserving the integrity of the biblical message.

Defining Prophecy

- **Prophecy**: A divinely-inspired message often containing foreknowledge of future events, divine judgments, promises, or moral teachings.

Recognizing Prophecy

Prophecy can appear in various parts of the Bible, notably in books specifically designated as prophetic (Isaiah, Jeremiah, Ezekiel, Daniel, and the twelve Minor Prophets), but also interspersed throughout historical books and even New Testament writings.

Scriptural Examples

1. **Isaiah's Suffering Servant**: In Isaiah 53, the prophecy of the suffering servant is a vivid depiction of the crucifixion of Jesus Christ, presented hundreds of years before the event.
2. **Daniel's Seventy Weeks**: Daniel 9:24-27 outlines a prophetic timeline concerning Israel and the coming Messiah, requiring meticulous attention to its apocalyptic language and historical context.
3. **End Times in Revelation**: The book of Revelation is replete with prophecies concerning the end times, including the rise of the Antichrist and the establishment of God's eternal kingdom.

Rules for Interpretation

1. **Context is King**: Understanding the historical and cultural context in which the prophecy was given is essential. Know the intended audience and what issues they were facing.

2. **Literal Interpretation**: When the plain sense of the text makes common sense, seek no other sense. Metaphorical or symbolic language should be understood as such only when the text indicates it.
3. **Scripture Interprets Scripture**: Often, the Bible itself will interpret its own prophecies. For instance, Old Testament prophecies concerning Christ are often explained in the New Testament.
4. **Covenantal Consideration**: Recognize the covenantal background against which many prophecies are made. For instance, prophecies concerning Israel should be interpreted with the Abrahamic and Mosaic covenants in mind.
5. **Historical Fulfillment**: Some prophecies have already been fulfilled, providing a model for interpreting similar future prophecies.

Common Pitfalls and How to Avoid Them

1. **Speculation**: It's tempting to speculate about dates, times, and specifics. However, if the Scripture is not explicit, it's prudent to avoid speculation.
2. **The Newspaper Syndrome**: Equating current events with biblical prophecy can be misleading. While it's essential to believe that the Bible speaks to all generations, not every event corresponds to a biblical prophecy.
3. **Isolation**: Interpreting a prophecy in isolation from the rest of Scripture can lead to misconstrued beliefs.
4. **Allegorization**: This method tends to obscure the intended, literal meaning of the text and replaces it with a subjective interpretation, often distorting the original message. While allegorical interpretation may seem to offer a symbolic, more profound meaning to biblical texts, it should be avoided due to its subjective nature. This method allows interpreters to assign any meaning they choose, which can lead to misleading or incorrect conclusions. Instead, scholars often prefer historical-grammatical interpretation, which relies more on the objective facts of the text, including its historical and grammatical context. Notably, while specific biblical authors like Paul used allegory, these were under divine inspiration and shouldn't be mimicked unless the interpretation is directly provided within the Scripture.
5. **Typological**: Typological interpretation, while it can seem to illuminate parallels between biblical entities and subsequent figures or events, should be avoided in Bible interpretation due to its subjective nature. Such interpretation can potentially distort the original, intended meaning of the text, as it's based more on the interpreter's perspectives than on objective analysis. Therefore, despite its occasional use by inspired New Testament

authors, it is typically only applied in cases where a clear typological pattern is established within the Scripture itself. Like allegorical interpretation, it should not replace the historical-grammatical approach that grounds interpretation in factual, contextual analysis.

Prophecy is a challenging but rewarding genre within the sacred canon of Scripture. It requires diligence, humility, and a firm grasp of interpretative principles grounded in the historical-grammatical method. We must be wary of the common pitfalls that can ensnare even the most vigilant readers. These include the temptation to speculate, to impose current events on ancient texts, or to allegorize the clearly stated prophetic messages.

Remember, the ultimate goal of studying prophecy is not merely to satisfy our curiosity about the future but to deepen our understanding of God's character and His redemptive plans for humanity. In this light, prophecy serves as both a warning and a beacon of hope, driving us toward holiness and the expectant realization of Jehovah's eternal kingdom. By adhering to these guidelines, we can approach the prophetic Scriptures with the reverence and seriousness they warrant, equipped to glean the deep truths they contain.

Rules for Interpreting Biblical Word Pictures

Biblical word pictures, also known as metaphors, similes, and idioms, are an essential literary device used throughout the Scriptures to convey deep truths about God, human nature, and the moral universe. Word pictures can provide insights into various theological truths when interpreted correctly.

Defining Biblical Word Pictures

- **Metaphor**: An expression that identifies something as being the same as some unrelated thing for rhetorical effect.
    - Example: Jesus referred to Himself as "the bread of life" (John 6:35).
- **Simile**: A figure of speech involving the comparison of one thing with another thing of a different kind.
    - Example: "As a deer pants for flowing streams, so pants my soul for you, O God" (Psalm 42:1).
- **Idiom**: An expression whose meanings cannot be inferred from the meanings of the words that make it up.

- Example: "To kick the bucket" doesn't literally mean to kick a bucket, but rather it's an idiom for dying.

Recognizing Biblical Word Pictures

It is essential to recognize when the Bible is using a word picture. This usually involves language that is not meant to be taken literally but conveys a deeper truth when understood metaphorically or idiomatically.

Scriptural Examples

1. **The Vine and the Branches (John 15:1-5)**: Jesus says, "I am the true vine, and my Father is the vinedresser." Here, the metaphor helps us understand the spiritual relationship between Christ and believers.
2. **Salt and Light (Matthew 5:13-14)**: Jesus tells His followers, "You are the salt of the earth" and "You are the light of the world." These metaphors suggest the preservative and enlightening influence of Christians in the world.
3. **Helmet of Salvation (Ephesians 6:17)**: The metaphor of the helmet in the Armor of God signifies the importance of salvation in spiritual warfare.

Rules for Interpretation

1. **Context Matters**: Understanding the cultural and historical context can often illuminate the meaning behind a word picture.
2. **Literal First**: Consider the literal meaning of the words used in the word picture. Sometimes the literal translation brings us close to the intended metaphorical meaning.
3. **Identify Purpose**: What is the underlying message or truth that the metaphor or simile is attempting to convey? This should be consistent with the broader teachings of Scripture.
4. **Scripture Interprets Scripture**: Use other passages to help clarify the meaning of a word picture. Often the Bible provides the interpretative key within the text itself or in other passages.
5. **Avoid Subjectivity**: It's tempting to apply personal interpretations to word pictures, but this can lead to misunderstandings. Always root your interpretation in the text and its context.

Common Pitfalls and How to Avoid Them

1. **Over-Spiritualization**: While it's easy to assign spiritual meanings to every element of a word picture, not every detail carries a hidden message. Stick to what the text emphasizes.
2. **Ignoring Context**: Context is crucial in determining whether language is metaphorical or literal. Ignoring it can lead to incorrect conclusions.
3. **Over-Literalization**: While literal interpretation is vital, insisting on a literal meaning where a metaphorical one is intended can distort the text's meaning.

Interpreting biblical word pictures requires a balanced approach that respects the text and its original intent. Recognizing and understanding metaphors, similes, and idioms in the Bible can open up a rich vein of theological and moral insight that is both intellectually satisfying and spiritually nourishing. While these word pictures can easily be misinterpreted or distorted, careful and disciplined study—grounded in the historical-grammatical approach—allows us to dig deeper into the text to uncover its layers of meaning. This method enables us to honor the divine inspiration of the Scriptures while navigating the human elements that make the Bible both complex and relatable. Proper interpretation of biblical word pictures is not just an academic exercise; it is a spiritual discipline that, when practiced faithfully, brings us closer to understanding the character of God and His purpose for humanity. Therefore, as we approach these illustrative elements of the sacred text, let us do so with diligence, humility, and a keen awareness of the potential pitfalls that can divert us from the path of true understanding.

Rules for Interpreting Biblical Narrative

Biblical narratives make up a significant portion of the Scriptures. They range from historical accounts such as the Exodus to biographies like the life of Jesus in the Gospels. Understanding how to interpret these narratives is essential for extracting the intended messages while maintaining respect for the text's historical and cultural context.

Definition of Biblical Narrative

A biblical narrative is a storytelling genre found in the Bible, often relaying historical events, lives of individuals, or moral lessons. Unlike parables or prophecies, narratives usually tell of actual happenings in a sequential manner.

Importance of Biblical Narrative

Biblical narratives are vital because they give us concrete examples of how God interacts with humanity and creation. They often serve as object lessons for spiritual, moral, and ethical principles. For example, the narrative of David and Goliath (1 Samuel 17) is not just a story about defeating giants but showcases faith, courage, and God's deliverance.

General Rules for Interpretation

1. **Context is King**: Knowing the historical and cultural context can greatly aid in understanding a narrative.
2. **Identify the Main Characters and Their Roles**: Knowing who is who helps in understanding what the narrative aims to convey.
3. **Understand the Plot**: Identifying the problem, the climax, and the resolution can help discern the main point of the narrative.
4. **Extract Principles, Not Laws**: Narratives usually offer principles that are generally true but are not to be taken as universally applicable commandments.
5. **Scripture Interprets Scripture**: Cross-reference related narratives or teachings elsewhere in the Bible for a fuller understanding.
6. **Observe, Interpret, and Apply**: First, make observations about what is explicitly stated in the text. Interpret these observations in their broader biblical context, and then consider how they apply today.

Scriptural Examples and Analysis

1. **Abraham's Sacrifice of Isaac (Genesis 22)**: In this dramatic story, Abraham's faith is tested when God commands him to sacrifice his son Isaac. Understanding the cultural importance of sacrifice and the Abrahamic covenant helps us grasp the depth of Abraham's faith and God's provision. The ram caught in the thicket symbolizes God's provision, and this theme recurs throughout Scripture as God provides for His people's needs.
2. **The Exodus (Exodus 1-15)**: This narrative shows God's miraculous deliverance of the Israelites from Egyptian slavery. The account is filled with God's interventions, from the plagues against Egypt to the parting of the Red Sea. Here, the main point is God's sovereignty and faithfulness to His promises.

3. **The Prodigal Son (Luke 15:11-32)**: This is a parable, which is a specific type of narrative. The prodigal son represents the repentant sinner, the father signifies God's loving and forgiving nature, and the older son symbolizes the self-righteous. The narrative teaches about repentance and the boundless grace of God.

Common Pitfalls and How to Avoid Them

1. **Moralizing**: One mistake is to turn every narrative into a moral lesson while ignoring the historical and literary context. For example, viewing the story of David and Goliath solely as a lesson on facing life's "giants" without recognizing its themes of faith and divine intervention can be misleading.
2. **Over-Spiritualizing**: Narratives should not be viewed as allegories with hidden spiritual meanings unless Scripture specifically interprets them that way.
3. **Fragmentation**: It's easy to focus on small portions of a narrative without considering the broader context, which can lead to misinterpretation.

Biblical narratives are rich tapestries that reveal God's character, humanity's challenges, and the theological and moral underpinnings that are essential for a robust faith. When interpreting these narratives, one must approach them with scholarly rigor, respect for their historical and cultural context, and an eye for literary elements like plot and character development. This balanced approach ensures that interpretations are grounded in the text itself, safeguarding against subjective or speculative conclusions. As we dive deep into these narratives, we learn not just about historical events but also about enduring truths that speak to the human condition. Proper interpretation of biblical narratives is a spiritual discipline that deepens our understanding of God and His interactions with humanity, guiding us toward a life of faithfulness and obedience.

Rules for Interpreting Symbolic, Numbers, Names, and Colors

The Bible contains a rich tapestry of literary styles and devices, including the use of symbolism, numbers, names, and colors. These elements are not just ornamental; they often carry substantive meaning integral to the interpretation of the text. However, these must be approached with caution and scholarly rigor to prevent subjective and speculative interpretations.

Symbols in Biblical Texts

Symbols are objects, characters, or events that represent something beyond their literal meaning. In biblical interpretation, symbols must be understood within their immediate context and the broader context of Scripture.

Examples

- **The Serpent in Genesis 3**: In the Genesis account, the serpent is more than a literal snake; it is symbolic of Satan or evil.
- **The Lamb in Revelation**: The lamb is a symbol of Jesus Christ, representing sacrifice and redemption (Revelation 5:6).

Interpretation Rules

1. Identify the symbol within its immediate context.
2. Cross-reference with other biblical passages where the symbol appears.
3. Avoid allegorical extrapolation unless explicitly warranted by the text or broader scriptural context.

Numbers in Biblical Texts

Numbers often bear symbolic significance in the Bible, but it's crucial not to overemphasize or arbitrarily assign meanings to numbers.

Examples

- **The Number 7**: Represents divine completeness or perfection. The seven days of creation (Genesis 1) indicate a complete creative act.
- **The Number 40**: Often appears in contexts of testing or trial, e.g., Israelites wandered for 40 years (Numbers 14:33), Jesus was tempted for 40 days (Matthew 4:1-11).

Interpretation Rules

1. Examine the immediate and broader context of the number.
2. Take into account its mathematical implications.
3. If symbolic, check other scriptural instances to understand its consistent meaning.

Names in Biblical Texts

Names in the Bible often have significance and can carry thematic weight or even prophetic meaning.

Examples

- **Isaac**: His name means "laughter," echoing Sarah's laughter at the news of her impending pregnancy in old age (Genesis 17:17, 21:3).
- **Jesus**: Means "Jehovah is salvation," describing His role as Savior (Matthew 1:21).

Interpretation Rules

1. Understand the original Hebrew or Greek meaning of the name.
2. Consider any textual commentary within Scripture about the name.
3. Evaluate how the name fits into the broader narrative or thematic development.

Colors in Biblical Texts

Like numbers and symbols, colors can have symbolic implications.

Examples

- **White**: Often symbolizes purity or holiness, as seen in Revelation 7:9.
- **Red**: Can symbolize blood, war, or judgment. Esau is described as "red" in Genesis 25:25, and red horses are found in Zechariah's vision (Zechariah 1:8).

Interpretation Rules

1. Note the color in its immediate narrative or prophetic context.
2. Compare with other instances of the same color in Scripture.
3. Avoid assigning meaning unless supported by scriptural evidence.

Common Pitfalls and How to Avoid Them

1. **Over-Symbolization**: Not every number, name, or color in the Bible has a symbolic meaning.
2. **Inconsistency**: It's critical to maintain a consistent method of interpretation throughout the Scriptures.
3. **Eisegesis**: Inserting one's own ideas into the text is to be avoided. Stick to what the text actually says and its broader context within Scripture.

The Bible's use of symbols, numbers, names, and colors enriches its message and deepens our understanding when approached carefully and conservatively. These elements are not mere ornaments but serve as additional layers of meaning that complement the literal text. By adhering to a disciplined, historical-grammatical method of interpretation and taking into account the broader scriptural context, one can arrive at an interpretation that is both faithful to the text and spiritually edifying. This approach also serves as a safeguard against the speculative and subjective methods that can lead us astray, ensuring that our interpretation remains grounded in the inerrant and authoritative Word of God.

Rules for Interpreting Dreams, Visions, and Revelations

Dreams, visions, and revelations are specialized genres found throughout the Bible. They provide unique insights into God's will, divine interventions, or prophecies. However, they are also susceptible to misinterpretation if not handled with scholarly caution. The historical-grammatical approach serves as a robust framework for interpreting these elements faithfully and accurately.

Dreams in Biblical Texts

Dreams in the Bible are often a means by which God communicates His plans, warnings, or promises to individuals.

Examples

- **Joseph's Dreams**: Joseph dreamt of his brothers' sheaves bowing down to his sheaf (Genesis 37:7). This dream was a divine revelation of Joseph's future prominence over his brothers.
- **Nebuchadnezzar's Dream**: The Babylonian king saw a great statue made of various metals, which Daniel interpreted as successive empires (Daniel 2).

Interpretation Rules

1. Examine the dream within its immediate historical and narrative context.
2. Consult scriptural cross-references that may shed light on specific symbols or figures in the dream.
3. Consider the purpose of the dream. Does it warn, instruct, or foretell?

Visions in Biblical Texts

Visions are similar to dreams but usually occur while the individual is awake. They often have a more significant prophetic or instructive function.

Examples

- **Isaiah's Temple Vision**: Isaiah saw the Lord seated on a throne, surrounded by seraphim, which signified his divine calling (Isaiah 6).
- **Peter's Vision**: Peter's vision of a sheet descending from heaven filled with unclean animals was an instruction to accept Gentiles into the faith (Acts 10:9-16).

Interpretation Rules

1. Contextualize the vision within its broader scriptural setting.
2. Identify any symbols or figures and refer to other biblical uses of these elements.
3. Understand the objective of the vision; is it prophetic, instructive, or corrective?

Revelations in Biblical Texts

Revelations are comprehensive disclosures from God, often encompassing intricate details about the future or the spiritual realm.

Examples

- **John's Revelation**: The Book of Revelation is a complex text filled with apocalyptic imagery that forecasts future events and spiritual realities.
- **Paul's Revelation**: Paul speaks of being caught up to the third heaven but refrains from detailing the experience (2 Corinthians 12:2-4).

Interpretation Rules

1. Approach the text cautiously, acknowledging its complex nature.
2. Distinguish between literal and symbolic language, always leaning toward a literal interpretation unless the context indicates otherwise.
3. Consult other scriptural revelations that may provide additional context or clarification.

Common Pitfalls and How to Avoid Them

1. **Over-Spiritualization**: Avoid attributing unwarranted spiritual meaning to every element in a dream, vision, or revelation.
2. **Isolation**: Don't interpret these phenomena in isolation from the rest of Scripture.

3. **Eisegesis**: Inserting personal beliefs or experiences into the text can lead to erroneous conclusions. Stick to the text and its broader scriptural context.

Dreams, visions, and revelations are specialized genres that offer unique insights into God's will and plans. However, they require rigorous exegetical scrutiny to avoid the pitfalls of misinterpretation. By adhering to the historical-grammatical method, interpreters can remain faithful to the text's original intent and the broader context of Scripture. This method serves as a safeguard against subjective and speculative interpretations, allowing the authority and inerrancy of Scripture to shine through. Therefore, when engaging with these intricate genres, one must employ a disciplined approach that respects both the literary aspects and the divine inspiration of the biblical text.

CHAPTER 6 Interpreting New Testament Writers Use of the Old Testament

Understanding a prophecy written in the Old Testament that's cited in the New Testament involves a multi-layered process. For instance, let's consider a prophecy from Isaiah about the birth of a child who would have a significant future role. While the prophecy might not have an immediate application for Isaiah's original audience, it still serves a purpose for them, much like how prophecies concerning Jesus' second coming serve to give hope to Christians today, despite the uncertainty about when that event will happen.

Key Principles for Interpretation

Single Meaning

In the grammatical-historical interpretation method, a text has only one meaning, and this is derived from:

1. **The Words Themselves**: Understanding the specific words that the author used is crucial. For example, if Isaiah used the term "Immanuel," understanding its meaning—'God with us'—is essential.

2. **Syntax and Sentence Structure**: How are these words arranged and constructed? Are they conditional clauses, imperatives, or statements of fact?

3. **Historical Context**: When and where was this written, and what was happening at that time? Context can dramatically affect the meaning of a text.

Additional Elements to Consider

Although we approach the text with the goal of objectivity, it's essential to remember that we're not inspired in the way the biblical writers were. Therefore, we must be cautious when applying our interpretations.

Three Areas to Examine

1. **Immediate Application**: Even if the prophecy doesn't have an immediate fulfilment, it still serves a purpose. The prophecy may have given hope or guidance to the people who first heard it. Similarly, prophecies in the New Testament about Jesus' return have offered hope to countless generations, even if the exact timing remains unknown.

2. **New Testament Usage**: Understanding how the New Testament writers used Old Testament prophecies is key. They were divinely inspired and often utilized Old Testament texts in ways that revealed further dimensions of their meaning. For example, Matthew cites Isaiah's prophecy about Immanuel to show it has been fulfilled through the birth of Christ (Matthew 1:23).

3. **Consistency in Interpretation**: Since we're not inspired, there's always the possibility of error. However, by consistently applying the principles of grammatical-historical interpretation, we can better align our understanding with the text's original meaning.

By approaching Old Testament prophecies and their New Testament references with these principles, we can gain a more in-depth understanding that respects the text's original context and intended meaning, while also appreciating its ongoing relevance.

When studying prophecies in the Bible, it's important to consider how these messages find their fulfillment. For instance, the New Testament often cites Old Testament prophecies to show how they've been fulfilled in Jesus Christ. In Luke 24:27, Jesus interprets "all the Scriptures" concerning Himself, which includes the prophetic writings. The Gospel of Matthew is particularly keen on highlighting these fulfillments.

Case Study: Hosea 11:1 and Matthew 2:15

Hosea 11:1 states, "When Israel was a [boy], I loved him, and out of Egypt I called my son." Matthew 2:15 cites this verse, saying, "and remained there until the death of Herod. This was to fulfill what the Lord had spoken by the prophet, 'Out of Egypt I called my son.'"

The question arises: Is Matthew suggesting that Hosea's original statement was a prophecy meant to be fulfilled by Jesus? Or is Matthew, under the inspiration of the Holy Spirit, giving Hosea's historical reference a fuller sense, a "sensus plenior"?

What Hosea Meant

It's important to understand what Hosea originally intended. He was not necessarily making a prophecy about the future; rather, he was likely referencing a historical event to make a point to his contemporary audience. His phrase "When Israel was but a boy" refers to the nation's early history, particularly their time in Egypt. Here, Jehovah is depicted as a loving Father who called Israel out of Egypt.

The Role of Inspired Sensus Plenior Application (ISPA)

New Testament writers often quote Old Testament passages, sometimes in line with the original context and meaning (i.e., adhering to the grammatical-historical interpretation). However, at other times, they apply or extend the text in a manner not originally intended by the Old Testament writer. This is what I refer to as Inspired Sensus Plenior Application (ISPA).

In ISPA, the New Testament writer, under divine inspiration, applies an Old Testament text to a new circumstance or gives it another layer of meaning. This doesn't negate the principle that every text has one single, original meaning. The Old Testament passage retains its original meaning, while the New Testament application offers a different, yet divinely inspired, understanding.

In the case of Hosea 11:1 and Matthew 2:15, it seems plausible that Matthew is employing ISPA. Hosea's original audience would have understood his statement as a historical reference to Israel's time in Egypt, guided by the principles of grammatical-historical interpretation. Matthew, under the inspiration of the Holy Spirit, extends this to show how it also points to Jesus, who lived in Egypt before returning to Israel.

Therefore, while Hosea might not have intended his statement to be prophetic, Matthew shows that it has found a fuller sense in the life of Jesus. This doesn't mean Hosea's original statement has two meanings, but rather that it has one meaning in its original context and another in the New Testament, both of which are valid within their respective frameworks.

When examining the use of Hosea 11:1 in Matthew 2:15, we must determine whether Matthew is (1) interpreting Hosea's words as prophetic or (2) applying a fuller or "sensus plenior" meaning to Hosea's historical reference via divine inspiration. The correct interpretation aligns with the second option. Hosea originally referred to a historical event—the Israelites' sojourn in Egypt—while Matthew amplifies this text with a new layer of meaning specific to Jesus Christ's life.

Dr. John H. Walton contends that it is crucial to differentiate between "message" and "fulfillment." In this context, Hosea's "message" was historical and easily comprehensible to his original audience. "Fulfillment," according to Walton, is not the content of the message but rather how God orchestrates His plan in history. Walton argues that grammatical-historical hermeneutics alone cannot identify a "fulfillment" merely by analyzing a prophecy. In essence, it's not necessary to force Matthew's meaning into Hosea's as if the latter were inherently prophetic, thereby validating Matthew's application. Both texts can maintain their distinct meanings without disrupting the unity of Scripture. Walton's stance resonates with Dr. Robert L. Thomas, although Thomas describes Matthew's application as a "completion," arguing that the relocation of Jesus from Egypt completes the original deliverance of Israel that commenced during Moses' time.

Considering that Hosea's initial words were not prophetic in nature, labeling Matthew's use as a "fulfillment" becomes problematic. How can there be a fulfillment when there was no prophecy to begin with? Rather, Matthew's use should be viewed as a "completion" of Hosea's historical reference. When Matthew attributes a new meaning to Hosea's words, it remains his unique interpretation. While this approach may seem subjective, it is fully warranted; Matthew was an inspired writer of Scripture, moved by the Holy Spirit. He wasn't reinterpreting Hosea's original message but offering a "sensus plenior," a fuller sense or completion, of what Hosea had initially penned.

The Greek term "pleroo" underpins the concept of "fulfillment" and carries multiple nuances: "to fulfill, to complete, to carry out to the full, to accomplish, and to perfect." Dr. Robert L. Thomas stresses that the English term "fulfill" doesn't fully encapsulate the semantic range of "pleroo." Specifically, in English, "fulfill" generally implies the historical occurrence of something previously promised or prophesied, whereas "pleroo" can signify much more.

New Testament scholar Douglas J. Moo furthers this point by saying that "pleroo" should not be narrowly construed to only denote the fulfillment of an Old Testament prophecy. In Matthew 2:15, a more apt translation might be, "This was to complete what the Lord had spoken by the prophet, 'Out of Egypt I called my son.'" Here, Matthew employs "pleroo" to signify the completion of a broader, "sensus plenior" meaning embedded in Hosea 11:1. This aligns with Thomas's assessment that Matthew, in essence, provides a "completion" of Hosea's historical reference about the Israelite's exodus from Egypt. The term "fulfill" could be misleading in this context.

Given these complexities, caution is warranted. Specifically, post-Apostolic interpretations—those after the death of the Apostle John in 100 C.E.—that claim to reveal allegorical, typological, or "fulfilled" meanings not explicitly stated by Bible authors should be viewed skeptically. The reason is simple: contemporary interpreters lack the divine authority and inspiration afforded to the original biblical authors. Consequently, no one today has the prerogative to issue interpretations that veer from the grammatical-historical method into the realm of allegory, typology, or "fulfillment" unless explicitly backed by Scripture itself.

While it is tempting to explore speculative interpretations, especially those promising to "unlock" future events or deeper meanings, such endeavors risk leading us astray. The New Testament writers were divinely inspired, and sometimes their interpretations diverged from strict grammatical-historical methods. We, however, don't possess that level of authority and should therefore avoid such interpretive liberties. It's critical to steer clear of subjective interpretations that are not expressly grounded in the biblical text.

The Use of Old Testament by New Testament Writers: A Recap

New Testament writers use Old Testament passages in one of two ways:

1. **Literal Fulfillment**: Here, the New Testament author adheres to the original, grammatical-historical interpretation of the Old Testament passage. This is what we commonly understand as the "fulfillment" of prophecy. The Old Testament passage, in this case, specifically foreshadows a future event rather than indicating an immediate fulfillment.

2. **Inspired Sensus Plenior Application (ISPA)**: This term, coined by Dr. Robert L. Thomas, describes instances where a New Testament writer extends the meaning of an Old Testament passage to make it relevant to a New Testament context. This is an inspired elaboration of the Old Testament text, making it more applicable to the writer's contemporary audience.

The concept of ISPA implies that the New Testament writers, while divinely inspired, didn't always strictly adhere to the grammatical-historical method. Nonetheless, the ISPA approach does not give us, contemporary interpreters, the license to mimic the hermeneutical tactics employed by New Testament writers.

The Ambiguity of the Term "Fulfillment"

The term "fulfillment" can be misleading when discussing these interpretations. For many conservative evangelical scholars, the idea of "fulfillment" extends beyond immediate or initial interpretations, sometimes spanning multiple generations. These prophetic messages have enduring relevance, though they might have been initially addressed to a specific audience. These prophecies could find another level of fulfillment in what the Bible describes as the "end times" or even during the millennial reign of Christ.

The Contextual Importance of Isaiah 65:17

To illustrate, consider Isaiah 65:17, which speaks of the creation of "new heavens and a new earth." While these words offered hope to the original audience, their fulfillment might not necessarily be immediate. In fact, it could have been almost two centuries later, when a remnant of Israelites returned from Babylonian captivity around 537 B.C.E.

Therefore, while prophecies like those in Isaiah might offer immediate hope and relevance to the people of that time, the "fulfillment" could extend beyond their lifetimes. It is crucial, however, to refrain from asserting any interpretive authority not explicitly provided by Scriptural writers. Doing so would risk straying from the objective, historical-grammatical method of interpretation that should guide our understanding of the Scriptures.

A Cautionary Note on Subjective Interpretation

It's essential to be wary of interpretations that claim to unlock the "hidden" meanings of Scripture, especially when they diverge from established methods of interpretation. We don't have the divine authority that New Testament writers possessed. Hence, let's remain anchored in the objective, historical-grammatical interpretation of the Bible, steering clear of subjective approaches that could distort its message.

In Conclusion

The relationship between the Old and New Testaments is one of profound continuity and divine orchestration. From a conservative perspective that adheres to a literal, historical-grammatical methodology, understanding how New Testament writers used Old Testament texts is crucial for responsible interpretation. We primarily observe two methods: Literal Fulfillment and Inspired Sensus Plenior Application (ISPA).

Literal Fulfillment: Aligning with Prophecy

In the case of Literal Fulfillment, New Testament writers follow the original meaning and intent of the Old Testament passage. One vivid example is the prophecy in Micah 5:2, which states that the Messiah would be born in Bethlehem. The Gospel of Matthew, in 2:1-6, explicitly acknowledges this fulfillment in the birth of Jesus. Here, there is a direct one-to-one correlation between prophecy and fulfillment. Both Micah and Matthew are on the same hermeneutical page, speaking of the same event but separated by time. The prophecy in Micah had only one fulfillment: the birth of Jesus, as confirmed by Matthew.

Inspired Sensus Plenior Application (ISPA): An Expanded Interpretation

The second method is what Dr. Robert L. Thomas coined as ISPA. Here, the New Testament writer takes liberties granted by divine inspiration to extend the original meaning of an Old Testament text. Take Psalm 110:1, where David says, "The Lord says to my Lord: 'Sit at my right hand, until I make your enemies your footstool.'" This verse is quoted multiple times in the New Testament, most notably by Jesus Himself in Matthew 22:44 and by Peter in Acts 2:34-35. In these instances, the New Testament writers are imbuing the text with a fuller sense, identifying Jesus as the Messiah who is both David's descendant and his Lord.

This ISPA approach does not give us, as contemporary interpreters, the latitude to make similar leaps in interpretation. The New Testament writers were inspired by the Holy Spirit, a privilege we do not possess. This maintains the integrity of the historical-grammatical method, emphasizing a single meaning for each text at the time it was written.

The Complexity of "Fulfillment"

The term "fulfillment" can be somewhat nuanced in Biblical hermeneutics. From a conservative viewpoint, prophecies in both the Old and New Testaments serve dual roles. They are both a guide for the original audience and a revelation for future generations. Consider Joel's prophecy of the outpouring of the Spirit in Joel 2:28-32. Peter cites this prophecy in Acts 2:17-21 on the Day of Pentecost, stating it was fulfilled through the coming of the Holy Spirit. However, many conservatives would argue that Joel's prophecy had a dual fulfillment: initially for the post-exilic community and also for the early church during Pentecost.

A Case Study: Isaiah 53 and its New Testament Implications

Isaiah 53 is one of the most striking prophecies about the suffering servant. The original audience likely understood it as a message of hope and future redemption, perhaps even associating the suffering servant with Israel itself. However, when we read the New Testament, particularly passages like Acts 8:32-35, the Ethiopian Eunuch specifically understands the prophecy in Isaiah as talking about Jesus. Philip confirms this interpretation. Therefore, what was originally a source of hope for Israel becomes, in the New Testament, a prophetic revelation of Jesus Christ's sacrifice for humanity.

Caution in Modern Interpretation

A vital principle to maintain in conservative hermeneutics is that the historical-grammatical interpretation does not permit the application of ISPA by contemporary readers. Unless a New Testament writer explicitly employs ISPA, claiming such an interpretation would be speculative at best, and irresponsible at worst. While we can observe how the New Testament writers applied ISPA, we don't have the license to extrapolate additional meanings from the text.

The hermeneutical methods employed by New Testament writers to interpret Old Testament texts provide us with valuable insights into the seamless continuity of the Scriptures. Through either Literal Fulfillment or Inspired Sensus Plenior Application (ISPA), these methods demonstrate divine orchestration in the revelation of God's will and plans. It is crucial for us, as interpreters committed to a conservative, historical-grammatical approach, to respect these methods and understand their limitations. This equips us to engage faithfully with the Scriptures, preserving their integrity and conveying their truth for generations to come.

SECTION 2 BIBLE TRANSLATION PHILOSOPHY

Digging Deeper

We put books here on this subject if one is interested in taking the subject deeper. This section gives you foundational knowledge to evangelize or engage people in conversation.

THE COMPLETE GUIDE TO BIBLE TRANSLATION: Bible Translation Choices and Translation Principles by Edward D. Andrews (2016)

https://www.amazon.com/dp/B01GD6ACQG

THE REVISIONS OF THE ENGLISH HOLY BIBLE: Misunderstandings and Misconceptions about the English Bible Translations by Edward D. Andrews and J. B. Lightfoot (2022)

https://www.amazon.com/dp/B0BF2MDJV4

HISTORY OF ENGLISH VERSIONS OF THE BIBLE by Edward D. Andrews and Frederick G. Kenyon (2019)

https://www.amazon.com/dp/1949586979

CHAPTER 7 The Steps of the Bible Translation Process

Preliminary Steps

Selection of Source Texts

The initial and foundational step in the Bible translation process is the selection of source texts. This phase involves gathering the best available manuscripts of the Hebrew, Aramaic, and Greek Scriptures to serve as the basis for translation.

Importance

The critical nature of selecting reliable source texts cannot be overstated. The chosen manuscripts will serve as the foundational layer upon which the entire translation effort will be built. Any error or deviation at this stage will have far-reaching implications for the theological integrity and fidelity to the original texts of the final translation. Hence, the primary goal is to be as accurate and faithful as possible to the original text.

Criteria for Selection

Manuscripts are selected based on several criteria: age, textual family, historical accuracy, and scholarly consensus. For the Old Testament, reliance is commonly placed on the Masoretic Text, a Hebrew text that has undergone rigorous scribal traditions to ensure its accuracy. For the New Testament, textual scholars often lean on the Nestle-Aland Greek New Testament, which represents a scholarly reconstruction closest to the original autographs.

Tools and Methods

Textual criticism plays a pivotal role in this phase. Scholars employ an array of critical methodologies to compare and contrast various manuscripts, examining the types of variants and their implications for understanding the text. These critical tools must be used judiciously and in alignment with a conservative, literal philosophy of translation to maintain fidelity to the original text.

Theological Implications

The selection of source texts is not a process that should be influenced by preexisting theological or doctrinal biases. Instead, the focus must strictly remain on the fidelity to the original texts. The goal is to select manuscripts that have been shown to be most reliable and closest to the original autographs, irrespective of the theological implications those texts might carry. By remaining unbiased in the selection process, the translation aims to provide a faithful representation of the original Scriptures, allowing doctrine to be extracted solely from the text itself rather than being read into it.

In this way, the theological integrity of the Scriptures is not a matter of preserving specific doctrines but rather of ensuring that the selected source texts are as accurate and reliable as possible. This, in turn, allows for the most authentic basis from which any theological or doctrinal understanding should be drawn.

Text Preparation

Once source texts have been selected, the next critical step in the Bible translation process is text preparation. This step can be likened to a goldsmith carefully sorting and purifying raw material before molding it into a treasured artifact. Likewise, the text must be meticulously prepared to ensure the integrity of the translation.

Initial Gathering

The first sub-step involves gathering the selected source texts. These manuscripts may be scattered across libraries, digital databases, and private collections worldwide. Scholarly cooperation is often essential at this stage to access and assemble these foundational texts.

Collation

Once the texts have been gathered, they are collated, meaning they are arranged and compared side by side. This is a detailed scholarly task that involves noting variations between texts, often at the minutiae level of individual words or letters. Any variations are carefully documented, providing an overview of textual witnesses.

Analysis

The texts are then subjected to rigorous analysis. At this stage, scholars delve into the grammar, syntax, and vocabulary of the original languages. The structure of the text is also carefully examined, including any poetic or narrative forms that might exist. Understanding the text's linguistic aspects helps create a framework for the translation task ahead.

Textual Criticism

While closely related to the selection of source texts, textual criticism continues to play a role in text preparation. Scholars utilize various methodologies to assess the reliability of the text, discerning which variants should be adopted or rejected. This process helps further refine the text, bringing it closer to its original form. This is done without allowing theological or doctrinal biases to influence the decisions.

Marking for Translation

After these preliminary steps, the text is marked for translation. This involves making decisions about how specific terms should be consistently translated, based on their usage in the original language. It is also the stage where any potential difficulties are flagged for further research or consultation.

Preparation for Teamwork

Finally, the prepared text is distributed to the translation team, along with any notes, guidelines, or other aids that will assist in the translation process. This collective effort ensures that multiple eyes scrutinize the text, thereby increasing the likelihood of a faithful translation.

In sum, text preparation is a thorough, labor-intensive process requiring scholarly rigor and an unwavering commitment to fidelity to the original text. This step serves to purify and prepare the text, setting a solid foundation for the translation work that will follow. As such, it is a crucial component in the chain of steps leading to a reliable and accurate Bible translation.

Assembling a Translation Team

Assembling a translation team is a critical juncture in the Bible translation process, as the individuals chosen for this task will be the ones to handle the deeply significant and delicate endeavor of rendering God's Word into a modern language. This assembly should be approached with the utmost diligence and discernment.

Expertise in Original Languages

First and foremost, team members must have a comprehensive understanding of the original languages: Hebrew for the Old Testament, and Greek for the New Testament. An understanding of Aramaic is also essential for certain sections of the Old Testament. These scholars should not only be versed in the grammar and syntax but also have a nuanced understanding of idiomatic expressions and cultural nuances present in the ancient texts.

Scholarly Credentials

Beyond linguistic capabilities, it is also crucial to consider the scholarly credentials of potential team members. This includes formal education, published works, and general recognition within the field of Biblical studies. These credentials often serve as a measure of a scholar's ability to contribute meaningfully to the project.

Theological Balance

While the translation should not be influenced by preexisting theological biases, assembling a team that represents a range of conservative, doctrinally sound perspectives can be helpful. This diversity can serve as a check against unintentional bias, ensuring that the translation remains faithful to the original text.

Complementary Skills

Ideally, the team will possess complementary skills that go beyond language and scholarship. Some may be experts in Old Testament poetry, others in Pauline epistles, and yet others in Biblical history or geography. This diversified expertise ensures that various aspects of the text are examined in depth, allowing for a more nuanced and comprehensive translation.

Compatibility and Team Dynamics

Lastly, the team should be able to work together effectively. Team dynamics can significantly influence the pace and quality of the translation process. Members should be compatible in terms of work ethics, commitment to the task, and openness to constructive criticism and scholarly debate.

In assembling a translation team, the aim is to bring together a group of individuals who share a mutual respect for the gravity of the task at hand: rendering God's thoughts into human language as faithfully as possible. Each member must be committed to the primary purpose of giving readers what God said through His human authors, maintaining the theological and textual integrity of the Scriptures throughout the process.

In essence, the assembling of a qualified, balanced, and harmonious team is instrumental in ensuring that the translation project is not only accurate but also held to the highest scholarly and theological standards. The team, thus assembled, lays the groundwork for a translation that stands the test of both academic rigor and spiritual fidelity.

Consulting with Experts

After assembling a qualified translation team, the next important step is to consult with experts in various fields related to the translation process. This additional layer of scholarly input serves multiple crucial functions and enhances the overall quality and accuracy of the translation.

Linguistic Specialists

Even with a proficient team, consultation with linguistic experts who specialize in Hebrew, Aramaic, and Greek can provide nuanced insights into difficult passages, idiomatic expressions, and variations in dialects. This helps ensure that the translation remains faithful to the original languages, adhering to the principles of literal translation.

Historical and Cultural Experts

Consulting scholars who specialize in the historical and cultural backgrounds of the Biblical text can offer invaluable context. This context is particularly important when translating terms or expressions that carried specific meanings or connotations in their original settings. The goal is to translate these in a manner that respects their historical and cultural significances yet remains comprehensible to a modern audience.

Textual Critics

The input of textual critics is essential, especially when dealing with variant readings among the manuscripts. These experts help in determining which readings are most likely to be closest to the original autographs. Their guidance can be instrumental in adhering to the principle of fidelity to the original texts.

Theological Consultants

Given the weighty implications of translating God's Word, consultation with theological experts who align with a conservative and literal perspective can be beneficial. They can provide additional layers of scrutiny to ensure that the translation does not inadvertently introduce doctrinal errors or misrepresentations, while maintaining the focus on textual integrity.

Peer Reviews

The translation process can also benefit from peer reviews. Respected scholars who are not directly involved in the project can offer an unbiased assessment of the work done, flagging any potential issues that the primary team might have overlooked. It's a form of checks and balances that adds credibility and integrity to the translation.

Practical Considerations

Consultations may take various forms, including in-person meetings, virtual conferences, or scholarly reviews of the translation drafts. Regardless of the method, what is paramount is the openness to constructive criticism and a commitment to the highest standards of accuracy and faithfulness to the original text.

Consulting with experts serves to augment the work of the translation team, providing a multifaceted, scholarly lens through which the text is examined and understood. Such consultations should be approached with a commitment to the principles of accuracy and fidelity to the original text, ensuring that the translation stands as a reliable and trustworthy representation of God's Word. By embracing this collaborative approach, the project aims to fulfill its highest responsibility: rendering God's thoughts into a modern language in a manner that is both academically rigorous and spiritually faithful.

Defining Target Audience and Purpose

One of the critical initial steps in Bible translation is defining the target audience and the purpose of the translation. While the ultimate aim is always to accurately convey the Word of God, different translations may have varying objectives and audiences in mind.

Target Audience

The target audience could range from academicians and scholars who seek rigorous linguistic accuracy to laypersons who may be reading the Bible for the first time. Some translations may aim to serve specific language-speaking communities, or even focus on age-specific groups like children or the elderly. Knowing the audience helps the translation team to anticipate the needs, limitations, and expectations that could affect the translation process.

Purpose

Identifying the purpose goes hand-in-hand with defining the audience. Are we aiming for a study Bible that provides in-depth analysis and commentary, or are we focusing on creating a text for devotional reading? While the primary goal remains the same—to be as accurate and faithful to the original text as possible—the purpose can guide specific translation decisions. For instance, in a study Bible, difficult Hebrew or Greek terms might be kept intact with footnotes explaining them, whereas in a Bible intended for broader public reading, more familiar language might be employed.

Importance of Fidelity to the Original Text

While defining the audience and purpose, it is crucial to remember that the primary responsibility is to render God's thoughts accurately into a modern language. This emphasis on fidelity to the original text serves as a non-negotiable standard against which all other considerations are measured. If a translation decision risks compromising this accuracy, it needs to be reconsidered, irrespective of the target audience or purpose.

Linguistic and Cultural Sensitivity

Once the target audience and purpose are defined, the translation team can proceed with heightened sensitivity to linguistic and cultural elements that may affect the reader's understanding. This could involve choosing vocabulary and syntax that are accessible to the audience while still maintaining the rigor and faithfulness to the original languages.

Defining the target audience and purpose does not in any way lessen the commitment to translating the Bible accurately. It simply helps in making informed decisions that can serve the readers more effectively. Every decision, from the selection of source texts to the choice of English vocabulary, is made with an unwavering commitment to accurately convey the Word of God. Thus, by clearly defining the audience and purpose, the translation team can better navigate the complexities involved in this monumental task, ultimately producing a translation that honors God by accurately conveying His Word.

YOUR GUIDE FOR DEFENDING THE BIBLE

Translation Philosophy and Style

Having established the target audience and the purpose of the translation, the next critical step is to clarify the translation philosophy and style that will guide the entire project.

Literal Translation Philosophy

The objective of a literal translation philosophy is to be as accurate and faithful to the original text as possible. This does not mean merely offering a word-for-word rendering of the Hebrew, Aramaic, and Greek texts; it involves a nuanced approach. The goal is to provide the reader with what God said through His human authors, allowing the interpreter (i.e., the reader) to glean the meaning from the text.

Context and Syntax

Literal translation pays keen attention to the original language syntax and the context in which words are used. The corresponding English words are carefully chosen to reflect the original words as much as possible. If the original author used a specific word order to convey or emphasize meaning, every effort is made to retain that emphasis in the translation.

Consistency in Rendering

One of the markers of a literal translation is the consistency in rendering specific terms. When an original language word appears multiple times in similar contexts, it is rendered with the same English term each time it occurs. This helps maintain the consistency and reliability of the translation.

Challenge of Clarity and Accessibility

While a literal translation aims to be as faithful as possible to the original text, challenges can arise when phrases or concepts from the original languages do not have direct equivalents in English or could be misunderstood. In such cases, the translation team must exercise discernment to produce a text that is both accurate and understandable, without sacrificing fidelity to the original.

Role of Theological and Doctrinal Neutrality

In line with the commitment to accurately render God's thoughts into a modern language, the translation philosophy avoids any doctrinal or theological biases. The selection of source texts and the translation process focus solely on the fidelity to the original manuscripts. This ensures that the Scriptures speak for themselves, providing a robust and authentic basis for any theological or doctrinal understanding.

The translation philosophy and style serve as the backbone of the entire translation project. By adhering to a literal translation philosophy, the team aims to produce a version that honors God's Word in its original form, thereby providing the reader with a reliable and faithful representation of the Scriptures. It's not just about translating words; it's about conveying the very thoughts of God, taking into account the linguistic, cultural, and theological complexities involved in this sacred task.

Choosing the Approach to Textual Criticism

For this author, textual criticism is the process of ascertaining the original words of the original texts. Establishing the approach for Old Testament textual criticism and New Testament textual criticism: Radical Eclecticism, Reasoned Eclecticism, Reasoned Conservatism, Radical Conservatism, The Documentary Method.

Radical Eclecticism: This approach is the most liberal and it allows for the greatest amount of freedom in choosing the readings of the text. It is based on the belief that the original text of the Bible is no longer extant and that the best we can do is to reconstruct it as best we can based on the available evidence.

Reasoned Eclecticism: This approach is more conservative than radical eclecticism and it attempts to find the most likely reading of the text based on the available evidence. It takes into account factors such as the age of the manuscripts, the geographic location of the manuscripts, and the theological perspective of the manuscripts.

Reasoned Conservatism: This approach is the most conservative of the five and it gives the highest priority to the oldest and best manuscripts. It is based on the belief that the original text of the Bible is still extant and that we can recover it with a high degree of accuracy.

Radical Conservatism: This approach is even more conservative than reasoned conservatism and it insists on using only the Masoretic Text for the Old Testament and the Textus Receptus for the New Testament. It is based on the belief that these are the most accurate copies of the original texts.

The Documentary Method NT: The documentary approach to New Testament textual criticism prioritizes external, documentary evidence over internal evidence for reconstructing the original text. This aligns with the views of scholars like Westcott, Hort, and Colwell. The discovery of the second-century papyrus 𝔓75, closely related to the fourth-century Codex Vaticanus, supports this method. It challenges the idea that the Alexandrian text is the result of a fourth-century recension, showing that a pure form of the text already existed by the late second century. This lends weight to the documentary approach over alternatives that focus more on internal evidence or categorize texts into less reliable "Western" and other types. Critics argue that preference for 𝔓75 and Vaticanus is subjective, but those who have closely analyzed manuscripts find them to be purer, less prone to errors and alterations than so-called Western manuscripts.

The Documentary Method OT: In Old Testament Textual Criticism, a similar emphasis on a documentary approach is crucial for approximating the original Hebrew text. The Masoretic Text (MT) stands as the principal witness, a product of meticulous scribal traditions dating back to the early centuries C.E., maintaining a Hebrew text that was likely in use well before its time. The Greek Septuagint (LXX), as a secondary witness, is essential not only for its antiquity but for understanding how early Jewish communities read the Hebrew text. It also provides variants that could offer insights into a different Vorlage, possibly reflecting a Hebrew text type that differed from the one that led to the MT. The Dead Sea Scrolls serve as a third weight, furnishing Hebrew texts from as early as the 2nd century B.C.E., some of which align closely with the MT, and others with the Septuagint, thereby adding layers to our understanding of the textual tradition. Other ancient versions, like the Targums, Vulgate, and Syriac Peshitta, fill supporting roles, often helping to settle cases where the primary texts are ambiguous or corrupt. While some scholars have argued in favor of the Septuagint or the Dead Sea Scrolls as more faithful in certain instances, the Masoretic Text, owing to its internal consistency and the rigorous methodology employed in its transmission, usually takes precedence. Caution is exercised against over-reliance on any single textual witness, maintaining the necessity for a balanced approach that takes into account all extant evidence. Skeptics often challenge the priority given to the Masoretic Text, suggesting that it represents a later 'recension' of the Hebrew Bible. However, the antiquity and consistency of the MT, supported by the Dead Sea Scrolls and its alignment with early citations in Rabbinic literature, affirm its prime role. Therefore, a documentary approach that heavily weighs the Masoretic Text, while taking into account the Septuagint, Dead Sea Scrolls, and other versions, is the most prudent method to approximate the original text of the Old Testament.

Translation Phase

Linguistic Analysis

Once the translation philosophy, textual method, and style have been determined, the next critical step is the Translation Phase, beginning with Linguistic Analysis. This is the stage where the rubber meets the road, and the foundational work is carried out to ensure the highest possible fidelity to the original texts.

Understanding the Original Languages

Before any rendering into the target language can occur, an in-depth understanding of the original languages (Hebrew, Aramaic, and Greek) is essential. This involves not merely understanding the dictionary definitions of words but also grasping the nuances, idioms, and particularities of the languages.

Textual Criticism and Manuscript Selection

At this stage, translators also engage in the practice of textual criticism, aiming to select the most reliable manuscripts closest to the original autographs. The focus here is strictly on the fidelity to the original texts and not influenced by any pre-existing theological or doctrinal biases.

Syntax and Semantics

Syntax (sentence structure) and semantics (meaning) are also closely analyzed. Each sentence is broken down into its constituent parts to understand how the words relate to each other and how they function within the larger units of verses, chapters, and books. This allows the translation team to render each phrase as faithfully as possible to the original, keeping in mind the rules of English grammar and syntax.

Lexical Choices

Translators scour lexicons to find the most accurate English equivalents for the original language words. This is a nuanced process. Each word is weighed not just for its basic meaning but also for its contextual implications. The goal is to render the original language word with the same corresponding English term each time it occurs in similar contexts, thereby maintaining consistency and reliability.

Special Considerations for Idioms and Cultural References

While the emphasis is on literal translation, some expressions in the original languages may not have direct equivalents in English or could lead to misunderstandings if rendered literally. In such cases, the translation team must exercise careful judgment to provide an accurate yet comprehensible rendering.

Cohesion and Internal Consistency

Cohesion and internal consistency are also vital. Translators cross-reference related passages to ensure that terminology and phrasing are consistent throughout the text. This provides a harmonious and coherent reading experience, which is critical for the reader's understanding and for maintaining the integrity of the Scriptures.

Linguistic Analysis is a rigorous and meticulous process that sets the stage for the subsequent steps in the translation project. This phase ensures that the translation will adhere closely to the original text, honoring the divine inspiration of the Scriptures and providing readers with the most reliable and faithful representation possible. It is indeed a sacred task that carries with it the weighty responsibility of rendering God's thoughts into a modern language.

Initial Draft and Translation

After the foundation is laid with Linguistic Analysis, the next crucial step is to create an Initial Draft and Translation of the text. Here, the theoretical groundwork and meticulous study of the original languages are put into action.

Crafting the Initial Draft

The Initial Draft is an important milestone. It is the first time the text from the original languages is rendered into the target language, which in the case of the Updated American Standard Version (UASV), is English. At this point, the work from the linguistic analysis phase bears its first fruits. Translators begin the careful work of transposing the Hebrew, Aramaic, and Greek texts into English, adhering to the literal translation philosophy.

Accuracy Over Readability

The goal is to be as accurate and faithful to the original text as possible. While some Bible translations aim for readability, often at the expense of accuracy, the guiding principle here is fidelity to the original languages. Readability is certainly considered but is secondary to the integrity of the text.

Consistency in Lexical Choices

Consistency is paramount, especially in lexical choices. Translators aim to use the same corresponding English word for an original language term each time it appears in similar contexts. This level of consistency aids in eliminating ambiguity and ensures the text is as faithful to the original as it can be.

Contextual Rendering

The translator will often engage in what is known as "contextual rendering," wherein the broader context of a passage, chapter, or book is considered when making translation choices. This ensures that the chosen English words accurately reflect the full scope of the original words' meanings.

The Role of the Translation Team

In most cases, an entire team is involved in crafting the Initial Draft. Multiple eyes on the text ensure that nothing is overlooked. Team members typically have specialized knowledge in various areas, such as Old Testament Hebrew, New Testament Greek, textual criticism, and English linguistics, which provides a well-rounded perspective.

Revision and Peer Review

Once the Initial Draft is completed, it undergoes multiple rounds of revisions. Peer review is an essential part of this process. The text is scrutinized for any potential errors, misunderstandings, or inconsistencies. This step is vital for refining the draft and further aligning it with the original texts.

The Weight of Responsibility

Creating the Initial Draft is a monumental task that carries with it a tremendous responsibility. Translators are acutely aware that they are rendering God's thoughts into a modern language, which demands the utmost care and precision. It is not a role that is taken lightly; rather, it is approached with a deep sense of reverence and commitment to providing the most accurate and faithful representation of the Scriptures possible.

By adhering to these guidelines and principles, the Initial Draft sets the stage for subsequent phases in the translation process, each of which aims to refine and perfect this most sacred and important task.

Using Computer-Aided Translation Tools

In the modern era, technology plays a significant role in the Bible translation process, enhancing both the efficiency and accuracy of the task. Using computer-aided translation tools is now an integral part of creating a faithful rendition of the Scriptures. However, it's essential to note that these tools serve as aids and are not a substitute for the scholarly rigor required for translating God's Word.

Role of Software in Textual Analysis

Computer software can quickly parse the Hebrew, Aramaic, and Greek texts, identifying the grammatical components and syntactical structures. This automation can save an enormous amount of time, allowing the translation team to focus more on ensuring the faithfulness of the translation.

Lexical Databases

Computer-aided translation tools often come equipped with comprehensive lexical databases. These databases are curated to include the range of meanings of words from the original languages, allowing translators to select the most appropriate corresponding English terms while adhering to a literal translation philosophy.

Comparing Manuscripts

One significant advantage is the ability to compare various source texts side-by-side quickly. This is crucial for ensuring fidelity to the original texts. Computer tools can highlight variations in different manuscripts, aiding in the selection of the most reliable sources.

Version Control and Collaboration

Software tools often have features for version control, enabling multiple team members to work on the same text without creating conflicts. This collaborative framework allows for a more streamlined translation process, as revisions can be tracked and reviewed efficiently.

Limitations of Computer-Aided Tools

While software is valuable, it comes with limitations. Algorithms cannot grasp the nuances and subtleties of human language entirely. They also can't appreciate the theological weight carried by the Scriptures. Thus, the use of these tools must be guided by a thorough understanding of the original languages and the theological implications of the text.

Ethical Considerations

The heavy responsibility of translating the Bible requires that these computer-aided tools be used ethically and responsibly. They should not be relied upon to the exclusion of human scholarship and should not bypass the painstaking process of ensuring fidelity to the original languages.

Caution and Balance

While technology offers many advantages, caution must be exercised. The ultimate goal remains to be as accurate and faithful to the original texts as possible. Computer-aided tools serve to assist in this task but should not replace the traditional skills of textual criticism, lexical analysis, and theological understanding.

By appropriately incorporating computer-aided translation tools into the process, translators are better equipped to meet the challenges posed by the task and to produce a more reliable and faithful rendering of God's Word.

Peer Review

The Peer Review phase is a critical step in the Bible translation process, ensuring that the translated text aligns closely with the original languages of Hebrew, Aramaic, and Greek. It adds an additional layer of scrutiny that helps to maintain the integrity, accuracy, and fidelity of the translation.

Importance of Multiple Eyes

No matter how skilled or experienced a translator might be, the human propensity for error necessitates multiple sets of eyes examining the text. Peer review is an avenue for these checks and balances. It allows for a range of expertise to be applied to the translation, which increases the likelihood of a faithful rendering.

Theological Examination

While the focus should remain on fidelity to the original text, the peer review process also serves as a safeguard against any inadvertent doctrinal bias that may creep in. The reviewers often come from a diverse set of theological backgrounds, offering different perspectives that help ensure the translated text is not slanted towards any particular doctrine.

Linguistic and Contextual Review

Experts in the field of ancient languages are usually part of the review team. Their role is to scrutinize the linguistic aspects, such as word choices and sentence structures, to ensure they are aligned with the literal translation philosophy. They also assess whether the translated text respects the context in which the original text was written.

Addressing Ambiguities

Peer review is particularly useful for addressing ambiguities in the text. If a word or phrase in the original language can be interpreted in multiple ways, reviewers can discuss the best approach for a literal and accurate rendering in English.

Consistency Check

Maintaining consistency in terminology and style is another vital role of the peer review process. The team checks whether the same original terms have been translated consistently throughout the text, which is important for the reader's understanding and for the theological integrity of the Scriptures.

Technical Validation

The review also includes a technical validation of the text. Footnotes, cross-references, and other supplementary materials are examined to ensure they aid in understanding the text without adding interpretative layers.

The Iterative Nature of Review

Peer review is often not a one-off process but an iterative one. Multiple rounds may be conducted, especially for complex or contested passages. Each round refines the text, bringing it closer to a faithful representation of the original.

Final Authority

While peer review is a collective effort, final decisions usually rest with a select committee or the chief translator. Their role is to take into consideration all the feedback and make the final call on the translated text, always with the goal of utmost fidelity to the original languages.

Through peer review, the translation project benefits from collective wisdom and multiple layers of expertise, which serve to create a more accurate and reliable rendition of God's Word.

Committee Review

After the Peer Review phase, the Bible translation project moves into the Committee Review stage. This is a critical juncture in the translation process, intended to bring additional layers of verification and rigor. The purpose is clear: to ensure that the translated text remains as close as possible to the original Hebrew, Aramaic, and Greek manuscripts.

Composition of the Committee

The committee is usually comprised of experts in Biblical languages, textual criticism, and theology. They are often individuals who have had extensive involvement in translation work and who are deeply committed to the principles of literal translation.

Role of the Committee

The Committee's primary function is to review the translated text in a comprehensive manner. Each member brings a unique expertise, whether it's in linguistic subtleties, the context of the original texts, or theological nuance.

Interpretive Decisions

One of the Committee's most sensitive tasks is to make interpretive decisions when the original languages offer more than one viable translation. The aim is to arrive at a consensus that most faithfully reflects the original text, avoiding subjective interpretations.

Checking for Consistency

Another vital role of the Committee is to check for consistency across books and chapters, especially when different translators have worked on various portions of the Scriptures. Ensuring that the same original words are translated consistently is critical for the reader's understanding and the integrity of the translation.

Final Review of Annotations

The Committee also reviews footnotes, cross-references, and other annotations. These need to be meticulously checked to ensure they are aligned with the original text and do not introduce any form of bias or interpretation.

Theology and Doctrine

While the focus remains staunchly on the literal translation philosophy, the Committee has the added responsibility to ensure that the translated text does not contradict established doctrine or introduce theological errors.

Resolving Disputes

In cases where disagreements arise, the Committee's role is to resolve them in a manner that is most faithful to the original languages. The objective is not to seek a middle ground but to adhere strictly to the text as it was written.

Final Approval

Once the Committee concludes its review, a final approval is given. This step signifies that the translated text has undergone rigorous evaluation and is considered to be a faithful and reliable representation of the original Scriptures. The approved text then moves on to the next phases of the translation process, such as typesetting and publication.

Through the Committee Review stage, the translation project gains an additional layer of rigor and meticulousness, further ensuring that the translated text stands as an accurate and reliable representation of God's Word.

Avoiding Theological Bias

An integral part of the translation process involves conscientiously avoiding theological bias. Given the gravity of translating the inspired Word of God, extra care must be exercised to ensure that one's theological perspectives do not influence the rendering of the original texts. Let's consider some of the key areas where this is crucial:

Source Text Selection

One of the initial steps where theological bias can creep in is during the selection of source texts. The manuscripts chosen should be those that are most reliable and closest to the original autographs, irrespective of the theological leanings they may appear to support.

Vocabulary and Syntax

Choosing the right words and sentence structures is a meticulous task. Bias can subtly enter into this stage if a translator opts for words or phrases that favor a certain theological viewpoint. The priority should always be to select terms that most accurately convey the original meaning, keeping in line with literal translation philosophy.

Annotations and Footnotes

The supplemental material like footnotes and annotations can be fertile ground for the insertion of theological bias. These must be carefully curated to ensure they merely elucidate the text rather than slant it towards a particular theological or doctrinal stance.

Doctrine and Theology

While a translator may have strong theological convictions, the text should not be manipulated to fit those convictions. The focus must be solely on what the original language texts say, not on what one wishes them to say. Allowing the text to speak for itself ensures that doctrine is derived directly and purely from the Scriptures, rather than being read into them.

Committee Oversight

The review committee should also be alert to any forms of theological bias, both in the translation and among its members. Checks and balances should be in place to question and review choices that seem to be leaning towards a particular theological interpretation.

Transparent Methodology

Transparency in the methodology used for translation can act as a deterrent against bias. The translation philosophy and methods should be explicitly stated, and deviations from this should be documented and justified.

Public Review

Finally, public or scholarly review can serve as an additional check against theological bias. Readers and scholars who have access to the translation can provide constructive feedback and point out potential areas where bias might have influenced the translation.

Avoiding theological bias is not just an ideal; it is a necessity for any translation that aims to faithfully represent the Word of God. By taking meticulous care at each step of the translation process, the result is a text that stands as an authentic and reliable representation of the original Scriptures.

Back Translation

The concept of back translation serves as a critical quality control measure in the Bible translation process. It provides an additional layer of scrutiny aimed at ensuring that the translation is as faithful as possible to the original texts. Here's a deeper look into this crucial step:

The Process

In a back translation, the text that has been translated into the target language is translated back into its original language (Hebrew, Aramaic, or Greek) by a different translator who has not been involved in the initial translation process. This "double-check" aims to reveal any inconsistencies, ambiguities, or errors that might have crept into the first-round translation.

Significance for Literal Translation

Back translation is particularly significant in the context of producing a literal translation like the Updated American Standard Version (UASV). Any deviations from the original text become glaringly apparent during this phase, thereby ensuring that the translation remains steadfast in its literal translation philosophy. This confirms that the text is not just a rewording or paraphrasing but a faithful representation of the original Scriptures.

Context and Syntax

One challenge that often arises in back translation is related to context and syntax. If the back translation returns a sentence structure or word choice that doesn't align well with the original text, it suggests that the translation may not have accurately captured the intended meaning or emphasis of the original authors.

Identifying Nuances

Back translation can help in identifying the nuanced meanings in the original text. If the back translation struggles to capture these, it serves as an indicator that perhaps the target language translation needs to be reevaluated and adjusted.

Committee Review

This step generally precedes a thorough review by the translation committee, which scrutinizes the back translation alongside the original text. Any discrepancies are discussed and resolved to maintain fidelity to the original text.

Theological Implications

Back translation can also serve as a check against unintentional theological bias. If a theological leaning appears in the back translation but is not present in the original text, it suggests that bias might have influenced the initial translation. Such issues can then be corrected to ensure that doctrine is drawn solely from what the Scriptures themselves say.

Limitations

It's important to note that while back translation is an invaluable tool, it is not foolproof. The back translation itself can introduce errors, and some idiomatic expressions may not translate back accurately. Therefore, it serves best as a part of a comprehensive review process.

In summary, back translation functions as an essential tool for quality control, especially for literal translations. It ensures the translated text adheres as closely as possible to the original Scriptures, thereby fulfilling the primary goal of faithfulness to the Word of God.

Public and Expert Review

The Public and Expert Review phase serves as another critical juncture in the Bible translation process. This stage acts as a final sieve, filtering the translated text through various levels of scrutiny before it gets published. Here are the essential components of this phase:

Public Review

A draft of the translated text is often made available to a broader audience for review. This could include laypersons, clergy, and scholars who are not part of the official translation team. The intention is to ensure that the translation resonates with the community for which it is intended while staying true to the original text.

Expert Review

Concurrent to the public review, the draft undergoes an in-depth evaluation by specialists in the fields of biblical languages, theology, exegesis, and hermeneutics. They meticulously examine the text to ensure that it adheres to the original languages faithfully. Such an endeavor aims to make the translation as accurate and reliable as possible, in line with the literal translation philosophy.

Transparency

Openness in the review process strengthens the credibility of the translation. It shows that the translation team is committed to accuracy and is willing to revise the text based on constructive feedback. This is crucial for maintaining a high standard of fidelity to the original text.

Identifying Problematic Renderings

The reviewers look for any instances where the meaning could be ambiguous or misunderstood. Their suggestions serve to refine the text and make it more precise. This is in keeping with the primary goal of being as faithful to the original as possible.

Theological Checks

Expert review provides an additional layer of assurance against theological bias. By assessing the text against the original languages, any inadvertent doctrinal influences can be identified and corrected.

Committee Evaluation

Following the public and expert review, the translation committee reviews the feedback collectively. This comprehensive evaluation aims to reconcile all the comments and recommendations in a manner that retains fidelity to the original Scriptures. Decisions are made through a process of discussion and consensus, with the primary aim being accuracy and faithfulness to the original text.

Importance for Literal Translations

In the context of literal translations like the Updated American Standard Version (UASV), the Public and Expert Review phase is indispensable. The rigor applied during this phase ensures that the translation remains closely aligned with the Hebrew, Aramaic, and Greek texts, providing the reader with a text that is as close as possible to what was originally written.

The Public and Expert Review phase plays an invaluable role in the Bible translation process. It gathers multiple perspectives and specialized expertise to refine the translated text. In doing so, it helps achieve the goal of producing a translation that is both accurate and faithful, offering the reader an authentic representation of God's Word.

Testing the Translation

The Testing the Translation phase is a decisive point that follows the Public and Expert Review stages. At this juncture, the translated text undergoes a series of rigorous evaluations designed to assess its fidelity to the original languages and its clarity in the receptor language. Below are the key elements that shape this phase.

Readability Testing

Given that the translation aims to be written at a 10th-12th grade level, it is vital to assess the readability of the text. Even though the primary objective is to remain faithful to the original text, readability tests help ensure that the translation isn't so complex as to be inaccessible to its intended audience.

Comprehension Testing

This involves subjecting the translation to a variety of readers to gauge their understanding of the text. Participants are asked to summarize or explain sections of the text in their own words. This helps identify any areas where the translation may be causing confusion or might be misunderstood, despite its commitment to literal rendering.

Consistency Testing

One hallmark of a reliable translation is its consistency in rendering terms and phrases. Testers scrutinize the text to ensure that identical or similar phrases in the original languages are translated consistently throughout the Scriptures. This is vital for a literal translation philosophy, which aims to carry the same corresponding English term for original language words whenever possible.

Cultural Sensitivity Testing

While the primary focus is on fidelity to the original texts, it's also important to ensure that the translation does not inadvertently introduce cultural biases or misinterpretations. Evaluators assess whether the text remains neutral and respectful of various cultural settings, avoiding any unnecessary stumbling blocks for readers.

Field Testing

Sometimes, drafts of the translation are sent to various groups or communities who represent the target audience of the translation. Their feedback provides practical insights into how the translation is being received and understood in real-world settings.

Theological Testing

Given the heavy responsibility of rendering God's thoughts into modern language, theological testing ensures that the translated text aligns with the original languages and does not introduce doctrinal biases. This is in harmony with the selection of source texts, which aims for the most reliable and closest manuscripts to the original autographs.

Feedback Integration

All findings from the tests are reviewed and analyzed. Any necessary adjustments are made to the text, always with the primary objective of maintaining accuracy and faithfulness to the original Scriptures.

The Testing the Translation phase is not merely a formality but a rigorous evaluation process. It serves as one of the last quality control steps to make certain that the translation is as close as possible to the original languages while still being understandable to modern readers. Through this detailed and multi-faceted testing procedure, the translation team assures that the finished product will stand as a reliable and faithful representation of God's Word.

Refinement Phase

Review and Editing

The Refinement Phase, specifically the Review and Editing section, is an essential step in the Bible translation process. This phase takes place after the "Testing the Translation" stage and serves as a final polishing process before the manuscript is ready for publication. It is during this phase that the translation team addresses a variety of elements to ensure the highest level of accuracy and faithfulness to the original text. Here's what this phase involves:

Linguistic Review

Firstly, experts on Hebrew, Aramaic, and Greek languages re-examine the translation to ensure that it remains linguistically faithful to the original text. This involves a meticulous review of word choices, grammar, and syntax. Adjustments are made where needed to achieve as close a representation to the original text as possible.

Stylistic Review

While the focus remains on being faithful to the original text, the translation also undergoes a stylistic review to ensure that the English language used is clear and understandable for the reader. Though the translation is aimed at a 10th-12th grade reading level, clarity and proper English syntax are still vital.

Peer Review

Another layer of scrutiny comes from a broader circle of translators, language experts, and conservative Bible scholars who have not been directly involved in the initial translation process. These external reviews offer a fresh perspective, potentially identifying subtleties or nuances that might have been overlooked.

Comparative Analysis

In this stage, the new translation is compared with other highly regarded literal translations to gauge its reliability and integrity. This serves as an additional benchmark and can help identify areas for improvement. It also helps ensure that the translation aligns closely with original texts that have been rigorously established as reliable and authentic.

Reconciliation of Feedback

Feedback from all these layers of review is collated, assessed, and applied to the manuscript. Decisions are made in accordance with the principles of fidelity to the original text, linguistic accuracy, and clarity for the modern reader.

Final Proofreading

After all adjustments have been made, the text undergoes a final proofreading. This step ensures that there are no typographical or formatting errors and that the text adheres to the literal translation philosophy.

Doctrinal Integrity Check

Before finalizing, an additional review is carried out to verify that the translation does not contain any theological biases or leanings. The text should allow the reader to extract doctrine solely from the words of Scripture, not from any interpretive layer added by the translator.

The Refinement Phase—Review and Editing serves as a rigorous, multi-layered process intended to produce a translation of the highest quality. Every step in this phase is designed to ensure that the final product is a trustworthy and reliable representation of the original languages of the Bible. With these meticulous steps, the translation team aims to provide the reader with a text that is as close to the original as possible, thus serving as a solid foundation for understanding God's Word.

Final Committee Review

The Final Committee Review is the culminating stage in the Refinement Phase of the Bible translation process. This is where all the meticulous labor, scholarly insight, and prayerful reflection converge to yield a translation that aspires to be both accurate and reliable. It is a stage that comes with the profound responsibility of ensuring that the Word of God is represented as faithfully as possible in a modern language. Let's delve into the core activities that are part of this crucial phase:

Assembling the Final Committee

This committee is usually composed of senior translators, linguistic experts, and conservative Bible scholars. The members should have been either directly involved in or closely following the translation project, ensuring they are fully aware of its guiding principles and objectives.

Comprehensive Evaluation

Each member reviews the final manuscript thoroughly, ensuring it meets the criteria established for a literal translation philosophy. They examine whether the text is both linguistically accurate and faithful to the original Hebrew, Aramaic, and Greek languages. This is the last opportunity to catch any potential errors or oversights, making this review critically important.

Consensus Building

During the committee's meetings, open dialogue and discussions are encouraged. The objective is to reach a unanimous or near-unanimous agreement on every aspect of the translation. Any discrepancies or disagreements are addressed and deliberated until consensus is reached.

Final Scrutiny for Doctrinal Integrity

Special attention is given to ensuring that the translation is free from theological or doctrinal biases. The committee evaluates whether the text allows the reader to extract doctrine solely from the Word itself, without any interpretation injected by the translators.

Final Validation Against Source Texts

The committee undertakes a final comparison with the source texts selected for the project. This comparison ensures the translated text remains aligned with the original autographs as closely as possible. Any last-minute adjustments needed for higher fidelity to the source texts are made at this point.

Verification of Readability and Syntax

While the primary objective is to offer a translation as close to the original as possible, the committee also ensures that the translation is coherent and understandable, targeted at a 10th-12th grade reading level.

Approval and Endorsement

After reaching a consensus and ensuring all criteria have been met, the committee provides its final approval and endorsement. This serves as the formal conclusion of the translation process and permits the project to move on to the publishing phase.

The Final Committee Review is the last but equally important line of defense in ensuring the translation's integrity. It serves as the capstone that validates the years of laborious work invested in translating the Bible. The aim is to produce a text that is not only reliable but also equips the reader to engage deeply with the Word, offering them a faithful representation of God's thoughts conveyed in the original languages.

Proofreading

Proofreading is an essential step in the Refinement Phase of Bible translation. While it might appear to be a purely mechanical process, it is integral to ensuring that the highest standards of accuracy and fidelity to the original text are maintained. Below are some key aspects of the proofreading phase:

Multiple Rounds of Review

Given the critical nature of the content, multiple rounds of proofreading are generally advised. The aim is to eliminate any typographical errors, grammatical issues, or inconsistencies that may have been overlooked in earlier stages.

Textual Integrity Check

Proofreaders must ensure that the translation reflects the original Hebrew, Aramaic, and Greek texts faithfully. Any deviation from the original languages, even if unintentional, could potentially compromise the text's integrity.

Consistency in Terminology

Uniformity in terminology is crucial, particularly in a literal translation. Words or phrases that appear repeatedly in the original language should ideally be represented by the same English terms, unless the context suggests otherwise. This helps maintain continuity and aids the reader in scriptural understanding.

Language and Syntax

The translation should aim for clarity while adhering to the complexity of the original languages. While the goal is not to produce an easy-to-read version, coherence and readability should still be checked, targeting a 10th-12th grade reading level.

Read-Aloud Tests

It's advantageous to include a step where the text is read aloud. This can reveal awkward phrasing or convoluted sentences that may not be immediately apparent during silent reading. Although readability is secondary to accuracy, the translation should not be unnecessarily cumbersome.

Peer Review

Aside from internal proofreading, it may be beneficial to have external conservative Bible scholars or linguistic experts review the text. This adds an extra layer of scrutiny and can highlight areas for improvement that internal team members may have missed.

Final Comparison with Source Texts

A last verification against the source texts ensures that no elements have been altered or lost during the translation and proofreading phases. This underscores the commitment to produce a translation that is as close as possible to the original autographs.

Sign-Off and Documentation

Once all members are satisfied that the text meets the required standards for accuracy and fidelity, they sign off on the proofreading phase. It is crucial to document all changes and discussions for future reference and for the sake of transparency.

The Proofreading step, while seemingly straightforward, serves as a final safeguard to ensure that the translated text meets the stringent criteria set forth for a literal translation. This phase ensures that the translation process culminates in a text that is both reliable and equips the reader to engage deeply with the Word of God, in as accurate a manner as possible, consistent with the original languages.

Publication Phase

Typesetting and Formatting

The publication phase, particularly typesetting and formatting, serves as the final step in transforming a carefully translated manuscript into a printed and electronic Bible that can be distributed to the public. The commitment to literal translation and accuracy must continue to be upheld even in this phase. Here are some key aspects to consider:

Text Layout and Design

The layout of the text should be designed to facilitate easy reference and readability, but without sacrificing the accuracy of the translated words. This often involves a balance between the number of words per line, the size and style of the font, and the use of headings and subheadings to help the reader navigate the text.

Verse Numbering and Cross-References

The inclusion of verse numbers is crucial for ease of navigation and cross-referencing. It's essential that these numbers align perfectly with the translated text. Adding cross-references can also be valuable in helping the reader to understand the Scripture more deeply, provided they are accurate and relevant.

Footnotes and Marginal Notes

Footnotes can provide additional context or explain translation choices for specific words or phrases. However, these should be used sparingly and should never serve as a substitute for a literal translation. Marginal notes may offer alternative readings based on the most reliable manuscripts.

Punctuation and Capitalization

Special attention must be given to punctuation, as these small marks can greatly influence the interpretation of a text. The challenge is to use punctuation that both reflects the original meaning and conforms to modern English usage. Also, capitalization rules must be consistent throughout, particularly for divine pronouns and key theological terms.

Review and Test Prints

Before mass printing, test copies should be printed and reviewed meticulously for any errors in typesetting or formatting. This involves both electronic versions and physical print, ensuring that the text displays correctly on various platforms and devices.

Usability Checks

Even in a translation that is designed for a 10th-12th grade reading level, checks should be done to ensure that the typesetting and formatting aid in comprehension rather than hinder it. While the focus is not on making the Bible easy to read, it should not be difficult to navigate.

Final Approvals

After exhaustive review, the typesetting and formatting are approved for publication. All decisions, changes, and justifications should be documented carefully for transparency and for any future editions that may be produced.

Typesetting and formatting in the Publication Phase may appear to be largely technical tasks, but they play a critical role in making sure that the translation reaches the reader in a format that is both usable and faithful to the original text. Even at this final stage, the commitment to translating truth accurately and faithfully must guide all decisions, ensuring that the end product is worthy of the sacred task of rendering God's Word into a modern language.

Publication

The actual publication of the Bible is the culmination of a long and meticulous process that has involved rigorous translation, review, and formatting efforts. Now, all these elements are assembled to release a complete Bible that will be accessible to the public. Here's a closer look at this phase.

Final Checks

Before proceeding with mass publication, one final round of checks is performed to confirm that the manuscript is error-free and that it aligns with the commitment to be as faithfully accurate to the original text as possible.

Printing and Digital Formats

A critical decision at this stage is the media formats in which the Bible will be published. This usually includes both print and digital versions. It's crucial that the high-quality standards are maintained across all formats, as each has its own set of challenges and opportunities.

Copyrighting

Given the sanctity and gravity of the text, copyrighting usually aims to protect the integrity of the translation rather than for commercial gain. This ensures that the text can't be altered or misused in ways that compromise its fidelity to the original languages.

Distribution Channels

The next step is deciding on the distribution channels. This may include religious institutions, online platforms, bookstores, and direct sales. The objective is to make the Bible as accessible as possible while maintaining the integrity of the translation.

Launch and Publicity

Even the most faithful translation won't be effective if people don't know about it. Therefore, a strategic plan is usually developed for the launch and publicity of the new translation. This could involve press releases, endorsements from reputable scholars, and various forms of media coverage.

Ongoing Review

The process of translation and publication doesn't necessarily end with the first edition. Readers' feedback, scholarly reviews, and advances in biblical linguistics and archaeology can all serve as bases for subsequent editions. However, any modifications must continue to adhere to the primary goal of literal and faithful translation.

User Engagement

While the translation is intended for a 10th-12th grade reading level, it's beneficial to gather data on how readers are engaging with the text. Are they finding it accessible? Is the literal translation aiding or hindering their study? This feedback can be invaluable for future editions.

The publication phase is not merely a logistical step but rather the moment when the years of scholarly effort finally reach the intended audience. This phase must be executed with the same diligence and reverence that have guided the translation process from its inception. The goal remains unwavering: to provide a translation that is as faithful as possible to the original text, thereby providing the reader with the most authentic representation of God's Word.

CHAPTER 8 Defining the Terms of the Bible Translation Debate

The Preference for Literal Bible Translation in Plenary Inspiration

The concept of plenary inspiration holds that every word in the Bible is inspired by God. This means that not just the ideas or themes, but the very words themselves are divinely inspired. As 2 Timothy 3:16-17 states, "All Scripture is breathed out by God and profitable for teaching, for reproof, for correction, for training in righteousness; so that the man of God may be fully competent, equipped for every good work." This belief underscores the seriousness and sacredness of the task of Bible translation.

Given that each word is inspired, a literal translation philosophy is the most appropriate way to honor this divine origin. It keeps as close as possible to the original text in Hebrew, Aramaic, and Greek, thereby preserving not just the message but the specific words that were inspired. By adhering to a literal translation methodology, the translator seeks to minimize the introduction of any human interpretation or bias into the text.

When the text is altered or paraphrased, it could inadvertently omit or add elements that were not in the original, thereby affecting the inspired nature of the Scripture. For instance, a non-literal translation might smooth out difficult or awkward phrases for the sake of readability, but in doing so, it risks losing the nuance or emphasis placed by the original author, who was guided by divine inspiration.

Moreover, the individual words in the original languages often carry deeper meanings or connotations that might be lost in a more "thought-for-thought" translation. These nuances might be essential for proper exegesis and doctrinal understanding. A literal translation respects the complexities and subtleties of the original languages and aims to bring them into the target language as faithfully as possible.

Given the solemn responsibility of translating God's inspired Word, a literal translation upholds the integrity of the text, respects its divine origins, and minimizes the risks of human error or interpretation influencing the translated work. Therefore, in line with the belief in plenary inspiration, a literal translation offers the most reliable and respectful rendering of the Scriptures.

"Literal" (or "Word-for-Word") Translation

In the realm of Bible translation, the term "literal" often evokes strong opinions, but it's vital to clarify what is meant by this term to engage in meaningful discourse. A "literal" or "word-for-word" translation aims to represent the original Hebrew, Aramaic, and Greek texts as faithfully as possible in the receptor language, which in this context is English. However, the term should not be reduced to a mere mechanical substitution of words; it should be understood within the realm of grammatical and syntactic rules of the target language.

Conceptual Integrity

The core objective of a literal translation is to maintain the conceptual integrity of the text. This is achieved by striving to retain the same semantic domain of each word in the original languages. For example, the Hebrew term "chesed," often rendered as "loving-kindness" or "steadfast love," carries a unique blend of love, loyalty, and covenant faithfulness. A literal translation would aim to capture these nuances rather than reducing it to just "love" or "mercy."

Grammatical and Syntactic Faithfulness

A literal translation is also committed to representing the grammar and syntax of the original languages. The famous phrase in Genesis 1:1, "In the beginning, God created the heavens and the earth," maintains the same subject-verb-object order as found in the Hebrew. This isn't mere aesthetics but serves to emphasize the actor and the action, thus influencing interpretation.

Word Order and Emphasis

The arrangement of words in a sentence can significantly influence its emphasis and the weight it carries. In biblical Greek, this is particularly true. Placing a word at the beginning of a sentence often serves to accentuate its importance, functioning as a means of emphasis.

Let's consider a different example from the New Testament: Romans 8:1, which in the UASV reads, "There is therefore now no condemnation for those who are in Christ Jesus." In the Greek, the word for "now" (νῦν) is placed at a position that gives it a level of emphasis, stressing the immediacy of the state of "no condemnation."

In a dynamic equivalent translation, the emphasis on "now" might be overlooked or diluted. A rendering might be, "So, there's no condemnation for those who belong to Christ Jesus," where the immediacy conveyed by "now" is missing. The placement of "now" in the original Greek serves to highlight the transformative power of being "in Christ Jesus," emphasizing that the absence of condemnation is not a future promise alone, but a present reality.

So why does this matter? Because these nuances—these small but profound emphases—are divinely orchestrated to convey a layered and rich meaning. They are an integral part of the text as inspired by God and penned by the human author. When a translation approach like dynamic equivalence glosses over these elements, it runs the risk of diminishing the depth of the original text. Therefore, a literal translation aims to preserve these nuances, giving readers the opportunity to engage with the text in a manner as close as possible to the original.

Vocabulary Consistency

Consistency in translating terms plays a significant role in a literal approach. The Hebrew word "nephesh," commonly translated as "soul," is often rendered uniformly across different contexts. Such consistency allows the reader to trace the concept throughout Scripture, permitting a more coherent biblical theology to emerge.

Limitations and Challenges

While striving for a word-for-word correspondence, translators acknowledge that it's sometimes necessary to deviate slightly to make the text comprehensible. For example, idioms or cultural references may not have direct equivalents in English. In these instances, the translator uses judgment to select an English term that conveys the closest meaning within the original context.

Dispelling Myths

1. **Worship of Words**: Critics argue that a literal approach "worships words." However, the focus is not on the words per se but on the meaning they convey. The words are vehicles of divine revelation and deserve faithful representation.

2. **Naivete**: Accusations of naivete overlook the fact that the ultimate aim is to convey truth, which sometimes requires complex or nuanced renderings.

3. **Transcription or Transliteration**: A literal translation is not a mere transcription. It involves understanding the original languages and applying that understanding to bring out the full meaning in English.

4. **All Translation is Interpretation**: While all translation involves some level of interpretation, a literal approach minimizes interpretive liberties, thus providing a text closer to the original.
5. **Obscurity**: While a literal translation can sometimes be challenging to read, it has the advantage of requiring the reader to delve deeply into the text. This is consistent with the expectation that understanding Scripture is an endeavor requiring earnest study.

Theological Implications

Maintaining a literal translation aligns with the notion of plenary inspiration, that every word of the Scriptures is God-breathed. This approach aids in the preservation of doctrinal purity, allowing theological positions to emerge from the text rather than being imposed upon it.

In summary, a literal or word-for-word translation seeks to bring as much of the original language into the target language as possible. It involves a delicate balance of maintaining linguistic fidelity and ensuring comprehensibility, guided by a deep respect for the divine inspiration of the text. This method provides the reader with the closest approximation to the original text, empowering them to engage in rigorous biblical study and accurate interpretation.

"Dynamic Equivalent" (or "Thought-for-Thought") Translation

The term "dynamic equivalence" is frequently invoked in discussions about Bible translation philosophy. Developed primarily by translation scholar Eugene A. Nida, this method seeks to convey the 'thought' or 'message' of the original text into the 'thought patterns' of the target audience. Dynamic equivalence does not aim for a word-for-word correspondence but emphasizes the reception of the text by the reader in their own cultural and linguistic context. It is a methodology more concerned with reader-response than with preserving the form or specific linguistic elements of the original text.

Theoretical Framework

Dynamic equivalence operates on the premise that language is primarily a vehicle for communication of meaning. As such, the focus is not necessarily on the form, syntax, or individual words in the text but on conveying the 'intended meaning' as understood by the translator. It is less concerned with reproducing the grammatical structure and more concerned with making the text easily understandable for the modern reader.

Practical Examples

Let's take a biblical example to illustrate. In the UASV, a literal translation, Matthew 6:11 reads: "Give us this day our daily bread." A dynamic equivalent version might render it as "Give us the food we need for today." Here, the thought is preserved, but the specific words and structure are not.

Another example can be seen in 1 Corinthians 7:1 which, in the ESV, reads: "It is good for a man not to have sexual relations with a woman." A dynamic equivalent might translate it as "It's a good thing for a man not to sleep with a woman." Here, the dynamic equivalent seeks to unpack the cultural and idiomatic subtleties in order to make the text more comprehensible for the contemporary reader.

The Updated American Standard Version is actually more literal. "It is good for a man not to touch a woman."[1]

[1] That is, not to have sexual relations with a woman.

So, it appears that even the ESV is dipping its toe into the pool of the interpretive translation philosophy. If we are going for the literal translation, the UASV is preferred, with a footnote that offers the meaning more clearly. We needed to make a valuable point about the distinctions among literal translations. While the ESV is generally considered to fall within the literal spectrum, it occasionally employs a degree of interpretive latitude, as demonstrated by its rendering of 1 Corinthians 7:1. The Updated American Standard Version (UASV) provides a more literal translation of the Greek word "haptesthai," which essentially means "to touch." This literal translation adheres more closely to the original text, leaving the task of interpretation to the reader, guided by a clarifying footnote.

This observation underscores the important idea that even within the realm of literal translation philosophy, there are varying degrees of adherence to the original words. It serves as a useful reminder that the primary goal of a literal translation is to offer the reader what God said through His human authors, not what the translator thinks God meant. This commitment to fidelity in translation is crucial, especially when certain versions may deviate, however slightly, from a strict literal approach.

Critiques of Dynamic Equivalence

1. **Loss of Nuance**: Dynamic equivalence often sacrifices the nuances and idiosyncrasies of the original text, potentially leading to a loss of depth in interpretation. Words carry theological, cultural, and literary weight that can be obscured when one opts for readability over textual fidelity.
2. **Interpreter vs. Translator**: A major point of contention is the role the translator plays in the interpretation of the text. In dynamic equivalence,

the translator takes on a more assertive role in interpreting the 'meaning' of the text for the reader, which some argue is not the translator's prerogative.

3. **Theological Concerns**: Given the focus on readability and cultural relevance, there's a risk that the translation might inadvertently introduce theological biases or misinterpretations. One word can have a range of meanings, each with its own theological implications. Dynamic equivalence can sometimes obscure these important distinctions.

4. **Difficulty with Complexity**: Some biblical texts are intentionally complex, filled with tensions and ambiguities. Dynamic equivalence tends to smooth out these difficulties, thereby depriving the reader of the opportunity to wrestle with the text as the original audience might have.

5. **Misuse of the 'All Translation is Interpretation' Principle**: While it's true that all translation involves some level of interpretation, the dynamic equivalent approach has been criticized for taking this principle too far, interpreting not just words but also meaning and intent, which should be left to the reader.

Dynamic equivalent translation, while popular and accessible, presents several challenges, particularly for those committed to a literal, word-for-word translation philosophy. The emphasis on readability and cultural relevance can sometimes come at the cost of textual and theological fidelity, making it a less than ideal choice for those who believe that every word of the Scriptures is God-breathed and serves an intentional, divinely orchestrated purpose. Therefore, while dynamic equivalence may serve as an auxiliary resource for the modern reader, it shouldn't replace the essential work of literal translations that aim to bring as much of the original text into the target language as possible.

Translations Fall Along a Spectrum

Bible translation is a subject that elicits strong opinions, and the debate over the "best" approach to rendering God's Word into modern languages often gets clouded by misunderstandings and myths. One crucial point to recognize is that translations exist along a spectrum—from the most literal to the most dynamic—and each philosophy of translation has its merits and limitations.

Literal Translations

At one end of the spectrum are literal translations. These aim to render the original Hebrew, Aramaic, and Greek texts as accurately and faithfully as possible, in keeping with English syntax and grammar. The Updated American Standard Version (UASV) is an example of a Bible that adheres rigorously to this philosophy. A literal translation takes the original language word and, in most instances, translates it with the same corresponding English term every time it occurs. Such translations often include footnotes to provide additional context or to clarify idiomatic expressions that might not carry over well into English. They don't aim for ease of reading at the expense of textual fidelity.

An example can be found in Romans 12:2, which in the UASV reads: "And do not be conformed to this world, but be transformed by the renewing of your mind." The word "conformed" in the original Greek is "syschēmatizesthe," which is a passive verb meaning to be fashioned in the same form as something else. A literal translation like the UASV keeps this word as "conformed," thereby preserving the author's original choice.

Dynamic Equivalent Translations

The other end of the spectrum includes dynamic equivalent translations. While still aiming for accurate conveyance of the original texts, these versions prioritize readability and comprehension for contemporary audiences. For instance, the New Living Translation (NLT) would render Romans 12:2 as: "Don't copy the behavior and customs of this world, but let God transform you into a new person by changing the way you think." While it captures the essence of the message, the term "copy the behavior and customs" is an interpretive move away from the word "conformed."

Middle-of-the-Road Translations

The New International Version (NIV) does indeed serve as a more "middle-of-the-road" translation, aiming for a balance between literal rendering and dynamic equivalence for the sake of modern readers. While the English Standard Version (ESV) and the Christian Standard Bible (CSB) lean more towards the literal side, they do make occasional concessions for readability and cultural comprehension.

- Literal: KJV, ASV, RSV, NASB, UASV

- Leans Literal: ESV, CSB, LEB

- Middle of the Road: NIV, NET

- Leans Interpretive: NRSV

- Interpretive Translations: CEV, NLT, TEV

This breakdown helps to illustrate the spectrum of Bible translations more accurately. Each category has its own strengths and weaknesses, but understanding where a translation falls on this continuum can assist the reader in making a more informed choice.

Myths and Misunderstandings

Several myths cloud the discussion about literal translations. Contrary to popular belief, striving for a literal translation is not a form of "word worship." Words are the carriers of meaning, and to dismiss the importance of words is to undermine the Scripture's own claim to the inspiration of its very words. Similarly, the charge that literal translations are mere "transcriptions" is misleading. The task involves nuanced decisions about syntax, semantics, and cultural context. Yet, the ultimate goal is not to make the text easy to read but to make it as accurately faithful to the original as possible.

The criticism that "all translation is interpretation" requires qualification. While it's true that some level of interpretation is inevitable in any act of translation, a literal approach minimizes this by sticking as closely as possible to the original words and structure of the text. Interpretation is the job of the reader, guided by the Holy Spirit-inspired Word of God, not the translator.

Textual Integrity and Theological Neutrality

The goal of a faithful translation should be theological neutrality. This means the selection of source texts should be based solely on their fidelity to the original languages, without regard to the theological implications. Thus, literal translations aim to provide an authentic basis for any theological or doctrinal understanding to be drawn. By sticking closely to the original languages, a literal translation ensures that the word of God is presented in a manner that is as unaltered as possible, allowing the reader to engage directly with the text as it was inspired.

No translation can claim absolute perfection, but those that strive for literal accuracy offer a closer approximation to the original text, placing the onus of interpretation where it belongs: on the reader. Understanding that translations fall along a spectrum can help us appreciate the merits and limitations of each approach, thereby making us more informed readers of God's Word.

The Claim Supported by the Bible's Teaching about Its Own Words

The Bible itself makes a potent case for its words, not just its thoughts, being divinely inspired. Understanding this key idea plays a pivotal role in the approach to Bible translation. We look to key verses to establish this: 2 Timothy 3:16, 2 Peter 1:20-21, Proverbs 30:5, Psalm 12:6, Matthew 4:4, and Revelation 22:18-19.

The Bible's Self-claims

Let's consider 2 Timothy 3:16: "All Scripture is breathed out by God and profitable for teaching, for reproof, for correction, and for training in righteousness." This verse clearly states that every word in the Scriptures is inspired by God, not merely the thoughts or ideas behind those words.

Similarly, 2 Peter 1:20-21 highlights that human interpretation is not the driving force behind the Scriptures: "No prophecy of Scripture comes from someone's own interpretation. For no prophecy was ever produced by the will of man, but men spoke from God as they were carried along by the Holy Spirit."

Proverbs 30:5 further attests, "Every word of God proves true; he is a shield to those who take refuge in him." Psalm 12:6 confirms this: "The words of Jehovah are pure words, like silver refined in a furnace on the ground, purified seven times."

Jesus Himself emphasized the importance of individual words in Matthew 4:4: "Man shall not live by bread alone, but by every word that comes from the mouth of God."

Lastly, Revelation 22:18-19 issues a dire warning against altering the words of Scripture: "I warn everyone who hears the words of the prophecy of this book: if anyone adds to them, God will add to him the plagues described in this book, and if anyone takes away from the words of the book of this prophecy, God will take away his share in the tree of life and in the holy city, which are described in this book."

The Importance of Words

The Bible's claim on the inspiration and importance of its words shapes the translation philosophy one should adopt. If a single word is changed or removed, the meaning can significantly shift. For instance, in John 14:6, Jesus says, "I am the way, and the truth, and the life. No one comes to the Father except through me." The word "the" before "way," "truth," and "life" is pivotal; changing it alters the exclusivity of Christ's claim.

Literal Translation Philosophy and Responsibilities

Translating God's Word requires a tremendous sense of responsibility. A literal translation like the Updated American Standard Version (UASV) aims for more than just a word-for-word rendering. It aligns with English grammar while staying faithful to the original text. It maintains the author's choice of words and structure unless they would be clearly misunderstood in the target language.

Source Texts and Doctrinal Integrity

The selection of source texts should remain unbiased and focused solely on fidelity to the original texts. This ensures that the theological integrity of the Scriptures is preserved, allowing for the most authentic basis for any theological or doctrinal understanding.

In conclusion, the Bible's own claims about the inspiration and sanctity of its words present a compelling argument for adopting a literal translation philosophy. This approach seeks to honor the very words of Scripture, in line with the teaching of the Bible about itself. Thus, the primary objective remains, above all, fidelity to the original text.

If Every Word Originates from God, Translators Must Faithfully Render Nothing Less Than the Original

The authority and inspiration of Scripture are established through a variety of passages. For example, 2 Timothy 3:16 declares, "All Scripture is breathed out by God," while 2 Peter 1:20-21 adds that "no prophecy of Scripture comes from someone's own interpretation." Further, Proverbs 30:5 asserts, "Every word of God proves true," Psalm 12:6 speaks of the purity of God's words, and Matthew 4:4 emphasizes the necessity of every word that comes from the mouth of God for spiritual sustenance. These texts affirm not only the inspiration of Scripture but also the criticality of its words.

The principle of verbal inspiration—that every word originates from God—is a pillar of conservative Christian doctrine. This concept undergirds the importance of rendering a translation that is as close to the original text as possible. The goal of a literal Bible translation, therefore, is not merely to convey thought but to present God's words in a way that is faithful to the original Hebrew, Aramaic, and Greek manuscripts.

Consequences of Altering a Single Word

The Bible's teaching about its own words suggests that even a single alteration can have a profound impact. For instance, consider the implications of changing the word "justify" in Romans 5:1, which in the ESV reads, "Therefore, since we have been justified by faith, we have peace with God through our Lord Jesus Christ." The word "justify" is a legal term implying a change of status, not merely a subjective experience. If a translator were to use a more "understandable" term like "made friends" instead of "justified," it would seriously distort Paul's argument, deviating from the original language and diluting the theological nuance.

Addressing the Myths

Several myths around the philosophy of literal translation need to be dispelled. The notion that literal translation is mere transcription or transliteration is a misunderstanding. The goal is not just to bring words from one language into another but to faithfully render the original languages into English according to the grammatical and syntactical norms of the target language. Still, the translation aims to be as faithful as possible to the original wording and structure.

The claim that "all translation is interpretation" also needs nuanced understanding. While it is true that the process of translation involves some level of interpretation, literal translation strives to minimize that. In other words, the meaning of a word is the responsibility of the interpreter (the reader), not the translator. Translators must ensure that they are not offering an interpretation of Scripture but a faithful representation of it.

High Reading Level and Complexity

Literal translation does not seek to simplify the text; it aims to make it understandable at a 10th-12th grade reading level. This approach is based on the premise that Scripture is meant to be studied and understood deeply. It encourages readers to grapple with the text, to wrestle with its complexities and unfamiliar features, rather than offering them a watered-down version that loses the nuances and profundities of the original languages.

Selection of Manuscripts and Theological Integrity

The choice of source texts is a fundamental step in ensuring fidelity to the original writings. This selection must be unbiased and based solely on the reliability and closeness of these manuscripts to the original autographs. By focusing on textual fidelity rather than preconceived theological positions, a literal translation provides the most authentic basis for theological understanding.

The task of translating the Bible is unparalleled in its weight and responsibility. Translators must remember that they are not rendering the thoughts of mere human authors but the very words of God. By adhering to a translation philosophy that seeks to maintain the utmost fidelity to the original text, we respect the divine origin of every word in Scripture. Given that these words are "breathed out" by God Himself, nothing less than a faithful, literal translation will suffice. Therefore, the primary goal is clear: to give the Bible readers what God said by way of His human authors, not what we think God meant. Translating truth—that is our highest calling.

Dynamic Equivalence Translations Frequently Omit the Meanings of Certain Words Present in the Original Text

One of the salient issues in Bible translation today is the question of how to best convey the nuances, subtleties, and semantic range of the original Hebrew, Aramaic, and Greek texts. In this debate, dynamic equivalence (DE) translations often come under scrutiny, specifically for their tendency to omit meanings of certain words present in the original text.

Dynamic equivalence aims to convey the "thought" or "idea" behind a sentence or phrase rather than focusing on a word-for-word translation. While this method can make the text more accessible for contemporary readers, it can also lead to the omission of specific meanings and nuances inherent in the original words. The central concern is that something God has communicated might be left out, potentially affecting the reader's understanding of Scripture.

Omissions in Word Choices

1. **Doulos (Greek: δοῦλος)**
   - Literal: "Slave" or "Bondservant"
   - Dynamic Equivalence Example: NLT translates it as "slave" in some contexts (e.g., Romans 1:1) but as "people" in Galatians 4:7, potentially omitting the element of submission and ownership.

2. **Sarx (Greek: σάρξ)**
   - Literal: "Flesh"
   - Dynamic Equivalence Example: The NIV translates it as "sinful nature" in Romans 7:18, which could be seen as an interpretive move that adds a psychological element not explicitly present in the original term.

Loss of Multiple Meanings

1. **Ruach (Hebrew: רוּחַ)**
   - Literal: "Spirit," "Wind," or "Breath"

- Dynamic Equivalence Example: The Message sometimes translates it as "God's Spirit" or "breath," depending on the context, potentially losing the layered meanings of the word.

2. **Logos (Greek: λόγος)**
   - Literal: "Word"
   - Dynamic Equivalence Example: The NLT translates it as "the Word" in John 1:1 but changes it to "the one" in John 1:14, which might miss the deeper theological implications.

Omitted Grammatical Features

1. **Genitive Case in Greek**
   - Literal: Varied meanings including possession, origin, or association.
   - Dynamic Equivalence Example: The NIV often simplifies genitive constructs. For instance, in Galatians 2:20, "faith of Christ" (literal) is rendered as "faith in Christ."

Fidelity to Theological Terms

1. **Justification (Greek: δικαίωσις)**
   - Literal: "To Declare Righteous"
   - Dynamic Equivalence Example: The CEV often translates it as "God accepts us," which may lack the judicial aspect present in the original term.

2. **Sanctification (Greek: ἁγιασμός)**
   - Literal: "Set Apart"
   - Dynamic Equivalence Example: The NLT uses "made holy" in 1 Thessalonians 4:3, which may lack the notion of being set apart for a special purpose.

These examples illustrate how dynamic equivalence translations can sometimes omit aspects of the original words' meanings. The translations provided above are not inherently "wrong," but they often sacrifice nuance or specific details for readability or contemporary relatability. Such omissions might miss out on the fullness of what was communicated in the original languages, hence underscoring the need for a more literal approach that aims for greater fidelity to the original text.

Translators bear the significant responsibility of rendering God's Word into a modern language, maintaining as much fidelity to the original text as possible. While dynamic equivalence translations strive for readability and relatability, these should not come at the expense of accuracy or completeness.

It is crucial to approach Bible translation with the utmost reverence for the original text, striving to convey not just the thoughts or ideas behind the words, but the words themselves. Words are the vehicle of meaning, and in the context of the Scriptures, these are words spoken to us by God Himself. Omitting any part of what God has said can be both a disservice to the reader and a deviation from the primary goal of Bible translation: to be accurate and faithful to the original text.

By focusing on a word-for-word or literal translation approach, translators offer readers the tools to engage with the text as it was initially written, allowing for a more robust understanding and interpretation. Only then can doctrine be extracted directly and authentically from the Scriptures, without the risk of human interference or omission. Therefore, a more literal approach to translation aligns closely with the ideal of preserving the integrity, depth, and richness of the God-breathed Scriptures.

Dynamic Equivalence Translations Often Add Meaning That Is Not in the Original Text

Dynamic equivalence, also known as functional equivalence or thought-for-thought translation, aims for ease of readability and comprehension. While these translations often serve as useful tools for new readers or those unfamiliar with biblical language and culture, they risk adding elements to the text that are not in the original. This stands in contrast to literal translations, where the primary goal is to retain as much of the original language, structure, and meaning as possible.

Added Interpretative Elements

1. **Ephesians 2:8-9 (Grace Through Faith)**
    - **Literal Translation (ESV)**: "For by grace you have been saved through faith. And this is not your own doing; it is the gift of God, not a result of works, so that no one may boast."
    - **Dynamic Equivalence (NLT)**: "God saved you by his grace when you believed. And you can't take credit for this; it is a gift from God. Salvation is not a reward for the good things we have done, so none of us can boast about it."

Here, the NLT adds the interpretative element "when you believed," which is not present in the original Greek. It emphasizes belief as the timing for salvation, which could potentially add another layer of interpretation that isn't in the original text.

2. **Proverbs 27:17 (Iron Sharpens Iron)**

    - **Literal Translation (ESV)**: "Iron sharpens iron, and one man sharpens another."
    - **Dynamic Equivalence (The Message)**: "You use steel to sharpen steel, and one friend sharpens another."

The Message adds the word "steel," which might introduce a modern material not specified in the original Hebrew. Also, it adds "friend," which is not explicitly stated in the original text, narrowing the potential relationships implied.

Added Cultural Context

1. **Matthew 6:11 (The Lord's Prayer)**

    - **Literal Translation (ESV)**: "Give us this day our daily bread,"
    - **Dynamic Equivalence (NLT)**: "Give us the food we need,"

Here, the term "daily bread" carries a multifaceted meaning in its original context, touching on physical sustenance and perhaps also spiritual sustenance. The NLT simplifies it to "food we need," potentially missing deeper theological implications.

2. **Acts 1:8 (Witnesses to Ends of the Earth)**

    - **Literal Translation (ESV)**: "But you will receive power when the Holy Spirit has come upon you, and you will be my witnesses in Jerusalem and in all Judea and Samaria, and to the end of the earth."
    - **Dynamic Equivalence (CEV)**: "But the Holy Spirit will come upon you and give you power. Then you will tell everyone about me in Jerusalem, in all Judea, Samaria, and everywhere in the world."

The CEV adds "then you will tell everyone about me," which may subtly change the focus from being witnesses to spreading verbal messages. The original word "witnesses" could entail more than just talking, including actions and lifestyles that testify to Christ's influence.

Theological Adjustments

1. **Romans 6:23 (Wages of Sin)**

    - **Literal Translation (ESV)**: "For the wages of sin is death, but the free gift of God is eternal life in Christ Jesus our Lord."

- **Dynamic Equivalence (NIV)**: "For the wages of sin is death, but the gift of God is eternal life in Christ Jesus our Lord."

The NIV removes the adjective "free" from "free gift." While the removal may seem minor, it can have theological implications, such as understanding the concept of grace and undeserved favor from God.

2. **1 Timothy 2:12 (Women in Church)**

    - **Literal Translation (ESV)**: "I do not permit a woman to teach or to exercise authority over a man; rather, she is to remain quiet."
    - **Dynamic Equivalence (NLT)**: "I do not let women teach men or have authority over them. Let them listen quietly."

The NLT adds "let them listen quietly," which adds a receptive element not present in the original text. This can lead to different applications and discussions regarding women's roles in the church setting.

In summary, while dynamic equivalence translations may improve readability, they can also introduce meanings not present in the original texts. The goal of a literal translation, in contrast, is to render the text as faithfully to the original languages as possible, leaving the interpretation up to the reader. This avoids the pitfalls of adding or omitting elements from the sacred text, thereby staying true to the goal of accurate and faithful translation.

Where Did We Get All These Dynamic Equivalence Translations?

Dynamic Equivalence as a translation methodology has a history that marks a shift from more traditional, word-for-word methods of translating biblical texts. Its emergence is not just a matter of linguistic theory; it also reflects broader cultural, technological, and commercial trends that influenced its development and reception.

The Theoretical Foundation: Eugene Nida and 'Dynamic Equivalence'

The term "Dynamic Equivalence" gained significant prominence through the work of Eugene Nida, who first advocated for this approach in the 1960s. He reasoned that the main goal of translation should be to convey the "equivalent effect" in the receptor language, making it relatable and understandable to modern readers. Nida's theories had a profound impact on several major translation projects.

Early Adoptions: Good News Bible (Today's English Version)

One of the first major translations to adopt a Dynamic Equivalence approach was the Good News Bible, also known as Today's English Version (TEV), published in 1976. This translation aimed to be highly readable and accessible, focusing on conveying the meaning of the text in contemporary language.

New International Version (NIV): A Milestone

Published initially in 1978, the New International Version aimed to strike a balance between word-for-word and thought-for-thought translation methods. However, it still incorporated Dynamic Equivalence principles, particularly in its later editions. For instance, in the ESV, Romans 3:24-25 reads, "and are justified by his grace as a gift, through the redemption that is in Christ Jesus, whom God put forward as a propitiation by his blood, to be received by faith." In the NIV, this reads, "and all are justified freely by his grace through the redemption that came by Christ Jesus. God presented Christ as a sacrifice of atonement, through the shedding of his blood—to be received by faith."

Controversial Iterations: Gender-Neutral and Inclusive Language

Starting in the late 20th and early 21st centuries, some Dynamic Equivalence translations began adopting gender-neutral or inclusive language. For example, the NRSV uses "brothers and sisters" where the original text simply has "brothers." These changes, while well-intentioned, have caused some concern over the fidelity to the original texts.

The Living Bible and The Message: Extremes in Dynamic Equivalence

The Living Bible (TLB) and The Message took Dynamic Equivalence to new heights by converting biblical text into paraphrases rather than direct translations. For example, the Lord's Prayer in The Message goes, "Our Father in heaven, Reveal who you are. Set the world right; Do what's best— as above, so below," which, while capturing the sentiment, can be a significant departure from more literal translations like the KJV or the ESV.

Technology and Accessibility

The rise of the Internet and digital publishing has also affected the spread and reception of Dynamic Equivalence translations. Online platforms and apps often feature multiple translations for easy comparison, giving readers the choice of more literal translations alongside Dynamic Equivalence versions.

The Impact on Doctrine and Study

While Dynamic Equivalence translations have made the Bible more accessible to many, they have also raised questions about theological depth and nuance. Simplifying complex terms or adjusting language to modern sensibilities can inadvertently lead to misunderstandings or misconceptions about key theological points.

The Role of Commercial Publishing

Commercial interests have also played a role in the spread of Dynamic Equivalence translations. Publishers often highlight the readability and "relatability" of these translations in their marketing strategies, aiming to reach broader audiences. While this has undoubtedly expanded the reach of the Bible, it has also raised concerns among scholars and laypeople alike about the sacrifice of textual accuracy for marketability.

The history of Dynamic Equivalence translations is a complex tapestry of linguistic theory, cultural change, technological advancement, and commercial interest. While these translations have brought the Word of God to countless individuals in a way that is easily understandable, the methodology has its drawbacks. The most significant among these is the potential compromise of fidelity to the original text—a matter of utmost importance for anyone who holds to the divine inspiration and inerrancy of Scripture. Thus, while Dynamic Equivalence has its place in the spectrum of Bible translations, it should be approached with discernment, particularly for serious study and doctrinal understanding.

The Impact and History of The Dynamic Equivalent

Dynamic Equivalence translations have proliferated over the years and become increasingly popular for various reasons. While this approach offers certain advantages, like readability and smoother flow in the target language, it also has notable shortcomings, especially from the perspective of fidelity to the original text.

Historical Background

The concept of Dynamic Equivalence gained prominence in the 20th century, particularly through the work of Eugene Nida, a linguist and translator. He argued that a translation should aim to reproduce the "dynamic equivalent" of the original text to make it relevant for a modern audience. This approach appealed to many and paved the way for translations like the New International Version (NIV), the New Living Translation (NLT), and the Good News Bible (GNB), among others.

Market Demand and Consumer Preferences

The rise in Dynamic Equivalence translations has also been fueled by market demand. Many readers prefer translations that are more "accessible" and "easy to understand," even at the expense of accuracy. Publishers are aware of this preference, and they produce translations that cater to these tastes, often emphasizing readability over fidelity to the original text. However, the goal of translation is not to simplify but to represent the original text as faithfully as possible.

Cultural and Linguistic Adaptation

Another factor contributing to the prevalence of Dynamic Equivalence translations is the rapid change in language and culture. Some argue that because societal norms and language evolve, the Bible must be "updated" to remain relevant. However, this perspective can easily lead to the sacrifice of textual accuracy for cultural adaptation, which is a risky trade-off.

Technological Advancements

Advancements in technology have also impacted the world of Bible translation. With software capable of performing complex linguistic analyses, some have felt emboldened to attempt more "dynamic" translations. However, technological finesse cannot replace the need for accurate and faithful translation of the original languages of Hebrew, Aramaic, and Greek.

Specific Examples of Dynamic Equivalence Impact

1. **Gender-Neutral Language:** Many Dynamic Equivalence translations have opted for gender-neutral language to align with modern cultural preferences. For instance, the NIV 2011 replaced "brothers" with "brothers and sisters" in many instances. While the aim may be inclusivity, this can introduce a layer of interpretation not present in the original text.

2. **Idiomatic Expressions:** Dynamic Equivalence often replaces idiomatic expressions in the Bible with contemporary alternatives. For example, Matthew 6:22 in The Message reads, "If you live squinty-eyed in greed and distrust, your body is a dank cellar." While attempting to be relatable, such translations can severely distort the original meaning.

3. **Theological Terms:** Substituting complex theological terms with simpler words can dilute the theological depth of the text. Romans 3:25 in the NLT

reads, "For God presented Jesus as the sacrifice for sin." While it captures the essence, it misses the depth of the original term "propitiation."

The Cost of Dynamic Equivalence

The major cost of Dynamic Equivalence is the potential for compromising the theological integrity of the Scriptures. By focusing more on the fluidity and relatability of the language, these translations may unintentionally strip the text of its theological and historical richness.

The proliferation of Dynamic Equivalence translations can be attributed to various factors: historical developments in the field of translation, market demands for easy-to-read versions, cultural and linguistic adaptations, and technological advancements. However, it's crucial to remember that readability should not come at the cost of faithfulness to the original text. For those serious about Bible study, this compromises the very essence of Scripture as the inerrant Word of God, and therefore such translations should be approached with caution.

We Cannot Trust Dynamic Equivalent Translations

When it comes to Bible translation, the stakes are incredibly high. We are dealing with the Word of God, divinely inspired and authoritative. A flawed translation can mislead the reader and distort the message that God intends to convey. Within the framework of Bible translation methodologies, two dominant paradigms exist: Dynamic Equivalence and Formal Equivalence, or as they are also known, "thought-for-thought" and "word-for-word" translation, respectively.

The Shortcomings of Dynamic Equivalence

Dynamic Equivalence aims to convey the thoughts of the original text rather than its exact words. While this approach may offer readability and flow in the target language, it often lacks precision and fidelity to the original text. This lack of strict adherence to the original wording can result in the imposition of the translator's own understanding or interpretation of the text. As a result, the primary purpose of giving the Bible readers what God said by way of His human authors is jeopardized. This compromises the text's reliability and should be a matter of grave concern for those who uphold the inerrancy and authority of the Scriptures.

Specific Examples

1. **Matthew 4:17 (NIV - Dynamic Equivalence):** "From that time on Jesus began to preach, 'Repent, for the kingdom of heaven has come near.'"

Matthew 4:17 (ESV - Formal Equivalence): "From that time Jesus began to preach, saying, 'Repent, for the kingdom of heaven is at hand.'"

The phrase "has come near" in the NIV may suggest a sense of immediacy or impending arrival, but the ESV's "is at hand" remains closer to the original Greek, capturing the eschatological tone better.

2. **Romans 3:20 (NLT - Dynamic Equivalence):** "For no one can ever be made right with God by doing what the law commands. The law simply shows us how sinful we are."

Romans 3:20 (ESV - Formal Equivalence): "For by works of the law no human being will be justified in his sight, since through the law comes knowledge of sin."

The NLT translation of Romans 3:20 takes considerable liberty by paraphrasing "the law simply shows us how sinful we are." This risks altering the theological emphasis of the text.

3. **Psalm 23:1 (The Message - Extreme Dynamic Equivalence):** "God, my shepherd! I don't need a thing."

Psalm 23:1 (ESV - Formal Equivalence): "The Lord is my shepherd; I shall not want."

The Message version of Psalm 23:1 significantly departs from the formal text and imposes an interpretation that can dilute the weight of the original phrasing.

Unreliable for Study

Given that every word in the Scriptures is of utmost importance, Dynamic Equivalence poses risks in biblical study. Since the reader has a role as an interpreter of the text, being presented with a translation that already contains interpretative elements can skew one's understanding. This is particularly problematic for those who wish to engage in serious theological or doctrinal study, as it introduces an additional layer of interpretation to navigate.

Source Text Selection

Moreover, it is crucial that the selection of source texts not be influenced by preexisting theological or doctrinal biases. When translators engage in Dynamic Equivalence, there is a heightened risk of such influence. This compromises the integrity of the Scriptures and creates an unstable foundation for theological or doctrinal understanding.

In summary, Dynamic Equivalent translations may be more accessible for the casual reader but are inadequate for those seeking to understand the theological depths of Scripture. It's imperative to use a translation that adheres closely to the original languages and maintains the complexity and nuance of the inspired Word of God. For these reasons, formal equivalence or "literal" translation methods, such as those employed by the ESV, are far more reliable and should be preferred for any serious study or application of the Bible.

CHAPTER 9 How the Bible Came to Down to Us

The Journey of the Bible: From Ancient Texts to Modern Hands - 440 BCE to 1300 CE

In a Humble Print Shop

Imagine a modest print shop where a printer and his young apprentices work diligently on a wood-frame press. Sheets of blank paper are placed on the typeface, and then examined for accuracy once printed. Across the room, cords stretch from one wall to another, holding up folded pages left to dry.

Suddenly, the door rattles with forceful pounding. With a sense of dread, the printer unlatches the door. A group of armed soldiers burst inside, scouring the shop for what was considered the most dangerous form of contraband—a Bible translated into the vernacular.

Fortunately, they arrive too late. The translator and his assistant had been tipped off, allowing them to grab bundles of pages before fleeing via the Rhine River. Though their work was endangered, it was not entirely lost.

The man behind this audacious effort was William Tyndale, who, in 1525, attempted to bring the New Testament to the English-speaking populace. Tyndale's plight was not unique. Across the span of nearly 1,900 years, countless individuals have risked their lives to translate and disseminate the Scriptures. How did we arrive at the Bibles we have today?

Edward D. Andrews

Copying and Translating Scriptures in Ancient Times

Respecting the Sanctity of the Text

Devoted believers have always revered Jehovah's Word. The *New Catholic Encyclopedia* concedes that early Christians, following the example set by Jesus and the Apostles, prioritized the reading and understanding of the Scriptures. This naturally necessitated the copying of the sacred texts.

In the time before Christ, meticulous scribes took on this task, treating any mistake as anathema. Their scrupulous methods set an example for all subsequent copyists, ensuring that the Scriptures remained as unblemished as possible.

Facing a Linguistic Challenge

During the fourth century B.C.E., a substantial shift occurred. Alexander the Great sought to spread Greek culture and language across his empire. The outcome was that Koine Greek became the lingua franca throughout the Middle East, leaving many Jews unable to read their Scriptures in Hebrew. Around 280 B.C.E., a solution was found when a group of scholars gathered in Alexandria, Egypt, to translate the Hebrew Bible into Koine Greek. This translation was eventually named the Septuagint.

Language and Early Christians

In the time of Jesus, Hebrew remained in use in Palestine, but Koine Greek was more pervasive. For the purpose of reaching a wider audience, the Christian Bible writers employed Koine Greek. They also liberally quoted from the Septuagint.

The early Christians used the Septuagint as a powerful tool in their missionary work, particularly for demonstrating that Jesus was the prophesied Messiah. This usage provoked the Jews to create new Greek translations that altered key passages to counter Christian arguments. For instance, in Isaiah 7:14, the word for "virgin" in the Septuagint was replaced by a term meaning "young woman" in these new translations. Ultimately, the tactic backfired, and the Jews reverted to promoting Hebrew. This decision inadvertently became a blessing for future Bible translations by preserving the Hebrew language.

The laborious and often perilous work of these early translators and scribes has provided us with the invaluable resource we hold in our hands today: a faithfully transmitted Bible. The text not only serves as a historical and spiritual guide but also as a testament to the determination and sacrifice of those who valued the Word of God above all else.

The Genesis of Christian Book Publishing: A Journey Through Time and Language

Innovations in Early Christian Publishing

The fervor of early Christians led to a flurry of Bible copying, all performed manually. Unlike their contemporaries, these religious pioneers adopted the *codex*, a precursor to the modern book, instead of traditional scrolls. The codex offered two main advantages: faster retrieval of specific passages and greater storage capacity—enough to hold all the Greek Scriptures or even the complete Bible.

The Formative Years of the Christian Canon

The canon of the Christian Greek Scriptures was officially completed around 98 C.E. with the apostle John's contributions. One of the oldest fragments of this canon is the Rylands Papyrus 457 (P52), which can be dated back to no later than 125 C.E. By 150 to 170 C.E., Tatian, a disciple of Justin Martyr, had compiled the *Diatessaron*, a harmonization of the four Gospels. This work indicates both the authenticity he attributed to these Gospels and their widespread distribution at the time. Around 170 C.E., the Muratorian Fragment, the earliest known list of New Testament books, was created, further affirming the canon.

Multi-Lingual Translations Emerge

The rapid expansion of Christianity ignited a demand for translations of both the Christian Greek and Hebrew Scriptures. Translations were made into a variety of languages, including Armenian, Coptic, Georgian, and Syriac. Some languages even had alphabets created specifically for this task. Ulfilas, a fourth-century bishop, is credited with inventing the Gothic script to facilitate Bible translation, although he controversially excluded the books of Kings to discourage the Goths' warlike propensities—a move that ultimately did not prevent the Goths from sacking Rome in 410 C.E.

Latin and Slavonic Bibles: The Evolution of Sacred Texts

Jerome's Authoritative Latin Bible

As Latin became increasingly crucial, several Old Latin Bible versions sprang up, varying in both style and accuracy. To remedy this, Pope Damasus in 382 C.E. commissioned Jerome to create an authoritative Latin translation.

Jerome first focused on revising the existing Latin translations of the Christian Greek Scriptures. For the Hebrew Scriptures, however, he was adamant about translating from the original Hebrew texts. Relocating to Bethlehem in 386 C.E., he mastered Hebrew with a rabbi's assistance, a move that sparked considerable debate in the religious community. Critics like Augustine considered the Septuagint to be divinely inspired and accused Jerome of "siding with the Jews." Undeterred, Jerome finished his translation around 400 C.E. His work, known as the Vulgate, became a cornerstone for centuries, as he employed translation techniques that were ahead of his time by nearly a millennium.

The Spread of the Slavonic Bible

In Eastern Christendom, many people were still able to read the Septuagint and the Christian Greek Scriptures. However, as Slavonic languages gained prominence in Eastern Europe, Cyril and Methodius, two Greek-speaking brothers, took on the task of translating the Bible into Old Slavonic. To accomplish this, they created the Glagolitic alphabet, later replaced by the Cyrillic alphabet, which paved the way for modern scripts like Russian, Ukrainian, Serbian, and Bulgarian. Although their Slavonic Bible served multiple generations, it eventually became archaic as languages evolved, rendering the text incomprehensible to the average reader.

This historical journey of the Bible, from its early hand-copied codices to its translation into multiple languages, illuminates the lengths to which individuals have gone to preserve and disseminate the Scriptures. These efforts have given us a treasure that has transcended time and language barriers.

Preservation Amidst Darkness: The Tenacity of the Hebrew Bible

Meticulous Craftsmanship of the Masoretes

During a pivotal period spanning the sixth to tenth centuries C.E., a Jewish sect known as the Masoretes took on the monumental task of safeguarding the integrity of the Hebrew Scriptures. Utilizing a rigorous method that involved counting each line and individual letter, and noting variations among manuscripts, they aimed to solidify an authentic text. Their scrupulous efforts were not in vain; a comparative study between the modern Masoretic texts and the Dead Sea Scrolls—dating from 250 B.C.E. to 50 C.E.—reveals that no doctrinal alterations occurred over a span of more than a millennium.

The European Context: Darkness and Isolation

Simultaneously, Europe was ensnared in what became known as the Dark Ages, a time when literacy and scholarly pursuits were severely hampered. Astonishingly, even members of the clergy lost their ability to read Church Latin and sometimes even their vernacular languages. The Jews, confined to ghettos during this era, maintained their scholarship in Biblical Hebrew, although this reservoir of knowledge remained largely inaccessible due to societal prejudices and the physical isolation of the ghettos.

The Diminishing Influence of Greek and Latin

As the Masoretic period concluded, Latin was fading into obsolescence. Yet, its importance was artificially sustained by the Western Church's near-deification of Jerome's Latin Vulgate. Greek, the language of the Christian Greek Scriptures, was also losing its hold over western Europe. Because Jerome's Latin Vulgate was considered the authoritative text, this amplified the already escalating issues concerning biblical literacy.

Setting the Stage for Conflict: A Thirst for Knowledge Reawakens

The deteriorating state of language proficiency and the isolation of the Jews with their valuable Hebrew scholarship conspired to create an environment ripe for conflict. As a burgeoning interest in the Scriptures began to resurface, the stage was set for an inevitable clash between tradition and the quest for authentic biblical knowledge.

The tension between these diverging currents—meticulous preservation on one hand and academic decline on the other—underscores the multifaceted journey the Bible underwent to emerge as the indomitable text we recognize today. With various groups fervently working either to protect or obstruct its diffusion, the Bible survived against incredible odds, testifying to its enduring relevance and resilience.

The Struggle for Bible Accessibility: Opposition and Resilience

Papal Resistance to Vernacular Translations

In the year 1079, Pope Gregory VII initiated a succession of ecclesiastical directives aimed at prohibiting the production—and in some instances, even the possession—of the Bible in vernacular languages. A particularly drastic measure was the revocation of permission to celebrate Mass in Slavonic, citing the inevitable need to translate portions of the Holy Scriptures. This stance starkly contradicted the ethos of early Christians. Pope Gregory VII declared, "It [has] pleased Almighty God that holy scripture should be a secret in certain places." Consequently, this became the Church's official stance, and those advocating for accessible Bible reading were increasingly marginalized as subversive elements.

Underground Circulation and Scriptural Memorization

Despite this unfavorable ecclesiastical climate, the tenacious copying and translating of the Bible into common tongues persisted. Manuscripts in multiple languages were discreetly distributed throughout Europe, reliant solely on manual copying techniques as movable-type printing had yet to be invented until the mid-15th century. These copies were not only rare but also costly, leading the average individual to feel fortunate if they possessed merely a fragment of a biblical book or just a few pages. In the face of these limitations, some devout believers went to great lengths to memorize expansive sections of the Bible, including the entirety of the Christian Greek Scriptures.

Toward Church Reformation: The Word of God Reclaims Its Place

Eventually, the winds of change began to blow as burgeoning movements called for widespread Church reforms. One of the driving forces behind these movements was the resurgent awareness of the Bible's fundamental role in spiritual and everyday life.

Anticipation: The Bible in the Age of Tyndale and Beyond

How did these reform movements and the advent of printing technology reshape the course of the Bible? And what was the ultimate fate of William Tyndale and his seminal translation work? The unfolding of this riveting narrative, leading up to contemporary times, will be explored below.

The oscillation between Church resistance and the tireless efforts to democratize the Word of God underscores the Bible's tumultuous journey through history. These struggles also attest to the ceaseless demand for the Scriptures, highlighting their enduring impact and significance.

Detailed Explanation of Key Dates in the Transmission of the Bible

The chart outlines significant events in the development, preservation, and dissemination of the Bible, segmented into periods before and after the Common Era (B.C.E. and C.E.).

BEFORE COMMON ERA (B.C.E.)

Hebrew Scriptures completed c. 440 B.C.E.: The Hebrew Scriptures, commonly known as the Old Testament, were completed around 443 B.C.E. These texts were meticulously copied and preserved by Jewish scribes and were the sacred texts of the Jewish people.

Alexander the Great (d. 323 B.C.E.): Alexander the Great's conquests in 323 B.C.E. led to the spread of Hellenism, a key factor in the subsequent translation of the Hebrew Scriptures into Greek (the Septuagint).

Septuagint begun c. 280-150 B.C.E.: Around 280 B.C.E., the Hebrew Scriptures began to be translated into Greek. This translation is known as the Septuagint and played a crucial role in making Jewish religious texts accessible to Greek-speaking populations.

100 B.C.E. Most Dead Sea Scrolls c. 100 B.C.E. to 68 C.E.: The Dead Sea Scrolls were written in this period, and they include some of the oldest known copies of the Hebrew Scriptures. These manuscripts corroborate the reliability of the text over centuries.

COMMON ERA (C.E.)

Jerusalem destroyed 70 C.E.: The destruction of Jerusalem by the Romans in 70 C.E. led to the dispersion of the Jewish people and their texts, adding another layer of complexity to the preservation of the Hebrew Scriptures.

Greek Scriptures completed 98 C.E.: By 98 C.E., the Christian Greek Scriptures, or the New Testament, were completed with the writings of John, the last surviving apostle.

Rylands Papyrus of John (b. 125 C.E.): This papyrus fragment contains portions of John's Gospel and dates back to around 125 C.E., confirming the early production and circulation of New Testament texts.

Jerome's Latin Vulgate c. 400 C.E.: Around 400 C.E., Jerome completed the Latin Vulgate, a Latin translation of both the Hebrew and Greek Scriptures. This became the authoritative text for the Western Church for centuries.

Masoretic Text Prepared: Between the 6th and 10th centuries C.E., the Masoretes, a group of Jewish scholars, took extreme care in preserving the Hebrew Scriptures, standardizing the text that became known as the Masoretic Text.

Cyril in Moravia 863 C.E.: In 863 C.E., Cyril and his brother Methodius began translating the Bible into Old Slavonic, thereby extending the reach of the Scriptures into Slavic lands.

Edict against vernacular Bible 1079 C.E.: In 1079 C.E., Pope Gregory VII issued an edict prohibiting the production and sometimes even the possession of the Bible in vernacular languages, effectively slowing down its widespread dissemination.

The chart provides a chronological overview of these major milestones, each of which contributed in some way to the Bible as we know it today. These events reveal the intricate process behind the preservation and transmission of a text that has been both deeply revered and fiercely contested.

How the Bible Came to Us: A Saga of Defiance and Devotion 1984 to 1611 CE

In a bizarre twist of fate, a fire roared against the backdrop of a moonlit night, its flames consuming Bibles. Clerics overseeing the spectacle thought they were quenching the Word of God. Ironically, they were inadvertently financing its dissemination; the funds used to buy those Bibles for destruction aided the translator, William Tyndale, in producing more editions.

This extraordinary event wasn't an isolated incident but part of a grander narrative, one rooted in the late Middle Ages and stretching into an era when **the Bible's impact on society would become monumental.**

A Pioneer Appears: John Wycliffe and His Revolutionary Ideas

John Wycliffe, a distinguished Oxford academic, was a pivotal figure who shook the religious establishment. Wycliffe used the authority of the Bible, which he referred to as 'God's law,' to critique the doctrinal and ethical missteps of the Catholic

Church. Through his disciples, known as the Lollards, Wycliffe propagated his beliefs and the Bible's message across England in the vernacular—common English.

Wycliffe's actions led the Church to view him as a dangerous heretic. Critics weren't merely bothered by his denunciations of clerical misconduct. They were outraged that he endorsed armed rebellions, although Wycliffe himself never advocated violence. His notoriety reached its zenith in 1412 when Archbishop Arundel penned a scathing letter to Pope John XXIII. Wycliffe was deemed a "herald and child of antichrist" for the apparent crime of translating the Bible into English.

International Influence and The Domino Effect

Wycliffe's translations weren't confined to England. *Anne of Bohemia*, who became Queen of England, used her position to further the Bible's reach internationally. Her interest in Wycliffe's work motivated Bohemian scholars to study at Oxford. These scholars returned to Prague University, carrying with them Wycliffe's teachings. This academic exchange laid the groundwork for **Jan Hus**, who contributed to the translation and dissemination of the Bible in Czech lands.

The Church Strikes Back: The Suppression of Dissent

Despite the efforts of these pioneering figures, the Church remained obstinate. The clergy took issue with the idea that the "bare text" of the Scriptures should take precedence over the "glosses," or traditional interpretations. They were wary of the Bible being made available to commoners in its *undiluted form*.

Hus found himself in hot water when he was lured to the Catholic Council of Constance under false pretenses of safe passage. Comprising a staggering 2,933 ecclesiastical figures, the council wasn't interested in a theological debate with Hus. He offered to recant his teachings if proven wrong by the Bible, but for the council, his mere challenge to their authority was reason enough to execute him.

The Council also delivered a posthumous insult to Wycliffe by decreeing his remains be exhumed and burned. Such a directive was so abhorrent that it wasn't executed until 1428, and only then due to papal insistence. Yet, as history shows, this vehement opposition only fanned the flames of resolve among those committed to making the Bible accessible to all.

This tale of fervor, struggle, and resilience demonstrates the extraordinary lengths to which individuals went to ensure the Bible's survival and dissemination, despite institutional challenges. It serves as a testament to the enduring power and significance of the Scriptures.

The Impact of Printing: A Technological Revolution and its Biblical Implications

By the mid-15th century, the invention of movable type by **Johannes Gutenberg** had revolutionized the way knowledge was disseminated. Among Gutenberg's earliest projects was the printing of the Latin Vulgate, completed around 1455. Within four decades, the Bible had been translated and printed in multiple languages, spanning German to Serbian. This technological leap gave incredible momentum to the circulation of the Scriptures.

One luminary in this period was **Desiderius Erasmus**, a Dutch scholar. In 1516, Erasmus published the first complete printed edition of the Greek New Testament. Despite his desire for the Bible to be "translated into all languages of all people," Erasmus hesitated to use his own popularity to produce such a translation.

William Tyndale: A Maverick for the English Bible

Breaking away from such hesitations was **William Tyndale**, an Oxford-educated scholar. Around 1521, Tyndale found employment as a tutor in the household of Sir John Walsh. Over dinner conversations, Tyndale frequently debated with local clergymen about theological matters, employing the Scriptures to make his points. The Walsh family became increasingly convinced by Tyndale's arguments, leading to a diminished welcome for the clergy, who naturally developed a deep-seated animosity toward Tyndale.

In one memorable debate, a clergyman provocatively claimed it would be better to be without God's laws than the Pope's. Tyndale's response was resolute: *"If God spare my life, ere many years I will cause a boy that driveth the plough shall know more of the Scripture than thou doest."* His mission was unambiguous: to establish the truth among laypeople, the Bible had to be available in English.

Up to that point, no complete Bible had been printed in English. In 1523, Tyndale sought the support of Bishop Tunstall in London for his English Bible project. After being turned away, Tyndale left for Cologne, Germany, where he ran into further opposition. Authorities raided his first printing effort, but he narrowly escaped, clutching some unbound pages. Eventually, Tyndale succeeded in printing at least 3,000 copies of his English New Testament in Worms, Germany. These were smuggled into England and began to circulate in 1526. Ironically, some of these Bibles ended up in the fire set by Bishop Tunstall—the same cleric who had rejected Tyndale's request for support. In doing so, Tunstall unwittingly financed Tyndale's ongoing efforts.

Tyndale's story is not just a biography of a courageous translator but an *epic of determination and ingenuity*, challenging societal norms and even risking life and limb to make the Bible accessible in the English language.

Unveiling the Scriptures: Tyndale's Rigorous Research

William Tyndale took great joy in his work, as noted by The Cambridge History of the Bible, which states, *"Scripture made him happy, and there is something swift and gay in his rhythm which conveys his happiness."* His aim was twofold: to present the Scriptures to the layperson in a straightforward manner and to illuminate meanings of Biblical terms that had been masked by ecclesiastical traditions. Undeterred by the imminent threat of death or by sharp criticisms from notable figures like Sir Thomas More, Tyndale fortified his translation with scholarly insights.

Tyndale based his translation on Erasmus' original Greek text instead of the Latin. Noteworthy changes he made include opting for "love" over "charity" to accurately capture the essence of the Greek term *a·ga'pe*. Tyndale also used "congregation" instead of "church," "repent" instead of "have penance," and "elders" instead of "priests." (1 Corinthians 13:1-3; Colossians 4:15, 16; Luke 13:3, 5; 1 Timothy 5:17) These seemingly minor alterations had major repercussions, weakening the institutional church's grip on religious doctrine and practices like confession.

Tyndale remained steadfast in using the term "resurrection," dismissing the notions of purgatory and consciousness after death as *unbiblical*. Addressing More, he articulated, *"In putting them in heaven, hell, and purgatory, [you] destroy the arguments wherewith Christ and Paul prove the resurrection."* This stance is rooted in Scriptures such as Matthew 22:30-32 and 1 Corinthians 15:12-19. Tyndale's viewpoint suggested that prayers to Mary and "saints" were futile, as these figures could not hear or intercede in their unconscious state.

Breaking New Ground: Tyndale and the Hebrew Scriptures

In 1530, Tyndale made another monumental contribution by publishing the Pentateuch, the first five books of the Hebrew Scriptures. He was the first to translate them directly from Hebrew to English. Notably, Tyndale was also the inaugural English translator to use the name *Jehovah*. David Daniell, a London scholar, observed, *"It would surely have struck Tyndale's readers forcibly that the name of God was newly revealed."*

Tyndale adhered to a literal translation philosophy, even when translating a single Hebrew word into various English equivalents to maintain clarity. He argued that the properties of the Hebrew language aligned more closely with English than with Latin, stating, *"The manner of speaking is both one; so that in a thousand places thou needest not but to translate it into the English, word for word."*

This meticulous approach introduced the English-speaking world to Hebrew expressions and idioms. While some might have seemed peculiar initially, they have now become ingrained in the English lexicon. Examples include phrases like "a man after his own heart" (as in 1 Samuel 13:14), "passover," and "scapegoat." More importantly, this exposure to Hebrew thought has enriched our understanding of the Scriptures, offering invaluable insights into the inspired Word.

The Threat of Accessible Scripture: Tyndale's Persecution and Legacy

The idea of having *access to the Scriptures in one's own language* was electrifying for the English people. They seized any copies that could be covertly brought into the country, often disguised as bundles of cloth or other merchandise. For the clergy, the prospect of the Bible becoming the ultimate authority spelled the end of their ecclesiastical power. As a result, the stakes were increasingly high, making it a matter of life and death for Tyndale and his supporters.

Continually pursued by both Church and State, Tyndale remained in hiding in Antwerp, Belgium. Despite the constant pressure, he dedicated two days a week to what he termed his "pastime"—ministering to English refugees, the impoverished, and the ailing. He channeled the majority of his resources toward these endeavors. However, before he could complete the translation of the latter half of the Hebrew Scriptures, Tyndale was betrayed for monetary gain by an Englishman posing as a friend. He was executed in Vilvoorde, Belgium, in 1536, with his dying words being, *"Lord! open the King of England's eyes."*

In a stunning reversal, King Henry VIII decreed in 1538 that Bibles should be available in every English church. Although Tyndale received no acknowledgment, the version selected was essentially his own work. According to *The Cambridge History of the Bible*, Tyndale's translation "determined the fundamental character of most of the subsequent versions" in English. As much as 90% of his work was incorporated directly into the King James Version of 1611.

Transformative Impact: England and Beyond

This newfound freedom to access the Bible marked a seismic shift in English society. Conversations about the Scriptures placed in churches became so intense that they sometimes disrupted church services. *A Concise History of the English Bible* notes that "Old people learned to read so that they might come directly to God's Word, and children joined their elders to listen." This era also witnessed an expansive distribution of the Bible in various European languages. However, the English Bible movement was destined to cast its influence globally.

Key Dates in the Transmission of the Bible: A Comprehensive Explanation

The chart outlines pivotal moments in the transmission of the Bible from the 14th century to the 17th century Common Era. These milestones reflect significant events that shaped the availability, translation, and dissemination of the Scriptures, affecting religious thought, practice, and governance for generations to come.

The Common Era

1. **Wycliffe Bible begun (b. 1384)**: John Wycliffe, an English theologian, initiated the first complete translation of the Bible into English. It was a massive undertaking and laid the foundation for future English translations.

2. **Hus executed 1415**: Jan Hus, a Bohemian theologian and Church reformer, was executed for heresy. His ideas would continue to influence the Protestant Reformation and the translations that followed.

3. **Gutenberg—first printed Bible c. 1455**: Johannes Gutenberg revolutionized the printing industry by creating the first printed Bible, known as the Gutenberg Bible. This made the Scriptures more accessible than ever before.

4. **Erasmus' Greek text 1516**: Dutch scholar Desiderius Erasmus published the first printed edition of the Greek New Testament. His work had a tremendous impact on Biblical scholarship and influenced subsequent translators, including Tyndale.

5. **Tyndale's "New Testament" 1526**: William Tyndale produced an English translation of the New Testament from Erasmus' Greek text. His work was controversial and led to his execution.

6. **Tyndale executed 1536**: Tyndale was executed for heresy, but his translation efforts significantly influenced future versions of the Bible in English.

7. **Henry VIII orders Bibles put in churches 1538**: King Henry VIII commanded that Bibles be placed in every English church, a move that essentially canonized Tyndale's work.

8. **King James Version 1611**: The King James Version, heavily influenced by Tyndale's translation, became the standard English Bible and has remained influential to this day.

Key Historical Figures

1. **John Wycliffe**: Known as the "Morning Star of the Reformation," Wycliffe was an English theologian and academic who argued that the Bible should be the primary authority for Christianity, challenging the dominant role of the clergy. He initiated the first complete English translation of the Bible, which was a significant milestone in the history of Biblical transmission.

2. **Jan Hus**: A Bohemian theologian and Church reformer, Hus was influenced by Wycliffe's writings. He advocated for Church reforms, including the use of vernacular language in Church rites. Condemned for heresy, he was burned at the stake, but his ideas lived on and were foundational for the Protestant Reformation.

3. **William Tyndale**: An Oxford-educated scholar, Tyndale produced the first printed English translation of the New Testament. His translation efforts were not only scholarly but also revolutionary, as they challenged the religious establishment. His work paved the way for future English translations of the Bible, even though he was executed for heresy.

4. **King Henry VIII**: The King of England who initially opposed Protestant reforms but later broke with the Catholic Church to form the Church of England. His 1538 decree to place Bibles in every English church made the Scriptures accessible to the common people and solidified the influence of the English Bible, particularly Tyndale's translation.

These individuals played pivotal roles in the transmission and transformation of the Bible, their contributions spanning from scholarly endeavors to royal decrees, setting the course for the study and understanding of the Scriptures for centuries to come.

The final question is: how have further discoveries and scholarly research impacted the Bibles we use today? This topic will be the focus below.

How the Bible Came to Us: A Journey Through Time and Trials

The Priceless Manuscript in Burma, 1824

In Burma, 1824, King's officials ransacked the home of missionaries Adoniram and Ann Judson. While they took many belongings, they failed to seize the most valuable asset: a translated Bible manuscript. Ann Judson ingeniously buried it underground to protect it. Later, she concealed the manuscript inside a pillow to protect it from humidity, ultimately saving it for posterity. This would later become part of the **first Burmese Bible**.

YOUR GUIDE FOR DEFENDING THE BIBLE

The Bible's Odyssey Across Centuries

The Bible has survived myriad challenges, spanning from its initial translation to the early 1600s. A critical question remains: would it ever be accessible to everyone? What role has various organizations, like the Watch Tower Society, played in this process?

Missionaries and the Surge of Bible Societies in the 1600s and 1700s

In England during the 1600s and 1700s, there was a notable rise in Bible engagement. *The Scriptures deeply influenced every stratum of society*, from royalty to commoners. England's maritime and colonial pursuits provided opportunities for Englishmen to take the Bible overseas, laying the foundation for broader Bible distribution.

Spiritual Awakening and Controversy in the Late 1700s

By the end of the 1700s, some in England began considering the spiritual well-being of indigenous people in British colonies. However, this perspective was not universally shared. The belief in predestination dissuaded some from missionary work. William Carey, unfazed by these criticisms, moved to India in 1793 and eventually translated the Bible into 35 Indian languages, proving the skeptics wrong.

The Catalytic Role of Mary Jones

In a twist of fate, a 16-year-old Welsh girl named Mary Jones triggered a movement that would have global repercussions. After saving for six years and walking 25 miles barefoot, she was devastated to find out that all the Bibles were sold out. A clergyman, moved by her disappointment, gave her one of his own Bibles. Inspired by Mary's quest, he consulted with friends about the scarcity of Bibles, culminating in the formation of the **British and Foreign Bible Society in 1804**. Their mission was clear: distribute affordable Bibles in vernacular languages, devoid of doctrinal notes to avert controversy.

Expanding the Horizon

Initially, the enthusiasm for Bible distribution was contagious, spreading across various European countries by 1813. It soon became apparent that the linguistic landscape was more diverse than initially thought—translators were facing languages by the thousands, not just a few major ones. The King James Version often served as a reference point for these new translations due to a lack of translators proficient in Hebrew and Greek.

In sum, the journey of the Bible from being a hidden treasure in a Burmese house to a globally accessible text has been fraught with challenges, but also marked by relentless human endeavor. The roles played by missionaries, ordinary individuals like Mary Jones, and organizations have been instrumental in shaping this journey, ensuring that the Word of God remains available to people in their own languages.

The Trials of One Translator: Challenges and Triumphs

Everyday Language and Unexpected Confusions

The Bible is largely composed of *narratives and illustrations grounded in common experience*, making it generally easier to translate than philosophical or abstract texts. However, this hasn't prevented occasional odd translations. For example, a certain translation led people in a part of India to conceive of God as a bluish figure. The term used for "heavenly" in "heavenly Father" got translated as "having the color of the sky"—reflecting the literal heavens!

Adoniram Judson's Herculean Task

In 1819, Adoniram Judson, an American missionary, described the challenges he faced translating the Bible. He pointed out that adapting a foreign language, without any dictionaries or interpreters, was a mammoth task. Judson and other translators like him played a **crucial role in making the Bible accessible globally**.

Personal Struggles of the Judsons

Ann Judson, Adoniram's wife, was an instrumental help in the translation process. But the challenges they faced were not merely academic. Ann was pregnant when Adoniram was jailed, and she spent 21 months petitioning for his release. Sadly, after Adoniram's release, Ann and their infant daughter passed away due to fever. Despite his heartbreak, Adoniram found strength in his faith and completed the Burmese Bible in 1835.

Controversy Surrounds the Bible: Faith Amidst Fire

The Bible in the Midst of Sociopolitical Storms

The 1800s were a hotbed of political and social controversies, often with the Bible at the center. For instance, the Russian Bible Society initially had the backing of the czar and the Russian Orthodox Church. But over time, both entities withdrew support and even banned the Society. The Orthodox clergy sought to cease the universal distribution of the Bible, claiming it threatened the Church and State authority. However, emerging revolutionary movements viewed the Bible not as a threat, but as a tool used by authorities to subdue the masses. Hence, the Bible faced attacks from **both ends of the spectrum**.

Intellectual Onslaughts on the Bible

The Bible also faced intellectual challenges during this period. Charles Darwin set sail in 1831 and later developed his theory of evolution, shaking traditional views on creation. In 1848, Marx and Engels issued the Communist Manifesto, framing Christianity as an oppressive force. Concurrently, higher critics started questioning the historical veracity and authenticity of the Scriptures.

The Defense of Scripture

Despite the multiplicity of attacks, some intellectuals recognized the flaws in theories rejecting God and the Bible. One such person was **Konstantin von Tischendorf**, a gifted German linguist who sought academic avenues to affirm the reliability of the Bible.

In summary, the story of Bible translation is a tapestry woven with linguistic puzzles, personal sacrifices, and social-political complexities. Through it all, the tireless efforts of translators and believers have ensured that the Word of God remains accessible and relevant in changing times.

Christian Publishing House and the Updated American Standard Version

Our primary purpose is to give the Bible readers what God said by way of his human authors, not what a translator thinks God meant in its place.—Truth Matters! Our primary goal is to be accurate and faithful to the original text. The meaning of a word is the responsibility of the interpreter (i.e., reader), not the translator.—Translating Truth!

Translating God's Word from Hebrew, Aramaic, and Greek original languages is a task unlike any other and should never be taken lightly. It carries with it the heaviest responsibility: the translator renders God's thoughts into a modern language. The **Updated American Standard Version (UASV)** is a literal translation. What does that mean?

A literal translation is certainly more than a word-for-word rendering of the original language of Hebrew, Aramaic, and Greek. The corresponding English words need to be brought over according to English grammar and syntax, but the translation at the same time must be faithful to the original word or as much as possible, for the author may have used word order to emphasize or convey some meaning. In most cases, the translator simply renders the original-language word with the same corresponding English term each time it occurs. The translator has used his good judgment to select words in the English translation from the lexicon within the context of the original-language text. The translator remains faithful to this literal translation philosophy unless it has been determined that the rendering will be misunderstood or misinterpreted. The translator is not tasked with making the text easy to read but rather to make it as accurately faithful to the original as possible.

Removing the Outdated

- Passages with the Old English "thee's" and "thou's" etc. have been replaced with modern English.

- Many words and phrases that were extremely ambiguous or easily misunderstood since the 1901 ASV have been updated according to the best lexicons.

- Verses with difficult word order or vocabulary have been translated into correct English grammar and syntax, for easier reading. However, if the word order of the original conveyed meaning, it was kept.

More Accurate

- The last 110+ years have seen the discovery of far more manuscripts, especially the papyri, with many manuscripts dating within 100 years of the originals.

- While making more accurate translation choices, we have stayed true to the literal translation philosophy of the ASV, while other literal translations abandon the philosophy far too often.

- The translator seeks to render the Scriptures accurately **without losing** what the Bible author penned by changing what the author wrote, by distorting or embellishing through imposing what the translator believes the author meant into the original text.

- Accuracy in Bible translation is being faithful to what the original author wrote (the words that he used), **as opposed to going beyond** into the meaning, trying to determine what the author meant by his words. The latter is the reader's job.

- The translator uses the most reliable, accurate critical texts (e.g., WH, NA, UBS, BHS) and the original language texts, versions, and other sources that will help him determine the original reading.

Why the Need for Updated Translations?

- New manuscript discoveries
- Changes in the language
- A better understanding of the original languages
- Improved insight into Bible translation

Why We Do Not Capitalize Personal Pronouns Referring to God

Choosing to capitalize personal pronouns in Scripture creates unnecessary difficulties at times. Note what the Pharisees say when speaking to Jesus (in the NASB), "We wish to see a sign from You." Thus, the meaning here would be that the Pharisees regarded Jesus as a deity when that is not the case. Some feel that it is honoring God to capitalize the personal pronouns. However, God has honor and authority purely because he is God. The Scriptures are filled with ways we are actually called to honor and worship God; we do not need to create others to show our reverence for God. We are not dishonoring God if personal pronouns referring to him are not capitalized. For those that decide to capitalize all personal pronouns referring to God, it is simply a matter of preference or style, not because the Scriptures obligate them to do so. Suppose we want to show respect, reverence, honor, and praise to God. In that case, it isn't through capitalizing personal pronouns that refer to him, but rather by personal Bible study, obedience to the Word of God, our service, church attendance, and carrying out the great commission to make disciples. (Matt. 24:14; 28:19-20; Acts 1:8) When we look at the ancient manuscripts, there is no effort made to differentiate the personal pronouns that refer to God. Sir Frederic Kenyon, in his book *Textual Criticism of the New Testament,* says, "Capital letters, which are occasionally used in business documents to mark the beginning of a clause, do not occur in literary papyri . . ."[10] Some might not even be aware that the translators of the highly valued *King James Version* always capitalized personal pronouns referring to God. It is a bit ironic that those translations that capitalize the personal pronouns referring to God out of reverence and respect remove the Father's personal name some 7,000 times in the Old Testament.

---

[10] Frederic G. Kenyon, *Handbook to the Textual Criticism of the New Testament* (London; New York: Macmillan and Co., 1901), 22.

Edward D. Andrews

CHAPTER 10 Manuscript Discoveries to Help Establish the Bible Text

The Bible has a divine origin in its content, but its history of writing and preservation is human. Moses began compiling the Scriptures around 1446 B.C.E., and it took over 1,600 years for the apostle John to finish writing it. As various religious communities formed, the demand for copies of the Bible increased. Scribes made handwritten copies for synagogues and later for Christian congregations. This was before the 15th century C.E., when printing became common. As a result, we refer to these handwritten copies as **manuscripts**.

Materials Used for Manuscripts

Bible manuscripts come in various materials like **leather, papyrus, and vellum**. The Dead Sea Scroll of Isaiah, for example, is made of leather. Papyrus, a paper made from plant fibers, was common until about the 4th century C.E. After that, vellum, which is a high-quality parchment usually made from animal skin, became the go-to material. **Codex Sinaiticus** and **Codex Vaticanus** are examples of vellum manuscripts.

Special Types of Manuscripts

Sometimes, an older manuscript was scraped to make room for new writing, creating what is known as a **palimpsest**. Scholars can often recover the erased writing using special techniques, like chemical reagents and photography. Another specialized type is the **lectionary**, which contains selected Bible readings for religious services.

Styles of Writing

Greek Bible manuscripts can be classified into **uncial and cursive** based on writing style. The older style, uncial, used large, separate capital letters, and it was common until the 9th century C.E. After that, cursive script, which involves smaller, flowing letters, became prevalent. This classification aids in dating the manuscripts.

Role of Copyists

No original manuscripts, or autographs, of the Bible exist today. Nevertheless, the Bible has been accurately preserved due to the meticulous work of **copyists**. These individuals viewed the Scriptures as divinely inspired and sought perfection in their work.

In ancient times, these copyists were called **scribes**. Ezra, for instance, is described in the Scriptures as "a skilled copyist" (Ezra 7:6). Some early scribes made deliberate changes to the Hebrew text. However, their successors, known as the **Masoretes**, identified these alterations and noted them in the margins of the **Hebrew Masoretic text**.

The legacy of these early scribes and their methods have left us with a highly reliable and accurate set of Scriptures. These manuscripts are a testament to the divine authority and the lasting relevance of the Bible, surviving the test of time and human imperfection.

Manuscripts of the Old Testament

The Old Testament, often referred to as the Hebrew Bible, is a collection of sacred texts that are foundational to Judaism and influential in Christianity. Despite its antiquity, the preservation of these Scriptures is a marvel of textual transmission. As a textual scholar committed to the objective Historical-Grammatical method of interpretation, it's critical to emphasize the ways in which Old Testament manuscripts have been transmitted, preserved, and studied.

The Original Autographs and Early Manuscripts

The Autographs: The Old Testament was initially penned by various authors such as Moses, David, Isaiah, and others who were divinely inspired. These original documents are called autographs. Unfortunately, no autographs survive today.

Scribes and Copying: Despite the absence of autographs, we have a rich collection of ancient manuscripts. The meticulous process of copying, primarily handled by scribes, ensures a high degree of accuracy. Among the early scribes was Ezra, who was "a skilled copyist" (Ezra 7:6). The reverence for Scripture led to an almost fanatical attention to detail in the copying process.

The Masoretic Text

The Masoretes: By the medieval period, a group of Jewish scribes known as the Masoretes played a pivotal role in textual transmission. Their work involved creating a stable Hebrew text, now known as the Masoretic Text.

Masora and Annotations: They included an array of textual notes known as the Masora, which were designed to safeguard the text from scribal errors. They even counted the number of times specific Hebrew letters appeared in the text to ensure accuracy.

Dead Sea Scrolls

Historical Importance: One of the most crucial manuscript discoveries is the Dead Sea Scrolls. Found between 1947 and 1956 near the Dead Sea, these scrolls date back to as early as the 2nd century B.C.E.

Comparison with Masoretic Text: The Scrolls provide a snapshot of the Hebrew Bible before the Masoretic Text's standardization. The remarkable consistency between the Scrolls and the Masoretic Text validates the latter's reliability. Notable among them is the Isaiah Scroll, a near-complete manuscript of the book of Isaiah.

Septuagint

Early Greek Translation: The Septuagint is an ancient Greek translation of the Hebrew Bible, created in the 3rd century B.C.E. for Greek-speaking Jews in Alexandria.

Textual Witness: Though a translation, the Septuagint serves as an important textual witness, providing insights into the Hebrew texts available at the time of its translation. It is occasionally cited by New Testament writers and was widely read in the early Christian church.

Samaritan Pentateuch

Samarian Tradition: Another noteworthy textual tradition is the Samaritan Pentateuch, used by the Samaritans. It consists only of the Torah—the first five books of the Hebrew Bible.

Divergences and Similarities: Although there are minor divergences between the Samaritan Pentateuch and the Masoretic Text, the similarities affirm the textual stability of the Hebrew Bible.

Targumim and Other Translations

Aramaic Targumim: As Aramaic replaced Hebrew in daily use, Targumim (Aramaic translations) were developed to assist in understanding the Hebrew Scriptures. These are not mere translations but include commentary and interpretation.

Latin Vulgate: Jerome's Latin Vulgate is another ancient translation that has influenced Western Christianity. Although not a primary textual witness to the Hebrew Bible, it played a significant role in the Bible's transmission history.

Textual Criticism and Modern Scholarship

Critical Apparatus: Scholars today use a critical apparatus to compare various manuscripts and translations. This helps in understanding the most likely original text.

Textual Families: Understanding the families of texts is essential for modern scholars. The Masoretic Text, the Dead Sea Scrolls, the Septuagint, and the Samaritan Pentateuch represent the major textual traditions, each with unique characteristics.

Scholarly Consensus: There is a strong scholarly consensus that the Hebrew Bible has been incredibly well-preserved. While no text can be entirely free from scribal errors, the Hebrew Bible's textual integrity is unparalleled.

In summary, the manuscripts of the Old Testament manifest a textual tradition that has been preserved with extraordinary care and fidelity. The multiplicity of ancient manuscripts—each bearing witness to the original texts in its unique way—contributes to our understanding and confidence in the Old Testament as the divinely inspired Word of God. Through these manuscripts, we discern not just the human effort in preserving these texts but also the providential hand of God ensuring that His Word endures for all generations.

Manuscripts of the New Testament

Understanding the New Testament involves more than interpreting its doctrines and teachings; it also entails a rigorous examination of the texts from which it is read. As a conservative New Testament textual scholar, I find that an exploration of the manuscript tradition of the New Testament is crucial for affirming its divine inspiration, historical reliability, and theological robustness.

The Autographs and Their Subsequent Loss

Original Writings: The New Testament was initially written by the apostles and other early Christian leaders. The original documents, known as autographs, were penned in Greek.

No Surviving Autographs: Regrettably, none of the autographs have survived. The reasons for their loss are manifold, including the perishable nature of the writing materials and the passage of time.

Manuscript Types and Categories

Papyrus Manuscripts: The earliest copies of the New Testament are found on papyrus, a type of paper made from plant fibers. These manuscripts are valuable because they often date back to within a few centuries of the original writings.

Uncial Manuscripts: Written in capital letters and often on more durable material like vellum, uncial manuscripts are significant for textual study. Notable examples include Codex Sinaiticus and Codex Vaticanus, both dating to the 4th century C.E.

Minuscule Manuscripts: These are later manuscripts, generally dating from the 9th century onward, written in a cursive style. They represent the majority of the extant New Testament manuscripts.

Lectionaries: Another type of New Testament manuscript is the lectionary, which contains selected passages arranged for liturgical reading.

Early Translations and Their Relevance

The Old Latin and Vulgate: Early Latin translations, known as the Old Latin, were succeeded by Jerome's Vulgate, which became the standard Latin Bible. While not primary textual witnesses, they are crucial for understanding the early reception and interpretation of the New Testament.

The Syriac Versions: Among early translations, the Syriac versions like the Peshitta are significant for studying textual variants and early Christian thought in the East.

Textual Families and Critical Texts

Alexandrian, Byzantine, and Western Texts: Manuscripts are often categorized into textual families. The Alexandrian family is generally considered the oldest and most reliable. The Byzantine family is the most numerous, while the Western family is noted for its unique variants.

Critical Texts: Modern textual scholars employ critical texts that compile readings from various manuscripts. The Nestle-Aland and UBS (United Bible Societies) Greek New Testaments are commonly used critical texts.

Textual Variants and Their Implications

Nature of Variants: Textual variants, or differences between manuscripts, are common but often inconsequential. The vast majority involve minor issues such as spelling and word order.

Handling Variants: Through textual criticism, scholars assess these variants to determine the most probable original reading. The endeavor is not to alter Scripture but to restore it to its original form as faithfully as possible.

The Importance of Early Church Quotations

A Secondary Witness: Church Fathers frequently cited New Testament passages in their writings. These quotations serve as a secondary but valuable witness to the text.

Manuscript Discoveries and Their Impact

The Chester Beatty Papyri and Bodmer Papyri: These discoveries have significantly expanded our knowledge of early New Testament texts. For example, Papyrus 46 (part of the Chester Beatty Papyri) is a nearly complete copy of Paul's epistles and is dated to around the 2nd century C.E.

Dead Sea Scrolls: While primarily significant for the Old Testament, the Dead Sea Scrolls also contain fragments of the New Testament, providing further confirmation of the text's integrity.

Final Thoughts: Divine Providence in Textual Transmission

Through the rigor of textual criticism and the wealth of manuscripts available, the New Testament's reliability has withstood the test of time. The differences that do exist among the manuscripts are minuscule and do not affect core doctrines. As such, it is evident that careful hands have been at work throughout the centuries to preserve these texts for future generations.

This process does not merely speak to the diligence of human scribes but also points to the divine providence ensuring the New Testament's preservation. Despite the many challenges these texts have faced—persecution, heresy, and the ravages of time—they have endured. The robust manuscript tradition of the New Testament serves not only as a testament to its human authors but more importantly, as a testament to its Divine Author.

The Text of the Old Testament: Its Transmission, Corruption, and Restoration

The Old Testament, often referred to as the Hebrew Bible, represents a fascinating interplay between divine inspiration and human effort. It has navigated through centuries, facing both meticulous transmission and unfortunate corruption, yet arriving in contemporary times in a remarkably preserved state. This scholarly journey into its textual history reveals the balance of divine providence and human agency.

The Inspired Transmission

Divine Origin, Human Hands: The Old Testament was penned by various authors, from Moses to the later prophets, under divine inspiration. Jehovah provided the framework, principles, and often the very words, ensuring that these texts held ultimate authority and intrinsic value.

Ancient Copies: The original manuscripts, known as autographs, have been lost to antiquity. However, the scrupulous work of early Jewish scribes provided the foundational copies and established a tradition of exacting textual transmission.

Timeline and Materials: Moses began writing in 1446 B.C.E., and the compilation continued over more than a millennium. The materials employed for writing included papyrus and animal skins. The Dead Sea Scrolls, for instance, were written on leather rolls.

The Phase of Corruption

Post-Exilic Period: While the early scribes were generally accurate, the period from 440 B.C.E. to 200 C.E. saw scribes taking liberties in textual alterations. This was a time when the Jewish community was scattered and undergoing significant social and religious changes.

Deliberate Changes: Some scribes made deliberate modifications for various reasons, including clarification, doctrinal emphasis, or harmonization of texts. These changes, although often well-intended, introduced variations and potential distortions into the text.

Hebrew Texts and Early Translations: The Samaritan Pentateuch and the Septuagint, an early Greek translation, occasionally show these textual discrepancies. For example, the Septuagint includes additional material not found in the Hebrew text.

The Masoretic Restoration

Masoretic Standardization: Between the 6th and 10th centuries C.E., Jewish scholars known as the Masoretes took it upon themselves to standardize the Hebrew text. Their mission was to preserve the text and correct any alterations.

Masora and Annotations: The Masoretes used a system of annotations, called the Masora, to indicate where they believed earlier scribes had altered the text. This allowed them to comment on the text without actually changing the sacred words. Their work culminated in the Masoretic Text, which has become the standard form of the Old Testament used today.

Vocalization: One of the major contributions of the Masoretes was the introduction of vowel points, as ancient Hebrew was written without vowels. This aided in the correct pronunciation and interpretation of the text.

Modern Textual Scholarship

The Renaissance and Beyond: Starting in the 16th century C.E., the advent of printing and increasing interest in biblical languages led to a renewed focus on Old Testament textual criticism.

Critical Editions: Projects like Biblia Hebraica Stuttgartensia have aimed to provide the most accurate text possible, often by comparing the Masoretic Text with other ancient manuscripts like the Dead Sea Scrolls.

Textual Variants: Modern scholars scrutinize differences between manuscripts to try and get as close as possible to the original text. The objective is not to modify the Scriptures but to recover their initial form.

Conclusion: A Testament to Divine Providence and Human Stewardship

The Old Testament's textual history reveals an extraordinary effort to preserve the Word of God through generations. While it has faced periods of corruption, the fidelity of early and later scribes, notably the Masoretes, has ensured its remarkable preservation. Modern textual criticism continues in this tradition, further testifying to the divine hand in the maintenance of these sacred texts.

In summary, the Old Testament has journeyed through times of inspired transmission, unfortunate corruption, and rigorous restoration. This arduous voyage underscores the balance between its divine authorship and human guardianship, making it not just a historical or religious text but a living testament to divine-human interaction.

The Text of the New Testament: Its Transmission, Corruption, and Restoration

Understanding the New Testament's textual history is like tracing a river back to its source. The New Testament is not merely a religious text but a living testament to the confluence of divine inspiration and human agency. The river, in this analogy, flows through three principal phases: Transmission, Corruption, and Restoration. Each phase carries with it complex tributaries that merit deep scholarly investigation.

Transmission: The Phase of Inspired Authors

Divine Inspiration, Human Authors: The New Testament was penned by inspired authors such as Matthew, John, Paul, and Peter, among others. They wrote under the guidance of divine inspiration, a belief held with conviction by conservative scholars and Christians alike.

Time and Material: These autographs were likely composed between 50 C.E. and 100 C.E. Early copies were often written on papyrus and sometimes on more durable materials like vellum or parchment as they became available.

Initial Dissemination: The early Christians highly valued these documents, using them for teaching, reproof, and edification. These texts were copied and disseminated to various Christian communities, often under adverse conditions that sometimes involved persecution.

Corruption: The Phase of Copyists' Liberties

Fourth to Fourteenth Centuries: This phase witnessed some liberties being taken by copyists. Though many scribes aimed for accuracy, the sheer volume of copying—especially once Christianity became the Roman Empire's state religion—led to inevitable errors and alterations.

Types of Changes: Variants arose due to unintentional mistakes, such as skipping lines (haplography) or duplicating them (dittography). There were also more deliberate changes like smoothing out grammatical rough edges, harmonizing parallel passages, or even inserting marginal notes into the text.

Text Families: Over time, these changes led to the formation of various text types or families. The Byzantine, Alexandrian, and Western text-types are the most prominent, each with its own set of variant readings.

Restoration: The Phase of Textual Criticism

17th to 19th Centuries

Pioneering Textual Critics: Early modern scholars like J. J. Wettstein, Johann Jakob Griesbach, and Richard Bentley initiated the process of examining these variant readings critically. They laid down principles for evaluating the quality of manuscripts and for making reasoned judgments about which readings were most likely original.

Methodological Advancements: Scholars like Karl Lachmann applied rigorous methodologies to textual criticism. Constantin von Tischendorf's monumental discovery of Codex Sinaiticus and the work of Westcott and Hort further revolutionized the field.

20th to 21st Centuries

Nestle-Aland and UBS: Building upon these foundations, Eberhard Nestle and later Kurt Aland produced editions of the Greek New Testament that have become academic standards. The United Bible Societies' (UBS) editions, in which

Bruce Metzger played a significant role, also stand as pillars in modern textual criticism.

Modern Tools and Technologies: Philip Comfort and other contemporary scholars have utilized papyrological advances and computational tools to analyze ancient manuscripts more precisely than ever before.

Conclusion: A River that Still Flows

The New Testament text is like a river that has flowed through various landscapes—calm plains of divine inspiration, rocky rapids of scribal alterations, and finally, the rigorous scrutiny of textual criticism. While we do not possess the autographs, the wealth of extant manuscripts and the science of textual criticism have allowed us to get exceedingly close to the "original" text.

This is not merely an academic exercise but a testament to the divine-human partnership. The text's survival and its painstaking restoration show that, despite human imperfections, the New Testament remains a reliable and authoritative document for understanding the teachings of Jesus Christ and the apostles. The conservative commitment to the text's divinely inspired origin keeps this river's flow pure, a source of spiritual nourishment for all who engage it deeply and thoughtfully.

Assurance of the Bible's Restoration: A Textual Scholar's Perspective

As a textual scholar specialized in both the Old and New Testaments, it's crucial to articulate the confidence we can have in the restoration of the Biblical text. The quest for textual integrity involves three interconnected realms: Quantity of Manuscript Evidence, Quality of Manuscript Tradition, and the Rigor of Textual Criticism.

Quantity of Manuscript Evidence

1. **Extensive Manuscript Pool**: The Bible has more manuscripts available for textual analysis than any other ancient text. We have thousands of Hebrew Old Testament manuscripts and thousands more of the Greek New Testament.
2. **Ancient Translations**: These include the Septuagint for the Old Testament and Latin Vulgate, Syriac Peshitta, and other versions for the New Testament, offering additional evidence for textual restoration.

3. **Early Citations**: Church Fathers and other ancient writers frequently cited the Scriptures, providing yet another layer of textual evidence.

Quality of Manuscript Tradition

1. **Proximity to the Autographs**: We have manuscripts that are close in time to the originals. The Dead Sea Scrolls date to as early as the 2nd century B.C.E. for the Old Testament. For the New Testament, the John Rylands papyrus (P52) dates to around 100-150 C.E., merely decades after the original autographs. We have many Greek New Testament manuscripts that date to the 2nd and 3rd centuries CE.
2. **Textual Families**: Over time, manuscripts have been grouped into "families" based on shared textual characteristics. This organization aids in tracking the history of textual changes and helps us get closer to the original.

Rigor of Textual Criticism

1. **Methodological Advances**: Both Old and New Testament textual criticism employ the Historical-Grammatical method, rigorously examining linguistic, grammatical, and historical contexts.
2. **Scholarly Contributions**: Masoretic scholars diligently worked on the Old Testament text between the 6th and 10th centuries C.E., while foundational New Testament scholars such as Westcott and Hort in the 19th century, and Bruce Metzger and Kurt Aland in the 20th century, have contributed significantly to textual restoration.
3. **Critical Editions**: Projects like the Biblia Hebraica Stuttgartensia for the Old Testament and the Nestle-Aland Novum Testamentum Graece for the New Testament represent the pinnacle of textual scholarship, incorporating diverse and ancient manuscripts, and noting significant textual variants for scholarly consideration.

Indicators of Divine Oversight

1. **Consistency across Time and Space**: Despite variations, the core message and key doctrines remain consistent across different textual traditions and periods. This integrity suggests a level of divine oversight in the transmission of the text.
2. **High-Level of Agreement**: Among the thousands of manuscripts, the level of textual agreement is extraordinarily high. Variants often involve minor issues like spelling or word order, rarely affecting doctrinal points.

Conclusion

The quantity and quality of manuscripts, combined with the rigorous methodology of textual criticism, offer compelling assurance that the Bible has been reliably restored. While we may not have the original autographs, we possess a text that is exceedingly close to them. In a divine-human partnership that defies the vicissitudes of history, the Scriptures have been preserved and restored in a form that warrants the highest level of confidence for study, teaching, and establishing doctrine.

Edward D. Andrews

SECTION 3 TEXTUAL CRITICISM OF THE OLD AND NEW TESTAMENT

Digging Deeper

We put books here on this subject if one is interested in taking the subject deeper. This section gives you foundational knowledge to evangelize or engage people in conversation.

FROM SPOKEN WORDS TO SACRED TEXTS: Introduction-Intermediate New Testament Textual Studies by Edward D. Andrews (2020)

- ISBN-13: 978-1949586985
- https://www.amazon.com/dp/1949586987

INTRODUCTION TO THE TEXT OF THE NEW TESTAMENT: From the Authors and Scribe to the Modern Critical Text by Edward D. Andrews (2019)

- ISBN-13: 978-1949586787
- https://www.amazon.com/dp/1949586782

MISREPRESENTING JESUS: Debunking Bart D. Ehrman's "Misquoting Jesus" by Edward Andrews (2019)

- ISBN-13: 978-1949586954
- https://www.amazon.com/dp/B07YN24CZY

THE ORIGINAL TEXT OF THE NEW TESTAMENT: Ascertaining the Original Words of the Original Greek New Testament Manuscripts by Edward D. Andrews (2022)

- ISBN-13: 979-8838283030
- https://www.amazon.com/dp/B0B4HGGTKP

THE TEXT OF THE NEW TESTAMENT: A Beginners Handbook to New Testament Textual Studies by Edward D. Andrews (2023)

- ISBN-13: 979-8397385831
- https://www.amazon.com/dp/B0C78L2ZK6

YOUR GUIDE FOR DEFENDING THE BIBLE

INTRODUCTION TO THE TEXT OF THE OLD TESTAMENT: From the Authors and Scribes to the Modern Critical Text by Edward D. Andrews (2023)

- ISBN-13: 979-8375131528
- https://www.amazon.com/dp/B0BT71ZZMB

INTRODUCTION TO OLD TESTAMENT TEXTUAL CRITICISM by Edward D. Andrews (2023)

- ISBN-13: 979-8398845891
- https://www.amazon.com/dp/B0C8JWNH1D

THE TEXTUS RECEPTUS: The "Received Text" of the New Testament by Edward D. Andrews (2023)

- ISBN-13: 979-8398458527
- https://www.amazon.com/dp/B0C86N38MK

THE SCRIBE AND THE TEXT OF THE NEW TESTAMENT: Scribal Activities in the Transmission of the Text of the New Testament by Edward D. Andrews (2023)

- ISBN-13: 979-8387004544
- https://www.amazon.com/dp/B0BYBQ9KXB

A JOURNEY THROUGH ANCIENT LETTER WRITING: A New Look at New Testament Letters in the Greco-Roman World by Edward D. Andrews (2023)

- ISBN-13: 979-8396921511
- https://www.amazon.com/dp/B0C6Y7BXRB

Edward D. Andrews

CHAPTER 11 Introduction to Textual Criticism

Defining Textual Criticism

The Quest for Authenticity: Why Textual Criticism Matters

Textual Criticism is the discipline concerned with identifying the original text of a document, particularly when multiple variants exist. In the field of biblical studies, this equates to a meticulous analysis of the extant manuscripts of the Scriptures in their original languages—Hebrew, Aramaic, and Greek. The objective is to determine, as closely as possible, the original words penned by the inspired authors, thus ensuring the fidelity of the text we have today. This endeavor is paramount because every doctrinal position rests upon the integrity of the underlying text. Given that the Bible claims to be the Word of God, even a minor corruption can have a profound impact on theology and practice.

Masoretic Text and the Old Testament

For the Old Testament, the Masoretic Text (MT) remains the foundational text, distinguished for its meticulous scribal practices. It contains consonantal Hebrew, augmented with diacritical marks that offer vowel sounds and cantillation—inserted by the Masoretes between the 6th and 10th centuries C.E. Even though the MT remains the base text, other versions like the Greek Septuagint (LXX) provide a valuable secondary witness. Additionally, the Dead Sea Scrolls have contributed significantly to Old Testament textual criticism by affirming the credibility of the MT, even though the scrolls occasionally align with the LXX or contain unique readings.

Corruptions did occur during the Old Testament's transmission. Copyists between 440 BCE and 200 CE sometimes took liberties with the text, perhaps to clarify or harmonize passages. The Masoretes, however, exercised great care in standardizing the text, applying various checks to avoid errors, thereby restoring much of the text's integrity.

Alexandrian Manuscripts and the New Testament

The New Testament textual criticism gives priority to Alexandrian manuscripts, particularly Codex Vaticanus and Codex Sinaiticus, along with early papyri like P75 and P66. These manuscripts generally represent a more conservative transmission history, free from many of the elaborations and harmonizations that characterize the Byzantine family of texts.

However, the New Testament text did not remain immune to corruption. Between 400 CE and 1400 CE, some copyists began to take liberties with the text. Whether to clarify a difficult passage or to harmonize disparate accounts, these changes introduced a degree of textual fluidity that requires scholarly scrutiny to resolve. Fortunately, the work of dedicated textual scholars from the 17th to the 21st centuries—such as Wettstein, Griesbach, Bentley, Lachmann, von Tischendorf, Westcott and Hort, and modern scholars like Aland, Metzger, and Comfort—has significantly clarified the New Testament's textual landscape.

Documentary Approach

In establishing the original reading, the Documentary Approach is primarily used. This method gives precedence to the actual documents—manuscripts, papyri, etc.—over internal evidence. However, internal considerations, such as the style and vocabulary of the author, are also crucial. The approach strikes a balance between the external manuscript evidence and the internal literary aspects to identify the most plausible original reading.

The Implications for Doctrine and Interpretation

Textual criticism is not merely an academic exercise; it has real-world implications for how Scripture is understood and applied. For example, the famous Comma Johanneum (1 John 5:7-8) is generally considered a later addition and is not included in most modern translations. Its exclusion has implications for the doctrine of the Trinity. Another example would be the Pericope Adulterae (John 7:53–8:11), the story of Jesus and the woman caught in adultery, which is absent in the earliest and most reliable manuscripts. Therefore, its doctrinal and ethical implications need to be carefully weighed.

Textual criticism is a fundamental discipline for anyone committed to understanding the Scriptures as they were originally inspired. It aims to remove the "noise" introduced over centuries of copying and transmission, restoring the signal—the original words of God, delivered through human authors. In a religious landscape filled with a multitude of doctrines and interpretations, having the most authentic text is crucial for doctrinal purity and the integrity of our faith. The task carries the heavy responsibility of dealing with the very words of God, necessitating a scholarly rigor guided by a reverential fear of God. Therefore, textual criticism matters because Truth matters.

Manuscript Evidence: Exploring the Sources of Biblical Texts

As the task of textual criticism is to reconstruct, as accurately as possible, the original words of the Scriptures, the value of manuscript evidence cannot be overstated. The richness and variety of these documents lay the foundation for the certainty and trust we place in the Bible. What follows is an exploration of the types of manuscripts that inform our understanding of the biblical text and why they are indispensable.

The Old Testament Manuscripts

Masoretic Text (MT)

The MT is the primary textual witness for the Old Testament. Developed between the 6th and 10th centuries C.E., it originates from the work of Jewish scholars and scribes known as the Masoretes. This text-type is based on what was then the traditional Hebrew text of the Old Testament, and it incorporates a complex system of scribal markings to preserve the text's pronunciation and chanting. The Aleppo Codex and the Leningrad Codex are among the most notable examples of the MT.

The Septuagint (LXX)

While the MT is the foundational text for the Old Testament, the Greek Septuagint plays a significant secondary role. The LXX is a translation of the Hebrew Scriptures into Koine Greek, dating from the 3rd century BCE. Its early use among Hellenistic Jews and the early Christian Church lends it historical and textual importance.

Dead Sea Scrolls

Discovered in the mid-20th century, the Dead Sea Scrolls offer invaluable insight into the state of the Hebrew text prior to the Masoretic tradition. Though the scrolls sometimes deviate from the MT, they often align closely with it, thereby affirming the MT's reliability.

Other Hebrew Manuscripts

Various other Hebrew manuscripts and fragments have come to light over the years, including the Samaritan Pentateuch, which corroborates parts of the MT but diverges in notable ways due to its Samaritan origins. These additional manuscripts add nuance to our understanding of the Old Testament text but are not given as much weight as the MT and the LXX.

The New Testament Manuscripts

Alexandrian Manuscripts

The New Testament textual tradition most relied upon is the Alexandrian text-type. Key manuscripts include Codex Vaticanus and Codex Sinaiticus, both dating from the 4th century C.E., as well as early papyri like P75 and P66. These are considered among the most reliable witnesses to the New Testament text due to their age and the conservative nature of their readings.

Byzantine Manuscripts

The Byzantine text-type, also known as the Majority Text, is characterized by a high degree of internal consistency but also exhibits expansions and explanatory glosses. Though not as ancient as the Alexandrian manuscripts, they are more numerous.

Western Manuscripts

The Western text-type is less uniform and includes Codex Bezae as a primary example. This text-type is noted for its tendency to paraphrase and expand upon the biblical text. Due to these traits, it is considered less reliable for determining the original text.

Caesarean Manuscripts

The Caesarean text-type is less distinct and more disputed among scholars. It is thought to be a "mixed" text-type with readings from both the Alexandrian and Western traditions.

The Documentary Approach

In evaluating these manuscripts, the Documentary Approach remains vital. This method prioritizes the document itself—its age, provenance, and textual character—over internal evidence, although internal factors like syntax and authorial style are still considered. This multifaceted approach is indispensable in ascertaining the most plausible original reading of a text.

Implications of Manuscript Evidence

The integrity of Scripture is bound to the integrity of its manuscripts. For instance, the ending of Mark is a contested text with multiple endings found in various manuscripts. The longer ending (Mark 16:9–20) is included in the Byzantine text-type but is absent in the Alexandrian manuscripts, most notably Codex Vaticanus and Codex Sinaiticus. Such cases require scrupulous analysis of the manuscript evidence to arrive at a reading that is as close as possible to the original.

Manuscript evidence serves as the backbone of textual criticism, furnishing scholars and believers alike with the resources to approach the Scriptures with both intellectual rigor and spiritual reverence. Through a careful study of these manuscripts, using established methodological approaches, we come ever closer to holding in our hands the Scriptures as they were first given—pure, unaltered, and divinely inspired. The value of this endeavor is immeasurable, for it directly impacts how we understand God, His will, and His ongoing work in the world. Therefore, every manuscript, every fragment, brings us one step closer to the original words penned by the inspired authors, fulfilling our unyielding quest for biblical authenticity.

Transmission of Scripture: How the Bible Has Come Down to Us

The sacred task of textual criticism seeks to reconstruct the original texts of the Scriptures, a process made more challenging—and rewarding—by the journey these texts have undergone throughout history. This journey, known as the transmission of Scripture, is marked by three distinct phases: its origination by inspired authors, the manifold corruption it encountered, and its subsequent restoration efforts. In each phase, the hand of Providence is evident, preserving God's Word for generations.

Old Testament Transmission

Inspired Authors

The Old Testament, written over approximately a millennium, has its origins in the inspired authors who, under divine guidance, penned its words. Whether it was Moses recording the Law, the prophets recounting visions, or the psalmists offering songs, each book originated from an author believed to be guided by Jehovah. This inspired content was initially passed down orally and then meticulously copied onto scrolls by scribes.

Corruption

The first layer of corruption entered the Old Testament text around 440 BCE to 200 CE when some copyists took liberties with the text. These changes ranged from simple scribal errors to intentional alterations for theological or interpretive reasons. However, it should be emphasized that such liberties were relatively rare, considering the scribes' high regard for the text.

Restoration

Between the 6th and 10th centuries C.E., Jewish scholars known as Masoretes embarked on a significant restoration process. The Masoretes aimed to standardize the Hebrew text, resulting in the Masoretic Text (MT). Their meticulous methods included counting verses and ensuring uniformity in the copying process. The MT thus became the primary text for Old Testament studies, supplemented by the Greek Septuagint and other texts like the Dead Sea Scrolls.

New Testament Transmission

Inspired Authors

The New Testament was penned within a much shorter timeframe, roughly between 45 and 95 C.E. Its authors, such as Peter, Paul, and John, were often writing within decades of the events they described. They wrote in Koine Greek on papyri and vellum, capturing the life, teachings, and works of Jesus Christ as well as the early history of the Christian Church.

Corruption

While the original manuscripts (autographs) were without error, corruption occurred when subsequent generations copied these texts. Between 400 CE and 1400 CE, more liberties were taken with the New Testament text. These changes include simple errors like misspellings, but also encompass more problematic issues like the Johannine Comma (1 John 5:7-8) and the Pericope Adulterae (John 7:53-8:11). Both passages are considered later additions and are generally not found in early Greek manuscripts, particularly those of the Alexandrian text-type.

Restoration

The work of restoration in the New Testament arena began with scholars in the 17th century and continued through the 19th and 21st centuries. Important figures include J. J. Wettstein, Johann Jakob Griesbach, and Karl Lachmann, who set the stage for the groundbreaking work of Westcott and Hort. Their work laid the foundation for the subsequent textual scholarship of Bruce Metzger, Kurt Aland, and others. The primary text used in these efforts is usually drawn from the Alexandrian text-type, including key manuscripts like Codex Vaticanus and Codex Sinaiticus.

Methodology: The Documentary Approach

In both the Old and New Testaments, the Documentary Approach is employed to sift through manuscript evidence. This method gives precedence to the external evidence of the document itself, including its age and provenance. Internal evidence, such as grammatical and stylistic considerations, is also factored in but given less weight compared to the document's own merits. The goal is to determine the reading closest to the original text, guided by the preeminent manuscripts in each testament: the Masoretic Text for the Old and Alexandrian manuscripts for the New.

Understanding the transmission of Scripture is crucial for any student or scholar engaged in textual criticism. Knowledge of how the Bible has been passed down through the ages enables us to appreciate the Herculean efforts that have been invested in preserving its text. Through meticulous scholarship and the providential preservation of key manuscripts, we come closer to ascertaining the original words of Scripture. This not only has implications for biblical studies but also for the faith and practice of believers who regard the Bible as the ultimate authority in life. Every discovery and restoration effort brings us closer to the divine message that was intended for all of humanity, solidifying our faith in the Scriptures as the inspired Word of God.

Purpose and Methodology: What Textual Critics Seek to Achieve

The most fundamental purpose of textual criticism is to ascertain the original words of the original texts of Scripture. This may seem like a daunting task given the thousands of years that separate us from these original writings, but it is an endeavor of incomparable importance. Christians consider the Bible the inspired Word of God, and as such, accurate knowledge of its text is crucial for both scholarly research and faith practice.

Old Testament

For the Old Testament, the Masoretic Text serves as the foundational text. For example, take the well-known passage of Isaiah 7:14, which in the Masoretic Text reads, "Behold, the virgin shall conceive and bear a son, and shall call his name

Immanuel." The Septuagint, the ancient Greek translation of the Old Testament, renders the Hebrew word for "virgin" as "parthenos," which is explicitly a virgin in Greek. This is one of the instances where the Masoretic Text and the Septuagint agree, thereby strengthening our confidence in the original wording.

New Testament

For the New Testament, the Alexandrian text-type manuscripts, especially Codex Vaticanus, Codex Sinaiticus, P75, and P66, hold priority. Consider the ending of the Gospel of Mark. Most Alexandrian manuscripts end at Mark 16:8, and this is deemed more likely to be the original ending. Other endings, found in different text-types, are considered later additions.

Methodology: The Documentary Approach

While the ultimate goal is the reconstruction of the original text, the means to this end is crucial. A methodical approach ensures that textual critics do not drift into the realm of subjectivity. Hence, the Documentary Approach is favored.

External Evidence

In the Documentary Approach, external evidence takes precedence. External evidence relates to the manuscripts themselves—things like the date of the manuscript, the geographical location it was found, and its text-type. For instance, Codex Vaticanus and Codex Sinaiticus are 4th-century manuscripts that are considered some of the most reliable for New Testament studies. They are given priority not merely due to their age but also because they belong to the Alexandrian text-type, which has been found to be more reliable in representing the original text.

Internal Evidence

While external evidence is important, internal evidence—such as the style and vocabulary of the author, context, and grammatical factors—is also considered. For instance, the shorter ending of Mark is favored not only because it is found in the oldest and most reliable manuscripts, but also because it is consistent with Mark's abrupt style throughout the Gospel.

Balancing Act

The Documentary Approach is a balancing act between respecting the integrity of ancient manuscripts (external evidence) and understanding the intrinsic factors that may affect textual transmission (internal evidence).

The Status of Restoration

Old Testament

Thanks to the dedicated work of scholars and the providential preservation of texts like the Dead Sea Scrolls, the Old Testament text has been restored to the point where it closely resembles its original form. It is often said to be 99.99% accurate when compared to what the original would have been. This enables us to affirm the stability and reliability of the Old Testament.

New Testament

For the New Testament, significant strides have been made since the work of 19th-century scholars like Westcott and Hort. For example, the 28th edition of the Nestle-Aland Greek New Testament (2012) is 99.5% the same as the 1881 Westcott and Hort Greek New Testament. The consistency here is remarkable and attests to the meticulous nature of textual restoration, aided by the discovery of 144 Greek New Testament papyri in the 20th century.

Textual criticism serves a dual role: it is an academic exercise, demanding rigorous methodological standards, but it is also a sacred duty for those who regard the Bible as the inspired Word of God. Utilizing the Documentary Approach, the field has reached a point where we can assert with high confidence that we possess a text that is a mirror-like reflection of the original. This allows for a deeper and more accurate understanding of the Scriptures, strengthening not only our scholarship but also our faith. Therefore, in pursuing the original words of the original texts, textual criticism is not merely a historical endeavor; it is an act of reverence, a homage to the divine Word that has been preserved for our edification and salvation.

The Old Testament Textual Criticism

The Hebrew Bible Manuscripts: Understanding the Sources

The Old Testament, also known as the Hebrew Bible, serves as the foundation of the Judeo-Christian tradition. Accurate knowledge of its text is therefore not just a scholarly concern but a matter of utmost religious significance. For this reason, Old Testament textual criticism stands as a cornerstone in biblical studies.

The Masoretic Text: The Pinnacle of Old Testament Manuscripts

The Masoretic Text (MT) is the gold standard for Old Testament scholarship. The Masoretes were Jewish scholars who worked from the 6th to the 10th centuries C.E., standardizing the Hebrew text to ensure its accurate transmission. Their scrupulous methods included counting not just lines but also letters to minimize the risk of errors.

Example: Psalm 22 in the MT opens with "My God, my God, why have you forsaken me?" The Masoretic Text here has shown its reliability in light of other sources, offering strong evidence that this was indeed the original wording of this crucial text.

The Greek Septuagint: A Secondary Source Yet Not Insignificant

The Septuagint (LXX) is an ancient Greek translation of the Hebrew Scriptures, originating around the 3rd to 2nd centuries BCE. While not considered as authoritative as the MT, the Septuagint serves as a valuable witness to the Hebrew text that preceded it.

Example: The Septuagint translates Deuteronomy 6:5 as, "You shall love the Lord your God with all your heart, and with all your soul, and with all your strength." Comparing this with the Masoretic Text, we find a remarkable consistency between the two, affirming the reliability of both sources.

Other Hebrew Manuscripts: Lesser-Known Yet Vital

Before the work of the Masoretes, various Hebrew manuscripts existed, which provide us with additional avenues for textual verification. However, these are less standardized and contain a greater degree of variation.

Example: In Genesis 4:8, some Hebrew manuscripts include the phrase, "Let us go out to the field," spoken by Cain to Abel. This phrase is absent in the Masoretic Text but does appear in the Septuagint, suggesting the possible originality of this reading.

The Dead Sea Scrolls: Window into the Second Temple Period

Discovered in 1947 near the Dead Sea, these ancient texts have revolutionized our understanding of the Hebrew Bible. Predating the Masoretic Text by about a thousand years, they offer an unprecedented glimpse into the textual world of the Second Temple period.

Example: The Great Isaiah Scroll from the Dead Sea Scrolls is almost identical to the Masoretic version of the Book of Isaiah, reinforcing our confidence in the MT's reliability.

Other Versions: Samaritan Pentateuch, Targums, and Beyond

While not primary sources, other versions like the Samaritan Pentateuch and Aramaic Targums provide secondary testimony to the text's historical transmission.

Example: The Samaritan Pentateuch has the Ten Commandments listed in a slightly different order than the MT. Although not considered authoritative, such variations help us understand the extent and limits of textual variation over time.

The Documentary Approach: Weighing the Manuscripts

Textual critics employ the Documentary Approach to weigh the value of these manuscripts, giving precedence to external evidence like date, geographical location, and textual family. For instance, while the Septuagint is valuable, its readings are weighed against the Masoretic Text, given the MT's closer connection to the original Hebrew.

The State of Restoration: A Mirror-like Reflection

The meticulous work of scholars from the 6th century to the present has restored the Hebrew Old Testament to a state that closely mirrors its original form, estimated to be 99.99% accurate. This accomplishment is not merely an academic feat; it's a tribute to the providence of God in preserving His Word.

The Task and Triumph of Old Testament Textual Criticism

Textual criticism is both a science and an art, employing rigorous methodologies and insightful interpretations. It's a field that has undergone significant evolution, from the painstakingly careful work of the Masoretes to the monumental discoveries of the Dead Sea Scrolls. By understanding the sources available for the Hebrew Bible, we are not just collecting data; we're engaging in a profound act of reverential scholarship, drawing ever closer to the original words that were "God-breathed" (2 Timothy 3:16, ESV).

In this pursuit, textual critics serve both the academic community and the body of believers, affirming the integrity of the Scriptures and fortifying the foundations of faith. Therefore, in the realm of Old Testament studies, textual criticism is not a peripheral endeavor but a central, unifying discipline that both challenges and rewards those who engage in its intricate but invaluable tasks.

Masoretic Text: The Standard Hebrew Bible Text

The Masoretic Text (MT) stands as the premier Hebrew text of the Old Testament. Produced between the 6th and 10th centuries C.E. by Jewish scholars known as the Masoretes, this text is pivotal for any Old Testament textual criticism. Its rigor, accuracy, and reliability make it the cornerstone upon which modern translations and scholarship are built.

Masoretes: The Guardians of the Text

The Masoretes were more than mere scribes. They functioned as textual scholars who established a comprehensive system of notes to safeguard the text's accurate transmission. These notes were attached to the consonantal text to guide pronunciation, intonation, and other phonetic aspects, thereby locking the text into a fixed form.

Example 1: Ketiv and Qere

One key feature of the Masoretic system is the Ketiv-Qere apparatus. "Ketiv" means "what is written," and "Qere" means "what is to be read." In several places, the Masoretes noted the text should be read differently than it is written, either for theological, traditional, or grammatical reasons.

For instance, in 1 Samuel 3:13, the Ketiv has "his sons brought a curse on themselves," but the Qere reads, "his sons made themselves contemptible." This ensures that the text's original intent is preserved.

Vocalization and Accent Marks: Binding the Oral Tradition

The Hebrew text was initially written with consonants only. Over time, the Masoretes added a system of dots and dashes under and above the letters. These marks codified the oral tradition of how the words should be pronounced and emphasized.

Example 2: Pronunciation of Jehovah's Name

The Masoretes employed a unique vocalization technique to signify that Adonai should be read in place of Jehovah's personal name (JHVH). This helped to guard against the misuse of the sacred name, ensuring its reverence.

Textual Stability: Minimized Variants

Because of their meticulous approach, the Masoretes achieved a high level of textual stability. This minimized textual variants and errors that had crept into the text over centuries.

Example 3: Stability in Numbers

A compelling example of this stability is found in the book of Numbers, where the Masoretes counted every word and letter to ensure accuracy. When compared with other versions, the level of agreement substantiates the Masoretic Text's reliability.

The Aleppo Codex and Leningrad Codex: Premier Manuscripts

Two primary codices dominate Masoretic studies—the Aleppo Codex (10th century) and the Leningrad Codex (11th century). Both have served as the base text for modern translations.

Example 4: The Song of the Sea

In Exodus 15, the Song of the Sea is presented in a poetic structure in these codices, illuminating the text's original form. Such insights are invaluable for both scholarly study and devotional reading.

External Validation: Dead Sea Scrolls and Other Texts

The MT finds robust validation from the Dead Sea Scrolls, which predate it by a millennium. Despite the time gap, the consistency between the MT and the Scrolls is astonishing, affirming the text's fidelity.

Example 5: Isaiah Scrolls

The Great Isaiah Scroll, part of the Dead Sea Scrolls, corroborates the MT, especially in key prophetic passages like Isaiah 53, often cited in messianic prophecies. This lends further credence to the MT as a reliable text.

The Documentary Approach: Integrating External and Internal Evidence

Textual critics favor the Documentary Approach, emphasizing the importance of the extant manuscripts but also scrutinizing internal evidence like grammar and context to establish the original reading. The MT, given its lineage and accuracy, often serves as the definitive voice in these deliberations.

Restoration and Current Status: Almost Mirror-like in Reflection

Through the painstaking work of the Masoretes, and subsequent scholars, the Hebrew Old Testament has been restored to an estimated 99.99% of its original state. This not only serves academic pursuits but also profoundly impacts theological understanding, apologetics, and devotional practices.

The Indispensable Role of the Masoretic Text

The Masoretic Text is not just a version of the Old Testament; it is the standard Hebrew Bible text. Its unsurpassed reliability makes it the foundational document for textual critics, translators, and scholars alike. The rigorous methodology employed by the Masoretes set a gold standard that succeeding generations have sought to emulate but seldom surpassed. As such, the MT provides both the academic and religious communities with a text that closely approximates the "God-breathed" original, enhancing our understanding and application of sacred Scripture.

Septuagint and Other Versions: Comparing the Ancient Translations

The Septuagint as a Secondary Standard

While the Masoretic Text (MT) holds the foundational position in Old Testament textual studies, the Septuagint (LXX), an ancient Greek translation of the Hebrew Scriptures, serves as an invaluable secondary source. Compiled in the 3rd to 2nd centuries BCE, it provides insights into textual variances, translation philosophies, and even early Jewish exegetical thought.

Why the Septuagint Matters

Understanding the LXX is essential for several reasons. First, it is one of the oldest translations of the Hebrew Scriptures, predating even the earliest Masoretic manuscripts. Second, it was widely used in the Hellenistic world and was influential in early Christianity. Many New Testament writers, when quoting the Old Testament, employed the LXX.

Example 1: Isaiah 7:14—Virgin or Young Woman?

One of the most debated examples of LXX usage in the New Testament is found in Isaiah 7:14. The MT uses the Hebrew word "almah," meaning "young woman," while the LXX translates it as "parthenos," which is more closely aligned with "virgin." This LXX translation is cited in Matthew 1:23, lending weight to the doctrine of the virgin birth of Christ.

The Septuagint and Documentary Approach

Applying the Documentary Approach to the LXX means evaluating its readings based on its agreement with the MT and other ancient texts. The LXX's significance is further illuminated when its readings help clarify ambiguous Hebrew terms or elucidate textual issues in the MT.

Example 2: Psalm 22:16—"Pierced" or "Like a Lion"?

The MT of Psalm 22:16 reads, "For dogs encompass me; a company of evildoers encircles me; they have pierced my hands and feet." However, some MT manuscripts read, "like a lion my hands and feet." The LXX supports the "pierced" reading, and this is considered prophetic in a messianic context, notably cited in the New Testament.

Other Versions: Targum, Vulgate, Syriac Peshitta

Besides the LXX, other ancient translations like the Aramaic Targums, Latin Vulgate, and Syriac Peshitta offer secondary yet valuable comparative material for textual criticism.

Example 3: Targum Jonathan on Isaiah 52:13-53:12

Targum Jonathan, an Aramaic paraphrase, presents a messianic interpretation of Isaiah 52:13-53:12, diverging from the MT but sharing similarities with the LXX. While not necessarily textual evidence for the original, it indicates early Jewish messianic expectations.

Textual Variants and Readings

In some cases, the Septuagint and other versions may contain readings not found in the MT, referred to as "plus verses" or expanded segments.

Example 4: 1 Samuel 16-18 and the Story of David and Goliath

In the story of David and Goliath (1 Samuel 17), the LXX includes textual variants and even entirely different verses. Some believe these to be additions, while others argue they might reflect an older form of the Hebrew text. Using the Documentary Approach, these divergences are carefully weighed against the MT.

Establishing Original Readings

By examining the MT and the ancient versions, scholars strive to ascertain the original text's wording. Where the MT and LXX (or other versions) diverge, the reading that best suits the historical, linguistic, and contextual criteria is often deemed the original.

The Septuagint and Christological Interpretation

Lastly, one cannot ignore the LXX's role in early Christological formulations. For instance, the LXX rendering of Psalm 110:1 is used by New Testament authors to substantiate the divinity of Christ.

A Tapestry of Witnesses

Textual criticism of the Old Testament is akin to weaving a tapestry of witnesses. While the MT holds the central thread, the Septuagint and other ancient translations offer additional colors and textures, enriching our understanding of the Scripture. These versions act as a mirror, reflecting both the world that produced them and illuminating our grasp of the original text. Thus, although the MT is foundational, the Septuagint and other versions are indispensable for anyone endeavoring to approach the Old Testament text both critically and devotionally.

Challenges in Old Testament Textual Criticism: Variants and Their Implications

Variants and Their Significance

Textual criticism of the Old Testament (OT) confronts several challenges, paramount among them being the textual variants—differences between various manuscripts. These variants have implications for our understanding of history, doctrine, and the unfolding plan of redemption as recorded in the OT Scriptures.

The Nature of Variants in Old Testament Texts

Textual variants in the OT arise from numerous factors including scribal errors, editorial activity, or the exigencies of copying lengthy and complicated manuscripts. The variants may involve substitutions, omissions, or additions of words, phrases, or even entire verses.

1. Spelling Variations and Vocalization

The earliest Hebrew texts were consonantal; vowels were added later by the Masoretes. Consequently, words could be read differently, affecting the text's meaning.

Example: The word for "God" in Hebrew can be vocalized as "Elohim" or "Eloah." While both refer to the same deity, the variant vocalizations might imply different nuances.

2. Transposition of Words and Phrases

Words or phrases are sometimes found in different sequences across manuscripts, altering the sentence's flow but not its meaning.

Example: 1 Samuel 13:1 in the Masoretic Text presents a chronological difficulty, appearing to say that Saul was one year old when he became king. Other textual traditions help clarify this apparent anomaly.

3. Deletion or Addition of Words and Phrases

Texts may exhibit words or phrases that are either missing or added.

Example: The Masoretic Text of Deuteronomy 32:43 has several clauses not found in some Septuagint manuscripts, affecting the text's doxological focus.

4. Substantive Variants

These are variants that could potentially affect the meaning or interpretation of the text in significant ways.

Example: 1 Samuel 17:50 states in some Masoretic manuscripts that David prevailed over Goliath with a sling and a stone, but other texts add "and with no sword in his hand."

Establishing the Original Text: A Case Study on Psalm 145

The Masoretic Text of Psalm 145 is an acrostic poem but is missing a verse for the letter "Nun." However, the Dead Sea Scrolls contain a verse at this point, completing the acrostic. The Documentary Approach would weigh these textual witnesses to ascertain the most likely original reading.

Theological Implications of Variants

1. **Monotheism**: Variants that touch on the nature and attributes of God have theological implications. For instance, different renderings of key passages like Deuteronomy 6:4 could affect our understanding of monotheism.

2. **Messianic Prophecies**: Variants in prophetic passages could have Christological consequences. Isaiah 53:11 in the Masoretic Text and the Septuagint offer slightly different views on the Suffering Servant, interpreted by many as a Messianic prophecy.

3. **Historicity**: When the chronology or specific events are affected by textual variants, this has implications for the historical reliability of the text. For example, the different numbers in the genealogies of Genesis 5 between the Masoretic Text and Septuagint have caused much debate.

Reliability of the Text and the Work of Textual Scholars

Given the high degree of precision employed by the Masoretes and the comparative analysis with secondary witnesses like the Septuagint and the Dead Sea Scrolls, we are confident that the OT text has been transmitted with a high degree of accuracy, reaching a near mirror-like reflection of the original.

Addressing Skepticism

Some critics claim that the presence of variants undermines the reliability of the Scriptures. However, through rigorous application of the Documentary Approach, we can establish that the original text has been faithfully preserved to a remarkable degree. Variants, rather than diminishing trust in Scripture, offer avenues for deeper study and understanding.

The challenges posed by textual variants in the Old Testament are real but not insurmountable. By applying rigorous, methodical scrutiny through the Documentary Approach, and by considering the Masoretic Text as our foundational document supported by other ancient witnesses, scholars can ascertain the text with an extraordinary degree of certainty. This lends both academic and spiritual credence to the Old Testament, as both a historical document and the inspired Word of Jehovah.

Edward D. Andrews

CHAPTER 12 Principles of Textual Criticism

Textual Variants and Their Causes

Scribal Errors: How Copyists Contributed to Variants

The Role of Copyists

The meticulous task of copying Scriptures fell upon scribes who worked diligently to replicate the text. However, humans are not immune to error, and despite the scribes' painstaking efforts, textual variants emerged over time. It is essential to understand these scribal errors as they are integral to textual criticism's aim: ascertaining the original words of the Scriptures.

Categories of Scribal Errors

1. Unintentional Errors

a. Errors of Sight

These occur when a scribe misreads the source manuscript.

Example: In Jeremiah 27:1, some manuscripts read "Zedekiah," while others read "Jehoiakim." A scribe might misread the original due to similar-looking letters or words.

b. Errors of Hearing

When the scribe is copying from oral dictation, misunderstandings can occur.

Example: In 1 Samuel 14:21, the Hebrew words for "Hebrews" and "Arameans" could be easily confused when spoken aloud.

c. Errors of Memory

This occurs when the scribe transcribes from memory.

Example: A famous instance occurs in the Ten Commandments, where "Remember the Sabbath" (Exodus 20:8) and "Keep the Sabbath" (Deuteronomy 5:12) differ, possibly due to memory lapse or oral transmission.

2. Intentional Errors

a. Harmonization

Scribes sometimes altered texts to make them conform to parallel passages.

Example: The Chronicles account often harmonizes with Samuel-Kings. In 2 Samuel 24:13, a three-day plague is mentioned, while 1 Chronicles 21:12 records "three days" more explicitly as "three days, the sword of Jehovah, even pestilence in the land."

b. Theological or Doctrinal Adjustments

Scribes might change text to align better with their theological views.

Example: The Tetragrammaton (the name of God) was often replaced by the Hebrew term for "Lord" to avoid potential misuse.

c. Scribal Glosses

Scribes sometimes added notes for clarification, which then became part of the text.

Example: The phrase "He who has ears, let him hear," found in the Gospels, could be a scribal gloss that eventually was integrated into the text.

Implications of Scribal Errors

1. Complexity in Establishing the Original Text

Scribal errors can make it challenging to discern the original text, requiring the application of textual criticism principles to sift through variants.

2. Theological Implications

While most variants are inconsequential, some can carry theological weight. For instance, different readings in key Messianic prophecies can influence our understanding of Christ's nature and work.

3. Historical Considerations

Scribal errors could affect the historical narrative, such as numbers and names, which requires careful scrutiny to establish a credible historical record.

Methodology: The Documentary Approach

Given that scribal errors are a natural part of the transmission process, employing the Documentary Approach is crucial. This method relies on evaluating the quality of the manuscripts where the variants are found. By prioritizing reliable texts like the Masoretic Text for the Old Testament and Alexandrian manuscripts for the New Testament, scholars can significantly minimize the impact of scribal errors.

The Integrity of the Text Despite Scribal Errors

The existence of scribal errors does not negate the reliability of the Scriptures. Rather, by understanding the nature and origin of these errors, textual scholars can work methodically to restore the text. The application of the Documentary Approach, in tandem with internal evidence, can help us arrive at a text that closely mirrors the original, maintaining both its theological depth and historical integrity.

Thus, while scribal errors present a challenge, they also serve as an impetus for rigorous scholarly engagement, affirming the enduring authority of the Scriptures.

Intentional Changes: Understanding Scribes' Corrections

Textual criticism often grapples with the enigma of intentional changes made by scribes during the process of manuscript transmission. This is a more perplexing concern than unintentional errors, as intentional changes are often made with a motive or reason that is not always easily discernible. Here, we will delve into the types of intentional changes scribes made and try to understand why they did so.

Types of Intentional Changes

1. Harmonization

Scribes sometimes sought to reconcile seemingly contradictory or dissimilar texts to achieve internal coherence within Scripture or across Testaments.

Example: In Matthew 3:11, John the Baptist declares that Jesus will baptize "with the Holy Spirit and fire." The parallel passage in Mark 1:8 mentions only the Holy Spirit, omitting "and fire." Some scribes might add "and fire" to Mark's account for harmony.

2. Theological Alterations

This involves changes aimed at affirming certain doctrinal stances or resolving perceived theological difficulties.

Example: The Comma Johanneum in 1 John 5:7-8 has additional wording supporting the doctrine of the Trinity in the Latin Vulgate, though it is absent in most ancient Greek manuscripts.

3. Scribal Glosses Becoming Text

Scribes occasionally added explanatory notes in the margins or between lines. Future copyists might integrate these into the text.

Example: In Romans 8:1, the phrase "who walk not after the flesh, but after the Spirit" appears in later manuscripts but not in the earliest ones like Codex Vaticanus. This may have started as a marginal note explaining what kind of people have "no condemnation."

4. Conflation

When scribes encountered divergent readings, they sometimes chose to include both to ensure that no inspired text was lost.

Example: In Mark 6:33, some manuscripts read "by land," others "on foot." Some later manuscripts contain both: "by land on foot."

5. Standardization of Language

Language evolves over time. Scribes might update archaic language to make the text more understandable to contemporary readers.

Example: The divine name in Hebrew, represented by the Tetragrammaton, is often rendered as "Jehovah" in English translations, but some manuscripts replace it with "Adonai" for reasons of reverence and changing linguistic norms.

6. Liturgical Adaptations

Text might be altered to fit liturgical recitations or hymns, affecting the manuscript tradition.

Example: The doxology in the Lord's Prayer ("For thine is the kingdom...") found in Matthew 6:13 is absent in early manuscripts but appears in later ones, possibly due to liturgical usage.

Reasons Behind Intentional Changes

Understanding why scribes made intentional changes can be as crucial as identifying the changes themselves. Several factors might motivate a scribe to alter the text:

1. **Theological Convictions**: Scribes, like any individuals, have personal beliefs. They might have changed text to align with their understanding of doctrine.
2. **Liturgical Utility**: Passages altered for liturgical reasons may not represent the original but were more suitable for public reading or singing.
3. **Harmonization**: The desire for internal consistency within Scripture is strong, and this has led to numerous instances of harmonization.
4. **Pedagogical Reasons**: A scribe might have made changes to clarify what they thought was ambiguous, especially for new converts or for the instruction of a community.

Methodology: Employing the Documentary Approach

Given the likelihood of intentional changes in the textual tradition, it becomes even more critical to apply a rigorous methodology like the Documentary Approach. This method relies on evaluating not just the age but the textual character of the manuscripts. Thus, Codex Vaticanus and Codex Sinaiticus for the New Testament, and the Masoretic Text for the Old Testament, are often given precedence, as they are closer to the originals.

While intentional changes can present substantial challenges to the textual critic, they are not insurmountable. Through a keen understanding of the types of intentional changes and the reasons behind them, coupled with rigorous methodology, we can come closer to recovering the original text of the Scriptures. These scribe-induced variants remind us of the human element in the transmission of the divine Word, making our endeavor not just a scholarly pursuit but a spiritual discipline. Thus, textual criticism serves as both a guardian and a guide to the original texts, helping the believer navigate through the complexities towards a more accurate understanding of the sacred Scriptures.

Harmonization and Expansion: Exploring Reasons for Changes

Textual criticism aims to restore the original text of the Scriptures to the fullest extent possible. Among the variants we find in our manuscript tradition, harmonization and expansion are two prevalent types of intentional changes. This discussion will focus on how these types of changes occur, their impact, and why they pose unique challenges in textual criticism.

Harmonization: A Closer Look

What is Harmonization?

Harmonization occurs when a scribe modifies a text to bring it into conformity with a parallel passage, either elsewhere in the same book or in another book of the Bible. This type of change often emerges out of a well-intentioned desire to preserve scriptural consistency.

Examples of Harmonization

1. **The Resurrection Accounts**: The accounts of Jesus' post-resurrection appearances differ slightly among the Gospels. A scribe, seeking uniformity, may add or omit details to make one Gospel account look more like another. For instance, the women at the tomb encounter different figures depending on the Gospel—sometimes an angel, sometimes two, and sometimes Jesus himself.

2. **Paul's Conversion Story**: Acts recounts Paul's conversion three times (Acts 9, Acts 22, Acts 26), and these accounts are not word-for-word identical. A scribe might alter one account to align it with another.

3. **Synoptic Parallels**: The Sermon on the Mount (Matthew) and the Sermon on the Plain (Luke) have similar content but are not identical. A scribe might insert phrases from one into the other for harmony.

Expansion: A Closer Look

What is Expansion?

Expansion involves adding phrases, sentences, or even larger passages to the text that were not part of the original. These additions may serve various purposes, such as clarifying a point, providing additional information, or emphasizing a particular doctrine.

Examples of Expansion

1. **The Long Ending of Mark**: Mark 16:9-20 is not present in the earliest manuscripts like Codex Vaticanus and Codex Sinaiticus. It seems to be a later addition aimed at providing a more 'complete' ending to Mark's Gospel.

2. **Pericope Adulterae**: The story of the woman caught in adultery (John 7:53-8:11) is absent in early Alexandrian manuscripts and appears to be a later expansion.

3. **Expansions in the Lord's Prayer**: The doxology ("For Yours is the kingdom...") in the Lord's Prayer (Matthew 6:13) is not found in earlier manuscripts but seems to have been added for liturgical reasons.

Exploring Reasons for Changes

Understanding why scribes introduced these changes is essential for textual criticism. Here are some considerations:

1. **Doctrinal Clarification**: A scribe may feel compelled to expand a text to clarify a point of doctrine. This can be problematic because while the intention may be noble, it deviates from the original text.

2. **Liturgical Use**: Some expansions seem designed for liturgical readings and could have been added for use in worship services.

3. **Textual Familiarity**: Scribes were deeply familiar with the Scriptures. Therefore, they could easily, even subconsciously, harmonize texts.

4. **Preservation and Loss Aversion**: In the face of multiple textual traditions, a scribe might include as much material as possible to avoid the loss of potentially inspired text.

Methodological Considerations

Given the presence of these intentional changes, the Documentary Approach becomes even more crucial. The priority given to key manuscripts like Codex Vaticanus, Codex Sinaiticus, and the Masoretic Text ensures that the original text is ascertained to the highest possible degree of certainty.

Harmonization and expansion present unique challenges in the quest for restoring the original text of the Scriptures. While these changes often arise from well-intentioned motives, they introduce complexities into the manuscript tradition. By understanding the types and reasons for these intentional changes and by adhering to rigorous methodological principles, we move closer to achieving the primary goal of textual criticism: the recovery of the original text. Thus, textual criticism does not merely serve an academic purpose but significantly impacts our understanding of doctrine, history, and the spiritual message of the Bible.

Oral Traditions and Memory: Their Role in Variants

Textual criticism has the noble aim of recovering the original words of the Scriptures. While much of the textual data comes from written manuscripts, oral traditions and memory also play a crucial role in the variance observed in the manuscript tradition. Understanding the impact of these factors can shed light on how the texts we possess today came to their current form.

Oral Traditions: Their Nature and Impact

What Are Oral Traditions?

Oral traditions refer to the stories, teachings, and doctrines passed down orally before they were eventually committed to writing. In cultures where writing materials were scarce or literacy rates low, oral tradition was the primary method of transmitting information.

Examples of Oral Traditions in Scripture

1. **Old Testament Histories**: Many Old Testament narratives, such as those concerning the Patriarchs and the Exodus, were likely passed down orally before they were codified in texts. We can consider the historical account of Abraham being called by God (Genesis 12) and the Exodus story (Exodus 1-15) as instances where oral tradition was likely involved.

2. **Teachings of Jesus**: Prior to the composition of the Gospels, the teachings and parables of Jesus were preserved orally. The Sermon on the Mount (Matthew 5-7) serves as an example where oral transmission likely played a role before the text was committed to writing.

3. **Apostolic Traditions**: Paul occasionally refers to oral traditions he received or delivered, such as the creed cited in 1 Corinthians 15:3-7, "For I delivered to you as of first importance what I also received: that Christ died for our sins in accordance with the Scriptures..."

Memory: An Underestimated Factor

The Role of Memory

Memory, both individual and collective, impacts how oral traditions are conveyed and eventually how they are written down. Memory is not a passive container but an active process involving interpretation, retention, and recall.

Examples of Memory in Scriptural Texts

1. **Parallel Accounts**: Variations in parallel accounts can often be attributed to memory. Consider the slight differences in the Synoptic Gospels in recounting the same events, such as the varying lists of the Twelve Apostles (Matthew 10:2-4; Mark 3:16-19; Luke 6:14-16).

2. **Paul's Recollection**: In 1 Corinthians 1:14-16, Paul first recalls baptizing only Crispus and Gaius and then remembers also baptizing the household of Stephanas. This provides a real-time example of the role of memory in recording events.

How Oral Traditions and Memory Lead to Variants

1. **Elaboration and Omission**: During oral transmission, details might be elaborated upon or omitted, which could lead to textual variants when these traditions are finally written down.
2. **Stylization**: Oral traditions often employ mnemonics, rhythm, and other poetic devices to aid in memorization. These elements can introduce changes when the traditions are transcribed.
3. **Transmission Errors**: The fidelity of memory isn't perfect. When coupled with the generational passage of oral traditions, errors can and do occur.
4. **Local Variants**: Different communities might have preserved slightly different versions of the same oral tradition, leading to textual diversity.

Methodological Considerations

Understanding the role of oral traditions and memory in the transmission of text enhances the application of the Documentary Approach. This method aims to prioritize documentary evidence over internal evidence but still considers the latter. Knowing that a text likely has its roots in oral tradition can affect how we weigh different kinds of internal evidence.

The impact of oral traditions and memory on textual variants cannot be ignored. While these factors do introduce complexities into our manuscript tradition, acknowledging them allows us to more robustly apply our methodologies and to get closer to the primary goal of textual criticism, namely the recovery of the original text. Far from being an academic exercise, these considerations add nuance to our understanding of Scripture, helping us to appreciate its rich history and the providential means through which it has been preserved.

Textual Criticism Methods

External Evidence: Evaluating Manuscript Quality and Quantity

Textual criticism seeks to reconstruct the original text of the Scriptures as faithfully as possible. The Documentary Approach allows us to give a certain priority to the evidence derived from manuscripts, which is what we refer to as external evidence. This section aims to delve into the critical aspects of evaluating the quality and quantity of manuscript evidence for both the Old and New Testaments.

Factors Affecting Manuscript Quality

1. **Age of the Manuscript**: Older manuscripts are generally closer to the autograph and may contain fewer copyist errors. For instance, the Codex Sinaiticus and Codex Vaticanus are valuable because of their 4th-century C.E. dating.
2. **Text-Type Affiliation**: Manuscripts belonging to a well-established text-type, such as the Alexandrian family for the New Testament, often carry more weight.
3. **Material**: Manuscripts on durable materials like vellum (e.g., Codex Vaticanus) are often better preserved than those on less durable materials like papyrus.
4. **Geographic Distribution**: Manuscripts that have a broad geographical distribution indicate a more widespread acceptance of a particular reading.
5. **Internal Consistency**: Manuscripts that consistently agree with other high-quality manuscripts are generally considered reliable.

Factors Affecting Manuscript Quantity

1. **Number of Manuscripts**: The more manuscripts available, the better we can reconstruct the original text. The New Testament, with its more than 5,800 Greek manuscripts, provides a wealth of data unparalleled in ancient literature.
2. **Geographical Spread**: Multiple manuscripts from diverse locations can affirm the stability and transmission of a text.
3. **Witness Across Languages**: Translations into other languages, like the Old Latin or Syriac Peshitta, serve as additional witnesses to the original text.

Evaluating Quality: Case Studies

1. **Codex Vaticanus (B)**: This is one of the oldest extant manuscripts of the Greek Bible and is of high quality due to its age, material, and consistency with other Alexandrian texts.
2. **Papyrus 75 (P75)**: Dated to around 175–225 C.E., this manuscript contains portions of the Gospels of Luke and John and is valued for its age and consistency with other early witnesses.
3. **Masoretic Text for the Old Testament**: Given its meticulous transmission and consistency over centuries, the Masoretic Text is considered a high-quality representation of the Old Testament.

Evaluating Quantity: Case Studies

1. **Greek New Testament**: With thousands of manuscripts, the New Testament stands as the best-attested document of antiquity. This sheer

number allows for a higher degree of certainty in reconstructing the original text.
2. **Septuagint**: While not as numerous as New Testament manuscripts, the copies of the Septuagint add valuable external evidence for the Old Testament, serving as secondary witnesses.
3. **Dead Sea Scrolls**: These provide a smaller but incredibly valuable set of Old Testament manuscripts, adding an additional layer of external evidence.

Balancing Quality and Quantity

While having a large number of manuscripts is advantageous, it's crucial to balance quantity with quality. A few high-quality manuscripts can outweigh a larger number of lesser-quality manuscripts. The Documentary Approach encourages us to consider both aspects critically but leans more towards the quality of the documents when making textual decisions.

Evaluating manuscript quality and quantity is a nuanced task, requiring careful attention to various factors, including age, material, consistency, and geographical distribution. These evaluations serve as the foundation upon which we can employ textual criticism methods like the Documentary Approach to reconstruct the original text of the Scriptures. The task, though intricate, serves a divine purpose: to recover the very words of God, as they were first revealed. This is not merely an academic endeavor but a theological imperative, aiding us in the proper understanding and teaching of the divine Word. Therefore, the efforts to weigh the external evidence are not just technical exercises but deeply spiritual undertakings, aligning our contemporary Bibles as closely as possible to the original texts.

Internal Evidence: Assessing Readings Based on Context and Grammar

While external evidence, rooted in the documentary material of manuscripts, forms an invaluable component of textual criticism, internal evidence—concerning the text itself—remains indispensable. These internal considerations often help textual scholars discern the original reading from among multiple variants. Internal evidence focuses on the text's internal coherence, evaluating readings based on context and grammar.

Importance of Context in Evaluating Readings

1. **Immediate Context**: Immediate context refers to the verses and chapters surrounding a given variant. Does the variant cohere with the immediate arguments, themes, or narration? For example, if we examine the long ending of Mark's Gospel (Mark 16:9-20), we find that its immediate context seems disjointed, leading many scholars to consider it a later addition.

2. **Broader Biblical Context**: This refers to the wider thematic, doctrinal, or narrative structures within the same book or even other books. Inconsistencies could signal a corrupted text. For example, the "Johannine Comma" (1 John 5:7–8) introduces Trinitarian language not found in other Johannine writings, rendering its authenticity suspect.

3. **Historical and Cultural Context**: Understanding the historical and cultural milieu often illuminates the text. For instance, understanding first-century Jewish practices can shed light on the meaning of the term "Sabbath" in the Gospels.

Importance of Grammar in Evaluating Readings

1. **Syntactical Consistency**: The syntax, or sentence structure, should align with the writing style of the given biblical author. For instance, Paul's usage of complex sentences and theological terms is a hallmark of his writings.

2. **Vocabulary**: Authentic readings should use vocabulary consistent with the author's known style. The usage of anachronistic or inconsistent terms can flag a variant. For example, the term "apostles" in the New Testament usually refers to a specific group. Variants using this term in a broader sense may be scrutinized.

3. **Concordance with Parallel Accounts**: For texts like the Synoptic Gospels, which often recount the same events, internal consistency across parallel accounts is vital. Variants that contradict other Synoptic accounts require special attention.

Practical Application: Case Studies

1. **Romans 5:1**: One variant reads "we have peace" (echomen), while another reads "let us have peace" (echōmen). The former is more likely the original reading given the immediate context of justification by faith and the broader Pauline theology.

2. **John 1:18**: The variants include "only begotten Son" (monogenēs huios) and "only begotten God" (monogenēs theos). The latter aligns better with John's high Christology and the immediate context of the prologue, making it the preferred reading.[11]

3. **Exodus 20:13**: The commandment is commonly rendered "You shall not kill," but a better translation considering Hebrew grammar and broader biblical context is "You shall not murder," which aligns with the specific prohibition against unlawful killing.

---

[11] The original words were μονογενὴς θεός or ο μονογενης θεος "only-begotten God" or "the only-begotten God" (P66 P75 ℵ B C* L 33 syr^hmp 33 cop^bo) A variant reading is ο μονογενης υιος "the only begotten Son" A C³ (W^s) Θ Ψ f^1, Maj syr^c).

Limits of Internal Evidence

Though valuable, internal evidence has its limits. It can be subjective, especially when dealing with vocabulary and style, which might evolve over an author's lifetime or be adapted for different audiences. Therefore, while internal evidence is a powerful tool, it is most effective when used in conjunction with external evidence.

Internal evidence serves as an indispensable companion to the external manuscript evidence in textual criticism. Assessing readings based on context and grammar aids in winnowing down the possible variants to the most likely original text. This exercise not only brings us closer to the text as it was initially penned but also enhances our understanding of the Bible as a divinely inspired yet humanly articulated document. By considering the context within the individual books and across Scripture as a whole, as well as focusing on the grammatical details, we can uphold the integrity of the original texts. While not without its limitations, the careful application of internal evidence plays a crucial role in our ongoing efforts to faithfully transmit the Word of God.

Comparative Analysis: Cross-Examining Variants Across Manuscripts

The principle of comparative analysis in textual criticism involves cross-examining textual variants across different manuscripts to ascertain which readings are likely original. This process often utilizes a set of criteria to weigh the evidence, blending both external documentary evidence and internal coherence. The comparative approach provides a way to triangulate the most probable reading.

Aligning Textual Families

Manuscripts often fall into distinct "families" or "types," based on shared readings and other characteristics.

1. **Alexandrian Text Type**: As exemplified by Codex Vaticanus and Codex Sinaiticus, these manuscripts are often older and considered by many scholars to be more reliable.
2. **Byzantine Text Type**: This family, usually represented by later manuscripts, tends to have longer readings and harmonizations.
3. **Western Text Type**: These manuscripts, often referenced but less relied upon, contain unique readings and possible paraphrases.

Criteria for Comparative Analysis

1. **Age and Provenance**: Older manuscripts are generally given more weight, especially if their geographical distribution is wide.
2. **Manuscript Agreement**: When multiple manuscripts from various families agree on a reading, the case for its originality strengthens.

3. **External Attestation**: Early church fathers' quotations, lectionaries, and other ancient translations like the Syriac Peshitta or the Latin Vulgate provide supplemental confirmation.
4. **Quantity of Manuscripts**: While not definitive on its own, the number of manuscripts containing a particular reading can be a factor.

Practical Applications: Case Studies

1. **John 7:53–8:11**: The story of the woman caught in adultery is absent in significant Alexandrian manuscripts and appears at different locations in other manuscripts, including in Luke in some. This evidence suggests it might be a later addition.
2. **Mark 16:9-20**: The longer ending is notably absent in the oldest and most reliable Alexandrian manuscripts. It also features vocabulary and style inconsistent with the rest of Mark, indicating it may not be original.
3. **1 Timothy 3:16**: Manuscripts differ on whether to read "God was manifest" or "He who was manifest." Alexandrian manuscripts like Codex Sinaiticus and Codex Vaticanus support the latter, making it more probable as the original reading.
4. **Matthew 24:36**: Some Byzantine manuscripts include the phrase "nor the Son" when speaking of who knows the day and the hour of the end. However, the best Alexandrian manuscripts lack this phrase, and its absence coheres more closely with Matthew's typical Christology.
5. **Psalm 22:16**: The reading "they have pierced my hands and feet" in some Masoretic Text manuscripts contrasts with "like a lion my hands and feet" in others. The Dead Sea Scrolls and the Septuagint lend weight to the "pierced" reading, which aligns with crucifixion, suggesting that it might be the original.

Limitations of Comparative Analysis

1. **Conflation**: Byzantine manuscripts, known for harmonization and conflations, may combine readings from different text types, complicating the identification of the original.
2. **Survival Bias**: Older manuscripts have had more time to be lost, damaged, or destroyed. Thus, their absence does not necessarily negate their reliability.
3. **Manuscript Anomalies**: Occasionally, a single manuscript might contain an idiosyncratic reading that neither fits with its textual family nor can be easily explained as a scribal error. These are often discounted but still present challenges to a streamlined comparative approach.

Comparative analysis stands as an essential technique in textual criticism. By cross-examining manuscript evidence, scholars can make educated judgments about the originality of variant readings. Although each manuscript family has its strengths and weaknesses, the comparative approach allows textual critics to glean insights that individual manuscripts alone cannot provide. The ongoing discovery of new manuscripts and the continuous refinement of critical editions further underline the vitality of this method in our unrelenting quest to restore the original text of Scripture. Therefore, while recognizing the limitations of the comparative approach, its utility in bringing us closer to the original writings remains irreplaceable.

History of the Transmission of the New Testament Text

Introduction to Textual Variants in Early Christian Writings

During the infancy of Christianity, *apostolic letters and gospels* served as primary religious texts. These documents were meticulously copied to broaden their impact and enrich more people's spiritual lives. However, *handwritten reproduction inevitably introduced variations*—some copies bore many discrepancies, while others had only a few. Such differences generally stemmed from accidental errors, such as confusing letters or words that looked alike. This is evident, for example, in discussions about 2 Peter 1:21.

Common Types of Accidental Mistakes

Visual Slip-ups: Homoioarcton and Homoioteleuton

Copyists occasionally skipped portions of the text because of visual tricks. In such cases, two lines might start or end with the same letters, or two similar words might be close to each other. The eyes could easily jump from one to the other, leading to omissions. These errors fall under two categories: **homoioarcton**, when similar letters occur at the beginnings of words, and **homoioteleuton**, when they occur at the ends.

Example of Homoioarcton

Refer to Mark 10:7 for an example where words might have been skipped because of homoioarcton.

Example of Homoioteleuton

In 1 Peter 3:14, certain words were left out due to homoioteleuton.

Mechanical Errors: Dittography and Haplography

Dittography is the accidental repetition of letters, syllables, or words, whereas **haplography** is their accidental omission. Sometimes it's hard to ascertain which has occurred.

Example of Dittography and Haplography

For instance, consider 1 Thessalonians 2:7, which mentions the words νήπιοι (infants) and ἤπιοι (gentle).

Phonetic Confusion: Itacism

Itacism refers to the misrepresentation of letters that sounded alike when spoken.

Examples of Itacism

See Colossians 2:13 and 1 Corinthians 15:54 for instances where such errors have been identified.

Challenges for Copyists

Numerous other challenges such as poor eyesight, distractions, and fatigue also contributed to mistakes. R.E. Brown noted the role of misreading by the individual dictating to the copyists as another potential source of error. The constant need to re-ink reed pens could also result in unintended errors.

Intentional Changes

Some changes were made deliberately to clarify ambiguous phrases or align the style with the prevailing linguistic norms.

Example of Intentional Change

In Romans 4:1, the words προπάτορα (ancestor) and πατέρα (father) serve as an example.

Harmonization and Assimilation

Harmonization or **assimilation** refers to the modification of a text to make it consistent with a parallel passage elsewhere in the New Testament or in the Septuagint, the Greek translation of the Old Testament.

Example of Harmonization

This is seen, for example, in Acts 3:22 and 1 Thessalonians 1:1.

Theological "Improvements"

Some changes were introduced to safeguard theological tenets, such as the virgin birth in the story of 12-year-old Jesus staying behind in Jerusalem in Luke 2:41-43.

Concluding Thoughts

As time passed after the New Testament documents were first penned, *thousands of variant readings emerged*. However, these variations serve more as a testament to the complexities of human transcription than as barriers to understanding the divine message.

The Journey of the New Testament Text Through History

In the infancy of the Christian church, apostolic letters and gospels were sent out to meet the spiritual needs of congregations or individuals. These valuable texts were hand-copied to maximize their reach and impact. However, human error was an inevitable part of this manual transmission process, leading to textual variants—*differences in wording* compared to the original documents.

Types of Copyist Errors

Several types of mistakes crept into the copied texts. Some were accidental, such as confusing similar-looking letters or words, leading to **homoioarcton** (similarity at the beginning of words) and **homoioteleuton** (similarity at the end of words). Another mistake is **dittography**, the accidental repetition of letters or words, and its opposite, **haplography**, where letters are accidentally omitted. **Itacism** occurred when similarly pronounced letters were mixed up.

Noteworthy Examples of Errors

- **Homoioarcton:** A copyist might skip text in Mark 10:7 due to similarities at the start of words.

- **Homoioteleuton:** An example can be found in 1 Pet 3:14, where certain words are skipped due to similar endings.

- **Dittography and Haplography:** 1 Thess 2:7 provides an example where it's hard to tell if a word has been repeated or omitted.

- **Itacism:** Issues with vowel sounds in Koine Greek led to confusion, as in 1 Cor 15:54 and Col 2:13.

Other Influencing Factors

As scholarly work by Head and Warren has shown, factors like the need to re-ink pens could lead to unintentional errors. In some cases, errors were deliberate attempts to improve the text's grammar, style, or theology.

Translations into Ancient Languages

As Christianity expanded geographically, there was a need for the Scriptures to be translated into local languages like Syriac, Latin, and various Coptic dialects. *Textual critics* refer to these translations as **ancient versions**. The reliability of these versions depended on two main elements: the translator's proficiency in both the original and target languages, and the diligence they applied to the translation process. Copyists of these versions sometimes made corrections based on their understanding of the text, further contributing to textual variants.

Research on Early Versions

For a comprehensive understanding of the role of these ancient versions in textual criticism, one can consult works such as "The Text of the New Testament in Contemporary Research" edited by Ehrman and Holmes.

Emergence of Local Texts and Text-Types

As Christian communities formed around major cities like Alexandria and Rome, localized versions of the New Testament texts, called **local texts**, began to develop. These would then be copied, *preserving and sometimes amplifying unique local readings*. By comparing manuscripts with the writings of Church Fathers who lived in these localities, modern scholars can identify these localized text-types.

However, *textual mixing* could occur if a manuscript from one region influenced the text in another. Yet, in the early centuries, there was a stronger tendency to preserve rather than mix text-types, leading to the development of various unique forms of New Testament texts.

Textual Criticism and Text-Types

In the meticulous field of textual criticism, scholars sift through hundreds of manuscripts and thousands of scribal errors to identify the most reliable versions of ancient texts. This process categorizes most New Testament manuscripts into one of three primary **text-types**. When manuscripts have strikingly similar readings, they're grouped into **families**. For example, Family 1 and Family 13 are collections of closely related manuscripts, labeled as **f1** and **f13** in critical apparatuses. The term **variant readings** signifies different readings appearing at the same location within a given verse. Manuscripts belonging to the same text-type consistently have identical variant readings when multiple options exist, known as a **unit of variation**.

Some manuscripts display different text-types for separate parts of the New Testament. Codex Alexandrinus, for instance, exhibits Byzantine text-type in the Gospels and Alexandrian text-type elsewhere. Scholars like Daniel Wallace and K. and B. Aland have created comprehensive charts that categorize manuscripts by century and text-type, aiding the study further.

Prominent Text-Types

Alexandrian Text

British scholars Westcott and Hort first termed this as the **Neutral text** in the 19th century. Today, it's often called the **Alexandrian text** or sometimes the "B text." It's largely considered the **most accurate and closest to the original writings**. It uses minimal words and lacks the stylistic polishing found in Byzantine text. Codex Vaticanus and Codex Sinaiticus were the primary witnesses until the discovery of the Bodmer Papyri in the mid-1950s, confirming its roots back to the early second century.

Western Text

Originally identified for its prevalence in the western Christian world, this is the **Western text**, also sometimes called the "D-text." Besides Western Europe, it was also present in Eastern Syriac-speaking churches and Egypt. **Key figures** like Marcion, Tatian, Irenaeus, Tertullian, and Cyprian employed this text-type. Its chief characteristic is **liberal paraphrasing**, freely changing, omitting, or inserting words, clauses, or entire sentences. Although prevalent, many scholars argue that its readings are too inconsistent to formally classify it as a distinct text-type.

Eastern Texts

Formerly termed as the **Caesarean text**, this text-type mixes Western and Alexandrian readings and doesn't command consensus as a standalone text-type today. Another Eastern type prevalent near Antioch is primarily found in Old Syriac manuscripts and quotations from fourth-century Syriac Church leaders.

Byzantine Text

Also known by several other names like the **Syrian text** or the **Majority text**, this is the **latest and most stylistically polished** of the text-types. Characterized by clarity and completeness, this text-type was prevalent throughout the Byzantine Empire. Despite its abundance in later manuscripts, it's generally not considered as authentic as the Alexandrian text-type.

Historical and Geographical Distribution

By 200 C.E., Latin, Coptic, and Syriac manuscripts were widely used in various parts of the Roman Empire. More than 8,000 Latin Vulgate manuscripts exist today, surpassing all known Greek manuscripts. By the end of the seventh century, the New Testament in Greek was mainly restricted to the Greek Orthodox Church in Constantinople, using the Byzantine text-type. Other regions switched to local languages and translations.

The Debate Over Dominant Text-Types

Some scholars argue that the **numerical majority of Byzantine manuscripts** implies greater authenticity. This argument overlooks the historical context where Greek was replaced by local languages in most of the Roman Empire. After the advent of the printing press, the Byzantine text became the standard, not because of its authenticity but due to its ready availability to early editors.

In sum, understanding these text-types is crucial for biblical studies, but one must carefully consider both the textual evidence and historical context when evaluating their reliability and origins.

The Evolution of Printed Greek New Testaments

Erasmus' Groundbreaking Edition

Desiderius Erasmus, a Dutch humanist scholar, produced the first printed edition of the Greek New Testament in Basel in 1516. Since he couldn't find a single manuscript containing the complete New Testament, Erasmus had to resort to a patchwork of various manuscripts. Interestingly, he mainly relied on two 12th-century manuscripts that were not of high quality. For the Book of Revelation, Erasmus had only one 12th-century manuscript and had to translate the missing last six verses from Jerome's Latin Vulgate. This resulted in readings that aren't found in any existing Greek manuscript.

Impact of Erasmus' Edition

The initial edition by Erasmus quickly sold out, prompting a second release in 1519. This second edition was the foundation for the German and English translations by **Martin Luther** in 1522 and **William Tyndale** in 1525, respectively. However, Erasmus' reliance on the Latin Vulgate in places means that this earlier translation actually has sections closer to the original text.

The Stephanus Editions

Later, **Robert Etienne**, known as Stephanus, published two significant editions of the Greek New Testament. His third edition in 1550 was the first to incorporate a *critical apparatus*—notations of variant readings across different manuscripts. His fourth edition in 1551 was the first to number verses within the New Testament text.

Beza's Influence

Theodore Beza, who succeeded Calvin in Geneva, was another prominent figure. He produced several editions between 1565 and 1604, and his work greatly influenced what came to be known as the *Textus Receptus (TR)*. This text was significantly utilized in the 1611 King James Version.

Textus Receptus and Its Reception

The term *Textus Receptus* originated with printers Bonaventura and Abraham Elzevir. It became a common term to describe the Byzantine text form, although the two are not identical. Most early editions of the printed Greek New Testament were based on this Byzantine form, a form that had accumulated numerous scribal changes over time.

Notable Scholars and Critical Editions

Johann A. Bengel initiated the practice of categorizing manuscripts and offered ways to evaluate variant readings. *Karl Lachmann* applied classic textual editing principles to the New Testament in 1831. Throughout the 19th and 20th centuries, various scholars like **Tischendorf**, **Westcott-Hort**, and **Nestle-Aland** released editions based on earlier and more reliable manuscripts.

Byzantine Text Proponents vs. Majority View

While the majority of scholars prefer editions like those by Westcott-Hort and Nestle-Aland, some, like **Z.C. Hodges and A.L. Farstad**, advocate for the Byzantine text form. However, their methodology and assumptions have not received widespread scholarly acceptance.

The Complex Nature of the Text

In summary, no single version of the Greek New Testament should be considered canonical in and of itself, as pointed out by scholar **Raymond Brown**. Instead, scholars generally rely on the United Bible Societies' edition or the Nestle-Aland Novum Testamentum Graece for their work, recognizing that these editions are the product of careful scholarly synthesis from various manuscripts.

Thus, the evolution of the printed Greek New Testament reflects both the complexities and the dedication involved in approximating the original texts of the New Testament as accurately as possible.

The Importance of the Documentary Approach: Approach to Reconstructing the Original Text

The Importance of External Evidence in Textual Criticism

Traditional Approaches to Textual Criticism

In the realm of Biblical textual criticism, the methods of "Reasoned Eclecticism" and the "Local-Genealogical" approach usually give precedence to internal evidence over external evidence, thus resulting in what's termed "atomistic eclecticism." In contrast, scholars Westcott and Hort argue that external evidence should be prioritized if the aim is to restore the original text of the New Testament. Hort wrote that *documentary evidence takes precedence over internal evidence*. This notion was also supported by Colwell in his article "Hort Redivivus: A Plea and a Program," where he called on scholars to reconstruct the history of manuscript tradition.

The Challenge of Reconstructing Manuscript Lineage

However, scholars have been reluctant to follow this approach, mainly because they believe it's impossible to reconstruct a manuscript "family tree" or stemma for the New Testament. This skepticism is often fueled by the criticism that Westcott and Hort received for their concept of a "Neutral" text originating from Codex Vaticanus (B) and tracing back to the original.

The Role of Manuscript Tradition

It's important to note that reconstructing early manuscript traditions *does not necessarily require tracing back to the original text*. This reconstruction provides valuable insights into the relationships between various manuscripts and might even indicate that some of the earliest manuscripts are indeed closest to the original text.

The Evidence of 𝔓75: A Second-Century Revelation

Second-Century Papyrus Changes the Game

One of the strongest arguments for reverting to a documentary approach is the second-century papyrus 𝔓75. This manuscript, which contains parts of the Gospels of Luke and John, has revealed a significant affinity with Codex Vaticanus. The textual agreement between 𝔓75 and B is around 83%, providing a compelling reason to re-examine previous assumptions about early manuscript traditions.

No Need for a 'Recension Theory'

Before the discovery of 𝔓75, scholars like Kenyon believed that the textual purity seen in Codex Vaticanus resulted from a scholarly revision process that spanned various manuscript traditions. The finding of 𝔓75 invalidated this theory, demonstrating that the text of Codex Vaticanus closely followed a second-century manuscript rather than a fourth-century scholarly revision.

Reassessing Other Textual Theories

The Western Text: A Loose Category

Some critics are still not convinced that the 𝔓75/B text type is superior to another early text type often called the "Western" text. This text type, however, is a loose collection of early texts rather than a distinct family. Therefore, the name "Western" is considered by some to be a misnomer.

Subjectivity vs. Objective Analysis

Skeptics argue that the preference for the 𝔓75/B text type may be based on a subjective evaluation, rather than on an objective analysis of early text transmission. However, those who have worked with these manuscripts point out that they contain fewer errors and interpolations compared to the so-called Western manuscripts.

In summary, the discovery of 𝔓75 has considerably *shifted the paradigm in New Testament textual criticism*, supporting the importance of external evidence and indicating that early and accurate manuscripts, like 𝔓75, can serve as reliable witnesses to the original text. This discovery underscores the need for a more balanced approach that includes both internal and external evidence in the quest for recovering the Biblical text.

YOUR GUIDE FOR DEFENDING THE BIBLE

CHAPTER 13 The New Testament Textual Criticism

New Testament Manuscripts

Papyrus Fragments: Discovering Early Witnesses to the New Testament

The discovery of papyrus fragments has significantly enriched the field of New Testament textual criticism. These early witnesses provide invaluable insights into the original text of the New Testament, primarily falling within the 2nd to 3rd centuries C.E. In this section, we will explore some key papyrus fragments that serve as essential landmarks in our journey towards the textual reconstruction of the New Testament.

The Importance of Papyrus

Before diving into specific examples, let's underscore the value of papyrus as a writing material. Papyrus was cheap, relatively durable, and widely used in the ancient Mediterranean world. These characteristics made it a prevalent choice for early Christian writings, including copies of New Testament texts.

P52 (John Rylands Papyrus: 110-150 C.E.)

Perhaps the most famous New Testament papyrus is P52, dating around 110-150 C.E. This fragment contains portions of John 18:31-33 and 18:37-38, dealing with Jesus' trial before Pilate. Its early date and the geographical distance from its likely place of origin (Ephesus) to its discovery site (Egypt) speak to the rapid dissemination of the Johannine Gospel.

P66 (Bodmer Papyrus II: 110-150 C.E.)

P66 is another noteworthy papyrus, particularly for its extensive coverage of the Gospel of John. It includes most of the text from John 1:1 to 21:9. Given its early dating and high-quality text, P66 offers important data points for textual scholars. This papyrus leans towards the Alexandrian text-type, often aligning with Codex Vaticanus and Codex Sinaiticus.

P75 (Bodmer Papyrus XIV–XV: 175-225 C.E.)

P75 is a prized fragment containing portions of the Gospels of Luke and John. What makes P75 especially important is its close textual affinity with Codex Vaticanus, suggesting a stabilized text tradition by the time of its production.

P45 (Chester Beatty I: 175-225 C.E.)

P45 is a fragmentary codex that includes texts from Matthew, Mark, Luke, John, and Acts. While it is more fragmentary and its text-type is less clearly Alexandrian, it still offers a crucial snapshot of how these texts were being read and understood in the early Christian communities.

P46 (Chester Beatty II: 125-150 C.E.)

This papyrus is remarkable for containing large portions of Pauline Epistles. It includes Romans, Hebrews, 1 and 2 Corinthians, Ephesians, Galatians, Philippians, Colossians, and 1 Thessalonians. Despite some textual variations, P46 provides some of the earliest extant evidence for the Pauline corpus.

P47 (Chester Beatty III: 200-250 C.E.)

P47 contains portions of the book of Revelation, specifically chapters 9-17. This is particularly significant since manuscripts of Revelation are scarce among early papyri.

P72 (Bodmer Papyrus VII–VIII: 200-250 C.E.)

This papyrus is unique for containing early portions of Jude and both Peter's epistles. This is significant in the study of the Catholic Epistles, an often-underrepresented section in the New Testament papyri.

Implications for Textual Reconstruction

1. **Alexandrian Priority**: The early dating and high quality of manuscripts like P66 and P75 strengthen the case for the priority of the Alexandrian text-type.

2. **Pauline Corpus**: P46 serves as an early witness to a substantial collection of Paul's letters, providing crucial data for textual critics.

3. **Rapid Distribution**: The geographical range and early dating of these fragments indicate that New Testament texts were disseminated quickly, counteracting claims that these books were late compositions.

4. **Textual Preservation**: The consistency between these early papyri and later codices like Vaticanus and Sinaiticus suggests a relatively stable transmission of the text, further confirmed by modern critical editions.

Papyrus fragments like P52, P66, P75, P45, P46, P47, and P72 are indispensible witnesses to the early text of the New Testament. They provide not only the foundation upon which critical editions are based but also a window into the early Christian world, where these sacred texts were read, copied, and preserved. These fragments play a vital role in attaining our primary objective: the most accurate possible reconstruction of the New Testament text. The ongoing work in papyrology and textual criticism continues to bring us closer to this goal.

Uncial Manuscripts: The Great Codices

The uncial manuscripts represent an invaluable asset to New Testament textual criticism. Written in large, uppercase Greek letters, these manuscripts serve as early witnesses to the New Testament text. Here, we focus on some of the great codices that have been at the epicenter of New Testament textual studies.

Codex Vaticanus (300-330 CE)

Regarded as one of the most important manuscripts, Codex Vaticanus resides in the Vatican Library. It includes almost the entire Greek Bible, though some portions are missing (e.g., Timothy, Titus, Revelation). The codex is written on fine vellum and demonstrates a high degree of scribal skill. Textual scholars give significant weight to its readings because of its antiquity and close adherence to the Alexandrian text-type.

Codex Sinaiticus (330-360 CE)

Discovered at St. Catherine's Monastery, this codex is another pillar in New Testament textual criticism. Like Vaticanus, it is closer to the Alexandrian family of texts. It contains the entire New Testament and a large portion of the Septuagint. The codex has undergone corrections over the years, offering scholars a glimpse into the scribal habits and textual changes in early Christianity.

Codex Bezae (c. 400 CE)

This codex is unique for containing the Gospels and Acts in both Greek and Latin. Unlike Vaticanus and Sinaiticus, Codex Bezae is usually classified under the Western text-type. It has many peculiar readings and seems to preserve an older form of the text in some instances. Despite its idiosyncrasies, it remains a valuable witness to the diversity of the early New Testament text.

Codex Claromontanus (6th century CE)

This bilingual manuscript contains parts of the New Testament in both Greek and Latin. The codex has been instrumental for textual scholars interested in the Pauline epistles, particularly in identifying textual variants.

Codex Washingtonianus I (5th century CE)

Housed in the Freer Gallery of Art in Washington, D.C., this codex contains the four Gospels. It has a mixed text-type, which means that it does not neatly fit into the primary categories of Alexandrian, Western, or Byzantine. This manuscript offers valuable insights into the textual transmission during a period of transition.

Codex Washingtonianus II (5th century CE)

Also housed in the Freer Gallery, this manuscript contains portions of the Pauline Epistles. It serves as another example of a mixed text-type, providing researchers with additional variants for consideration.

Codex Alexandrinus (5th century CE)

This codex, held in the British Library, is one of the earliest complete New Testaments. It has Byzantine leanings but also contains elements typical of the Alexandrian text-type. While not as old as Vaticanus or Sinaiticus, its comprehensive nature makes it an important resource for textual critics.

Codex Ephraemi Syri Rescriptus (Codex Ephraemi, 5th century CE)

This is a palimpsest, meaning that the original writing was scraped off and overwritten. However, the underwriting contains portions of every New Testament book except 2 Thessalonians and 2 John. Its textual character is generally Alexandrian but shows some Western and Byzantine influences.

These great codices are crucial for understanding the New Testament text. They serve as the foundation upon which textual critics build their reconstructions. Each codex has its unique features, scribal habits, and textual characteristics, and thus, they contribute to a multi-dimensional understanding of the text.

In summary, these uncial manuscripts are instrumental for textual scholars aiming to restore the New Testament text to its original form. They serve as windows into the early textual history, helping us come closer to the autographs. By meticulously analyzing these manuscripts, scholars are able to substantiate the New Testament text we possess today as a near mirror-like reflection of what the original would have been, aligning closely with our commitment to a literal, objective Historical-Grammatical method of interpretation.

Minuscule Manuscripts: The Majority of New Testament Copies

The study of New Testament textual criticism is significantly aided by the plethora of minuscule manuscripts that we have at our disposal. Comprising the majority of extant copies, these minuscule manuscripts—written in lowercase, cursive Greek script—emerged around the 9th century CE and continued to be produced until the advent of the printing press. While not as ancient as their uncial counterparts, they constitute the overwhelming majority of our textual witnesses and are vital in ascertaining the original text.

Origin and Importance

The development of minuscule script was likely influenced by the need for more economical use of materials and more efficient copying. Before this period, uncial manuscripts, written in large, uppercase letters, were the norm. The minuscule manuscripts facilitated easier reading and faster writing. Although most are Byzantine in text-type, their sheer number and the relatively late period they cover make them indispensable in cross-checking readings and in corroborating or questioning findings from older manuscripts.

Categories and Examples

1. **Continuous Text Manuscripts**: These are the complete New Testament documents or those containing large portions. A good example is Minuscule 33, often called the "Queen of the Minuscules," dating to the 9th century CE. It is highly esteemed for its accuracy and is sometimes considered to align more closely with the Alexandrian text-type than with the Byzantine.

2. **Lectionaries**: These are church-use manuscripts that contain passages of Scriptures arranged according to the liturgical calendar. While not strictly continuous-text manuscripts, lectionaries are nevertheless crucial for understanding how the text was read and understood in the life of the Church.

3. **Commentary Manuscripts**: These contain the New Testament text along with patristic commentaries. Minuscule 1241, for example, has extensive scholia (marginal notes) and offers a window into how certain passages were interpreted.

4. **Luxury Manuscripts**: These are ornately decorated and often have gold or silver inlays, like Minuscule 565, which is known for its unique textual features and beautiful artistry.

Relationship with Other Text Types

While the majority of minuscules are Byzantine in text-type, it's essential to note that some contain "mixed" text forms. They offer a unique blend of Alexandrian, Western, and Byzantine readings. The thorough examination of these manuscripts can yield interesting perspectives on the text's transmission history. Minuscule 1739, for example, displays a complex mixture of text-types, making it valuable for understanding the interplay of textual families over time.

Challenges and Criticisms

Some textual critics argue that the sheer number of minuscules may not necessarily mean that their readings are closer to the original text. This is mainly due to the late date of these manuscripts and their overwhelming alignment with the Byzantine text-type, which some scholars view as less reliable than the Alexandrian. Nonetheless, given that these manuscripts represent centuries of textual transmission, their importance in textual criticism cannot be understated.

Role in Textual Criticism

1. **Corroboration of Earlier Witnesses**: Despite their later date, minuscules often corroborate earlier uncial manuscripts, thereby strengthening the confidence in certain textual readings.

2. **Identifying Textual Variants**: With thousands of minuscules available, the identification of variants is significantly aided. Even a single manuscript

can offer a previously unrecognized variant that may aid in determining the original text.
3. **Textual Families and Groupings**: The large number of minuscule manuscripts allows scholars to identify patterns and groupings, helping to trace the development and movement of textual families over time.
4. **Liturgical and Theological Insights**: Lectionaries and commentary manuscripts offer more than just the text; they provide an understanding of how Scriptures were used and understood in worship and teaching.

In sum, minuscule manuscripts, while later in origin, form the backbone of New Testament textual witnesses. Their number and diversity contribute significantly to our efforts to reconstruct the New Testament text. Through careful examination and comparison with older manuscripts and other text-types, they play a vital role in our endeavor to come as close as possible to the original writings. Like the ancient uncial manuscripts, these minuscule texts form part of a complex but highly informative tapestry that textual critics must analyze in a meticulous, objective manner. As a result, they provide an indispensable resource that brings us closer to affirming the New Testament text we possess today as a nearly mirror-like reflection of what the original would have been.

Patristic Quotations, Lectionaries, and Early Versions: Expanding the Sources

While the primary focus in New Testament textual criticism has often been on Greek manuscripts, particularly those of the Alexandrian tradition, other crucial sources should not be overlooked. Patristic quotations, lectionaries, and early versions provide a rich tapestry of evidence that complements and sometimes clarifies the readings found in Greek manuscripts. These additional sources play vital roles in cross-referencing, verifying, or challenging the readings we find in Greek texts.

Patristic Quotations

The writings of the Church Fathers, commonly referred to as the "Patristic" writings, contain a treasure trove of quotations from the New Testament. These quotations serve multiple purposes:

1. **Corroborating Greek Manuscripts**: Patristic writings often include citations or allusions to New Testament texts. For instance, Origen's works are replete with such quotations, helping scholars establish a benchmark against which other readings may be measured.
2. **Unique Variants**: Church Fathers sometimes offer readings not found elsewhere. These may be indicative of localized text types or unique transmission paths.

3. **Geographic and Temporal Range**: Different Church Fathers wrote in different locales and during different centuries, thus providing insights into the text's geographical and temporal dissemination.
4. **Scriptural Interpretation**: While the primary focus is on recovering the original text, patristic quotations offer valuable insights into early understandings of the text.
5. **Examples**: Clement of Rome, Ignatius of Antioch, and Justin Martyr are early witnesses whose citations have been instrumental in corroborating or challenging the readings in Greek manuscripts.

Lectionaries

Lectionaries are essentially ecclesiastical books containing Scripture readings arranged according to the liturgical calendar. The importance of lectionaries lies in:

1. **Stability of Text**: Since these were used in a liturgical setting, there was less room for scribal "creativity," making them a stable source for the text.
2. **Community Verification**: Their public use means that lectionaries underwent a form of community scrutiny, which could serve as a corrective measure against potential scribal errors.
3. **Liturgical Context**: They give us an insight into the text's use in early Christian communities, helping us understand the functional aspect of Scripture within the Church.
4. **Examples**: The Byzantine Lectionary, known for its use in the Eastern Orthodox Church, often reflects the Byzantine text-type and serves as an important witness to this text form.

Early Versions

Non-Greek translations, such as the Latin Vulgate, the Syriac Peshitta, and the Coptic translations, are invaluable for textual criticism.

1. **Language Transition**: When the text was translated into another language, scholars can study how Greek terms were understood and rendered, sometimes shedding light on ambiguous passages.
2. **Localization of Text**: Early versions reflect the form of the text that was in use in specific linguistic and geographic communities.
3. **Textual Variants**: These versions can contain unique readings, which either present a variant not found in the Greek manuscripts or corroborate a Greek reading that has fewer witnesses.
4. **Examples**: Jerome's Latin Vulgate has often been used to shed light on difficult readings, while the Old Latin versions predate the Vulgate and offer even earlier witness to the text. The Syriac Peshitta is another

invaluable resource, especially for the texts of the Eastern Christian tradition.

Challenges and Opportunities

1. **Limited Scope**: Not all New Testament books are equally represented in these sources, which can be a limitation.

2. **Secondary Nature**: Being translations or quotations, these sources are considered secondary compared to Greek manuscripts, yet they offer valuable supporting evidence.

3. **Contextual Interpretation**: The way Scripture is quoted or translated could be influenced by the theological or liturgical context, which needs to be considered in textual analysis.

Patristic quotations, lectionaries, and early versions are secondary yet significant resources in New Testament textual criticism. Their contributions are not to be underestimated, particularly when they corroborate or challenge readings found in primary Greek witnesses.

Through a nuanced use of these sources, textual critics can achieve a fuller understanding of the text's transmission history, its geographical spread, and its interpretation in the early Church. Consequently, these additional sources are invaluable tools that assist in achieving the ultimate goal: a New Testament text that mirrors, as closely as possible, what the original authors wrote. With these additional layers of evidence, we come closer to a text that is a nearly exact reflection of the original, fulfilling the rigors of the Documentary Approach in textual criticism.

The Nestle-Aland and UBS Greek Texts: Modern Critical Editions

In the landscape of New Testament textual criticism, few names are as pivotal as Nestle-Aland and the United Bible Societies (UBS) Greek New Testament. These critical editions aim to approximate the original text of the New Testament as closely as possible by drawing on a wide array of manuscript evidence and scholarly analysis. These texts are foundational tools for anyone engaged in New Testament studies, from scholars to translators working on literal Bible translations.

Nestle-Aland Greek New Testament

1. **Origins and Evolution**: The Nestle-Aland edition has its roots in the work of Eberhard Nestle, who published the first edition in 1898. It has since gone through several revisions and updates, the latest being the 28th edition released in 2012.

2. **Manuscript Base**: This edition prioritizes the Alexandrian text-type, giving significant weight to Codex Vaticanus, Codex Sinaiticus, P66, and P75 among others, in alignment with the Documentary Approach.

3. **Apparatus**: One of its defining features is the critical apparatus, which documents variant readings among the manuscripts, thus allowing scholars to make informed decisions about the text.

4. **Examples**:

- In Matthew 24:36, the Nestle-Aland includes the phrase "nor the Son" based on its presence in Codex Vaticanus and Codex Sinaiticus, even though the phrase is absent in some Byzantine manuscripts.

- In Mark 1:1, the title "Son of God" is bracketed to indicate its disputed status. It is found in many manuscripts but is absent in Codex Sinaiticus and others.

5. **Impact and Usage**: The Nestle-Aland edition has been adopted as the base text for many modern translations and is a primary text used in academic settings.

United Bible Societies (UBS) Greek New Testament

1. **Origins and Goals**: Initiated by the United Bible Societies, the first edition was published in 1966. The text is designed to be user-friendly for translators, providing a text critically established from ancient manuscripts.

2. **Manuscript Base**: Like Nestle-Aland, UBS also relies heavily on the Alexandrian text-type, but its apparatus is simplified for easier usage, focusing mainly on variants that have implications for translation.

3. **Textual Decisions**: The UBS includes a grading system (A, B, C, D) to indicate the level of certainty for each textual decision.

4. **Examples**:

- In 1 John 5:7-8, the UBS text does not include the Comma Johanneum ("in heaven: the Father, the Word, and the Holy Ghost"), indicating this with a grade of 'A' to signify high certainty.

- In John 7:53–8:11, the Pericope Adulterae is bracketed and accompanied by a 'D' rating, signifying high uncertainty but acknowledging its historical significance.

5. **Impact and Usage**: This text is often used by Bible translators and is also recommended for students and pastors for its readability and straightforward apparatus.

Comparison and Interdependence

1. **Similarity of Text**: The UBS and Nestle-Aland texts are almost identical; in fact, from the fourth edition of the UBS text onwards, the two have shared the same base text.

2. **Differences in Apparatus**: While the Nestle-Aland provides an exhaustive apparatus useful for academic work, the UBS is designed to be more accessible, with a focus on translation-relevant issues.
3. **Scholarly Contributions**: Over the years, the work of scholars like Kurt Aland, Bruce Metzger, and more recently, Philip Comfort, has shaped these editions. Their rigorous methodologies and commitment to high standards of scholarship have led to a text that closely approximates the original New Testament writings.

Challenges and Criticisms

1. **Eclectic Methodology**: Some critics argue that the eclectic approach, which weighs different readings from different text types, can sometimes yield a text that never existed in any single manuscript.
2. **Overreliance on Alexandrian Texts**: Some scholars have criticized the strong preference for Alexandrian manuscripts, although this remains the mainstream view given their antiquity and reliability.
3. **Subjectivity in Grading**: Especially in the UBS text, the grading system has been called into question for potentially introducing a level of subjectivity into what should be an objective scholarly enterprise.

The Nestle-Aland and UBS Greek texts are monumental achievements in the field of New Testament textual criticism. These editions have been methodologically rigorous and are rooted in extensive manuscript evidence, aligning closely with the principles of the Documentary Approach. Their apparatuses serve as invaluable guides for scholars and translators alike, making complex textual data accessible and understandable. As close approximations to the original text of the New Testament, they stand as indispensable tools for anyone engaged in the serious study of the New Testament Scriptures.

Key New Testament Variants

The Pericope Adulterae (John 7:53-8:11): An Example of a Significant Variant

The Pericope Adulterae, found in John 7:53-8:11, is a passage that has drawn substantial attention within New Testament textual criticism. Although this account of Jesus sparing a woman caught in adultery has been widely cited for ethical and theological reasons, a careful analysis of both manuscript and internal evidence strongly indicates that it is not original to the Gospel of John.

Manuscript Evidence

1. **Absence in the Earliest Manuscripts**: The most compelling evidence against the authenticity of this passage is its absence from early Alexandrian manuscripts, like Codex Vaticanus and Codex Sinaiticus. Important papyri, P66 and P75, also do not include the Pericope Adulterae.
2. **Presence in Later Manuscripts**: The passage is found in later Byzantine texts, and even in these, it is often accompanied by critical marks indicating doubt regarding its authenticity.
3. **Textual Displacement**: A critical red flag is that the passage occasionally appears in different locations within John's Gospel or even within the Gospel of Luke, highlighting its unstable history.

Internal Evidence

1. **Stylistic Anomalies**: The structure and language of the passage differ from the rest of John's Gospel. This discrepancy in style and vocabulary points toward a later interpolation.
2. **Contextual Disruption**: When this pericope is removed, the thematic and narrative flow of John's Gospel becomes more coherent, reinforcing the argument that the passage is a later insertion.

Church Fathers and Early Citations

1. **Early Silence**: Early Church Fathers, who frequently cited the Gospel of John, curiously omit this story. It raises questions about the passage's absence from their available manuscripts.
2. **Late Inclusion**: Only from the 4th century C.E. do we find Church Fathers, like Augustine, mentioning this text. Even then, it was suggested that its inclusion could have been purposeful to avoid any misunderstanding that Jesus condoned adultery.

Scholarly Opinion and Bible Translation

1. **Elimination in Critical Texts**: Given the absence in early and reliable manuscripts, this passage should not be part of the New Testament text. Maintaining it in critical texts like the Nestle-Aland and UBS Greek New Testaments—despite being bracketed—violates the principle of textual purity.
2. **Integrity Over Popularity**: The passage may be popular, but retaining it contradicts the guidelines of textual criticism. If it were an unknown phrase, the same scholars who keep it in the Nestle-Aland and UBS texts would likely exclude it without hesitation.
3. **Ethical and Theological Implications**: While the message of the story seems to align with the broader teachings of Jesus, that alone does not validate its inclusion. Doing so risks undermining the integrity of Scripture

and contradicts the apostle John's stern warning against adding to God's Word (Revelation 22:18-19).

Practical Implications for Bible Translation

1. **Relegate to Footnotes**: Consistent with a rigorous approach to textual criticism, Bible translations should not include this passage in the main text. Instead, a footnote can inform the reader of its dubious status and non-originality.

The Pericope Adulterae serves as a crucial case study in New Testament textual criticism. It demonstrates why textual integrity must not be compromised, even when a passage has gained popular or theological significance. Retaining it in critical texts and translations perpetuates a textual corruption that should have been corrected, thus straying from the textual critic's primary goal: to establish the original words of the original texts. Therefore, based on the available manuscript evidence and internal indicators, this passage should be relegated to footnotes in translations and omitted from critical texts of the New Testament.

The Longer Ending of Mark (Mark 16:9-20): A Controversial Passage

The Longer Ending of Mark's Gospel, encompassing Mark 16:9-20, remains one of the most hotly debated passages in New Testament textual criticism. Its textual status has puzzled scholars, generated polemics, and deeply influenced Bible translation philosophies. Given the primacy of ascertaining the original words of the original texts in textual criticism, an in-depth analysis of this passage is essential.

Manuscript Evidence: The Indicators

1. **Absence in Early Manuscripts**: The most glaring issue with the Longer Ending of Mark is its absence in critical early Alexandrian manuscripts, such as Codex Vaticanus and Codex Sinaiticus. Also, papyri such as P45, which contains portions of Mark, omit this section. This absence calls into question its authenticity from the Documentary Approach, which prioritizes early manuscripts.

2. **Presence in Later Manuscripts**: While the Longer Ending does find its way into later Byzantine manuscripts, its appearance is not universal across this textual family. Even within Byzantine tradition, the passage is often marked with asterisks or obeli, signifying doubt about its canonical status.

3. **Ancient Translations**: Translations like the Syriac Peshitta and some copies of the Latin Vulgate exclude the Longer Ending, further contributing to the manuscript evidence against its originality.

Internal Evidence: Narrative and Style

1. **Stylistic Differences**: A careful analysis reveals that the vocabulary and style in Mark 16:9-20 differ markedly from the rest of Mark's Gospel. Phrases and words unique to this passage are not found elsewhere in Mark, contributing to the notion that this section was a later addition.

2. **Narrative Discontinuity**: Mark's Gospel is renowned for its fast-paced narrative style, encapsulated in the frequent use of the Greek word "εὐθὺς" ("immediately"). The Longer Ending lacks this sense of urgency and introduces resurrection appearances and signs that are not consistent with Mark's earlier narrative focus.

Testimonies of the Church Fathers

1. **Early Silence**: Early Church Fathers such as Origen and Clement of Alexandria, who were prolific in their use of Mark's Gospel, make no mention of this Longer Ending. This suggests that the earliest available manuscripts to them likely did not contain this passage.

2. **Late Acknowledgment**: Eusebius and Jerome noted that the passage was missing in most of the Greek manuscripts available to them, further indicating its dubious status. However, it is worth mentioning that some later Church Fathers like Augustine did use the Longer Ending, but this was in a period when the Byzantine text-type had become more widespread.

Scholarly Opinion and Bible Translation

1. **Textual Integrity**: In line with the Documentary Approach, the manuscript and internal evidence should take precedence over the popularity or theological attractiveness of a passage. Just as one wouldn't include an appealing but spurious phrase, the Longer Ending should not be included in the main text of critical editions or Bible translations.

2. **Accountability and Reverence**: Retaining this text in the main body, as done even in critical texts like the Nestle-Aland and UBS Greek New Testaments, undermines the integrity of the Scripture. This practice contradicts the apostolic injunction found in Revelation 22:18-19 against adding to God's Word, potentially holding scholars and translators accountable for such an addition.

3. **Footnote, Not Main Text**: For maintaining a text that is as close as possible to the original, the Longer Ending should be relegated to a footnote or an appendix, with an explanation concerning its disputed status. This respects the reader's right to be informed while preserving the integrity of the canonical text.

The Longer Ending of Mark serves as a litmus test for the principles and methodologies employed in New Testament textual criticism. A commitment to restoring the New Testament text to its original form, which is 99.99% achievable based on extensive manuscript evidence, requires us to critically evaluate every textual variant, no matter how theologically significant or traditionally revered it may be. This critical evaluation strongly suggests that Mark 16:9-20 was a later addition, not part of the original Gospel of Mark. As such, it should not be included in the main text of New Testament editions but should be consigned to footnotes or appendices, where its complex history and disputed status can be adequately explained.

Comma Johanneum (1 John 5:7-8): Tracing a Notable Interpolation

The Comma Johanneum, found in 1 John 5:7-8, is one of the most debated passages in the realm of New Testament textual criticism. The passage reads, "For there are three that bear record in heaven, the Father, the Word, and the Holy Ghost: and these three are one. And there are three that bear witness in earth, the Spirit, and the water, and the blood: and these three agree in one." At the heart of the debate is whether these verses were part of the original text penned by the Apostle John or a later interpolation.

Manuscript Evidence: The Crux of the Issue

1. **Late Manuscript Support**: In the vast landscape of Greek manuscripts, the Comma Johanneum is notably absent in all Greek manuscripts prior to the 14th century, except for a few that are suspected to have been modified to include it. It is also missing in the early critical Alexandrian manuscripts, such as Codex Vaticanus and Codex Sinaiticus.

2. **Latin Vulgate**: The passage finds its most ancient support in some manuscripts of the Latin Vulgate. However, even early Vulgate manuscripts and Old Latin versions are devoid of this passage. When the passage does appear, it's often in manuscripts that have heavy theological annotations, possibly suggesting a theological motivation for its inclusion.

3. **Syriac and Coptic**: The passage is also absent from ancient translations like the Syriac Peshitta and Coptic versions, casting further doubt on its originality.

Internal Evidence: Style and Content

1. **Theological Statements**: The Comma Johanneum is often cited in Trinitarian arguments, as it appears to be an explicit statement of the Trinity. However, no other New Testament passage encapsulates the doctrine in such a direct and systematic way, which is atypical for the biblical writers.

2. **Vocabulary and Syntax**: The Greek language used in the passage shows a level of grammatical and syntactical sophistication not seen in the rest of 1 John. This discrepancy could be an indicator that it was penned by a different hand.

Church Fathers and Early Citations

1. **Silence from the Ante-Nicene Fathers**: Early Christian authors who dealt with Trinitarian issues, like Irenaeus, Tertullian, and Origen, never cite the Comma Johanneum. This suggests that they were likely unaware of its existence or did not consider it to be authoritative Scripture.

2. **Medieval Acknowledgment**: The passage gains more traction in the works of medieval theologians, a period when the Latin Vulgate had become authoritative and the Greek text was not as accessible. However, this is well after the early formative period of the New Testament canon.

Theological Implications and Translations

1. **The Danger of Doctrinal Anachronism**: Importing this text into modern Bibles could present a theological anachronism, making it seem as if the Trinity was explicitly taught in the earliest layers of the Christian church. Although the doctrine is rooted in biblical concepts, the explicit formulation came later.

2. **Literal Translation Philosophy**: A commitment to a literal translation philosophy that aims to produce a text that mirrors the original as closely as possible necessitates the exclusion of the Comma Johanneum from the main body of the text.

3. **Modern Translations**: The ESV, in line with other critical translations, excludes the Comma Johanneum from its main text but often includes a footnote to indicate that the passage is included in later manuscripts.

Conclusion

In aligning with a strict documentary approach to textual criticism that seeks to present a New Testament text as close to the original as humanly possible, the Comma Johanneum cannot be included in the main text. Its absence in early Greek manuscripts, its late appearance in the manuscript tradition, and its non-citation by early Church Fathers collectively make a compelling case against its authenticity.

Furthermore, it's worth noting that while the 1881 Westcott and Hort text and the 28th edition of the Nestle-Aland Greek New Testament may differ in minor ways (they agree 99.5%), they are in agreement about the exclusion of this passage. Today's reconstructed Greek New Testament texts, based on exhaustive scholarly work, do not include the Comma Johanneum in the main text, supporting the notion that our New Testament today is a 99.99% mirror-like reflection of the original autographs. Thus, while the passage may continue to be of interest in historical or theological discussions, it does not belong in the main text of a New Testament that seeks to be faithful to the original writings.

Understanding Theological Variants: Their Influence on Doctrine

The field of New Testament textual criticism is not merely an academic endeavor; it holds vast implications for the life of the Church and its doctrine. A subset of variants that attract particular attention are "theological variants," which could potentially affect the Church's understanding of key doctrines.

The Case of 1 Timothy 3:16

One of the most debated passages in this regard is 1 Timothy 3:16. The textual issue boils down to whether the original text read "God was manifested in the flesh" or "He who was manifested in the flesh." The majority of Alexandrian manuscripts, including Codex Sinaiticus and Codex Vaticanus, support "He who," while the Textus Receptus, which influenced the King James Version, reads "God."

While the essence of the doctrine of the Incarnation isn't necessarily overthrown by either reading, the stronger claim, "God was manifested," would certainly offer a more explicit proof-text for the deity of Christ. Therefore, it becomes vital to establish the most authentic reading through rigorous textual criticism.

Mark 1:1 and the Son of God

Another instance is Mark 1:1. The phrase "the Son of God" is found in most translations but is missing in some manuscripts, including Codex Sinaiticus. The absence of the phrase wouldn't negate the doctrine of Jesus as the Son of God, given that it's abundantly supported elsewhere in Scripture. However, its inclusion or exclusion in this specific text could influence how one understands the prologue and thematic thrust of Mark's Gospel.

The Ending of the Lord's Prayer (Matthew 6:13)

The doxology at the end of the Lord's Prayer ("For yours is the kingdom and the power and the glory, forever. Amen.") is absent in important Alexandrian manuscripts but is included in the majority of Byzantine manuscripts. While this doxology doesn't introduce any new doctrine, its inclusion shapes the liturgical life of the Church and encapsulates a theological framework for the prayer.

James 2:1 and the "Lord of Glory"

The epistle of James refers to Jesus as the "Lord of glory" in 2:1. Some textual critics argue that the original text might simply refer to "the Lord," without the additional title "of glory." This title serves as an indirect affirmation of Christ's deity, making its textual validity a question of theological import.

Implications for Doctrine

So, what do these theological variants tell us about the influence on doctrine? Several key points emerge:

1. **Apologetic Utility**: An accurate text is vital for apologetics. Defending the deity of Christ, for instance, becomes more straightforward with a text that has been rigorously scrutinized.

2. **Systematic Consistency**: Theological variants can influence how systematic theology is constructed. A missing or added term could have a ripple effect on theological categories.

3. **Liturgical Impact**: Words and phrases that are recited weekly in churches can shape the congregation's theology subtly but profoundly over time.

4. **Doctrinal Integrity**: Establishing the most reliable text is essential for preserving the integrity of Christian doctrine, especially in the face of heresies that may seek to exploit textual uncertainties.

5. **Trustworthiness of Scripture**: Finally, establishing the most accurate text builds confidence in the Scriptures as the reliable Word of God.

The methodology used in textual criticism, such as the Documentary Approach focusing on manuscript evidence, is indispensable for resolving these issues. Although the differences among the Greek New Testament manuscripts are minor and do not affect any major doctrine, every word matters in the life of the Church.

Through the labors of scholars from the 17th century to the present, we can be confident that we possess a New Testament text that very closely approximates the original autographs. This should embolden Christians to proclaim the doctrines of the faith, firmly rooted in a text that has stood the test of rigorous academic scrutiny.

Edward D. Andrews

CHAPTER 14 Applying Textual Criticism

Using Textual Criticism Tools

Bible Translations: How Textual Criticism Impacts Your Bible

The impact of textual criticism reaches far beyond the academic sphere; it directly influences the Bibles that believers hold in their hands for study, reflection, and worship. Textual criticism seeks to establish the most authentic text possible, and this critically determined text serves as the basis for modern Bible translations. When considering the impact of textual criticism on Bible translations, the focus should not be on loss but on restoration and accuracy. Through meticulous textual analysis, the aim is to arrive at a version of the Bible that is as close to the original autographs as possible.

Role of Manuscripts in Bible Translation

The first step in Bible translation is selecting the text to be translated. When it comes to the New Testament, translations oriented toward fidelity to the original languages generally opt for the Nestle-Aland Greek New Testament, which draws primarily from Alexandrian manuscripts like Codex Vaticanus and Codex Sinaiticus. These editions are compiled after extensive textual criticism, utilizing the Documentary Approach that balances both internal and external evidence.

Textual Basis and Translation Philosophy

Translators must choose not just the textual basis but also their translation philosophy. Given the priority of ascertaining the original words of the original text, a "literal" translation philosophy that adheres closely to the word-for-word rendering of the original language is often the most suitable. Translations like the UASV, which aims for "word-for-word" accuracy, are good examples of this approach.

Specific Textual Choices and Their Impact

Acts 8:37: The Ethiopian eunuch's confession of faith in Jesus as the Son of God is present in some manuscripts but absent in earlier ones, including key Alexandrian witnesses. This variant affects how one understands the necessity of a confession of faith in the context of baptism.

Acts 20:28: The textual variant "church of God" vs. "church of the Lord" may seem minor but has implications for Christology and the divine nature of Christ.

Both readings have strong manuscript support, and a Bible translation's choice here reflects its textual foundation as well as its theological leanings.

Romans 5:1: The textual variant "we have peace" vs. "let us have peace" with God offers different understandings of the peace that comes from justification. The first implies it is a given; the second suggests it is an ongoing process. Here, the translator's view of soteriology could influence which variant is chosen.

Matthew 6:13: "For Yours is the kingdom and the power and the glory forever. Amen." This doxology at the end of the Lord's Prayer is a textual variant that's not found in early manuscripts. Including or excluding this doxology can affect liturgical practices and how the prayer is used in corporate worship settings.

1 Corinthians 14:34-35: Some manuscripts place these verses at the end of the chapter or in the margin, leading some to question their original placement. Their location in the text could influence one's view on the role of women in the church, making it crucial to rely on the best manuscripts for a faithful rendering of Paul's instruction.

James 2:18: The phrase "by my works" appears in varying forms in the manuscripts, and the choice of wording can subtly change the emphasis of James' argument about faith and works. The phrase "I will show you my faith by my works" stresses the evidence of faith in works, aligning more coherently with the theme of the epistle. The textual choice here refines our understanding of the relationship between faith and works.

Translation Footnotes: A Crucial Aid

Footnotes in modern Bible translations play an essential role in helping the reader understand the choices made by translators. These notes often indicate textual variants and provide information about the weight of manuscript evidence supporting each reading. For example, footnotes may flag verses that are not found in the earliest manuscripts, guiding readers to approach such verses with the understanding that they may not be part of the original text.

In Summary

The art and science of textual criticism serve to refine the text of the New Testament to its most original form, allowing for more accurate and reliable translations. While the textual variations do not materially affect core doctrines, they do offer nuances that can deepen our understanding of Scriptural truths. By working to establish the most accurate text possible, textual critics offer an invaluable service to believers who seek to understand the Word of God as it was first given. Thus, the field of New Testament Textual Criticism holds a significant and practical role in the life of the church, directly impacting the Bibles that are used for teaching, reproof, correction, and training in righteousness (2 Timothy 3:16).

Online Resources and Software: Accessing Manuscript Data and Tools

As technological advancements progress, the field of biblical textual criticism has increasingly benefited from the digitization of manuscripts and the creation of sophisticated software tools. These advancements significantly aid scholars, pastors, and laypeople in studying the text more efficiently and thoroughly. In this chapter, we will focus on key online resources and software tools that facilitate deeper study into the realm of textual criticism.

Digital Libraries and Repositories

Center for the Study of New Testament Manuscripts (CSNTM)

The CSNTM hosts high-quality digital images of New Testament manuscripts, enabling researchers to view them online. This is particularly useful for comparing early Alexandrian manuscripts like Codex Sinaiticus and Codex Vaticanus, which are foundational to most modern critical texts.

Website: CSNTM

The Leon Levy Dead Sea Scrolls Digital Library

This online platform provides access to high-resolution images of the Dead Sea Scrolls, invaluable for studying the Old Testament text. These scrolls often serve as secondary but vital witnesses, especially when weighed against the Masoretic Text.

Website: Dead Sea Scrolls Digital Library

The Vatican Library

Home to Codex Vaticanus and other valuable manuscripts, the Vatican Library has made strides in digitizing its extensive collection, offering unparalleled insight into various textual traditions.

Website: Vatican Library

Software Tools

Logos Bible Software

Logos offers a wide array of resources, including text-critical commentaries, early manuscripts, and even modules that allow you to compare textual variants side-by-side. It is an indispensable tool for both Old and New Testament textual criticism.

Website: Logos

Accordance Bible Software

Accordance provides specialized modules focused on textual criticism, including tagged texts of the Hebrew Bible and Greek New Testament. The platform also supports the documentary approach, facilitating comparison between manuscripts of different textual families.

Website: Accordance

BibleWorks (discontinued but still useful)

Although discontinued, BibleWorks has features that remain invaluable. It includes various text-critical apparatuses and databases that help users delve into the nitty-gritty of textual variants.

Website: BibleWorks

Online Manuscript Collations

The New Testament Virtual Manuscript Room (NTVMR)

This is an excellent platform for comparing New Testament manuscript data. Users can collate multiple manuscripts to view variants and even perform searches based on specific criteria.

Website: NTVMR

Institute for New Testament Textual Research (INTF)

This institute offers scholarly resources, including an online apparatus for the Nestle-Aland Greek New Testament, which is a key text for modern translations and aligns well with the Documentary Approach of textual criticism.

Website: INTF

The Online Critical Pseudepigrapha

Although not part of the biblical canon, the study of pseudepigrapha can provide context and a wider scope when assessing the text of both Old and New Testaments.

Website: Online Critical Pseudepigrapha

In Summary

The current technological landscape has equipped textual scholars and interested laypeople with a plethora of tools for rigorous study. From digital libraries to advanced software tools and online collation platforms, these resources enable us to be more accurate and thorough in our textual criticism tasks. Given that the New Testament text as it stands today in the 28th edition of the Nestle-Aland Greek New Testament is a close reflection of the original, and the Old Testament text of the Masoretic Text has been faithfully transmitted, these digital tools serve as both a confirmation and a means of further refining our understanding of the Scriptures. Therefore, investing time and resources in familiarizing oneself with these tools is highly beneficial for anyone dedicated to studying the Bible at a deeper level.

Critical Apparatus: Understanding the Information in Critical Editions

Navigating the labyrinthine details of a critical edition of the biblical text can be a daunting task, especially for those unfamiliar with the intricacies of textual criticism. However, a critical apparatus—the set of notes and symbols usually found at the bottom or margins of the page—serves as an invaluable guide for those committed to understanding the text at a deeper, more granular level. Let's delve into how to comprehend the information provided in a critical apparatus.

Symbols and Abbreviations

A first step is familiarizing oneself with the symbols and abbreviations used in the critical apparatus. Common symbols you may encounter include:

- **Square Brackets [ ]**: These usually indicate that the enclosed words are considered doubtful or disputed.
- **Curly Braces { }**: Used less frequently, these indicate text that is considered to have been added later.
- **The Dagger (†)**: This symbol typically marks a variant reading that is considered spurious or incorrect.

Understanding Manuscript Sigla

Critical editions also make use of specific abbreviations or "sigla" to refer to manuscripts. For instance:

- **ℵ**: Codex Sinaiticus
- **B**: Codex Vaticanus
- **P66**: Papyrus 66

Case Studies: Examples of Textual Variants

John 1:18 - Theos vs. Huios

The UASV reads, "No one has seen God at any time; the only begotten God who is in the bosom of the Father, that one has made him fully known." However, some early manuscripts, like P66 and P75, read "only begotten God," while others read "only begotten Son" (huios). Both Alexandrian manuscripts (B, ℵ) and others like the Latin Vulgate contain the variant "God." This shows the importance of considering the weight of manuscript evidence in the apparatus. The original words were μονογενὴς θεός or ο μονογενης θεος "only-begotten God" or "the only-begotten God" (P66 P75 ℵ B C* L 33 syr^{hmp} 33 cop^{bo}) A variant reading is ο μονογενης υιος "the only begotten Son" A C³ (W^s) Θ Ψ f¹, Maj syr^c).

1 Samuel 13:1

In the UASV, this verse reads: "Saul was […] years old when he began to reign, and for […] he reigned over Israel." The age of Saul at the time of his ascension and the number of years he reigned are missing in the Masoretic Text. The Septuagint and the Dead Sea Scrolls do not provide a clear answer either. The critical apparatus alerts the reader to these issues. **MT** has a corrupt reading of "a son of a year," for it means Saul was one year old when he began to reign; **LXX** a few **MSS** "thirty," most **LXX** lack the verse, a few others "one year;" **SYR** "twenty-one years old," which is impossible when we consider the age of Saul's son in the next verse. The **LXX's** "thirty" is possible but unlikely. Because Saul's son Jonathan was old enough to be a military leader, the 1901 ASV has offered a conjectural emendation of "forty years."

Matthew 24:36

In the UASV, this verse reads: "But of that day and hour no one knows, not even the angels of the heavens, nor the Son, but the Father only." The phrase "nor the Son" is omitted in some early Alexandrian manuscripts like Codex Sinaiticus (א). While the phrase is present in Codex Vaticanus (B), the apparatus notes this significant textual variant, urging the reader to investigate further. א*, B D Θ f¹³ it MSS^(according to Jerome) "nor the Son" Other MSS (א¹ L W f¹ 33 Maj syr cop) omit "nor the Son."

Romans 8:1

In the UASV, this verse reads: "There is therefore now no condemnation for those who are in Christ Jesus." A significant textual variant is the long ending, "who walk not after the flesh, but after the Spirit," found in the King James Version. This ending is not supported by early Alexandrian manuscripts like B and א. The apparatus reveals this discrepancy, guiding the researcher to prioritize early and reliable manuscripts. The original words were ("Christ Jesus") (א* B C D* (F G with space for addition) 1739 it^(b,*) cop) Two variant readings are (1) "not walking according to the flesh" (A D¹ Ψ syr) and (2) "not walking according to the flesh, but according to Spirit" (א² D² 33^(vid) Maj syr).

Reading the Apparatus for Textual Weights

Critical editions often provide a textual weight, either explicitly or implicitly, indicating how strong or weak a particular reading is based on the manuscript evidence. We must remember that while Alexandrian manuscripts like Codex Vaticanus and Codex Sinaiticus often take precedence, other manuscript families are not entirely disregarded. In some instances, multiple manuscripts from different families may corroborate a specific reading, thereby increasing its textual weight.

Final Considerations

Using a critical apparatus is not just about knowing what symbols mean; it is about understanding the history of the text—its transmission, corruption, and restoration. Recognizing how different manuscripts contribute to our understanding can significantly bolster the study of Scriptures, both in personal study and scholarly research. We should approach the apparatus as an analytical tool that aids us in the quest for the original text, given that the primary goal of textual criticism is to ascertain the original words of the original texts. The apparatus, thus, is not merely an academic novelty but an essential instrument for anyone serious about understanding the Scriptures as they were first penned.

Practical Application: How to Apply Textual Criticism Insights

Textual criticism, while academic in nature, has significant and meaningful practical applications, particularly for those committed to upholding the integrity of the Scriptures. Here are some ways in which the findings of textual criticism can be applied practically in the study and teaching of the Bible.

1. More Informed Exegesis

The first and most direct application of textual criticism is in the area of exegesis—the interpretation of biblical passages. When you engage in exegesis, understanding the textual history can illuminate the original meaning. For example, knowing that the longer ending of Mark (Mark 16:9–20) is not found in early Alexandrian manuscripts like Codex Vaticanus and Codex Sinaiticus allows for a more nuanced interpretation of the Gospel as a whole.

2. Translation Work

For those involved in Bible translation, textual criticism serves as an invaluable tool. For example, knowing that 1 John 5:7-8, often cited as a prooftext for the doctrine of the Trinity, is not supported by early manuscripts could lead to a different translation choice, one that is faithful to the oldest and most reliable manuscripts.

3. Teaching and Preaching

Textual criticism can also provide greater depth and nuance in teaching and preaching. When pastors and educators are aware of textual variants, they can offer a richer, more nuanced message. For instance, discussing the pericope adulterae (John 7:53–8:11) not being present in many early manuscripts might open the door for a broader discussion on how texts were transmitted and why this story, though valuable, might not have been part of John's original Gospel.

4. Apologetics and Evangelism

Textual criticism can be a formidable tool in the arsenal of Christian apologists and evangelists. By understanding the text at a deeper level, one can more effectively counter criticisms regarding supposed contradictions or errors in the Bible. This is crucial in dialogues concerning the inerrancy of Scriptures.

5. Doctrine and Theology

Doctrines often hinge on specific wordings of biblical texts. A well-known example is the debate over the nature of Christ. The textual variant in John 1:18—whether it should be "the only God" or "the only begotten Son"—has implications for Christology. Being aware of such variants helps theologians construct doctrines that are more in line with the original intent of the text.

6. Ethical and Moral Decisions

Ethical implications can also be drawn from textual criticism. For example, a key passage often cited regarding the role of women in the church is 1 Corinthians 14:34-35. Knowing that these verses are a textual variant and not present in some early manuscripts can impact the church's stance on the issue.

7. Historical Studies

Textual criticism allows us to be more precise in reconstructing the historical context in which the Bible was written and later copied. For instance, the variations between the Masoretic Text and the Septuagint in books like Jeremiah can offer insights into the different historical settings in which these texts were produced.

8. Personal Devotion and Study

Last but not least, for the individual believer, understanding the roots and development of the biblical text can deepen one's appreciation for the Scriptures. The rich tapestry of its transmission over time testifies to its enduring significance and divine inspiration.

10. Liturgy and Worship

For those who are responsible for crafting liturgical texts, knowing which passages are likely to be original and which are not can guide the selection of Scripture readings. The integrity of worship is maintained when the words read and reflected upon are those that are closest to what was originally written.

In conclusion, textual criticism is not an esoteric field irrelevant to the church or the average Christian. Its findings have broad and meaningful applications that can deepen our understanding, sharpen our teaching, and fortify our faith. By grounding ourselves in the best manuscript evidence available, we can approach the biblical text with both intellectual integrity and spiritual fervor, always seeking to be as faithful as possible to the original words of the original texts.

Textual Criticism in Apologetics

Answering Skeptical Challenges: Addressing Questions About the Bible's Reliability

In the contemporary world, the reliability of the Bible often comes under intense scrutiny, both from scholars of varying fields and from laypeople skeptical of its claims. As conservative textual scholars, it's essential to provide well-reasoned, evidence-based answers to these skeptical challenges. Textual criticism plays an indispensable role in demonstrating the Bible's reliability. Below are some ways it does so:

1. Defending the Integrity of the Text

Skeptics often claim that the Bible has been significantly altered over time, sometimes to the point of being unreliable. Textual criticism refutes this by showing the high degree of accuracy preserved in the transmission of the text. For example, the Isaiah Scroll from the Dead Sea Scrolls closely matches the Masoretic Text of Isaiah, affirming the fidelity with which the Old Testament text has been preserved.

2. Addressing Alleged Contradictions

Skeptics often point to what they perceive as contradictions within the text as evidence of its unreliability. Textual criticism can sometimes resolve these supposed contradictions. For instance, 1 Samuel 17:50 and 2 Samuel 21:19 appear to present two different killers of Goliath. However, the textual evidence shows that the latter passage is a textual corruption and should refer to Elhanan killing Lahmi, the brother of Goliath, resolving the contradiction. **MT** "the son of Jaare-oregim, the Bethlehemite, struck down Goliath" **1 Chron. 20:5** "the son of Jair struck down Lahmi the brother of Goliath"

3. Demonstrating Consistency Across Manuscripts

Questions regarding the Bible's reliability often hinge on the idea that there are vast differences between manuscripts. In reality, the consistency across ancient manuscripts, whether it's Codex Vaticanus and Codex Sinaiticus for the New Testament or the Masoretic Text and Dead Sea Scrolls for the Old, is remarkably high, thereby demonstrating the Bible's textual integrity.

4. Refuting Claims of Late Additions

One frequent skeptical claim is that significant doctrines or stories were later additions to the text. For example, the story of Jesus and the woman caught in adultery (John 7:53-8:11) is often cited. Textual criticism can clarify that while this passage is not be part of the original Gospel of John, its absence does not affect core Christian doctrines. Critics will act as though they are disclosing some new discovery to you when, in fact, these textual issues have been known about for centuries. Moreover, they are resolved.

5. Confirming Historical Accounts

Textual criticism can validate the historical accounts found in the Bible. For example, there are claims that the events of the New Testament were myths developed centuries after the supposed events. However, the early dating of manuscripts like P66 (d. 110-150 CE) and P75 (d. 175-225 CE), which include portions of the Gospels, provide evidence that these accounts were circulating within the lifetimes of contemporaneous witnesses.

6. Validating Quotations from External Sources

Skeptics often claim that the New Testament authors fabricated quotes from the Old Testament to support their arguments. Textual criticism can show that the quotations align very closely with ancient versions of the Old Testament texts, thus affirming their authenticity.

7. Counteracting Hyper-Skepticism

Some skeptics adopt a level of scrutiny towards the Bible that they do not apply to other ancient documents. Textual criticism allows us to show that if we apply the same level of skepticism to other ancient texts like the works of Plato or Homer, they would fare far worse in terms of manuscript support and consistency.

8. Assessing Claims of Lost Books or Gospels

There are claims that certain "lost books" should be part of the Bible, thereby suggesting its incompleteness. Textual criticism helps by evaluating the validity, antiquity, and reliability of these texts, most of which are found to be of late origin and lacking the rigorous manuscript evidence that supports canonical Scriptures. Note the following statements by scholars on these noncanonical books:

"There is no question of any one's having excluded them from the New Testament: they have done that for themselves."—M. R. James, *The Apocryphal New Testament,* pages xi, xii.

"We have only to compare our New Testament books as a whole with other literature of the kind to realize how wide is the gulf which separates them from it. The uncanonical gospels, it is often said, are in reality the best evidence for the canonical."—G. Milligan, *The New Testament Documents,* page 228.

"It cannot be said of a single writing preserved to us from the early period of the Church outside the New Testament that it could properly be added to-day to the Canon."—K. Aland, *The Problem of the New Testament Canon,* page 24.

9. Demonstrating Textual Restorations

By explaining the process of textual restoration carried out rigorously by scholars across centuries, we can confirm that today's text is a mirror-like reflection of what the original would have been, thus bolstering the Bible's reliability.

10. Reinforcing the Unchanged Message

Lastly, it's vital to emphasize that while there are textual variants, none affect central doctrines of the faith. Whether it's the nature of God, the resurrection of Christ, or the plan of salvation, the key messages of the Bible remain consistent across all reliable manuscripts.

In summary, textual criticism is a crucial discipline for defending the reliability of the Scriptures. It not only responds to critiques but also positively affirms the fidelity with which these sacred texts have been transmitted. Thus, a thorough understanding of textual criticism equips us to address skeptical challenges effectively, affirming our commitment to the inerrancy and trustworthiness of the Word of God.

Building Confidence in Scripture: How Textual Criticism Supports Faith

Textual criticism may initially sound like a discipline designed to tear apart the very fabric of Scripture, to cast doubts and poke holes in the reliability of the Word of God. However, in reality, it serves as a formidable ally in bolstering the faith of believers and affirming the integrity of the Bible. Below are several ways in which the meticulous practice of textual criticism serves to build, rather than dismantle, confidence in the Scriptures.

1. Reinforcing the Accuracy of Transmission

Textual criticism helps affirm the extreme care with which the biblical texts have been transmitted over centuries. The Masoretic Text of the Old Testament, for instance, shows a remarkable consistency with the Dead Sea Scrolls, which are over a thousand years older. This demonstrates that the text we have today mirrors what was initially written, thus affirming the reliability of the Old Testament Scriptures.

2. Authenticating Core Doctrines

One of the common objections to the trustworthiness of the Bible is the notion that core doctrines are built on shaky textual grounds. However, through rigorous analysis, textual critics affirm that none of the essential Christian doctrines—like the deity of Christ, the nature of God, or the plan of salvation—are affected by textual variants. This should fortify the faith of believers, reassuring them that the doctrines they hold dear are grounded in a stable text.

3. Unveiling Original Authorial Intent

Through the lens of textual criticism, we are better positioned to apprehend the original words of the biblical authors. For instance, in the New Testament, we give priority to Alexandrian manuscripts like Codex Vaticanus and Codex Sinaiticus. This allows us to come closer to what apostles like Paul, Peter, and John originally penned, thereby enriching our understanding of their teachings and enhancing our faith.

4. Discerning Authenticity

With a plethora of ancient manuscripts at our disposal, textual criticism allows us to sift through textual families and better understand which readings are likely original and which are later interpolations or errors. For example, the absence of the "Comma Johanneum" (1 John 5:7-8) in earlier manuscripts gives us confidence that the doctrine of the Trinity is not dependent on a textually dubious passage.

5. Fostering Unity in Interpretation

Textual criticism helps to minimize divisions that arise from differing interpretations based on faulty texts. By striving to return to the original wording of the text, we provide a firmer foundation upon which to build our theology, thereby fostering unity within the Body of Christ.

6. Providing a Counterpoint to Skeptical Criticisms

The rigor of textual criticism gives Christians a robust framework to counteract skeptical claims regarding the Bible's reliability. The discipline does not merely engage in apologetics; it provides factual evidence and logical coherence to affirm that our current Bibles are overwhelmingly faithful to the original manuscripts.

7. Enhancing Personal Devotion

Knowing that the text of the Bible has been meticulously studied and that it closely mirrors the original provides Christians with greater confidence in their personal study and devotion. A believer can read the words of Isaiah or the letters of Paul knowing that they are engaging with text nearly identical to what was originally inspired by God.

8. Illuminating Historical Context

Textual criticism often goes hand-in-hand with understanding the historical circumstances surrounding a text. Knowing that the text we read today closely reflects its original form enables us to better appreciate its historical context, thereby enriching our understanding and application of Scripture.

9. Empowering Apologetics

Armed with the tools and findings of textual criticism, Christians are better equipped to defend their faith. Whether it's demonstrating the reliability of Old Testament prophecies or substantiating the claims of the New Testament, the discipline provides a robust foundation for Christian apologetics.

10. Deepening Worship

Ultimately, the exercise of textual criticism should lead us to a place of deepened worship. Knowing that we have a reliable text allows us to engage with God's Word not as a distant, corrupted document, but as the living, active revelation of God. It assures us that when we read the Bible, we are indeed hearing the very words of God, just as they were inspired thousands of years ago.

In sum, far from being an enemy of faith, textual criticism serves as an essential ally in strengthening our trust in the Scriptures. It enhances our understanding, fuels our worship, and equips us to engage skeptically minded critics. It confirms, rather than contradicts, the notion that the Scriptures are the reliable, inerrant Word of God, worthy of our full trust and wholehearted devotion.

Engaging with Critics: Strategies for Apologetics Based on Textual Criticism

One of the most challenging but necessary aspects of being a student of the Bible, especially for those committed to its authority, is the task of engaging with critics. Textual criticism provides a foundational set of tools that can greatly aid in responding to these challenges, enabling a robust defense of the Scriptures. Here are some strategies to employ:

Understanding the Limits and Scope of Textual Criticism

First, it's essential to delineate what textual criticism can and cannot do. It can attempt to recover the original text of the Scriptures. However, it is not in itself a tool to prove the divine inspiration of these texts. Understanding this can help when critics misuse textual criticism to debunk Scriptural authority.

Demonstrating the Robust Nature of the Textual Evidence

One of the strongest points in favor of the Bible's reliability is the sheer volume of manuscripts available. For the New Testament, we have over 5,800 Greek manuscripts, more than any other ancient text. These include key Alexandrian manuscripts like Codex Vaticanus and Codex Sinaiticus. For the Old Testament, the Masoretic Text serves as a cornerstone, and the discovery of the Dead Sea Scrolls provides additional validation. Presenting these facts can undercut critics who argue that the Bible has been drastically changed over time.

Addressing Variants Head-On

Instead of sidestepping the issue of textual variants, directly addressing them can actually strengthen your apologetic approach. Most textual variants are inconsequential and don't affect doctrinal truths. For example, the infamous "Johannine Comma" (1 John 5:7-8) is not found in any Greek manuscript before the 14th century C.E., and most modern translations omit this interpolation. By admitting and explaining such variants, you demonstrate intellectual honesty and show that the essential Christian doctrines are not at stake.

Historical Corroboration

Another powerful strategy is highlighting how historical accounts outside of the Bible align with the Biblical narrative. For instance, historians like Josephus mention figures like Jesus and Herod, providing an extra layer of validation to the Scriptural accounts. While these external accounts don't confirm matters of faith, they do add credibility to the historicity of the Bible.

Citing Scholarly Consensus on Key Texts

The work of textual scholars from the 17th to the 21st centuries has largely confirmed the accuracy of foundational texts. For example, the Westcott and Hort Greek New Testament (1881) is 99.5% identical to the 2012 28th edition of the

Nestle-Aland Greek New Testament. Citing this type of scholarly work adds an extra layer of authority and also counters criticisms that might suggest a wide disparity in Biblical texts over time.

Addressing Alleged Contradictions

Critics often point to supposed contradictions within the Bible. A thorough understanding of the languages, cultures, and contexts of the Biblical world can often resolve these issues. For instance, some point to varying numbers in the Old Testament, such as in 2 Samuel 24:13 and 1 Chronicles 21:12, as contradictions. However, textual criticism reveals that these can be reconciled through understanding scribal errors or different numbering methods used in ancient times.

Ethical and Doctrinal Integrity

It's crucial to maintain a high level of ethical integrity in your apologetic endeavor. Avoid overstating your case or employing straw man arguments. Stay committed to the original texts, even if it requires admitting to difficult or uncomfortable truths. Upholding a high standard of integrity will only strengthen your apologetic position and the perceived reliability of the Scriptures.

The Resilience of Core Doctrines

Finally, a central point to make is that despite the challenges posed by textual criticism, core doctrines such as the resurrection, the divinity of Christ, and salvation by grace through faith remain uncompromised. The reliability of critical texts ensures that these doctrines are solidly grounded in the original manuscripts, bolstering the overall argument for the trustworthiness of Scripture.

Engaging with critics requires courage, intellectual rigor, and a deep commitment to truth. Armed with the tools of textual criticism, you can approach these debates with confidence, secure in the knowledge that the Scriptures have withstood the most stringent of examinations and remain a reliable guide for faith and practice.

Interfaith Dialogues: The Role of Textual Criticism in Discussions with Other Religions

The Bible's Perspective on Interfaith Relationships

"Be peacemakers," Jesus taught, indicating the importance of peaceful coexistence (Matthew 5:9). Indeed, Jesus himself was a paragon of nonviolence and took a message of harmony to a religiously diverse audience (Matthew 26:52). Those who accepted this message shared a deep, unifying love (Colossians 3:14). But did Jesus intend to merely forge social ties between various religious communities, or to endorse the blending of religious practices?

Jesus faced strong opposition from the religious sects of the Pharisees and the Sadducees. They not only disagreed with him but also sought to kill him. His response was unambiguous. He told his disciples to "Let them alone. They are blind guides" (Matthew 15:14). Clearly, Jesus did not recognize any spiritual kinship with such individuals.

Fast forward to the Christian community in Corinth, Greece. The city was known for its diverse religious landscape. How should Christians navigate this complicated environment? Paul's guidance was clear: "Do not be yoked together with unbelievers" (2 Corinthians 6:14). He further reasoned, "What harmony has Christ with Belial, or what has a believer in common with an unbeliever?" Paul's directive was explicit: "Therefore, come out from their midst and separate from them" (2 Corinthians 6:14, 15, 17).

In light of these passages, it's clear that the Bible does not support the practice of interfaith. While many proponents of interfaith argue that no single religion has a monopoly on truth, the Bible's position is different. Jehovah is declared as "the God of truth," who states, "I do not change" (Psalm 31:5; Malachi 3:6). About God, Jesus affirmed, "Your word is truth" (John 17:17). This truth is not a human construct; it is divinely revealed through the Scriptures, equipping us "for every good work" (2 Timothy 3:16, 17).

Thus, the Bible doesn't align with the modern view that all religions are paths to the same truth. Rather, it underscores the necessity of distinctness in spiritual matters and warns against the dilution of Christian doctrine through interfaith participation. So, why do we use the term interfaith a number of times throughout this publication. It is only for apologetic and evangelist purposes. It is definitely **not** to see some pluralistic, multireligious culture, not to become unevenly yoked with unbelievers or supposed "believers."

In the arena of interfaith dialogue, textual criticism can serve as a valuable instrument to bridge gaps, clarify misunderstandings, and create a basis for honest discussion. The focus here is on the role of textual criticism in facilitating conversations between Christianity and other world religions.

Establishing Common Ground

One of the starting points in any interfaith dialogue is establishing common ground. Textual criticism can aid in this by demonstrating the historical reliability of certain texts that multiple traditions might revere. For instance, the Old Testament, particularly the Torah, is a shared text between Jews and Christians, and its discussion can also pave the way for engaging with Muslims who honor biblical figures like Moses and Abraham in their tradition.

Credibility and Authority

Engaging in textual criticism helps defend the credibility of the Scriptures. When in conversation with adherents of other faiths, the credibility of one's sacred texts often becomes a discussion point. For instance, the Qur'an claims to be the literal word of God as revealed to Muhammad, and it has been preserved in a textually consistent form. By discussing the thousands of Greek New Testament manuscripts and the Masoretic Text of the Old Testament, Christians can likewise demonstrate the textual fidelity of the Bible, establishing its credibility.

Resolving Apparent Contradictions

Interfaith dialogues often stall over apparent contradictions or differences in sacred texts. For example, in dialogue with Muslims, the Bible's portrayal of Jesus as the Son of God conflicts with the Islamic view of Jesus as merely a prophet. Textual criticism can play a role here by making it clear what the original texts actually say and what interpretations or variations arose later. This approach helps to delineate between what is central to the Christian faith and what might be later interpretative traditions.

Clarifying Misinterpretations

Often, religious texts are quoted out of context or misunderstood. An example would be the numerous passages in both the Old and New Testaments that have been cited either to support or to denigrate various modern stances. Textual criticism allows scholars to clarify what the text most likely originally said, shedding light on its proper context. This can be particularly helpful in dialogues with groups that rely on partial or decontextualized quotations from Christian Scripture.

Handling Variants and Translation Issues

Textual variants and translation issues often surface in interfaith discussions. For example, Psalm 22:16 has been cited in dialogues with Jews concerning its messianic implications. The Masoretic Text reads, "like a lion, my hands and feet," whereas the Septuagint and some Dead Sea Scrolls read, "they pierced my hands and feet." Textual criticism allows us to address these variants critically and responsibly.

Demonstrating Doctrinal Consistency

A critical aspect of interfaith dialogue involves the defense of key Christian doctrines, such as the deity of Christ, the resurrection, and the doctrine of salvation. Textual criticism reassures that these doctrines are not based on late or questionable textual traditions but are firmly rooted in the earliest and most reliable manuscripts.

Revealing the Historical Jesus

The "Historical Jesus" is often brought up in discussions, especially with skeptics and members of non-Christian faiths. Utilizing textual criticism, scholars can confidently affirm the credibility and historicity of the Gospel accounts. This can be particularly influential in dialogues with those who may question the existence or the portrayal of Jesus in Christian Scriptures.

Acknowledging Similarities and Differences

Finally, textual criticism can be useful in honestly acknowledging both the similarities and the differences between religious texts. This level of honesty builds trust and can lead to more fruitful dialogue. For instance, while there are stories common to both the Bible and the Qur'an (such as the story of Noah), the textual critical approach can highlight how each tradition's text came to be and where they diverge in their portrayals.

Textual criticism, therefore, serves as an essential tool in interfaith dialogues. It allows for the establishment of common ground, defense against criticisms, and the clarification of misunderstandings, among other benefits. It provides an academically rigorous, historically grounded basis upon which meaningful dialogues can occur, making it an indispensable resource in any discussion between Christianity and other world religions in an apologetic and evangelistic sense.

CHAPTER 15 The Future of Textual Criticism

Advancements in Technology

Digital Imaging and Analysis: New Tools for Manuscript Study

In the constantly evolving field of textual criticism, technological advancements like digital imaging and analysis represent revolutionary shifts that could change the landscape of manuscript study for years to come. These tools offer promising prospects for those committed to ascertaining the original words of the biblical texts.

High-Resolution Imaging

One of the most important advancements is high-resolution imaging, which enables scholars to see minute details in manuscripts that were previously undetectable. For example, the Codex Sinaiticus has undergone extensive digital imaging, revealing corrections and nuances that could have implications for understanding the text. This technology can even illuminate faint or erased writings known as palimpsests, offering a fuller picture of the text's transmission history.

Multispectral Imaging

Multispectral imaging takes this a step further by capturing images at different wavelengths. This method can be particularly valuable in studying badly damaged or faded manuscripts. The Dead Sea Scrolls are a case in point. Utilizing multispectral imaging, scholars can now decipher sections that were illegible, thereby gaining a fuller understanding of these ancient documents.

Computational Analysis

Digital tools also facilitate computational textual analysis. By employing algorithms and machine learning, scholars can perform more nuanced collations of manuscripts, even predicting likely variants where manuscripts are missing or damaged. For instance, computational analysis can identify patterns of textual variants across multiple manuscripts, effectively narrowing down which readings might be closer to the original text.

Virtual Reconstructions

Another breakthrough is virtual reconstruction. Fragments from various locations can be digitally assembled to recreate 'lost' manuscripts. This has been especially important in the case of the Dead Sea Scrolls, where hundreds of fragments can now be virtually aligned to reconstruct whole books or sections of Scripture.

3D Imaging and Virtual Reality

Beyond 2D scans, 3D imaging and virtual reality offer immersive experiences that could fundamentally change how scholars engage with manuscripts. With 3D scans, it becomes easier to understand the physical context of a manuscript — how ink penetrated the papyrus or velum, how corrections were made, or how a manuscript was bound. Virtual reality could even allow scholars to 'walk through' a digital library of ancient texts, examining them as if they were physically present.

Crowd-Sourced Analysis

Digital imaging also opens the door for crowd-sourced textual criticism. High-resolution images made available online can be examined by scholars and trained amateurs alike. This collaborative approach accelerates the process of collation and can lead to faster identification of textual variants and their significance.

Archiving and Preservation

The digital age has also resolved some of the problems of archiving and preserving ancient manuscripts. Unlike physical copies that decay over time, digital images can be stored indefinitely, facilitating long-term study and safeguarding these invaluable resources for future generations.

Challenges and Ethical Considerations

However, this digitization wave is not without its challenges. Questions regarding the ethics of digital reproduction, copyright issues, and data security remain to be addressed. Who gets access to these digital resources, and how they are used, are questions that will have to be tackled as these technologies become more prevalent.

Integration with Traditional Methods

Digital tools don't negate the necessity for traditional methods of textual criticism; rather, they complement them. For example, the Documentary Approach, which prioritizes manuscript evidence while also considering internal evidence, can be significantly enhanced through the use of digital tools. Complex algorithms can be designed to weigh various kinds of evidence, further refining our understanding of what the original text likely said.

Digital imaging and analysis are driving a new era in textual criticism, offering powerful new tools for manuscript study. These technological advancements have enormous potential to refine our understanding of the biblical texts. They represent an evolutionary leap in the methods we can employ to approach our unchanging goal: the most accurate possible reconstruction of the original texts of Scripture.

By embracing these tools, future textual scholars will not only expedite but also improve the accuracy of their work, bringing us ever closer to the original words of the Old and New Testaments. The field of textual criticism is on the cusp of a technological revolution, one that promises to usher in unprecedented levels of accuracy and understanding in the study of the Scriptures.

Machine Learning and AI: The Potential for Automated Textual Criticism

As the landscape of textual criticism is progressively shaped by technological innovations, machine learning and artificial intelligence (AI) emerge as pioneering tools with immense potential to transform the way we approach the text of Scripture. These advancements stand poised to revolutionize traditional methodologies, potentially accelerating the fulfillment of our longstanding goal: identifying the original words of the original texts as accurately as possible.

Identifying Textual Families

Machine learning algorithms can analyze thousands of manuscripts rapidly, segregating them into families based on commonalities and differences. For example, an algorithm could sift through numerous manuscripts of the New Testament, highlighting those that closely align with the Alexandrian textual family, including significant manuscripts like Codex Vaticanus and Codex Sinaiticus. The benefit is not merely speed but also a potentially higher degree of accuracy in categorizing manuscripts.

Variant Analysis

Machine learning tools can also be programmed to identify textual variants and predict their probable origins. In a database of Greek New Testament manuscripts, for example, AI could recognize instances where the Documentary Approach would favor one reading over another. Through pattern recognition algorithms, machine learning could forecast which variants are more likely to be original based on the extant manuscript evidence.

Collating Manuscripts

Machine learning could expedite the collation process dramatically. Manually comparing manuscripts is a laborious task, subject to human error. Automated systems could collate manuscripts with high speed and accuracy, identifying points of divergence and agreement among thousands of manuscripts, thus aiding scholars in assembling a critical text that hews closely to the original.

Automated Paleography

Paleographic dating of manuscripts is often a subjective and time-consuming endeavor. Machine learning algorithms could be trained to recognize specific forms of letters, writing styles, and even ink compositions, thereby providing more precise dating of manuscripts. More accurate dating leads to better understanding of a text's transmission history, which is crucial for textual criticism.

Error Identification and Correction

AI can be trained to recognize common scribal errors like haplography, dittography, or metathesis. By cross-referencing multiple manuscripts, AI can identify likely errors and suggest corrections, potentially revealing readings that are closer to the original text.

Integrating Multiple Data Points

Another exciting possibility is the integration of linguistic analysis, manuscript dating, textual variants, and even historical context into one comprehensive AI model. Such a model could weigh each data point to provide an overall likelihood score for a given reading being original, incorporating all these aspects into a single evaluative measure.

Ethical and Methodological Considerations

With great power comes great responsibility. Automation raises questions about the future role of human scholars. Would machine learning models replace human judgment, or would they serve as supplementary tools? Moreover, machine learning algorithms are only as good as the data they are trained on. Poorly digitized manuscripts or biased training data could skew results. Therefore, methodological rigor is crucial to ensure the responsible use of AI in textual criticism.

Potential Pitfalls

Machine learning and AI are not without limitations. They are tools that can aid but never entirely replace human expertise. Interpretive decisions still require a nuanced understanding of theology, language, and culture—something that AI currently cannot replicate. Moreover, there is always the danger of 'overfitting' where the machine becomes too adapted to the training set of manuscripts and is less effective with new, unseen data.

Collaborative Synergy

The ultimate strength of machine learning and AI in textual criticism may lie in their collaborative synergy with human scholars. AI can handle the quantitative, data-heavy aspects, freeing scholars to focus on qualitative, interpretive elements. For example, machine learning could quickly sift through the myriad of textual variants, allowing scholars to spend more time using the Documentary Approach to evaluate the significance of these variants.

Conclusion

Machine learning and AI hold remarkable promise for the field of textual criticism. These technologies offer tools that can automate and refine processes that have traditionally been manual and time-consuming. Their potential to revolutionize how we study the text of Scripture is enormous, but they must be used responsibly, ethically, and in collaboration with human expertise.

While they may not fully replace traditional methods, they can vastly augment them, providing scholars with new ways to achieve the ancient goal of getting as close as possible to the original text of Scripture. As these technologies continue to advance, their integration into the field of textual criticism is not just likely but inevitable, heralding an era of unprecedented precision and depth in our engagement with the Word of God.

Collaborative Projects: International Efforts in Manuscript Digitization

As the discipline of textual criticism looks to the future, the role of technological innovation cannot be overstated. One of the most promising areas where this integration is manifesting is in international efforts to digitize manuscripts. While the past few centuries of textual scholarship have been grounded in the physical examination of manuscripts, the digitization process opens new possibilities for the study of ancient texts. It also increases the accessibility and preservation of materials that could otherwise be lost to time, weather, or socio-political upheaval.

The CSNTM and Digitization

One of the leading organizations in this endeavor is the Center for the Study of New Testament Manuscripts (CSNTM). They have initiated global projects to digitize New Testament manuscripts, making high-quality images available for textual scholars. Their efforts have increased the scope of accessible materials, especially considering the priority given to Alexandrian manuscripts like Codex Vaticanus and Codex Sinaiticus.

Cooperation with Libraries and Monasteries

International cooperation is indispensable for these digitization initiatives. Manuscripts often reside in monasteries, private collections, or libraries across different countries. Take, for example, Codex Sinaiticus, which is distributed across four locations: the British Library, Leipzig University Library, the National Library of Russia, and St. Catherine's Monastery in the Sinai Peninsula. Comprehensive digitization can only be achieved through international collaboration.

The Leon Levy Dead Sea Scrolls Digital Library

Similarly, the Leon Levy Dead Sea Scrolls Digital Library is another example of an ambitious digitization project, albeit focused on the Old Testament. This endeavor aims to provide public access to the Dead Sea Scrolls, which are instrumental for Old Testament textual criticism. Given the foundational nature of the Masoretic Text in Old Testament studies, these scrolls help scholars verify the integrity of the Masoretic Text by providing manuscripts that predate it.

Standardization and Metadata

One of the challenges of such widespread digitization projects is the need for standardization. Metadata—the background information about each manuscript, such as its date, location, and material—needs to be systematically documented. This standardization ensures that scholars worldwide can understand the context of the manuscript, which is crucial when determining textual variants and their significance.

Interdisciplinary Collaboration

Digitization fosters interdisciplinary cooperation between textual scholars, computer scientists, and data analysts. While the focus remains on establishing the original text of the Scriptures, computational methods can augment traditional scholarship. For example, machine learning algorithms can sift through the myriad of textual variants more efficiently, albeit under the supervision of skilled textual critics.

Ethical and Legal Considerations

It's important to remember that digitization involves legal and ethical challenges, particularly regarding the rights to digital reproductions. Countries, libraries, or religious institutions that house these manuscripts may have specific guidelines or reservations about digitization. Navigating these concerns requires a careful, respectful approach, recognizing the religious and historical significance of the texts involved.

Pros and Cons

Pros:

1. **Accessibility:** Digitized manuscripts are accessible to scholars and the general public worldwide.

2. **Preservation:** Digital copies ensure the long-term safety of these invaluable texts.

3. **Data Analysis:** Metadata and digital formats facilitate new types of data analysis.

Cons:

1. **Cost:** Digitization is an expensive venture.

2. **Inaccuracy:** There is always the risk of introducing errors during the digitization process.

3. **Limitation:** Not all texts can or will be digitized due to various constraints, including but not limited to, ethical, religious, or geopolitical reasons.

As we look to the future, the digitization of manuscripts through international collaborations promises to be a groundbreaking development in the field of textual criticism. While this process comes with challenges and limitations, its potential for advancing our understanding of ancient texts is immense. Through digitization, scholars are better equipped to scrutinize textual variants against primary source documents, whether it's the foundational Masoretic Text for the Old Testament or the priority Alexandrian manuscripts for the New Testament. Such collaborative projects are not merely academic exercises but are vital for upholding the integrity and authenticity of the Scriptures for generations to come.

Ethical Considerations: Challenges and Responsibilities in the Digital Age

The digital age has revolutionized almost every facet of our lives, and the field of biblical textual criticism is no exception. With the advent of digital technologies, the range of possibilities has dramatically expanded for scholars striving to ascertain the original words of the biblical texts. However, these innovations bring their own unique set of ethical challenges and responsibilities. Here, we'll delve into some of these issues, recognizing that any tool—no matter how advanced—is only as good as the ethics that guide its use.

Ethical Obligation to Accuracy

In our endeavor to discover the original biblical text, the obligation to maintain high standards of accuracy is non-negotiable. The temptation may arise to use digital means to alter textual data or to enhance it in a way that is not faithful to the original manuscript. Manipulation of digital images can create a misleading representation, calling into question the credibility of critical scholarship. This not only endangers the integrity of the work but can have longstanding theological ramifications as well.

Cultural Sensitivity and Ownership

Many ancient manuscripts are housed in countries with cultural and religious perspectives different from those of scholars. As such, there is an ethical obligation to respect the cultural and religious significance these texts may hold for communities in their native locations. One has to navigate the complex terrain of rights and permissions, often treading the line between scholarly need and cultural sensitivity.

Data Privacy and Security

The digitization of manuscripts and the creation of online databases open up the risk of unauthorized access and plagiarism. There is an ethical responsibility to implement robust security measures to protect these valuable resources. Scholars and academic institutions must ensure that the digital manuscripts are securely stored and that access is appropriately regulated.

Commercialization and Accessibility

The potential for commercialization of digitized manuscripts is a growing concern. While organizations may need funding for preservation and further study, the commercialization of biblical texts can create ethical dilemmas. The Scriptures belong to the collective heritage of humanity and their primary purpose is not for profit. Creating paywalls around digital manuscripts can restrict scholarly access and hinder the dissemination of knowledge.

Intellectual Honesty

Digital tools also offer the ability to cross-reference manuscripts at an unprecedented scale, and this makes it tempting to take shortcuts in research. It's possible, for example, to employ algorithms to identify parallels and variants. However, scholars have an ethical responsibility to acknowledge the limitations of these tools. They must maintain intellectual honesty by not overstating what digital analysis can achieve, as compared to traditional scholarly methods.

Collaboration and Crediting

International efforts in digitization often involve collaboration between multiple institutions, scholars, and technical experts. Ethical collaboration demands clarity in roles, responsibilities, and credit attribution. Failing to appropriately credit contributions can lead to misunderstandings and devalue the collective endeavor.

Ethical Considerations in Teaching and Pedagogy

With the digital age making a wealth of resources available, educators also face the challenge of ethical use of these materials in teaching. They must be transparent about the sources of digital materials, and guide students in understanding the importance of ethics in scholarly work, including the commitment to ascertain the original words of the biblical texts.

Long-term Preservation and Sustainability

Finally, as we move increasingly toward a digital future, there's the question of long-term sustainability. How will these digital resources be preserved for future generations? What if the organizations or institutions storing these files cease to exist? Planning for long-term digital preservation is an ethical responsibility that current scholars owe to future generations.

As we strive to fulfill our primary purpose in textual criticism, which is to ascertain the original words of the Scriptures, we find that the digital age offers both unprecedented opportunities and significant ethical challenges. The application of digital tools must be guided by a commitment to scholarly rigor, cultural sensitivity, and ethical integrity. Failing in these responsibilities can compromise the credibility of the scholarly community and, more importantly, the integrity of the biblical text. Therefore, as we navigate this digital landscape, let us do so with a sense of the weighty ethical responsibilities that accompany these promising technological advancements.

Continuing Research and Discovery

Unexplored Manuscripts: Potential Finds in Libraries and Archives

The study of biblical textual criticism hinges on the manuscripts and textual witnesses at our disposal. As of now, we have thousands of manuscripts for the New Testament and a significant, though less voluminous, amount for the Old Testament. But the world is filled with libraries, archives, monasteries, and other repositories that remain largely untapped. The prospect of discovering new manuscripts or forgotten textual witnesses that could further enlighten our understanding of the biblical text is both exciting and daunting. Let's explore this uncharted terrain of potential finds in libraries and archives.

The Significance of Unexplored Manuscripts

Unexplored or newly discovered manuscripts carry immense potential to either confirm our existing critical texts or challenge them, thus refining our understanding. For instance, the discovery of the Dead Sea Scrolls in the mid-20th century provided remarkable confirmation for the Masoretic Text of the Old Testament. Conversely, newly found papyri like P66 and P75 have been invaluable in strengthening the preference for the Alexandrian text-type in New Testament textual criticism.

Old Testament: A Goldmine Waiting to be Unearthed

Although the Hebrew Old Testament has been restored to a state closely mirroring the original text, any new discoveries could provide further clarity or even resolve longstanding issues. The desert regions of the Middle East, as well as ancient monastic libraries, could still hold manuscripts or fragments that would augment our textual base.

New Testament: What Lies in Unopened Drawers?

Many of the existing manuscripts for the New Testament were not discovered in large-scale archeological digs but rather found in monastic libraries or university collections, sometimes mislabeled or poorly described. These manuscripts, especially those from the Alexandrian family, can contribute significantly to our understanding of the New Testament text.

Eastern Christian Traditions: A Neglected Area

Eastern Christian traditions have unique textual witnesses that are often overlooked. The textual traditions of the Syriac, Coptic, and Ethiopian churches, for instance, can offer variant readings and new perspectives. These traditions are especially relevant when exploring the early translations of the New Testament and should not be neglected.

The Role of Private Collections

Not all manuscripts are housed in public institutions. Private collectors sometimes possess significant manuscripts, which might be made available for scholarly study either through purchase or loan. Here too, ethical considerations are paramount; any acquisition must be done legally and transparently.

The Power and Limitation of Digital Cataloging

Digital technology allows for a global catalog of manuscripts, but the actual process of cataloging can be slow and laborious. Many libraries, particularly in economically disadvantaged areas, may lack the resources to properly catalog and digitize their collections. It may fall upon textual critics and philanthropic organizations to aid in this vital task.

Risks and Challenges

While the potential rewards are great, there are also risks. Manuscripts are delicate and can be easily damaged if not handled properly. Moreover, not all manuscript finds are authentic; forgeries have been produced throughout history, requiring scholars to exercise caution and employ rigorous authentication methods.

Implications for Textual Criticism

New manuscript finds have the power to reshape our critical editions of the biblical text, and therefore, they can significantly influence biblical translations as well. While the documentary approach is crucial for establishing the primacy of certain manuscripts, new discoveries may alter the balance, making some texts more preferable based on a broader manuscript base.

The unexplored manuscripts lying in the world's libraries and archives represent a frontier in biblical textual criticism. They hold the promise of sharpening our understanding of what the original texts likely said, thereby getting us closer to the words that were inspired by God. As textual critics, it is our task to continue this quest, to venture into unexplored libraries and archives, ever in search of that elusive original text. Care must be taken to handle these potential finds ethically, cautiously, and respectfully, acknowledging the weight of our responsibility to both history and faith.

Revisiting Established Texts: Ongoing Evaluations of Critical Editions

The field of textual criticism is a discipline of perpetual refinement. Even though we have critical editions that are very close to the original autographs, the task of ongoing evaluation is crucial for sharpening our understanding. Revisiting established texts not only ensures academic rigor but also contributes to the ecclesiastical objective of ascertaining what the original writers intended to convey.

Why Revisit Established Texts?

1. **New Manuscript Finds**: Newly discovered manuscripts can introduce readings that might be older or better attested than those in the current editions. For example, the discovery of P75 significantly impacted the study of the Gospel of Luke and the Gospel of John, corroborating earlier preferences for certain Alexandrian readings.

2. **Improved Philological and Linguistic Knowledge**: As our understanding of ancient languages grows, it might necessitate reevaluation. For instance, semantic changes in Hebrew or Greek words could influence the translation and interpretation of specific verses.

3. **Technological Advancements**: With the rise of digital humanities and computational methods, we have more efficient ways to collate manuscripts, perform phylogenetic analyses, and even detect interpolations or scribal errors that might have eluded earlier scholars.

The Masoretic Text and its Perennial Evaluation

The Masoretic Text serves as the foundational document for Old Testament studies. Its fidelity to the original Hebrew Scriptures is widely accepted, but ongoing research is essential. The Dead Sea Scrolls, for example, provided additional material for evaluating the Masoretic Text, confirming its reliability but also offering variant readings that required scholarly attention. Constant reassessment ensures that the text remains a mirror-like reflection of the original, which is especially crucial given the liberties taken by copyists between 440 BCE and 200 CE.

The Alexandrian Manuscripts and the New Testament

The Alexandrian family of manuscripts, particularly Codex Vaticanus and Codex Sinaiticus, holds a special place in New Testament textual criticism. However, the field has witnessed significant changes with the discovery of early papyri like P66 and P75. These have mostly vindicated the work done by scholars like Westcott and Hort but have also led to minor adjustments in the critical text.

Role of Modern Editions: Nestle-Aland and Others

Modern editions like the 28th edition of the Nestle-Aland Greek New Testament are not static but constantly revised to incorporate new findings and scholarship. While the 1881 Westcott and Hort Greek New Testament is 99.5% the same as the 2012 28th edition of the Nestle-Aland Greek New Testament, that 0.5% warrants scholarly attention, ensuring that our modern editions are the closest possible reflection of the original text.

Importance of the Documentary Approach

Given the priority to manuscripts in our methodological approach, any new addition to our corpus of manuscripts can result in changes to the critical edition. The Documentary Approach maintains a fine balance between respecting the weight of the documents and considering internal evidence. It assures that no reading is preserved merely for its theological or traditional appeal but for its authenticity and fidelity to the original text.

Translations and the Chain of Trust

Revisiting established texts has a downstream effect on Bible translations. Most translations are based on a specific edition of the Hebrew or Greek text. As these editions are revised, so too must the translations be reevaluated to ensure they remain true to the original words and intent.

Ethical Considerations

The ongoing reevaluation of established texts must be conducted transparently and ethically. Scholarship should never be driven by a doctrinal agenda but by the quest for truth. Given the deep-seated beliefs and the eternal implications attached to the text, the responsibility is enormous.

The textual landscape we navigate is not set in stone. It is a dynamic field, subject to change and refinement. As new evidence comes to light, and as our tools and techniques evolve, revisiting established texts becomes not just an option but a scholarly and ecclesiastical necessity. This constant reevaluation serves to sharpen our understanding and bring us ever closer to the original words penned by the inspired authors, thus fulfilling our primary purpose in textual criticism. Therefore, the future of this discipline lies in its ability to adapt, refine, and, if needed, reform our textual bases, ensuring that what we have today is, as closely as possible, what was originally meant to be conveyed.

Interdisciplinary Approaches: The Integration of Textual Criticism with Other Fields

As textual criticism has matured over the centuries, its reach has grown to encompass various academic disciplines. The complexity of deciphering ancient manuscripts cannot be contained within the boundaries of a single field. Thus, the future of textual criticism, particularly in relation to biblical studies, is increasingly becoming interdisciplinary. This interdisciplinary approach integrates the findings from linguistics, archaeology, paleography, and even computational sciences with textual criticism to achieve a more holistic understanding of the texts in question. Below are specific examples and instances where the integration with other fields has borne or may bear significant fruit.

Linguistics

Understanding the languages in which the Bible was originally written (Hebrew, Aramaic, and Greek) goes hand in hand with textual criticism. Linguistics helps in understanding the semantic range of words, syntax, and the rhetorical devices used by the authors. This is crucial when evaluating variant readings. For instance, when comparing the textual variants of Matthew 5:32, some manuscripts use the term "πορνεία" (porneia) to refer to marital unfaithfulness, while others do not. Linguistic studies can offer insight into how this term was understood in the first-century context.

Archaeology

Archaeological findings can validate or question the historical context suggested by the text. The Dead Sea Scrolls, discovered between 1947 and 1956, offered older Hebrew manuscripts of the Old Testament and shed light on the Jewish practices and beliefs during the Second Temple period. These findings influenced textual critics to re-evaluate the Masoretic Text and the Septuagint and their respective places in Old Testament criticism.

Paleography

The study of ancient writing systems and handwriting, paleography assists textual scholars in dating manuscripts. A well-known example is P52, a fragment of the Gospel of John. Paleographic dating helped to establish that this papyrus could be dated to as early as the first half of the 2nd century C.E., providing significant implications for the dating of the Gospel of John and, consequently, the reliability of the New Testament texts.

Computational Sciences

With the advent of computers and machine learning algorithms, textual scholars now have tools for conducting analyses that would be inconceivable manually. Computational methods can sort through thousands of manuscript variants in seconds, offering statistical models for assessing the most likely original reading. This was seen in the preparation of the Editio Critica Maior of the Greek New Testament, where computational tools assisted in collating multiple manuscripts and evaluating readings.

Ethical Considerations

While interdisciplinary approaches open up exciting opportunities, they also come with responsibilities. Textual critics must handle these auxiliary sciences with care, respecting their methodologies and limitations. Additionally, the integration of these various disciplines should never compromise the primary purpose of textual criticism: to ascertain the original words of the original texts. Critics must resist the temptation to use these interdisciplinary findings to infuse the text with meanings that it did not originally have.

Future Outlook

The integration of textual criticism with other disciplines provides a more rounded approach to the Bible's text. But we must remember that each field has its own sets of assumptions and methodologies, which must be integrated cautiously into the framework of textual criticism.

To sum up, the future of textual criticism lies not only in deepening specialization but also in broadening interdisciplinary approaches. Such integration offers the promise of not just textual but also holistic historical and cultural understanding of the Scriptures, allowing for a more nuanced and comprehensive approach to the study of God's Word.

Implications for Biblical Studies: How Textual Criticism Shapes Scholarship

Textual criticism holds profound implications for biblical studies. In our quest to ascertain the original words of the original texts, every advancement in this field has a domino effect on biblical exegesis, theology, and ultimately, Christian practice. In what follows, we will examine the ways textual criticism influences various aspects of biblical scholarship.

For Biblical Exegesis

The exegete's first task is to engage directly with the biblical text, and the quality of that engagement is largely dependent on the quality of the text being studied. Textual criticism ensures that exegetes are working with a text that is as close as possible to the original, allowing for a more accurate interpretation.

For instance, consider the passage from Mark 16:9-20, known as the Longer Ending of Mark. Many early manuscripts, including Codex Vaticanus and Codex Sinaiticus, do not contain this passage. Excluding these verses has a substantial impact on how one interprets the Gospel of Mark and its message about the Resurrection.

For Historical Studies

Textual criticism serves as the bedrock for reconstructing the historical context in which the Bible was written and later transmitted. Understanding the original text helps to set the cultural, religious, and geopolitical context that inspired it.

Take, for example, the "Woman Caught in Adultery" in John 7:53-8:11. This passage is absent in early manuscripts like P66 and P75 and does not appear until later. The absence or inclusion of such a passage has significant historical implications, especially when studying the social norms and judicial practices of the period.

For Theological Formulation

One of the most significant contributions of textual criticism to biblical studies is in the realm of theology. Textual variants can impact theological discourse significantly. Consider 1 Timothy 3:16, where some manuscripts read "God was manifest in the flesh," while others read "He was manifest in the flesh." The former reading supports the doctrine of Christ's divinity more explicitly than the latter.

For Canonical Discussions

Textual criticism can also inform discussions about the canon of Scripture. While the canon of the Old and New Testaments has been largely fixed for centuries, the rigorous work of textual criticism ensures that the texts within that canon are reliable. It also raises questions about passages found in some manuscripts but not others, influencing our understanding of what the original canonical text likely included.

For Ethical and Moral Teachings

Textual criticism affects not only what Christians believe but also how they live. Passages that pertain to ethics and moral decisions must be critically examined. For example, the differing accounts of the Ten Commandments in Exodus and Deuteronomy have been the subject of much textual scrutiny, affecting how these commandments are understood and applied today.

For Apologetics

In the realm of Christian apologetics, the reliability of the biblical text is a frequent point of discussion. Apologists can make stronger cases for the authenticity and reliability of Christian Scriptures when they can confidently assert that the texts have been rigorously examined and found to be reliable representations of the original.

For Translations and Global Christianity

Finally, textual criticism holds major implications for Bible translation, which in turn, affects global Christianity. Translations based on a carefully critiqued text can faithfully convey the intended message of the original authors, affecting the spiritual lives of millions around the world.

Textual criticism is far from a solitary discipline, confined to the perusal of scholars. It is a linchpin that holds multiple facets of biblical studies together. The rigors of textual criticism provide the basis upon which reliable exegesis, sound theology, and faithful Christian practice are built. Therefore, any advances in textual criticism are not just academic exercises but contribute to a more profound understanding and application of the eternal Word of God in the lives of believers today.

SECTION 4 BIBLE DIFFICULTIES

Digging Deeper

We put books here on this subject if one is interested in taking the subject deeper. This section gives you foundational knowledge to evangelize or engage people in conversation.

BIBLE DIFFICULTIES: How to Approach Difficulties In the Bible by Edward D. Andrews (2020)

ISBN-13: 979-8611089118

https://www.amazon.com/dp/B084DLSBZ2

CHAPTER 16 Bible Difficulties Explained

IT SEEMS THAT the charge that the Bible contradicts itself has been made more and more in the last 20 years. Generally, those making such claims are merely repeating what they have heard because most have not even read the Bible, let alone done an in-depth study of it. I do not wish, however, to set aside all concerns as though they have no merit. There are many who raise legitimate questions that seem, on the surface anyway, to be about well-founded contradiction. Sadly, these issues have caused many to lose their faith in God's Word, the Bible. The purpose of this chapter is, to help its readers to be able to defend the Bible against Bible critics (1 Pet. 3:15), to contend for the faith (Jude 1:3), and help those, who have begun to doubt. – Jude 1:22-23.

Before we begin explaining things, let us jump right in, getting our feet wet, and deal with two major Bible difficulties, so we can see that there are reasonable, logical answers. After that, we will delve deeper into explaining Bible difficulties.

Is God permitting Human Sacrifice?

Judges 11:29-34, 37-40? Updated American Standard Version (UASV)

29 Then the Spirit of the Lord was upon Jephthah, and he passed through Gilead and Manasseh; and passed on to Mizpah of Gilead, and from Mizpah of Gilead he passed on to the sons of Ammon. 30 And Jephthah **made a vow** to Jehovah and said, "If You will indeed give the sons of Ammon into my hand, 31 then it shall be that **whatever** comes out of the doors of my house to meet me when I return in peace from the sons of Ammon, it shall be Jehovah's, and I will offer it up as a burnt offering." 32 So Jephthah crossed over to the sons of Ammon to fight against them; and Jehovah gave them into his hand. 33 He struck them with a very great slaughter from Aroer as far as Minnith, twenty cities, and as far as Abel-keramim. So the sons of Ammon were subdued before the sons of Israel.

34 When Jephthah came to his house at Mizpah, behold, **his daughter was coming out to meet him** with tambourines and with dancing. Now she was his one and only child; besides her he had no son or daughter.

37 And she said to her father, "Let this thing be done for me: leave me alone two months, that I may go up and down on the mountains and weep because of my virginity, I and my companions." 38 And he said, "Go." So he sent her away for two months; and **she left with her companions, and wept on the mountains because of her virginity.** 39 At the end of two months she returned to her father, who **did to**

her according to the vow that he had made; and she never known a man.[12] Thus it became a custom in Israel, [40] that the daughters of Israel went year by year **to commemorate**[13] **the daughter** of Jephthah the Gileadite four days in the year.

It is true; to infer that having the idea of an animal sacrifice would really have not been an impressive vow, which the context requires. Human sacrifice will be repugnant if we are talking about taking a life. Jephthah had no sons, so he likely knew it was the daughter, who would come to greet him.

First, the text does not say he killed his daughter. The idea of some that he did kill her is concluded only by inference. While it is not good policy to interpret backward, using Paul on Judges, he does say humans are to be "**as a living sacrifice.**" Therefore, Jephthah could have offered his daughter at the temple, "as a living sacrifice" in service, like Samuel.

This is not to be taken dismissively, because, under Jewish backgrounds, it is no small thing to offer a **perpetual virginity** as a sacrifice. This would mean Jephthah's lineage would not be carried on, the family name, was no more.

Second, the context says she went out to weep for two months, not mourn her death. It says, "she left with her companions, and **wept on the mountains because of her virginity.**"

If she was facing imminent death, she could have married, and spent that last two months as a married woman. There would be absolutely no reason for her to mourn her virginity if she were not facing perpetual virginity. – Exodus 38:8; 1 Samuel 2:22

Third, it was completely forbidden to offer a human sacrifice. – Leviticus 18:21; 20:2-5; Deuteronomy 12:31; 18:10

Imagine an Israelite believing that he could please God with a human sacrifice that was intended to offer up a human life. To do so would have been a rejection of Jehovah's Sovereignty (the very person you are asking for help), and a rejection of the Law that made them a special people. Worse still, this interpretation would have us believe that Jehovah knew this was coming, allowed the vow, and then aided this type of man to succeed over his enemies.

The last point is simple enough. If such a man as one who would make such a vow, in gross violation of the law, and then carry it out; there is no way he would be mentioned by Paul in Hebrews chapter 11 among the most faithful men and women in Israelite history.

In review, there is no way God would have granted and helped in Jephthah's initial success knowing the vow that was coming because both Jehovah and Jephthah would be as bad as the Canaanites. There is no way that God would accept such a

---

[12] I.e., *never had relations with a man*
[13] Or *lament*

vow and then go on to help Jephthah with his enemies yet again. Then, to allow such a vow to be carried out, to then put Jephthah on the wall of star witnesses for God in Hebrews chapter 11.

Does Isaiah 45:7 mean that God Is the Author of Evil?

Isaiah 45:7 King James Version (KJV) 7 I form the light, and create darkness: I make peace, and **create evil**: I the Lord do all these things.	Isaiah 45:7 English Standard Version (ESV) 7 I form light and create darkness, I make well-being and **create calamity**, I am the Lord, who does all these things.[14]

Encarta Dictionary: (Evil) (1) morally bad: profoundly immoral or wrong (2) deliberately causing great harm, pain, or upset

QUESTION: Is this view of evil always the case? No, as you will see below.

Some apologetic authors try to say, 'we do not understand Isaiah 45:7 correctly, because there are other verses that say God is not evil (1 John 1:5), cannot look approvingly on evil (Hab. 1:13), and cannot be tempted by evil. (James 1:13)' Well, while all of these things are Scripturally true, the question at hand is not: Is God evil, can God approvingly look on evil, or can God be tempted with evil? Those questions are not relevant to the one at hand, as God cannot be those things, and at the same time, he can be the yes to our question. The question is, is God the author, the creator of evil?

We would hardly argue that God was **not just** in his bringing "calamity" or "evil" down on Adam and Eve. Thus, we have Isaiah 45:7 saying that God is the creator of "calamity" or "evil."

Let us begin simple, without trying to be philosophical. When God removed Adam and Eve from the Garden of Eden, he sentenced them and humanity to sickness, old age, and death. (Rom. 5:8; i.e., enforce penalty for sin), which was to bring "calamity" or "evil" upon humankind. Therefore, as we can see "evil" does not always mean wrongdoing. Other examples of God bringing "calamity" or "evil" are Noah and the flood, the Ten Plagues of Egypt, and the destruction of the Canaanites. These acts of evil were not acts of wrongdoing. Rather, they were righteous and just, because God, the Creator of all things, was administering justice to wrongdoers, to sinners. He warned the perfect first couple what the penalty was for sin. He warned the people for a hundred years by Noah's preaching. He warned the Canaanites centuries before.

Nevertheless, there are times, when God extends mercy, refraining from the execution of his righteous judgment to one worthy of calamity. For example, he warned Nineveh, the city of blood, and they repented, so he pardoned them. (Jonah

---

[14] See Jeremiah 18:11, Lamentations 3:18, and Amos 3:6

3:10) God has made it a practice to warn persons of the results of sin, giving them undeservedly many opportunities to change their ways. – Ezekiel 33:11.

God cannot sin; it is impossible for him to do so. So, when did he create evil? Without getting into the eternity of his knowing what he was going to do, and when, let us just say, evil did not exist when he was the only person in existence. We might say the idea of evil existed because he knew what he was going to do. However, the moment he created creatures (spirit and human), the potential for evil came into existence because both have free will to sin (fall short of perfection). Evil became a reality the moment Satan entertained the idea of causing Adam to sin, to get humanity for himself, and then acted on it.

God has the right and is just to bring the *calamity of* or *evil* down on anyone that is an unrepentant sinner. God did not even have to give us the underserved kindness of offering us his Son. God is the author or agent of evil regardless of the source books that claim otherwise. If he had never created free will beings, evil would have never gone from the idea of evil to the potential of evil, to the existence of evil. However, God felt that it was better to get the sinful state out of angel and human existence, recover, and then any who would sin thereafter; he would be justified in handing out evil or calamity to only that person or angel alone.

Who among us would argue that he should have created humans and angels like robots, automatons with no free will? The moment he chose the free will, he moved evil from an idea to a potential, and Satan moved it to reality. God has a moral nature that does not bring about evil and sin when he is the only person in existence. However, the moment he created beings in his image, which had the potential to sin, he brought about evil. The moment we have a moral code of good and evil that is placed upon one's with free will; then, we have evil as a potential.

In English, the very comprehensive Hebrew word ra' is variously translated as "bad," "downcast (sad, NASB)," "ugly," "evil," "grievous (distressing, NASB)," "sore," "selfish (stingy, HCSB)," and "envious," depending upon the context. (Gen 2:9; 40:7; 41:3; Ex 33:4; Deut. 6:22; 28:35; Pro 23:6; 28:22)

Evil as an adjective **describes** the **quality of** a class of people, places, or things, or of a specific person, place, or thing

Evil as a noun, **defines** the **nature** of a class of people, places, or things, or of a specific person, place, or thing (e.g., the evil one, evil eye).

We can agree that "evil" is a thing. Create means to bring something into existence, be it people, places, or things, as well something abstract, for lack of a better word at the moment. We would agree that when God was alone evil was not a reality; it did not exist? We would agree that the moment that God created free will creatures (angels and humans), creating humans in his image, with his moral nature, he also brought the potential for evil into existence, and it was realized by Satan?

Inerrancy: Can the Bible Be trusted?

If the Bible is the Word of God, it should be in complete agreement throughout; there should be no contradictions. Yet, the rational mind must ask, why is it that some passages appear to be contradictions when compared with others? For example, Numbers 25:9 tells us that 24,000 died from the scourge, whereas at 1 Corinthians 10:8, the apostle Paul says it was 23,000. This would seem to be a clear error. Before addressing such matters, let us first look at some background information.

Full inerrancy in this book means that the original writings are fully without error in all that they state, as are the words. The words were not dictated (automaton), but the intended meaning is inspired, as are the words that convey that meaning. The Author allowed the writer to use his style of writing, yet controlled the meaning to the extent of not allowing the writer to choose a wrong word, which would not convey the intended meaning. Other more liberal-minded persons hold with *partial inerrancy*, which claims that as far as faith is concerned, this portion of God's Word is without error, but that there are historical, geographical, and scientific errors.

There are several different levels of inerrancy. *Absolute Inerrancy* is the belief that the Bible is fully true and exact in every way; including not only relationships and doctrine, but also science and history. In other words, all information is completely exact. *Full Inerrancy* is the belief that the Bible was not written as a science or historical textbook, but is phenomenological, in that it is written from the human perspective. In other words, speaking of such things as the sun rising, the four corners of the earth or the rounding off of number approximations are all from a human perspective. *Limited Inerrancy* is the belief that the Bible is meant only as a reflection of God's purposes and will, so the science and history is the understanding of the author's day, and is limited. Thus, the Bible is susceptible to errors in these areas. *Inerrancy of Purpose* is the belief that it is only inerrant in the purpose of bringing its readers to a saving faith. The Bible is not about facts, but about persons and relationships, thus, it is subject to error. *Inspired: Not Inerrant* is the belief that its authors are human and thus subject to human error. It should be noted that this author holds the position of full inerrancy.

For many today, the Bible is nothing more than a book written by men. The Bible critic believes the Bible to be full of myths and legends, contradictions, and geographical, historical, and scientific errors. University professor Gerald A. Larue had this to say, "The views of the writers as expressed in the Bible reflect the ideas, beliefs, and concepts current in their own times and are limited by the extent of knowledge in those times."[15] On the other hand, the Bible's authors claim that their writings were inspired of God, as Holy Spirit moved them along. We will discover shortly that the Bible critics have much to say, but it is inflated or empty.

---

[15] Gerald Larue, "The Bible as a Political Weapon," *Free Inquiry* (Summer 1983): 39.

2 Timothy 3:16-17 Updated American Standard Version (UASV)

¹⁶ All Scripture is inspired by God and profitable for teaching, for reproof, for correction, for training in righteousness; ¹⁷ so that the man of God may be fully competent, equipped for every good work.

2 Peter 1:21 Updated American Standard Version (UASV)

²¹ for no prophecy was ever produced by the will of man, but men carried along by the Holy Spirit spoke from God.

The question remains as to whether the Bible is a book written by imperfect men and full of errors, or is written by imperfect men, but inspired by God. If the Bible is just another book by imperfect man, there is no hope for humankind. If it is inspired by God and without error, although penned by imperfect men, we have the hope of everything that it offers: a rich, happy life now by applying counsel that lies within and the real life that is to come, everlasting life. This author contends that the Bible is inspired of God and free of human error, although written by imperfect humans.

Before we take on the critics who seem to sift the Scriptures looking for problematic verses, let us take a moment to reflect on how we should approach these alleged problem texts. The critic's argument goes something like this: 'If God does not err and the Bible is the Word of God, then the Bible should not have one single error or contradiction, yet it is full of errors and contradictions.' If the Bible is riddled with nothing but contradictions and errors as the critics would have us believe, why, out of 31,173 verses in the Bible, should there be only 2-3 thousand Bible difficulties that are called into question, this being less than ten percent of the whole?

First, let it be said that it is every Christian's obligation to get a deeper understanding of God's Word, just as the apostle Paul told Timothy:

1 Timothy 4:15-16 Updated American Standard Version (UASV)

¹⁵ Practice these things, be absorbed in them, so that your progress will be evident to all. ¹⁶ Pay close attention to yourself and to your teaching; persevere in these things, for as you do this you will ensure salvation both for yourself and for those who hear you.

Paul also told the Corinthians:

2 Corinthians 10:4-5 Updated American Standard Version (UASV)

⁴ For the weapons of our warfare are not of the flesh[16] but powerful to God for destroying strongholds.[17] ⁵ We are destroying speculations and every lofty thing

---

[16] That is *merely human*

[17] That is *tearing down false arguments*

raised up against the knowledge of God, and we are taking every thought captive to the obedience of Christ,

Paul also told the Philippians:

Philippians 1:7 Updated American Standard Version (UASV)

⁷ It is right for me to feel thus about you all, because I hold you in my heart, for you are all partakers with me of grace, both in my imprisonment and in the defense and confirmation of the gospel.

In being able to defend against the modern-day critic, one has to be able to reason from the Scriptures and overturn the critic's argument(s) with mildness. If someone were to approach us about an alleged error or contradiction, what should we do? We should be frank and honest. If we do not have an answer, we should admit such. If the text in question gives the appearance of difficulty, we should admit this as well. If we are unsure as to how we should answer, we can simply say that we will look into it and get back to them, returning with a reasonable answer.

However, we do not want to express disbelief and doubt to our critics, because they will be emboldened in their disbelief. It will put them on the offense and us on the defense. With great confidence, we can express that there is an answer. The Bible has withstood the test of 2,000 years of persecution and interrogation and yet it is the most printed book of all time, currently being translated into 2,287 languages. If these critical questions were so threatening, the Bible would not be the book that it is.

When we are pursuing the text in question, be unwavering in purpose, or resolved to find an answer. In some cases, it may take hours of digging to find the solution. Consider this: as we resolve these difficulties, we are also building our faith that God's Word is inerrant. Moreover, we will want to do preventative maintenance in our personal study. As we are doing our Bible reading, take note of these surface discrepancies and resolve them as we work our way through the Bible. We need to make this part of our prayers as well. I recommend the following program. Below are several books that deal with difficult passages. As we daily read and study our Bible from Genesis to Revelation, do not attempt it in one year; make it a four-year program. Use a good exegetical commentary like *The Holman Old/New Testament Commentary* (HOTC/HNTC) or *The New American Commentary* set, and *The Big Book of Bible Difficulties* by Norman L. Geisler, as well as *The Encyclopedia of Bible Difficulties* by Gleason Archer.

We should be aware that men under inspiration penned the originally written books. In fact, we do not have those originals, what textual scholars call autographs, but we do have thousands of copies. The copyists, however, were not inspired; therefore, as one might expect, throughout the first 1,400 years of copying, thousands of errors were transmitted into the texts that were being copied by imperfect hands that were not under inspiration when copying. Yet, the next 450 years saw a restoration of the text by textual scholars from around the world.

Therefore, while many of our best literal translations today may not be inspired, they are a mirror-like reflection of the autographs by way of textual criticism.[18] Therefore, the fallacy could be with the copyist error that has simply not been weeded out. In addition, we must keep in mind that God's Word is without error, but our interpretation and understanding of that Word is not.

It should be noted that the Bible is made up of 66 smaller books that were hand-written over a period of 1,600 years, having some 40 writers of various trades such as shepherd, king, priest, tax collector, governor, physician, copyist, fisherman, and a tentmaker. Therefore, it should not surprise us that some difficulties are encountered as we casually read the Bible. Yet, if one were to take a deeper look, one would find that these difficulties are easily explained. Let us take a few pages to examine some passages that have been under attack.

This chapter's objective is not to be exhaustive, not even close. What we are looking to do is cover a few alleged contradictions and a couple of alleged mistakes. This is to give us a small sampling of the reasonable answers that we will find in the above recommended books. Remember, our Bible is a sword that we must use both offensively and defensively. One must wonder how long a warrior of ancient times would last who was not expertly trained in the use of his weapon. Let us look at a few scriptures that support our need to learn our Bible well so will be able to defend what we believe to be true.

When "false apostles, deceitful workmen, disguising themselves as apostles of Christ" were causing trouble in the congregation in Corinth, the apostle Paul wrote that under such circumstances, we are to *tear down their arguments* and *take every thought captive*. (2 Corinthians 10:4, 5; 11:13–15) All who present critical arguments against God's Word, or contrary to it, can have their arguments overturned by the Christian, who is able and ready to defend that Word in mildness. – 2 Timothy 2:24–26.

1 Peter 3:15 Updated American Standard Version (UASV)

[15] but sanctify Christ as Lord in your hearts, always being prepared to make a defense[19] to anyone who asks you for a reason for the hope that is in you; yet do it with gentleness and respect;

Peter says that we need to be prepared to make a *defense*. The Greek word behind the English 'defense' is *apologia*, which is actually a legal term that refers to the defense of a defendant in court. Our English apologetics is just what Peter spoke of, having the ability to give a reason to any who may challenge us, or to answer those who are not challenging us but who have honest questions that deserve to be answered.

---

[18] Textual criticism is the study of copies of any written work of which the autograph (original) is unknown, with the purpose of ascertaining the original text. Harold J. Green, Introduction to New Testament Textual Criticism (Peabody, MA: Hendrickson, 1995), 1.

[19] Or *argument*, or *explanation*

2 Timothy 2:24-25 Updated American Standard Version (UASV)

24 For a slave of the Lord does not need to fight, but needs to be kind to all, qualified to teach, showing restraint when wronged 25 with gentleness correcting those who are in opposition, if perhaps God may grant them repentance leading to accurate knowledge[20] of the truth,

Look at the Greek word (*epignosis*) behind the English "knowledge" in the above. "It is more intensive than *gnosis* (1108), knowledge because it expresses a more thorough participation in the acquiring of knowledge on the part of the learner."[21] The requirement of all of the Lord's servants is that they be able to teach, but not in a quarrelsome way, and in a way to correct his opponents with mildness. Why? Because the purpose of it all is that by God, and through the Christian teacher, one may come to repentance and begin taking in an accurate knowledge of the truth.

Inerrancy: Practical Principles to Overcoming Bible Difficulties

Below are several ways of looking at the Bible that enable the reader to see he is not dealing with an error or contradiction, but rather a Bible difficulty.

Different Points of View

At times, you may have two different writers who are writing from two different points of view.

Numbers 35:14 Updated American Standard Version (UASV)

14 You shall give three cities across the Jordan and three cities you shall give in the land of Canaan; they will be cities of refuge.

Joshua 22:4 Updated American Standard Version (UASV)

4 And now Jehovah your God has given rest to your brothers, as he spoke to them; therefore turn now and go to your tents, to the land of your possession, which Moses the servant of Jehovah gave you beyond the Jordan. [on the other side of the Jordan, ESV]

Here we see that Moses is speaking about the east side of the Jordan when he says "on this side of the Jordan." Joshua, on the other hand, is also speaking about

---

[20] *Epignosis* is a strengthened or intensified form of *gnosis* (*epi,* meaning "additional"), meaning, "true," "real," "full," "complete" or "accurate," depending upon the context. Paul and Peter alone use *epignosis.*

[21] Spiros Zodhiates, *The Complete Word Study Dictionary: New Testament,* Electronic ed. (Chattanooga, TN: AMG Publishers, 2000, c1992, c1993), S. G1922.

the east side of the Jordan when he says "on the other side of the Jordan." So, who is correct? Both are. When Moses was penning Numbers the Israelites had not yet crossed the Jordan River, so the east side was "this side," the side he was on. On the other hand, when Joshua penned his book, the Israelites had crossed the Jordan, so the east side was just as he had said, "on the other side of the Jordan." Thus, we should not assume that two different writers are writing from the same perspective.

A Careful Reading

At times, it may simply be a case of needing to slow down and carefully read the account, considering exactly what is being said.

Joshua 18:28 Updated American Standard Version (UASV)

28 and Zelah, Haeleph and the Jebusite (that is, Jerusalem), Gibeah, Kiriath; fourteen cities with their villages. This is the inheritance of the sons of Benjamin according to their families.

Judges 1:21 Updated American Standard Version (UASV)

21 But the sons of Benjamin did not drive out the Jebusites who lived in Jerusalem; so the Jebusites have lived with the sons of Benjamin in Jerusalem to this day.

Joshua 15:63 Updated American Standard Version (UASV)

63 But as for the Jebusites, the inhabitants of Jerusalem, the sons of Judah could not drive them out; so the Jebusites live with the sons of Judah at Jerusalem until this day.

Judges 1:8-9 Updated American Standard Version (UASV)

8 And then the sons of Judah fought against Jerusalem and captured it and struck it with the edge of the sword and set the city on fire. 9 And afterward the sons of Judah went down to fight against the Canaanites living in the hill country and in the Negev[22] and in the Shephelah.[23]

2 Samuel 5:5-9 Updated American Standard Version (UASV)

5 At Hebron he reigned over Judah seven years and six months, and in Jerusalem he reigned thirty-three years over all Israel and Judah.

6 And the king and his men went to Jerusalem against the Jebusites, the inhabitants of the land, and they said to David, "You shall not come in here, but the blind and lame will turn you away"; thinking, "David cannot come in here." 7 Nevertheless, David captured the stronghold of Zion, that is the city of David. 8 And David said on that day, "Whoever would strike the Jebusites, let him

---

[22] I.e. *South*

[23] I.e., lowland

get up the water shaft to attack 'the lame and the blind,' who are hated by David's soul." Therefore it is said, "The blind and the lame shall not come into the house." ⁹ And David lived in the stronghold and called it the city of David. And David built all around from the Millo and inward.

There is no doubt that even the advanced Bible reader of many years can come away confused because the above accounts seem to be contradictory. In Joshua 18:28 and Judges 1:21, we see that Jerusalem was an inheritance of the tribe of Benjamin, yet the Benjamites were unable to conquer Jerusalem. However, in Joshua 15:63 we see that the tribe of Judah could not conquer them either, with the reading giving the impression that it was a part of their inheritance. In Judges 1:8, however, Judah was eventually able to conquer Jerusalem and burn it with fire. Yet, to add even more to the confusion, we find at 2 Samuel 5:5–8 that David is said to have conquered Jerusalem hundreds of years later.

Now that we have the particulars let us look at it more clearly. The boundary between Benjamin's inheritances ran right through the middle of Jerusalem. Joshua 8:28 is correct, in that what would later be called the "city of David" was in the territory of Benjamin, but it also in part crossed over the line into the territory of Judah, causing both tribes to go to war against this Jebusite city. It is also true that the tribe of Benjamin was unable to conquer the city and that the tribe of Judah eventually did. However, if you look at Judges 1:9 again, you will see that Judah did not finish the job entirely and moved on to conquer other areas. This allowed the remaining ones to regroup and form a resistance that neither Benjamin nor Judah could overcome, so these Jebusites remained until the time of David, hundreds of years later.

Intended Meaning of the Writer

First, the Bible student needs to understand the level that the Bible intends to be exact in what is written. If Jim told a friend that 650 graduated with him from high school in 1984, it is not challenged, because it is all too clear that he is using rounded numbers and is not meaning to be exactly precise. This is how God's Word operates as well. Sometimes it means to be exact, at other times, it is simply rounding numbers, in other cases, the intention of the writer is a general reference, to give readers of that time and succeeding generations some perspective. Did Samuel, the author of judges, intend to pen a book on the chronology of Judges, or was his focus on the falling away, oppression, and the rescue by a judge, repeatedly. Now, it would seem that Jeremiah, the author of 1 Kings was more interested in giving his readers an exact number of years.

Acts 2:41 Updated American Standard Version (UASV)

⁴¹ So those who received his word were baptized, and there were added that day about three thousand souls.

As you can see here, numbers within the Bible are often used with approximations. This is a frequent practice even today, in both written works and verbal conversation.

Acts 7:2-3 Updated American Standard Version (UASV)

² And Stephen said:

"Brothers and fathers, hear me. The God of glory appeared to our father Abraham when he was in Mesopotamia, before he lived in Haran, ³ and said to him, 'Go out from your land and from your kindred and go into the land that I will show you.'

If you were to check the Hebrew Scriptures at Genesis 12:1, you would find that what is claimed to have been said by God to Abraham is not quoted word-for-word; it is simply a paraphrase. This is a normal practice within Scripture and in writing in general.

Numbers 34:15 Updated American Standard Version (UASV)

¹⁵ The two and a half tribes have received their inheritance beyond the Jordan opposite Jericho, eastward toward the sunrising."

Just as you would read in today's local newspaper, the Bible writer has written from the human standpoint, how it appeared to him. The Bible also speaks of "to the end of the earth" (Psalm 46:9), "from the four corners of the earth" (Isa 11:12), and "the four winds of the earth" (Revelation 7:1). These phrases are still used today.

Unexplained Does Not mean Unexplainable

Considering that there are 31,173 verses in the Bible, encompassing 66 books written by about 40 writers, ranging from shepherds to kings, an army general, fishermen, tax collector, a physician and on and on, and being penned over a 1,600 year period, one does find a few hundred Bible difficulties (about one percent). However, 99 percent of those are explainable. Yet no one wants to be so arrogant to say that he can explain them all. It has nothing to do with the inadequacy of God's Word but is based on human understanding. In many cases, science or archaeology and the field of custom and culture of ancient peoples has helped explain difficulties in hundreds of passages. Therefore, there may be less than one percent left to be answered, yet our knowledge of God's Word continues to grow.

Guilty Until Proven Innocent

This is exactly the perception that the critic has of God's Word. The legal principle of being "innocent until proven guilty" afforded mankind in courts of justice is withheld from the very Word of God. What is ironic here is that this policy has contributed to these Bible critics looking foolish over and over again when something comes to light that vindicates the portion of Scripture they are challenging.

Daniel 5:1 Updated American Standard Version (UASV)

¹ Belshazzar the king made[24] a great feast for a thousand of his nobles, and he was drinking wine in the presence of the thousand.

Bible critics had long claimed that Belshazzar was not known outside of the book Daniel; therefore, they argue that Daniel was mistaken. Yet it hardly seems prudent to argue error from absence of outside evidence. Just because archaeology had not discovered such a person did not mean that Daniel was wrong, or that such a person did not exist. In 1854, some small clay cylinders were discovered in modern-day southern Iraq, which would have been the city of Ur in ancient Babylonia. The cuneiform documents were a prayer of King Nabonidus for "Bel-sar-ussur, my eldest son." These tablets also showed that this "Bel-sar-ussur" had secretaries as well as a household staff. Other tablets were discovered a short time later that showed that the kingship was entrusted to this eldest son as a coregent while his father was away.

He entrusted the 'Camp' to his oldest (son), the firstborn [Belshazzar], the troops everywhere in the country he ordered under his (command). He let (everything) go, entrusted the kingship to him and, himself, he [Nabonidus] started out for a long journey, the (military) forces of Akkad marching with him; he turned towards Tema (deep) in the west."[25]

Ignoring Literary Styles

The Bible is a diverse book when it comes to literary styles: narrative, poetic, prophetic, and apocalyptic; also containing parables, metaphors, similes, hyperbole, and other figures of speech. Too often, these alleged errors are the result of a reader taking a figure of speech as literal, or reading a parable as though it is a narrative.

Matthew 24:35 Updated American Standard Version (UASV)

³⁵ Heaven and earth will pass away, but my words will not pass away.

If some do not recognize that they are dealing with a figure of speech, they are bound to come away with the wrong meaning. Some have concluded from Matthew 24:35 that Jesus was speaking of an eventual destruction of the earth. This is hardly the case, as his listeners would not have understood it that way based on their understanding of the Old Testament. They would have understood that he was simply being emphatic about the words he spoke, using hyperbole. What he was conveying is that his words are more enduring than heaven and earth, and with

---

[24] I.e., held

[25] J. Pritchard, ed., *Ancient Near Eastern Texts* (1974), 313.

heaven and earth being understood as eternal, this merely conveyed even more so that Jesus' words could be trusted.

Two Accounts of the Same Incident

If you were to speak to officers that take accident reports for their police department, you would find that there is cohesion in the accounts, but each person has merely witnessed aspects that have stood out to them. We will see that this is the case as well with the examples below, which is the same account in two different gospels:

Matthew 8:5 Updated American Standard Version (UASV)

⁵ When he[26] had entered Capernaum, a centurion came forward to him, imploring him,

Luke 7:2-3 Updated American Standard Version (UASV)

² And a centurion's[27] slave, who was highly regarded[28] by him, was sick and about to die. ³ When he heard about Jesus, he sent some older men of the Jews[29] asking him to come and bring his slave safely through.[30]

Immediately we see the problem of whether the centurion or the elders of the Jews spoke with Jesus. The solution is not really hidden from us. Which of the two accounts is the most detailed account? You are correct if you said, Luke. The centurion sent the elders of the Jews to represent him to Jesus, so; that whatever response Jesus might give, it would be as though he were addressing the centurion; therefore, Matthew gave his readers the basic thought, not seeing the need of mentioning the elders of the Jews aspect. This is how a representative was viewed in the first century, just as some countries see ambassadors today as being the very person they represent. Therefore, both Matthew and Luke are correct.

Man's Fallible Interpretations

Inspiration by God is infallible, without error. Imperfect man and his interpretations over the centuries, as bad as many of them have been, should not cast a shadow over God's inspired Word. The entire Word of God has one meaning and one meaning only for every penned word, which is what God willed to be conveyed by the human writer he chose to use.

---

[26] That is *Jesus*

[27] I.e., army officer over a hundred solderiers

[28] Lit *to whom he was honorable*

[29] Or *Jewish elders*

[30] I.e., *save the life of his slave*

YOUR GUIDE FOR DEFENDING THE BIBLE

The Autograph Alone Is Inspired and Inerrant

It has been argued by conservative scholars that only the autograph manuscripts were inspired and inerrant, not the copying of those manuscripts over the next 3,000 years for the Old Testament and 1,500 years for the New Testament. While I would agree with this position as well, it should be noted that we do not possess autographs, so to argue that they are inerrant is to speak of nonexistent documents. However, it should be further understood that through the science of textual criticism, we can establish a mirror reflection of the autograph manuscripts. B. F. Westcott, F. J. A. Hort, F. F. Bruce, and many other textual scholars would agree with Norman L Geisler's assessment: "The New Testament, then, has not only survived in more manuscripts than any other book from antiquity, but it has survived in a purer form than any other great book—*a form that is 99.5 percent pure.*"[31]

An example of a copyist error can be found in Luke's genealogy of Jesus at Luke 3:35–37. In verse 37 you will find a Cainan, and in verse 36 you will find a second Cainan between Arphaxad (Arpachshad) and Shelah. As one can see from most footnotes in different study Bibles, the Cainan in verse 36 is seen as a scribal error, and is not found in the Hebrew Old Testament, the Samaritan Pentateuch, or the Aramaic Targums, but is found in the Greek Septuagint. (Genesis 10:24; 11:12, 13; 1 Chronicles 1:18, but not 1 Chronicles 1:24) It seems quite unlikely that it was in the earlier copies of the Septuagint, because the first-century Jewish historian Josephus lists Shelah next as the son of Arphaxad, and Josephus normally followed the Septuagint.[32] So one might ask why this second Cainan is found in the translations at all if this is the case? The manuscripts that do contain this second Cainan are some of the best manuscripts that are used in establishing the original text: 01 B L A^1 33 (Kainam); A 038 044 0102 A^{13} (Kainan).

The Bible Was Miraculously Restored, not Miraculously Preserved

The Hebrew text was like the Greek NT; it had accumulated copyist errors, a few intentional, a good number accidental, between the Malachi days of 440 BCE and Rabbi Judah ha-Nasi (135 to 217 CE). The same thing happened to the Greek New Testament from about 400 CE to 1550 CE, a period of copyist errors. The good news is for the NT is fourfold: (1) the 144 NT papyri discovered in the early part of the 20th century, (2) a number of them dated within decades of the originals, and the great Codex Vaticanus (300-330 CE) and Codex Sinaiticus (330-360 CE), (3) that we have 5,898 Greek NT MSS; (4) then, there was the era of many dozens of textual scholars, from 1550 to the present who restored the text to its original words.

---

[31] Norman L. Geisler and William E. Nix: *A General Introduction to the Bible* (Chicago, Moody Press, 1980), 367. (Emphasis is mine.)

[32] *Jewish Antiquities,* I, 146 [vi, 4].

So, the Hebrew OT corruption ran in earnest between 440 BCE to 220 CE. At that time, the Greek Septuagint, a translation of the Hebrew Scriptures, was produced between 280 – 150 BCE, which became favored by the Jews to the point that they claimed it was inspired. However, the fact that the lingua franca of the Roman Empire ran from 330 BCE to 330 CE, the Christians in the first century CE wisely used the Greek Septuagint to evangelize, to show that Jesus Christ was the long-awaited Messiah. Then, Jerusalem was destroyed by General Titus and the Roman army in 70 CE, killing one million one hundred thousand Jews and carrying another seventy thousand back to Rome as slaves. No temple led to the creation of the Mishnah, an authoritative collection of exegetical material embodying the oral tradition of Jewish law and forming the first part of the Talmud. During the 150 years in the wake of the temple's destruction in Jerusalem in 70 CE, rabbinic sages throughout Israel at once were quick to seek out a new source for preserving Jewish practice. They debated and combined various traditions of their oral law. Growing this foundation, they set new constraints, boundaries, and requirements for Judaism. This gave the Jewish people direction for their day-to-day life of holiness, even though they lacked a temple. This new spiritual structure was summarized in the Mishnah, which Judah ha-Nasi compiled by about 200-217 CE.

In addition, the Jewish scholars set about creating a corrected text of the Hebrew Old Testament because they realized it had some textual variants from the sopherim (scribes). But it was the greatest textual scholars who have ever lived, the Masoretes, who made corrected copies from 500 to 900 CE. Below is an article about them. The beauty is that they did not erase the manuscripts with the errors; they kept them, then simply put the corrections in the margin, called the Masorah. So, the Hebrew text was corrected just as the Greek text was. And then, in 1947, we found the Dead Sea Scrolls, which dated as early as the 3rd century BCE and validated the Masoretic text. And ironically at this same time, many of the **best** NT papyri were coming to light that validated the work of Johann Jakob Wettstein [1693-1754 A.D.], Karl Lachmann [1793-1851], Samuel Prideaux Tregelles [1813-1875], Friedrich Constantin von Tischendorf [1815-1874], and especially Westcott and Hort of 1881.

MIRACULOUS RESTORATION, NOT MIRACULOUS PRESERVATION

OLD TESTAMENT
Transmission: 1500 BCE – 440 BCE
Corruption: 440 BCE – 220 CE
Restoration: 500 – 900 CE – Present
Corroboration MSS (Dead Sea Scrolls): 1947

NEW TESTAMENT
Transmission: 45 CE – 98 CE
Corruption: 440 CE -1550 CE
Restoration: 1550 CE – Present
Corroboration MSS (NT Papyri): 1900s-1960s-Present

A Lack of <u>Preservation</u> Does Not Mean a Lack of <u>Inspiration</u>

- The Bible **was miraculously inspired** as men were moved along by the Holy Spirit (*Absolute Inerrancy*)
- The Bible **was not miraculously preserved** as men's human imperfection gave us corruption (*Limited Inerrancy*)
- The Bible **was restored** through tens of millions of hours by many hundreds of (men) textual scholars from the 16th to the 21st centuries. (*Absolute Inerrancy Restored*)

The **men who restored the text** are no more perfect than the **men who** intentionally and unintentionally **corrupted the text**. However, even hundreds of **imperfect men**, through dozens of lifetimes of sweat and toil, arrived at **a perfect text** that was lost but now is found. With the copyists, you have tens of thousands of men **focusing on their work as an individual** in reproducing a copy; with the textual scholars, it is teams of hundreds of men focusing on all of the manuscripts to ascertain the original words of the original texts.

Many of the above scholars gave their entire lives to God and the Hebrew and Greek text.[33] Each of these could have an entire book devoted to them and their work alone. The amount of work they accomplished before the era of computers is nothing short of astonishing. Rightly, the preceding history should serve to strengthen our faith in the authenticity and general integrity of the Hebrew Scriptures and the Greek New Testament. Unlike Bart D. Ehrman, men like Sir Frederic Kenyon have been moved to say that the books of the Greek New Testament have "come down to us substantially as they were written." And all this is especially true of the critical scholarship of the almost two hundred years since the days of Karl Lachmann. All today can feel confident that what they hold in their hands is a mirror reflection of the Word of God that was penned in twenty-seven books, some two thousand years ago.

It is true that the Jewish copyists and the later Christian copyists were not led along by the Holy Spirit, and therefore their manuscripts were not inerrant, infallible. Errors (textual variants) crept into the manuscripts unintentionally and intentionally. However, the vast majority of the Hebrew Old Testament and Greek New Testament has not been infected with textual errors. For the portions impacted with textual errors, it is the many tens of thousands of copies that we have to help us to weed out the errors. How? Well, not every copyist made the same textual errors. Hence, by comparing the work of different copyists and different manuscripts, textual scholars can identify the textual variants (errors) and remove those, leaving us with the original content.

---

[33] **The Climax of the Restored Text**

Yes, it would be the greatest discovery of all time if we found the actual original five books that were penned by Moses himself, Genesis through Deuteronomy. However, there would be no way of establishing that they were the originals. The fact is, we do not need the originals. We do not need those original documents. What is so important about the documents? The documents are not important; it is the content on the original documents that we are after. And truly, miraculously, we have more copies than needed to do just that. We do not need miraculous preservation because we have miraculous restoration. We now know beyond a reasonable doubt that the Hebrew Old Testament and the Greek New Testament critical texts are a 99.99% reflection of the content that was in those ancient original manuscripts. Some textual scholars might say that I am exaggerating with the 99.99%. An example of how that is not so can be found in the 1881 Westcott and Hort critical Greek NT, which is 99.5% the same as the 2012 28th edition of the critical Greek NT. The discovery of the NT papyri from the 1900s to the 1960s and up to the present has validated Westcott and Hort's Greek NT and let us know that the 2012 Nestle-Aland Greek NT is a mirror-like reflection of the original. To be frank, there are about 100+ textual variants where Westcott and Hort were correct, and the Nestle-Aland text is likely not correct. This is because they took the textual eclecticism method of determining the original, which was to focus on both external and internal evidence. Still, they leaned heavily on internal evidence, which is a bit more subjective. Regardless, we have the apparatus in the 28th edition of the Nestle-Aland that gives the translator the variants, allowing him to make an objective determination. Therefore, the 100+ textual variants can be decided on a case-by-case basis. So, yes, what we have is 99.99% reflective of the original.

The critical text of Westcott and Hort of 1881 [(FENTON JOHN ANTHONY HORT (1828 – 1892) and BROOKE FOSS WESTCOTT (1825 – 1901)] has been commended by leading textual scholars over the last one hundred and forty years, and still stands as the standard. Numerous additional critical editions of the Greek text came after Westcott and Hort: Richard F. Weymouth (1886), Bernhard Weiss (1894–1900); the British and Foreign Bible Society (1904, 1958), Alexander Souter (1910), Hermann von Soden (1911–1913); and Eberhard Nestle's Greek text, *Novum Testamentum Graece*, published in 1898 by the Württemberg Bible Society, Stuttgart, Germany. The Nestle in twelve editions (1898–1923) to subsequently be taken over by his son, Erwin Nestle (13th–20th editions, 1927–1950), followed by Kurt Aland (21st–25th editions, 1952–1963), and lastly, it was coedited by Kurt Aland and Barbara Aland (26th–28th editions, 1979, 1993, 2012).

Look at the Context

Many alleged inconsistencies disappear by simply looking at the context. Taking words out of context can distort their meaning. *Merriam-Webster's Collegiate Dictionary* defines context as "the parts of a discourse that surround a word or passage and can throw light on its meaning."[34] Context can also be "the circumstances or events that form the environment within which something exists or takes place." If we were to look in a thesaurus for a synonym, we would find "background" for this second meaning. At 2 Timothy 2:15, the apostle Paul brings home the point of why context is so important: "Do your best to present yourself to God as one approved, a worker who has no need to be ashamed, rightly handling the word of truth."

Ephesians 2:8-9 Updated American Standard Version (UASV)

[8] For by grace you have been saved through faith; and that not of yourselves, it is the gift of God; [9] not from works, so that no man may boast.

James 2:26 Updated American Standard Version (UASV)

[26] For as the body apart from the spirit[35] is dead, so also faith apart from works is dead.

So, which is it? Is salvation possible by faith alone as Paul wrote to the Ephesians, or is faith dead without works as James wrote to his readers? As our subtitle brings out, let us look at the context. In the letter to the Ephesians, the apostle Paul is speaking to the Jewish Christians who were looking to the works of the Mosaic Law as a means to salvation, a righteous standing before God. Paul was telling these legalistic Jewish Christians that this is not so. In fact, this would invalidate Christ's ransom because there would have been no need for it if one could achieve salvation by meticulously keeping the Mosaic Law. (Rom. 5:18) But James was writing to those in a congregation who were concerned with their status before other men, who were looking for prominent positions within the congregation, and not taking care of those that were in need. (Jam. 2:14–17) So, James is merely addressing those who call themselves Christian, but in name only. No person could truly be a Christian and not possess some good works, such as feeding the poor, helping the elderly. This type of work was an evident demonstration of one's Christian personality. Paul was in perfect harmony with James on this. – Romans 10:10; 1 Corinthians 15:58; Ephesians 5:15, 21–33; 6:15; 1 Timothy 4:16; 2 Timothy 4:5; Hebrews 10:23-25.

Inerrancy: Are There Contradictions?

Below I will follow this pattern. I will list the critic's argument first, followed by the text of difficulty, and conclude with an answer to the critic. What should be kept at the forefront of our mind is this: one is simply looking for the best answer, not absoluteness. If there is a reasonable answer to a Bible difficulty, why are the

---

[34] Merriam-Webster, Inc: *Merriam-Webster's Collegiate Dictionary*. Eleventh ed. (Springfield, Mass.: Merriam-Webster, Inc. 2003).

[35] Or *breath*

critics able to set them aside with ease? Because they start with the premise that this is not the Word of God, but only a book by imperfect men and full of contradictions; thus, the bias toward errors has blinded their judgment.

Critic: The critic would argue that there was an Adam and Eve, and an Abel who was now dead, so, where did Cain get his wife? This is one of the most common questions by Bible critics.

Genesis 4:17 Updated American Standard Version (UASV)

¹⁷ Cain had sexual relations[36] with his wife and she conceived, and gave birth to Enoch; and he built a city, and called the name of the city Enoch, after the name of his son, Enoch.

Answer: If one were to read a little further along, they would come to the realization that Adam had a son named Seth; it further adds that Adam "became father to sons *and daughters*." (Genesis 5:4) Adam lived for a total of 800 years after fathering Seth, giving him ample opportunity to father many more sons and daughters. So it could be that Cain married one of his sisters. If he waited until one of his brothers and sisters had a daughter, he could have married one of his nieces once she was old enough. In the beginning, humans were closer to perfection; this explains why they lived longer and why at that time there was little health risk of genetic defects in the case of children born to closely related parents, in contrast to how it is today. As time passed, genetic defects increased and life spans decreased. Adam lived to see 930 years. Yet Shem, who lived after the Flood, died at 600 years, while Shem's son Arpachshad only lived 438 years, dying before his father died. Abraham saw an even greater decrease in that he only lived 175 years while his grandson Jacob was 147 years when he died. Thus, due to increasing imperfection, God prohibited the marriage of closely related people under the Mosaic Law because of the likelihood of genetic defects.—Leviticus 18:9.

Critic: If God is here hardening Pharaoh's heart, what exactly makes Pharaoh responsible for the decisions he makes?

Exodus 4:21 Updated American Standard Version (UASV)

²¹ Jehovah said to Moses, "When you go and return to Egypt see that you perform before Pharaoh all the wonders which I have put in your hand; but I will harden his heart so that he will not let the people go.

Answer: This is actually a prophecy. God knew that what he was about to do would contribute to a stubborn and obstinate Pharaoh, who was going to be unwilling to change or give up the Israelites so they could go off to worship their God. Therefore, this is not stating what God is going to do; it is prophesying that Pharaoh's heart will harden because of the actions of God. The fact is, Pharaoh allowed his own heart to harden because he was determined not to agree with Moses' wishes or accept Jehovah's request to let the people go. Moses tells us at Exodus 7:13

---

[36] Lit *knew*

(ESV) that "Pharaoh's heart was hardened, and he would not listen to them, as the Lord had said." Again, at 8:15 we read, "When Pharaoh saw that there was a respite, he hardened his heart and would not listen to them, as the Lord had said."

Critic: The Israelites had just received the Ten Commandments, with one commandment being: "You shall not make for yourself a carved image or any likeness of anything that is in heaven above, or that is in the earth beneath, or that is in the water under the earth." Therefore, how is the bronze serpent not a violation of this commandment?

Numbers 21:9 Updated American Standard Version (UASV)

⁹ And Moses made a bronze serpent and set it on the standard;[37] and it came about, that if a serpent bit any man, when he looked to the bronze serpent, he lived.

Answer: First, an idol is "a representation or symbol of an object of worship; *broadly*: a false god."[38] Second, it should be noted that not all images are idols. The bronze serpent was not made for the purpose of worship, or for some passionate devotion or veneration. There were times, however, when images were created with absolutely no intention of it receiving devotion, veneration, or worship, yet were later made into objects of veneration. That is exactly what happened with the copper serpent that Moses had formed in the wilderness. Many centuries later, "in the third year of Hoshea son of Elah, king of Israel, Hezekiah the son of Ahaz, king of Judah, began to reign. He removed the high places and broke the pillars and cut down the Asherah. And he broke in pieces the bronze serpent that Moses had made; for until those days the people of Israel had made offerings to it (it was called Nehushtan)."—2 Kings 18:1, 4.

Critic: Deuteronomy 15:11 (NET) says: "*There will never cease to be some poor people in the land;* therefore, I am commanding you to make sure you open your hand to your fellow Israelites who are needy and poor in your land." Is this not a contradiction of Deuteronomy 15:4? Will there be no poor among the Israelites, or will there be poor among them? Which is it?

Deuteronomy 15:4 Updated American Standard Version (UASV)

⁴ However, there will be no poor among you, since Jehovah will surely bless you in the land which Jehovah your God is giving you as an inheritance to possess,

Answer: If you look at the context, Deuteronomy 15:4 is stating that if the Israelites obey Jehovah's command to take care of the poor, "there should not be any poor among" them. Thus, for every poor person, there will be one to take care of that need. If an Israelite fell on hard times, there was to be a fellow Israelite ready to step in to help him through those hard times. Verse 11 stresses the truth of the imperfect world since the rebellion of Adam and inherited sin: there will always be

---

[37] I.e., *pole*

[38] Merriam-Webster, Inc: *Merriam-Webster's Collegiate Dictionary*. Eleventh ed. (Springfield, Mass.: Merriam-Webster, Inc., 2003).

poor among mankind, the Israelites being no different. However, the difference with God's people is that those who were well off financially were to offset conditions for those who fell on difficult times. This is not to be confused with the socialistic welfare systems in the world today. Those Jews were hard-working men, who labored from sunup to sundown to take care of their families. But if disease overtook their herd or unseasonal weather brought about failed crops, an Israelite could sell himself into the service of a fellow Israelite for a period of time; thereafter, he would be back on his feet. And many years down the road, he may very well do the same for another Israelite, who fell on difficult times.

Critic: Joshua 11:23 says that Joshua took the land according to what God had spoken to Moses and handed it on to the nation of Israel as planned. However, in Joshua 13:1, God is telling Joshua that he has grown old and much of the Promised Land has yet to be taken possession of. How can both be true? Is this not a contradiction?

Joshua 11:23 Updated American Standard Version (UASV)

²³ So Joshua took the whole land, according to all that Jehovah had spoken to Moses, and Joshua gave it for an inheritance to Israel according to their divisions by their tribes, and the land had rest from war.

Joshua 13:1 Updated American Standard Version (UASV)

13 Now Joshua was old and advanced in years, and Jehovah said to him, "You are old and advanced in years, and there remains yet very much land to possess.

Answer: No, it is not a contradiction. When the Israelites were to take the land, it was to take place in two different stages: the nation as a whole was to go to war and defeat the 31 kings of this land; thereafter, each Israelite tribe was to take their part of the land based on their individual actions. (Joshua 17:14–18; 18:3) Joshua fulfilled his role, which is expressed in 11:23 while the individual tribes did not complete their campaigns, which is expressed in 13:1. Even though the individual tribes failed to live up to taking their portion, the remaining Canaanites posed no real threat. Joshua 21:44, *ASV,* reads: "Jehovah gave them rest round about."

Critic: The critic would point out that John 1:18 clearly says that "*no one has ever seen God,*" while Exodus 24:10 explicitly states that Moses and Aaron, Nadab and Abihu, and seventy of the elders of Israel "*saw the God of Israel.*" Worse still, God informs them in Exodus 33:20: "You cannot see my face, for man shall not see me and live." The critic with his knowing smile says, 'This is a blatant contradiction.'

John 1:18 Updated American Standard Version (UASV)

¹⁸ No one has seen God at any time; the only begotten god³⁹ who is in the bosom of the Father,⁴⁰ that one has made him fully known.

Exodus 24:10 Updated American Standard Version (UASV)

¹⁰ and they saw the God of Israel; and under his feet was what seemed like a sapphire pavement, as clear as the sky itself.

Exodus 33:20 Updated American Standard Version (UASV)

²⁰ But he [God] said, "You cannot see my face, for no man can see me and live!"

Answer: Exodus 33:20 is one-hundred percent correct: No human could see Jehovah God and live. The apostle Paul at Colossians 1:15 tell us that Christ is the image of the invisible God, and the writer informs us at Hebrews 1:3 that Jesus is the "exact representation of His nature." Yet if you were to read the account of Saul of Tarsus (the apostle Paul), you would see that a mere partial manifestation of Christ's glory blinded Saul – Acts 9:1–18.

When the Bible says that Moses and others have seen God, it is not speaking of *literally* seeing him, because first of all He is an invisible spirit person. It is a *manifestation* of his glory, which is an act of showing or demonstrating his presence, making himself perceptible to the human mind. In fact, it is generally an angelic representative that stands in his place and not him personally. Exodus 24:16 informs us that "the glory of the Lord dwelt on Mount Sinai," not the Lord himself personally. When texts such as Exodus 24:10 explicitly state that Moses and Aaron, Nadab and Abihu, and seventy of the elders of Israel "*saw the God of Israel*," it is this "glory of the Lord," an angelic representative. This is shown to be the case at Luke 2:9, which reads: "And *an angel of the Lord* appeared to them, and *the glory of the Lord shone around them* [the shepherds], and they were filled with fear."

Many Bible difficulties are cleared up elsewhere in Scripture; for example, in the New Testament, you will find a text clarifying a difficulty from the Old Testament, such as Acts 7:53, which refers to those "who received the law *as delivered by angels* and did not keep it." Support comes from Paul at Galatians 3:19: "Why then the law? It was added because of transgressions until the offspring should come to whom the promise had been made, and it was put in place through angels by an intermediary." The writer of Hebrews chimes in at 2:2 with "For since the message *declared by angels* proved to be reliable, and every transgression or disobedience received a just retribution...." As we travel back to Exodus again, to 19:19 specifically, we find support that it was not God's own voice, which Moses heard; no, it was an angelic representative, for it reads: "Moses was speaking, and God was answering him with a voice." Exodus 33:22–23 also helps us to appreciate that it was

---

³⁹ Jn 1:18: "only-begotten god", P⁶⁶א*BC*Lsyr^hmg,p; **[V1]** "the only-begotten god," P⁷⁵33אcop^bo; **[V2]** "the only-begotten Son." AC³(W^s)QYf1,¹³ MajVgSyr^c

⁴⁰ Or *at the Father's side*

the back of these angelic representatives of Jehovah that Moses saw: "While my glory passes by . . . Then I will take away my hand, and you shall see my back, but my face shall not be seen."

Exodus 3:4 states: "God called to him out of the bush, 'Moses, Moses!' And he said, 'Here I am.'" Verse 6 informs us: "I am the God of your father, the God of Abraham, the God of Isaac, and the God of Jacob." Yet, in verse 2 we read: "And the angel of the Lord appeared to him in a flame of fire out of the midst of a bush." Here is another example of using God's Word to clear up what seems to be unclear or difficult to understand at first glance. Thus, while it speaks of the Lord making a direct appearance, it is really an angelic representative. Even today, we hear such comments, as 'the president of the United States is to visit the Middle East later this week.' However, later in the article it is made clear that he is not going personally, but it is one of his high-ranking representatives. Let us close with two examples, starting with,

Genesis 32:24-30 Updated American Standard Version (UASV)

24 And Jacob was left alone, and a man wrestled with him until daybreak. 25 When he saw that he had not prevailed against him, he touched the socket of his thigh; so the socket of Jacob's thigh was dislocated as he wrestled with him. 26 Then he said, "Let me go, for the dawn is breaking." But he said, "I will not let you go unless you bless me." 27 And he said to him, "What is your name?" And he said, "Jacob." 28 And he said, "Your name shall no longer be called Jacob, but Israel,[41] for you have struggled with God and with men and have prevailed." 29 Then Jacob asked him and said, "Please tell me your name." But he said, "Why is it that you ask my name?" And he blessed him there. 30 So Jacob named the place Peniel,[42] for he said, "I have seen God face to face, yet my soul has been preserved."

It is all too obvious here that this man is simply a materialized angel in the form of a man, another angelic representative of Jehovah God. Moreover, the reader of this book should have taken in that the Israelites as a whole saw these angelic representatives and spoke of them as though they were dealing directly with Jehovah God himself.

This proved to be the case in the second example found in the book of Judges where an angelic representative visited Manoah and his wife. Like the above mentioned account, Manoah and his wife treated this angelic representative as if he were Jehovah God himself: "And Manoah said to the angel of the Lord, 'What is your name, so that, when your words come true, we may honor you?' And the angel of the Lord said to him, 'Why do you ask my name, seeing it is wonderful?' Then Manoah knew that he was the angel of the Lord. And Manoah said to his wife, "We shall surely die, *for we have seen God.*" – Judges 13:3–22.

---

[41] Meaning *he contends with God*

[42] Meaning *face of God*

Inerrancy: Are There Mistakes?

I have addressed the alleged contradictions, so it would seem that our job is done here, right? Not hardly. Yes, there are just as many who claim that the Bible is full of mistakes.

Critic: Matthew 27:5 states that Judas hanged himself, whereas Acts 1:18 says, "Falling headlong, he burst open in the middle and all his intestines gushed out."

Matthew 27:5 Updated American Standard Version (UASV)

5 And he threw the pieces of silver into the temple and departed; and he went away and hanged himself.

Acts 1:18 Updated American Standard Version (UASV)

18 (Now this man acquired a field with the price of his wickedness, and falling headlong, he burst open in the middle and all his intestines gushed out.

Answer: Neither Matthew nor Luke made a mistake. What you have is Matthew giving the reader the manner in which Judas committed suicide. On the other hand, Luke is giving the reader of Acts, the result of that suicide. Therefore, instead of a mistake, we have two texts that complement each other, really giving the reader the full picture. Judas came to a tree alongside a cliff that had rocks below. He tied the rope to a branch and the other end around his neck and jumped over the edge of the cliff in an attempt at hanging himself. One of two things could have happened: (1) the limb broke plunging him to the rocks below, or (2) the rope broke with the same result, and he burst open onto the rocks below.

Critic: The apostle Paul made a mistake when he quotes how many people died.

Numbers 25:9 Updated American Standard Version (UASV)

9 The ones who died in the plague were twenty-four thousand.

1 Corinthians 10:8 Updated American Standard Version (UASV)

8 Neither let us commit sexual immorality, as some of them committed sexual immorality, only to fall, twenty-three thousand of them in one day.

Answer: We must keep in mind the above principle that we spoke of, the *Intended Meaning of the Writer*. We live in a far more precise age today, where specificity is highly important. However, we round large numbers off (even estimate) all the time: "there were 237,000 people in Time Square last night." The simplest answer is that the number of people slain was in between 23,000 and 24,000, and both writers rounded the number off. However, there is even another possibility, because the book of Numbers specifically speaks of "all the chiefs of the people" (25:4-5), which could account for the extra 1,000, which is mentioned in Numbers 24,000. Thus, you have the people killing the chiefs of the people and the plague killing the people. Therefore, both books are correct.

Critic: After 215 years in Egypt, the descendants of Jacob arrived at the Promised Land. As you recall they sinned against God and were sentenced to forty years in the wilderness. But once they entered the Promised Land, they buried Joseph's bones "at Shechem, in the piece of land that *Jacob bought* from the sons of Hamor the father of Shechem," as stated at Joshua 24:32. Yet, when Stephen had to defend himself before the Jewish religious leaders, he said that Joseph was buried "in the tomb that *Abraham had bought* for a sum of silver from the sons of Hamor." Therefore, at once it appears that we have a mistake on the part of Stephen.

Acts 7:15-16 Updated American Standard Version (UASV)

¹⁵ And Jacob went down to Egypt and died, he and our fathers. ¹⁶ And they were brought back to Shechem and buried in the tomb that Abraham had bought for a sum of silver from the sons of Hamor in Shechem.

Genesis 23:17-18 Updated American Standard Version (UASV)

¹⁷ So Ephron's field, which was in Machpelah, which faced Mamre, the field and cave which was in it, and all the trees which were in the field, that were in all its border around, were made over ¹⁸ to Abraham for a possession in the presence of the sons of Heth, before all who went in at the gate of his city.

Genesis 33:19 Updated American Standard Version (UASV)

¹⁹ And he bought the piece of land where he had pitched his tent from the hand of the sons of Hamor, Shechem's father, for one hundred qesitahs.⁴³

Joshua 24:32 Updated American Standard Version (UASV)

³² As for the bones of Joseph, which the sons of Israel brought up from Egypt, they buried them at Shechem, in the piece of land that Jacob bought from the sons of Hamor the father of Shechem for one hundred qesitahs.⁴⁴ It became an inheritance of the sons of Joseph.

Answer: If we look back to Genesis 12:6-7, we will find that Abraham's first stop after entering Canaan from Haran was Shechem. It is here that Jehovah told Abraham: "To your offspring I will give this land." At this point Abraham built an altar to Jehovah. It seems reasonable that Abraham would need to purchase this land that had not yet been given to his offspring. While it is true that the Old Testament does not mention this purchase, it is likely that Stephen would be aware of such by way of oral tradition. As Acts chapter seven demonstrates, Stephen had a wide-ranging knowledge of Old Testament history.

---

⁴³ Or *pieces of money*; money of unknown value

⁴⁴ Or *pieces of money*; money of unknown value

Later, Jacob would have had difficulty laying claim to the tract of land that his grandfather Abraham had purchased, because there would have been a new generation of inhabitants of Shechem. This would have been many years after Abraham moved further south and Isaac moved to Beersheba, and including Jacob's twenty years in Paddan-aram (Gen 28:6, 7). The simplest answer is that this land was not in use for about 120 years because of Abraham's extensive travels and Isaac's having moved away, leaving it unused; likely it was put to use by others. So, Jacob simply repurchased what Abraham had bought over a hundred years earlier. This is very similar to the time Isaac had to repurchase the well at Beersheba that Abraham had already purchased earlier. – Genesis 21:27–30; 26:26–32.

Genesis 33:18–20 tells us that 'Jacob bought this land for a hundred pieces of money, from the sons of Hamor.' This same transaction is also mentioned at Joshua 24:32, in reference to transporting Joseph's bones from Egypt, to be buried in Shechem.

We should also address the cave of Machpelah that Abraham had purchased in Hebron from Ephron the Hittite. The word "tomb" is not mentioned until Joshua 24:32, and is in reference to the tract of land in Shechem. Nowhere in the Old Testament does it say that Abraham bought a "tomb." The cave of Machpelah obtained by Abraham would eventually become a family tomb, receiving Sarah's body and, eventually, his own, and those of Isaac, Rebekah, Jacob, and Leah. (Genesis 23:14–19; 25:9; 49:30, 31; 50:13) Gleason L. Archer, Jr., concludes this Bible difficulty, saying:

> The reference to a *mnema* ("tomb") in connection with Shechem must either have been proleptic [to anticipate] for the later use of that shechemite tract for Joseph's tomb (i.e., 'the tomb that Abraham bought' was intended to imply 'the tomb location that Abraham bought"); or else conceivably the dative relative pronoun *ho* was intended elliptically [omission] for *en to topo ho onesato Abraam* ("in the place that Abraham bought") as describing the location of the *mnema* near the Oak of Moreh right outside Shechem. Normally Greek would have used the relative-locative adverb *hou* to express 'in which' or 'where'; but this would have left o*nesato* ("bought") without an object in its own clause, and so *ho* was much more suitable in this context. (Archer 1982, 379–81)

Another solution could be that Jacob is being viewed as a representative of Abraham, for he is the grandson of Abraham. This was quite appropriate in Biblical times, to attribute the purchase to Abraham as the Patriarchal family head.

Critic: 2 Samuel 24:1 says that God moved David to count the Israelites, while 1 Chronicles 21:1 Satan, or a resister did. This would seem to be a clear mistake on the part of one of these authors.

2 Samuel 24:1 Updated American Standard Version (UASV)

¹ Now again the anger of Jehovah burned against Israel, and it incited David against them to say, "Go, number Israel and Judah."

1 Chronicles 21:1 Updated American Standard Version (UASV)

¹ Then Satan stood up against Israel and moved David to number Israel.

Answer: In this period of David's reign, Jehovah was very displeased with Israel, and therefore he did not prevent Satan from bringing this sin on them. Often in Scripture, it is spoken of as though God did something when he allowed an event to take place. For example, it is said that God 'hardened Pharaoh's heart' (Exodus 4:21), when he actually allowed the Pharaoh's heart to harden.

Inerrancy: Are There Scientific Errors?

Many truths about God are beyond the scope of science. Science and the Bible are not at odds. In fact, we can thank modern day science as it has helped us to better under the creation of God, from our solar system to the universes, to the human body and mind. What we find is a level of order, precision, design, and sophistication, which points to a Designer, the eyes of many Christians, to an Almighty God, with infinite intelligence and power. The apostle Paul makes this all too clear, when he writes, "For his invisible attributes, namely, his eternal power and divine nature, have been clearly perceived, ever since the creation of the world, in the things that have been made. So they are without excuse." – Romans 1:20.

Back in the seventeenth century, the world-renowned scientist Galileo proved beyond any doubt that the earth was not the center of the universe, nor did the sun orbit the earth. In fact, he proved it to be the other way around (no pun intended), with the earth revolving around the sun. However, he was brought up on charges of heresy by the Catholic Church and ordered to recant his position. Why? From the viewpoint of the Catholic Church, Galileo was contradicting God's Word, the Bible. As it turned out, Galileo and science were correct, and the Church was wrong, for which it issued a formal apology in 1992. However, the point we wish to make here is that in all the controversy, the Bible was never in the wrong. It was a misinterpretation on the part of the Catholic Church and not a fault with the Bible. One will find no place in the Bible that claims the sun orbits the earth. So where would the Church get such an idea? The Church got such an idea from Ptolemy (b. about 85 C.E.), an ancient astronomer, who argued for such an idea.

As it usually turns out, the so-called contradiction between science and God's Word lies at the feet of those who are interpreting Scripture incorrectly. To repeat the sentiments of Galileo when writing to a pupil–Galileo expressed the same sentiments: "Even though Scripture cannot err, its interpreters and expositors can, in various ways. One of these, very serious and very frequent, would be when they always want to stop at the purely literal sense."[45] I believe that today's scholars, in hindsight, would have no problem agreeing.

While the Bible is not a science textbook, it is scientifically accurate when it touches on matters of science.

The Circle of the Earth Hangs on Nothing

Isaiah 40:22 Updated American Standard Version (UASV)

[22] It is he who sits above **the circle of the earth**,
and its inhabitants are like grasshoppers;
who stretches out the heavens like a curtain,
and spreads them like a tent to dwell in.

More than 2,500 years ago, the prophet Isaiah wrote that the earth is a circle or sphere. First, how would it be possible for Isaiah to know the earth is a circle or sphere, if not from inspiration? Scientific America writes, "As countless photos from space can attest, Earth is round–the "Blue Marble," as astronauts have affectionately dubbed it. Appearances, however, can be deceiving. Planet Earth is not, in fact, perfectly round."[46] Scientifically speaking, the sun is not perfectly, absolutely 100 percent round but in everyday speech, this verse is both acceptable and accurate, when we keep in mind it is written from a human perspective, not from a scientific perspective. Moreover, Isaiah was not discussing astronomy; he was simply making an inspired observation that man came to realize once he was in space, looking back at the earth, it is round. See the section about title, "Intended Meaning of Writer."

Job 26:7 Updated American Standard Version (UASV)

[7] "He stretches out the north over empty space
and hangs the earth on nothing.

Here the author describes the earth as hanging upon nothing. Many have never heard of the Greek mathematician and astronomer Eratosthenes. He was born in about 276 B.C.E. and received some of his education in Athens, Greece. In 240 B.C., the "Greek astronomer, geographer, mathematician and librarian Eratosthenes calculates the Earth's circumference. His data was rough, but he wasn't far off."[47] While man very early on used their God given intelligence to arrive at some outstanding conclusion that was actually very accurate, we learn two points here. Eratosthenes was a very astute scientist, while Isaiah, who wrote some 500 years

---

[45] Letter from Galileo to Benedetto Castelli, December 21, 1613.

[46] Charles Q. Choi (April 12, 2007). Scientific America. Strange but True: Earth Is Not Round. Retrieved Monday, August 03, 2015.

http://www.scientificamerican.com/article/earth-is-not-round/

[47] Alfred, Randy (June 19, 2008). "June 19, 240 B.C.E: The Earth Is Round, and It's This Big". Wired. Retrieved Monday, August 03, 2015.

earlier, was no scientist at all. Moreover, Moses, who wrote the book of Job over 1,230 years before Eratosthenes, knew that the earth hung upon nothing.

How Is the Sun Standing Still Possible?

Joshua 10:13 Updated American Standard Version (UASV)

¹³ And the sun stood still, and the moon stopped,
   until the nation avenged themselves of their enemies.

Is this not written in the Book of Jashar? The sun stopped in the midst of heaven and did not hurry to set for about a whole day.

The Canaanites had besieged the Gibeonites, a group of people that gained Jehovah God's backing because they had faith in Him. In this battle, Jehovah helped the Israelites continue their attack by causing "the sun [to stand] still, and the moon stopped, until the nation took vengeance on their enemies." (Jos 10:1-14) Those who accept God as the creator of the universe and life can accept that he would know a way of stopping the earth from rotating. However, there are other ways of understanding this account. We must keep in mind that the Bible speaks from an earthly observer point of view, so it need not be that he stopped the rotation. It could have been a refraction of solar and lunar light rays, which would have produced the same effect.

Psalm 136:6 Updated American Standard Version (UASV)

⁶ to him who spread out the earth above the waters,
   for his lovingkindness is everlasting;

Hebrews 3:4 Updated American Standard Version (UASV)

⁴ For every house is built by someone, but the builder of all things is God.

2 Kings 20:8-11 Updated American Standard Version (UASV)

⁸ And Hezekiah said to Isaiah, "What shall be the sign that Jehovah will heal me, and that I shall go up to the house of Jehovah on the third day?" ⁹ And Isaiah said, "This shall be the sign to you from Jehovah, that Jehovah will do the thing that he has spoken: shall the shadow go forward ten steps or go back ten steps?" ¹⁰ And Hezekiah answered, "It is an easy thing for the shadow to decline ten steps; no, but let the shadow turn backward ten steps." ¹¹ And Isaiah the prophet cried to Jehovah, and he brought the shadow on the steps back ten steps, by which it had gone down on the steps of Ahaz.

How is it that the stars fought on behalf of Barak?

Judges 5:20 Updated American Standard Version (UASV)

²⁰ From heaven the stars fought, from their courses they fought against Sisera.

Judges 4:15 Updated American Standard Version (UASV)

¹⁵ And Jehovah routed Sisera and all his chariots and all his army with the edge of the sword before Barak; and Sisera alighted from his chariot and fled away on foot.

In the Bible, you have Biblical prose, and Biblical poetry.

Prose: language that is not poetry: (1) writing or speech in its normal continuous form, without the rhythmic or visual line structure of poetry **(2)** ordinary style of expression: writing or speech that is ordinary or matter-of-fact, without embellishment.

Poetry: literature in verse: (1) literary works written in verse, in particular verse writing of high quality, great beauty, emotional sincerity or intensity, or profound insight **(2) beauty or grace:** something that resembles poetry in its beauty, rhythmic grace, or imaginative, elevated, or decorative style.

We have a beautiful example of both of these forms of writing communication in chapters four and five of the book of Judges. Judges, Chapter 4 is a prose account of Deborah and Barak, while Judges Chapter 5 is a poetic account. As we have learned from the above, poetry is less concerned with accuracy than evoking emotions. Poetry has a license to say things like what we find in of 5:20, which is in the poetry chapter: "from heaven the stars fought." This can be said, and the reader is expected not to take the language literally. What we can surmise from it though, is that God was acting against Sisera in some way, there was divine intervention.

Procedures for Handling Biblical Difficulties

1. You need to be completely convinced a reason or understanding exists.

2. You need to have total trust and conviction in the inerrancy of the Scripture as originally written down.

3. You need to study the context and framework of the verse carefully, to establish what the author meant by the words he used. In other words, find the beginning and the end of the context that your passage falls within.

4. You need to understand exegesis: find the historical setting, determine author intent, study key words, and note parallel passages. You need to slow down and carefully read the account, considering exactly what is being said

5. You need to find a reasonable harmonization of parallel passages.

6. You need to consider a variety of trusted Bible commentaries, dictionaries, lexical sources, encyclopedias, as well as books on Bible difficulties.

7. You should investigate as to whether the difficulty is a transmission error in the original text.

8. You must always keep in mind that the historical accuracy of the biblical text is unmatched; that thousands of extant manuscripts some of which date back to the second century B.C. support the transmitted text of Scripture.

9. We must keep in mind that the Bible is a diverse book when it comes to literary styles: narrative, poetic, prophetic, and apocalyptic; also containing parables, metaphors, similes, hyperbole, and other figures of speech. Too often, these alleged errors are the result of a reader taking a figure of speech as literal or reading a parable as though it is a narrative.

10. The Bible student needs to understand what level that the Bible intends to be exact in what is written. If Jim told a friend that 650 graduated with him from high school in 1984, it is not challenged, because it is all too clear that he is using rounded numbers and is not meaning to be precise.

YOUR GUIDE FOR DEFENDING THE BIBLE

CHAPTER 17 View of Bible Difficulties

By R. A. Torrey

Updated By Edward D. Andrews

Every careful student and every thoughtful reader of the Bible finds that the words of the Apostle Peter concerning the Scriptures, that there are some things in them hard to be understood is true. The apostle Peter says of Paul's letters, "as also in all his [Paul's] letters, speaking in them of these things, in which are some things **hard to understand**, which the untaught and unstable distort, as they do also the rest of the Scriptures, to their own destruction." (2 Peter 3:16, UASV) If this were true of Peter, how much more so of us 2,000 years removed, of a different language and culture? This is abundantly true for us! Who of us has not found things in the Bible that have puzzled us, yes, that in our early Christian experience have led us to question whether the Bible was, after all, the Word of God? We find some things in the Bible, which it seems impossible to reconcile with other things in the Bible. We find some things, which seem incompatible with the thought that the whole Bible is of divine origin and absolutely inerrant.

It is not wise to attempt to conceal the fact that these difficulties exist. It is the part of wisdom, as well as of honesty, to frankly face them and consider them.

What shall we say concerning these difficulties that every thoughtful student will eventually encounter?

The first thing we have to say about these difficulties in the Bible is that from the very nature of the case *difficulties are to be expected*.

Some people are surprised and staggered because there are difficulties in the Bible. For my part, I would be more surprised and staggered if there were not. What is the Bible? It is a revelation of the mind and will and character and being of an infinitely great, perfectly wise and absolutely holy God. God, Himself is the Author of this revelation. However, one would ask, to who specifically is the revelation made? To men, to finite beings who are imperfect in intellectual development and consequently in knowledge, and who are imperfect in character and consequently in spiritual discernment. The wisest man measured on the scale of eternity is only a babe, and the holiest man compared with God is only an infant in moral development.

Therefore, there must from the very necessities of the case, be difficulties in such a revelation from such a source made to such persons. In addition, when the finite is attempting to understand the infinite, there is bound to be a difficulty. When the ignorant contemplate the utterances of one perfect in knowledge, there must be many things hard to be understood, and some things, which to their immature and inaccurate minds appear absurd. When beings whose moral judgments as to the hatefulness of sin and as to the awfulness of the penalty that it demands, listen to the demands of an absolutely holy Being, they are bound to be staggered at some of His demands, and when they consider His dealings, they are bound to be staggered at some of His dealings. These dealings will appear too severe, too stern, and too harsh.

It is plain that there must be difficulties for us in such a revelation as the Bible has proved to be. If someone should hand me a book that was as simple to me as the multiplication table, and say, "This is the Word of God; in it He has revealed His whole will and wisdom," I should shake my head and say, "I cannot believe it; that is too easy to be a perfect revelation of infinite wisdom." There must be in any complete revelation of God's mind and will and character and being, things hard for the beginner to understand; and the wisest and best of us are but beginners.

The second thing to be said about these difficulties is that a difficulty in a doctrine, or a grave objection to a doctrine, does not in any way prove the doctrine untrue.

Many people think that it does. If they come across some difficulty in the way of believing in the divine origin and absolute inerrancy and infallibility of the Bible, they at once conclude that the doctrine is exploded. That is very illogical. They should stop a moment and think, and learn to be reasonable and fair.

There is scarcely a doctrine in science generally believed today, that has not had some great difficulty in the way of its acceptance.

When the Copernican theory (the earth revolves around the sun and not vice versa), now so universally accepted, was first proclaimed, it encountered a very grave difficulty. If this theory were true, the planet Venus should have phases as the moon has, but the best glass could discover no phases then in existence. However, the positive argument for the theory was so strong that it was accepted in spite of this apparently unanswerable objection. When a more powerful glass was made, it was found that Venus had phases after all. The whole difficulty arose, as most; all of those in the Bible arise, from man's ignorance of some of the facts in the case.

The nebular hypothesis (the formation of the solar system) is commonly accepted in the scientific world today. Nevertheless, when this theory was first announced, and for a long time afterward, the movements of the planet Uranus could not be reconciled with the theory. Uranus seemed to move in just the opposite direction from that in which it was thought it ought to move in accordance with the demands of the theory. However, the positive arguments for the theory were so strong that it was accepted in spite of the inexplicable movements of Uranus.

If we apply to Bible study the commonsense logic recognized in every department of science (with the exception of Biblical criticism, if that be a science), then we must demand that if the positive proof of a theory is conclusive, it must be believed by rational men in spite of any number of difficulties in minor details. He is a shallow thinker who gives up a well-attested truth because there are some apparent facts, which he cannot reconcile with that truth. In addition, he is a very shallow Bible scholar who gives up his belief in the divine origin and inerrancy of the Bible because there are some supposed facts that he cannot reconcile with that doctrine. There are in the theological world today many shallow thinkers of that kind.

The third thing to be said about the difficulties in the Bible is: there are many more, and much greater, difficulties in the way of the doctrine that holds the Bible to be of human origin, and hence fallible, than there are in the way of the doctrine that holds the Bible to be of divine origin, and hence infallible.

Turning the Tables

Oftentimes a man will put forth some difficulty and say, "How do you explain that, if the Bible is the Word of God?" You may not be able to answer him satisfactorily. Then he thinks he has you cornered. Not at all, turn on him, and ask him, "How do you account for the fulfilled prophecies of the Bible if it is of human origin? How do you account for the marvelous unity of the Book? How do you account for its inexhaustible depth? How do you account for its unique power in lifting men up to God?" For every insignificant objection he can bring to your view of the Bible, you can bring very many more deeply significant objections to his view of the Bible. Moreover, any candid man who desires to know and obey the truth will have no difficulty in deciding between the two views.

Some time ago a young man, who was of a bright mind and unusually well read in skeptical, critical, and agnostic literature, told me he had given the matter a great deal of candid and careful thought, and as a result, he could not believe the Bible was of divine origin.

I asked him, "Why not?"

He pointed to a certain teaching of the Bible that he could not and would not believe to be true.

I replied, "Suppose for a moment that I could not answer that specific difficulty; that would not prove that the Bible is not of divine origin. I can bring you many things far more difficult to account for on the hypothesis that the Bible is not of divine origin than on the hypothesis that the Bible is of divine origin. You cannot deny the fact of fulfilled prophecy. How do you account for it if the Bible is not God's Word? You cannot shut eyes to the marvelous unity of the sixty-six books of the Bible, written under such divergent circumstances and at periods of time so remote from one another. How do you account for it if God is not the real Author of the Book back of the forty or more human authors? You cannot deny that the Bible has a power—to save men from sin, to bring men peace and hope and joy, to lift men up to God—that all other books taken together do not possess. How do you account for it if the Bible is not the Word of God in a sense that no other book is the Word of God?"

The objector did not answer. The difficulties that confront one who denies that the Bible is of divine origin and authority are far more numerous and vastly more weighty than those which confront the one who believes it to be of divine origin and authority.

The fourth thing to be said about the difficulties in the Bible is: *the fact that you cannot solve a difficulty does not prove it cannot be solved, and the fact that you cannot answer an objection does not prove at all that it cannot be answered.*

It is remarkable how often we overlook this very evident fact. There are many, who meet a difficulty in the Bible and give it a little thought and can see no possible solution, at once jump to the conclusion that a solution is impossible, and so they give up their faith in the inerrancy of the Bible and in its divine origin. Any man should have a sufficient amount of modesty, being so limited in knowledge, to say, "Though I see no possible solution to this difficulty, someone a little wiser than I might easily find one."

If we would only bear in mind that we do not know everything, and there are a great many things that we cannot solve now which we could very easily solve if we only knew a little more, it would save us from all this foolishness. We ought never to forget that there may be a very easy solution to infinite wisdom even for that which to our finite wisdom—or ignorance—appears unsolvable. What would we think of a beginner in algebra who, having tried in vain for half an hour to solve a difficult problem, declared that there was no possible solution to the problem because he could find none!

A man of unusual experience and ability one day left his work and drove a long distance to see me, as he was in great uneasiness of mind because he had discovered what he believed to be a flat contradiction in the Bible. He had lain awake all night thinking about it. It had defied all his attempts at reconciliation, but when he had fully stated the case to me, in very few moments I showed him a very simple and satisfactory solution of the difficulty. He went away with a happy heart. Nevertheless, why had it not occurred to him at the outset that, though it appeared impossible to him to find a solution, after all, someone else might easily discover a solution? He supposed that the difficulty was an entirely new one, but it was one that had been faced and answered long before either he or I were born.

The fifth thing to be said about the difficulties in the Bible is that *the seeming defects of the Book are exceedingly insignificant when put in comparison with its many and marvelous areas of excellence.*

It certainly reveals great perversity of both mind and heart that men spend so much time focusing on and exaggerating such insignificant points, which they consider defects in the Bible, and pass absolutely unnoticed the incomparable beauties and wonders that adorn and glorify almost every page. This is even taking place in some prominent institutions of learning, where men are supposed to be taught to appreciate and understand the Bible and where they are sent to be trained to preach its truth to others. These institutions are spending much more time on minute and insignificant points that seem to point toward an entirely human origin of the Bible than is spent on studying and understanding and admiring the unparalleled glories that make this Book stand apart from all other books in the world. What would we think of any man who in studying some great masterpiece of art concentrated his whole attention upon what looked like a flyspeck in the corner? A large proportion of the much boasted about "critical study of the Bible" is a laborious and scholarly investigation of supposed flyspecks. The man who is **not** willing to squander the major portion of his time in this intellectualized investigation of flyspecks but prefers to devote it to the study of the unrivaled beauties and majestic splendors of the Book is counted in some quarters as not being "scholarly and up to date."

The sixth thing to be said about the difficulties in the Bible is that *they have far more weight with superficial readers than with profound students.*

Take a man like Colonel Ingersoll, who was very ignorant of the real contents and meaning of the Bible, or that class of modern preachers who read the Bible for the most part for the sole purpose of finding texts to serve as pegs to hang their own ideas. To such superficial readers of the Bible these difficulties seem of immense importance, but to one who has learned to meditate upon the Word of God day and night they have scarcely any weight at all. That rare man of God, George Müller, who had carefully studied the Bible from beginning to end more than one hundred times, was not disturbed by any difficulties he encountered; but to the man who is reading it through for the first or second time there are many things that perplex and stagger.

The seventh thing to be said about the difficulties in the Bible is that *they rapidly disappear upon careful and prayerful study.*

How many things there are in the Bible that once puzzled and staggered us, but which have since been perfectly cleared up and no longer present any difficulty whatever! Every year of study finds these difficulties disappear more and more rapidly. At first, they go by ones, and then by twos, and then by dozens, and then by scores. Is it not reasonable then to suppose that the difficulties that remain will all disappear upon further study?

CHAPTER 18 Some Types of Bible Difficulties

By R. A. Torrey

Updated by Edward D. Andrews

All the difficulties found in the Bible can be included under ten general headings:

The Text from Which our English Bible was Translated

No one, as far as I know, holds that the English translation of the Bible is absolutely infallible and inerrant. The doctrine held by many is that the Scriptures as originally given were absolutely infallible and inerrant, and that our English translation is a *substantially accurate* rendering of the Scriptures as originally given.

We do not possess the original manuscripts of the Bible. These original manuscripts were copied many times with great care and exactness, but naturally, some errors crept into the copies that were made. We now possess so many good copies that by comparing one with another, we can tell with great precision just what the original text was. Indeed, for all practical purposes the original text is now settled.

Update: After Torrey's death in 1928, we have made the extremely important discovery over 100 papyrus manuscripts that date before 300 C.E. Quite a few date to the second century, with one small fragment being dated to about 125 C.E. The modern textual scholar can now say with certainty that we have establish the Greek New Testament to a ninety-nine percent reflect of the originally publish book(s). Moreover, we have more than 100 English translations today, with many of them being a very good representation of the Hebrew and Greek in English: NASB, ESV, HCSB, LEB, and especially the UASV. **Edward D. Andrews**

There is not one important doctrine which hangs upon any doubtful reading of the text. However, when our Authorized Version (KJV) was published in 1611, some of the best manuscripts were not within reach of the translators, and the science of textual criticism was not so well understood as it is today, and so the translation was made from an imperfect text. Not a few of the apparent difficulties in the Bible arise from this source.

For example, we are told in John 5:4 that "an angel went down at a certain season into the pool and troubled the water: whosoever then first after the troubling of the water stepped in was made whole of whatsoever disease he had." This statement for many reasons seems improbable and difficult to believe, but upon investigation, we find that it is all a mistake of the copyist. Some early copyists, reading John's account, added in the margin his explanation of the healing properties of this intermittent medicinal spring. A late copyist embodied this marginal note in the body of the text, and so it came to be handed down and got into the Authorized Version (KJV). Very properly, it has been omitted from the Revised Version.

Note: It is omitted from almost all of our modern-day translations as well, with the exception of the NASB and the HCSB, which retained it out of esteem to the KJV. **Edward D. Andrews**

The discrepancies in figures in different accounts of the same events as, for example, the differences in the ages of some of the kings as given in the text of Kings and Chronicles, doubtless arise from the same cause, errors of copyists. Such an error in the matter of figures would be very easy to make, as in the Hebrew; letters, and letters that appear very much alike have a very different value as figures denote numbers. For example, the first letter in the Hebrew alphabet denotes one, and with two little points above it, no larger than flyspecks, it denotes a thousand. The twenty-third or last letter of the Hebrew alphabet denotes four hundred, but the eighth letter of the Hebrew alphabet that looks very much like it and could be easily mistaken for it, denotes eight. A very slight error of the copyist would therefore make an utter change in figures. The remarkable thing when one contemplates the facts in the case is that so few errors of this kind have been made.

Inaccurate Translations

For example, in Matthew 12:40 Jonah is spoken of as being in "the whale's belly." Many a skeptic has made a mockery over the thought of a whale with the peculiar construction of its mouth and throat swallowing a man. However, if the skeptic had only taken the trouble to look the matter up, he would have found the word translated "whale" really means "sea monster" [or great fish] without any definition as to the character of the sea monster. We will take this up more in detail in considering the story of Jonah. Therefore, the whole difficulty arose from the translator's mistake and the skeptic's ignorance. Many skeptics today are so densely ignorant of matters clearly understood by many Sunday school children that they are still harping in the name of scholarship on this supposed error in the Bible.

False Interpretations of the Bible

What the Bible teaches is one thing, and what men interpret it to mean is oftentimes something widely different. Many difficulties that we have with the Bible arise not from what the Bible actually says, but from what men interpret it to mean.

A striking illustration of this is found in Genesis 1. If we were to take the interpretation put upon this chapter by many, it would indeed be difficult to reconcile it with much that modern science regards as established. However, the difficulty is not with what Genesis 1 says, but with the interpretation put upon it. There is no contradiction whatever between what is really proven by science and what is really said in Genesis 1.

Another difficulty of the same character is with Jesus' statement that He would be three days and three nights in the heart of the earth. Many interpreters would have us believe that He died Friday and rose early Sunday morning, and the time between these two is far from being three days and three nights. However, it is a matter of biblical interpretation, and the trouble is not with what the Bible actually says, but with the interpretation that men put upon the Bible. We will take this matter up at length below by Edward D. Andrews.

Matthew 12:40 How many days was Jesus in the tomb?

Some argue for three days, based on Jesus' words,

Matthew 12:40 English Standard Version (ESV)

⁴⁰ For just as Jonah was three days and three nights in the belly of the great fish, so will the Son of Man be three days and three nights in the heart of the earth.

This would seem to suggest a full 72 hours. However, we should not set aside similar expressions that may allow us to get at the intent of the words. Many times in Scripture, three days does not always mean a full 72 hours of three days. For example, look at the words of Rehoboam,

1 Kings 12:5, 12 English Standard Version (ESV)

⁵ He said to them, "Go away for three days, then come again to me." So the people went away. ¹² So Jeroboam and all the people came to Rehoboam the third day, as the king said, "Come to me again the third day."

You see that the king told the people to go away for three days, and then return to him. But you also will notice that they returned on the third day, which was not a full 72 hours of three days. Now, consider what Jesus said of himself, something that Scripture repeatedly says,

Luke 24:46 English Standard Version (ESV)

⁴⁶ and said to them, "Thus it is written, that the Christ should suffer and **on the third day** rise from the dead

Now, if he had remained in the grave for a full 72 hours of three days, it mean that he would have been raised on the fourth day. Jewish days ran from sundown to sundown. Jesus died on Friday afternoon about 3:00 p.m., Nisan 14, 33 C.E.

- Jesus' death Friday Nisan 14, about 3:00 p.m. (Matt 27:31-56; Mk 15:20-41; Lu 23:26-49; Jn 19:16-30)

- Jesus was in Tomb before sundown Friday evening (Matt 27:57-61; Mk 15:42-47; Lu 23:50-56; Jn 19:31-42)
- Jesus in tomb all of Nisan 15th from sundown Friday to sundown Saturday, which began Nisan 16 (Matt 27:62-66)
- Jesus resurrected early Sunday morning of Nisan 16th (Matt 28:1; Mk 16:1; Lu 24:1; Jn 20:1)

Therefore, Jesus was dead and in the tomb for at least a period of time on Friday Nisan 14, was still in the tomb during the course of the whole day of Nisan 15, and spent the nighttime hours of Nisan 16 in the tomb.

- Now after the Sabbath, toward the dawn of the first day of the week, Mary Magdalene and the other Mary went to see the tomb. (Matt 28:1)
- When the Sabbath was past, Mary Magdalene, Mary the mother of James, and Salome bought spices, so that they might go and anoint him. (Mk 16:1)
- But on the first day of the week, at early dawn, they went to the tomb, taking the spices they had prepared. (Lu 24:1)
- Now on the first day of the week Mary Magdalene came to the tomb early, while it was still dark, and saw that the stone had been taken away from the tomb. (Jn 20:1)

Certain women came to the tomb on Sunday morning, it was still dark, he had already been resurrected. Thus, Jesus had been in the tomb for parts of three days.

A Wrong Conception of the Bible

Many think that when we say the Bible is the Word of God, of divine origin and authority, we mean that God is the speaker in every utterance it contains; but this is not what is meant at all. Oftentimes, it simply records what others say, i.e., what good men say, what bad men say, what inspired men say, what uninspired men say, what angels and demons say, and even what the devil says. The record of what they said is from God and absolutely true, but what those other persons are recorded as saying may be true or may not be true. It is true that they said it, but what they said may not be true.

For example, the devil is recorded in Genesis 3:4 as saying, "You will not surely die." It is true that the devil said it, but what the devil said is not true, but an infamous lie that shipwrecked our race. That the devil said it is God's Word, but what the devil said is not God's word but the devil's word. It is God's Word that this was the devil's word.

Very many careless readers of the Bible do not notice who is talking, God, good men, bad men, inspired men, uninspired men, angels or devil. They will tear a verse right out of its context regardless of the speaker and say, "There, God said that." However, God said nothing of the kind. God's Word says that the devil said it or a bad man said it or a good man said it or an inspired man said it, or an uninspired man said it, or an angel said it. What God says is true, namely, that the devil said it, or a bad man, or a good man, or an inspired man, or an uninspired man, or an angel. However, what they said may or may not be true.

It is very common to hear men quote what Eliphaz, Bildad or Zophar said to Job as if it were necessarily God's own words because it is recorded in the Bible, in spite of the fact that God disavowed their teaching and said to them, "you have not spoken of me what is right" (Job 42:7). It is true that these men said the thing that God records them as saying, but often they gave the truth a twist and said what is not right. A very large share of our difficulties thus arises from not noticing who is speaking. The Bible always tells us, and we should always note it. Below, under the subheadings of "the Case of Job" and "The Comforters" Andrews demonstrates how the erroneous interpretations come about.

The Case of Job

What we have covered thus far will help us understand one of the more complex books of the Bible, the book of Job.

Job was a "blameless and upright man, who fears God and turns away from evil." Job was living the happy life; he had seven sons and the daughters. He was a wealthy landowner. "He possessed 7,000 sheep, 3,000 camels, 500 yoke of oxen, and 500 female donkeys, and very many servants, so that this man was the greatest of all the people of the east." (1:3) Even so, he is not a materialistic person; he was simply following a proverb like the above, 'if you work hard, your efforts will be blessed.'

Job 1:13-19; 2:7-8 English Standard Version (ESV)

[13]Now there was a day when his sons and daughters were eating and drinking wine in their oldest brother's house, [14]and there came a messenger to Job and said, "The oxen were plowing and the donkeys feeding beside them, [15]and the Sabeans fell upon them and took them and struck down the servants with the edge of the sword, and I alone have escaped to tell you." [16]While he was yet speaking, there came another and said, "The fire of God fell from heaven and burned up the sheep and the servants and consumed them, and I alone have escaped to tell you." [17]While he was yet speaking, there came another and said, "The Chaldeans formed three groups and made a raid on the camels and took them and struck down the servants with the edge of the sword, and I alone have escaped to tell you." [18]While he was yet speaking, there came another and said, "Your sons and daughters were eating and drinking wine in their oldest brother's house, [19]and behold, a great wind came across the wilderness and struck the four corners of the house, and it fell upon the young people, and they are dead, and I alone have escaped to tell you." [2:7]So Satan went out from the presence of the LORD and struck Job with loathsome sores from the sole

of his foot to the crown of his head. ⁸And he took a piece of broken pottery with which to scrape himself while he sat in the ashes.

The Comforters

Job 4:7-8 English Standard Version (ESV)

⁷"Remember: who that was innocent ever perished? Or where were the upright cut off? ⁸As I have seen, those who plow iniquity and sow trouble reap the same.

Eliphaz in an attempt at dealing with Job's atrocities assumes Job's tragedies are a result of his own actions. Eliphaz has reasoned wrong by taking a proverb and making it an absolute. In essence, he asks Job, 'do those that are innocent die? When have those that live a righteous life been destroyed?' Eliphaz goes on by saying, 'my experience suggests that it is those who are doing wrong and entertain bad that will get back what they gave out.' In other words, Eliphaz is assuming that only the wicked reap bad times.

Job 5:15 English Standard Version (ESV)

¹⁵But he saves the needy from the sword of their mouth and from the hand of the mighty.

Eliphaz again assumes that Job is at fault. Eliphaz is assuming that it was Job's great riches, which were ill gotten, and this is why he is suffering. Is Eliphaz's statement wrong in and of itself? No, God does rescue the poor from the oppressive, by their following his counsel on the right way to live. However, this is no absolute; saying all who live by God's will and purposes will never be mistreated. Moreover, the whole idea is misplaced, in that maybe Job is the rich oppressor and this is his punishment from God.

Job 8:3-6 English Standard Version (ESV)

³Does God pervert justice? Or does the Almighty pervert the right? ⁴If your children have sinned against him, he has delivered them into the hand of their transgression.⁵If you will seek God and plead with the Almighty for mercy, ⁶if you are pure and upright, surely then he will rouse himself for you and restore your rightful habitation.

Bildad too is stating true statements, but in absolute terms that are misplaced when it comes to Job, or anyone. Certainly, God does not pervert justice. Therefore, Bildad is right on that, but his application and understanding is what is twisted, as he assumes that children died because they had sinned, and justice was being meted out to them. Again, in verse 5-6, we have a true thought, in that if one is in an impure state, and turns to God with pleadings, he will restore them. However, in verses 5-6, Bildad is assuming that Job is unrighteous, because he sees that proverb as an absolute.

As can be seen from the above, one must be aware that proverbs are not absolutes, but are general truths. True enough, there are likely a couple of exceptions to this rule, but that would not negate this rule, and approach of correct interpretation of proverbs.

In the Psalms, we have sometimes, what God said to man and that is always true; but on the other hand, we often have what man said to God, and that may or may not be true. Sometimes, and far oftener than most of us see, it is the voice of the speaker's personal vengeance or despair. This vengeance may be and often is prophetic, but it may be the wronged man committing his cause to Him to whom vengeance belongs (Romans 12:19), and we are not obliged to defend all that he said. In the Psalms, we have even a record of what the fool said, "There is no God" (Psalm 14:1). Now it is true that the fool said it, but the fool lied when he said it. It is God's Word that the fool said it, but what God reports the fool as saying is not God's own word at all but the fool's own word.

Therefore, in studying our Bible, if God is the speaker we must believe what He says. If an inspired man is the speaker, we must believe what he says. If an uninspired man is the speaker, we must judge for ourselves, it is perhaps true, perhaps false. If it is the devil who is speaking, we do well to remember that he was a liar from the beginning; but even the devil may tell the truth sometimes.

The Language in Which the Bible was Written

The Bible is a book of all ages and for all kinds of people, and therefore it was written in the language that continues the same and is understood by all, the language of the common people and of appearances. It was not written in the terminology of science.

Thus, for example, what occurred at the Battle of Gibeon (Joshua 10:12–14) was described in the way it appeared to those who saw it, and the way in which it would be understood by those who read about it. There is no talk about the refraction of the sun's rays, and so forth, but the sun is said to have *"stood still"* (or tarried) in the midst of heaven. It is one of the perfections of the Bible that it was not written in the terminology of modern science. If it had been, it would never have been understood until the present day, and even now it would be understood only by a few. Furthermore, as science and its terminology are constantly changing, the Bible if written in the terminology of the science of today would be out of date in a few years; but being written in just the language chosen, it has proved the Book for all ages, all lands and all conditions of men.

Other difficulties from the language in which the Bible was written arise from the fact that large portions of the Bible are poetical and are written in the language of poetry, the language of feeling, passion, imagination and figure. Now if a man is hopelessly matter-of-fact, he will inevitably find difficulties with these poetical portions of the inspired Word.

For example, in Psalm 18 we have a marvelous description of a thunderstorm, but let the dull, matter-of-fact fellow get hold of that, for example, verse 8: "Smoke went up from his nostrils, and devouring fire from his mouth; glowing coals flamed forth from him," and he will be head over heels in difficulty at once. However, the trouble is not with the Bible, but with his own stupid, thickheaded plainness.

Our Defective Knowledge of the History, Geography and Usages of Bible Times

For example, in Acts 13:7 Luke speaks of "the deputy" (more accurately "the proconsul," see English Standard Version) of Cyprus. Roman provinces were of two classes, imperial and senatorial. The ruler of the imperial provinces was called a propraetor, of a senatorial province a proconsul. Up to a comparatively recent date, according to the best information we had, Cyprus was an imperial province and therefore its ruler would be a propraetor, but Luke calls him a proconsul. This certainly seemed like a clear case of error on Luke's part, and even the conservative commentators felt forced to admit that Luke was in slight error, and the destructive critics were delighted to find this "mistake." Further and more thorough investigation has brought to light the fact that just at the time of which Luke wrote the senate had made an exchange with the emperor whereby Cyprus had become a senatorial province, and therefore its ruler was a proconsul. Luke was right after all, and the literary critics were themselves in error.

Repeatedly further researches and discoveries, geographical, historical and archaeological, have vindicated the Bible and put to shame its critics. For example, the book of Daniel has naturally been one of the books that unbelievers and destructive critics have most hated. One of their strongest arguments against its authenticity and truthfulness was that such a person as Belshazzar was unknown to history, that all historians agreed that Nabonidus was the last king of Babylon, and that he was absent from the city when it was captured. Therefore, Belshazzar must be a purely mythical character, and the whole story legendary and not historical. Their argument seemed very strong. In fact, it seemed unanswerable. However, Sir H. Rawlinson discovered at Mugheir and other Chaldean sites clay cylinders on which Belshazzar (Belsaruzar) is named by Nabonidus as his eldest son. Doubtless he reigned as regent in the city during his father's absence, an indication of which we have in his proposal to make Daniel third ruler in the kingdom (Daniel 5:16). He himself being second ruler in the kingdom, Daniel would be next to him. So the Bible was vindicated again.

The critics asserted most positively that Moses could not have written the Pentateuch because writing was unknown in his day. However, recent discoveries have proved beyond a question that writing far antedates the time of Moses. So the critics have been compelled to give up their argument, though they have had the bad grace to hold on stubbornly to their conclusion.

The Ignorance of Conditions under Which Books Were Written and Commands Given

For example, to one ignorant of the conditions, God's commands to Israel as to the extermination of the Canaanites seem cruel and horrible. However, when one understands the moral condition to which these nations had sunk, the utter hopelessness of reclaiming them and the weakness of the Israelites themselves, their extermination seems to have been an act of mercy to all succeeding generations and to themselves.

The Many-Sidedness of the Bible

The broadest-minded man is one-sided, but the truth is many-sided, and the Bible is all-sided. Therefore, to our narrow thought one part of the Bible seems to contradict another.

For example, religious men as a rule are either Calvinistic or Arminian in their mental makeup. In addition, some portions of the Bible are decidedly Calvinistic and present great difficulties to the Arminian type of mind, while other portions are decidedly Arminian and present difficulties to the Calvinistic type of mind. However, both sides are true. Many men in our day are broad-minded enough to be able to grasp at the same time the Calvinistic side of the truth and the Arminian side of the truth; but some are not, so the Bible perplexes, puzzles and bewilders them. The trouble is not with the Bible, but with their own lack of capacity for comprehensive thought.

Expansion: These schools of doctrinal positions are initially established religious leaders and their followers, such as John Calvin and Jacob Arminius. There are even more, such as the Lutheran, from Martin Luther, The Wesleyan, from John Wesley, and the Mennonites, from Menno Simons, and Society of Friends (Quakers) under George Fox. Actually, I would disagree with Torrey here, I believe that he should have used his earlier point of argument, it boils down to the truth of the Bible as being absolute, but man may misinterpret that truth. Therefore, it will lay concealed until discovered. This misinterpretation does not refute the infallibility or inerrancy of Scripture. Actually, doctrine plays no part in inerrancy of Scripture. Whether one believes the earth was created in six literal 24-hour days, or six creative periods called days, has no impact on the doctrine of inerrancy. The Bible is inerrant and one of those interpretations is wrong and the other is correct. This has to do with the person interpreting the Bible, not the inerrancy of the Bible. **Edward D. Andrews**

Therefore, Paul seems to contradict James, and James seems sometimes to contradict Paul; and what Paul says in one place seems to contradict what he says in another place. However, the whole trouble is that our narrow minds cannot take in God's large truth.

The Bible has to do with the Infinite, and our Minds are Finite

It is necessarily difficult to put the facts of infinite being into the limited capacity of our finite intelligence, just as it is difficult to put the ocean into a pint cup. To this class of difficulties belong those connected with the Bible doctrines of the Trinity and of the divine-human nature of Christ. To those who forget that God is infinite, the doctrine of the Trinity seems like the mathematical monstrosity of making one equal three. However, when one bears in mind that the doctrine of the Trinity is an attempt to put into forms of finite thought the facts of infinite being, and into material forms of expression the facts of the spirit, the difficulties vanish. The simplicity of the Unitarian conception of God arises from its shallowness.

The Dullness of our Spiritual Perception

The man who is farthest advanced spiritually is still so immature that he cannot expect to see everything yet as an absolutely holy God sees it, unless he takes it upon simple faith in Him. To this class of difficulties belong those connected with the Bible doctrine of eternal punishment. It often seems to us as if this doctrine cannot be true, must not be true, but the whole difficulty arises from the fact that we are still so blind spiritually that we have no adequate conception of the awfulness of sin, and especially of the awfulness of the sin of rejecting the infinitely glorious Son of God. However, when we become so holy, so like God, that we see the enormity of sin as He sees it, we shall have no difficulty with the doctrine of eternal punishment.

Expansion: Torrey is like many other Calvinist or Lutheran minded individuals, he wishes to follow the evidence, but instead, desires to call those, who do not find this doctrine Biblical, spiritually blind. I hope that even the most conservative reader can see that as dismissive. Without arguing the evidence, I will say that once again, the truth is biblical, and we must follow it objectively, and not allow theological bias to cloud our judgment. I am recommending that you read, *WHAT IS HELL? Basic Bible Doctrines of the Christian Faith* by Edward D. Andrews[48]

---

[48] http://www.christianpublishers.org/apps/webstore/products/show/5346167

As we look back over the ten classes of difficulties, we see they all arise from our imperfection, and not from the imperfection of the Bible. The Bible is perfect, but we, being imperfect, have difficulty with it. As we grow more and more into the perfection of God, our difficulties grow ever less and less, and so we are forced to conclude that when we become as perfect as God is, we shall have no more difficulties whatever with the Bible.

CHAPTER 19 Dealing With Bible Difficulties

By R. A. Torrey

Updated By Edward D. Andrews

Honestly

Whenever you find a difficulty in the Bible, frankly, acknowledge it. Do not try to obscure it. Do not try to dodge it. Look it square in the face. Admit it openly and honestly to whoever mentions it. If you cannot give a good, square, honest explanation, do not attempt any at all. In their zeal for the infallibility of the Bible, those who have attempted explanations of difficulties that do not commend themselves to the honest, fair-minded man have done untold harm. People have concluded that if these are the best explanations, there are really no explanations. And the Bible, instead of being helped, has been injured by the unintelligent zeal of foolish friends. Suppose you are not really convinced that the Bible is the Word of God. In that case, you can far better afford to wait for a real solution to a difficulty than you can afford to attempt a solution that is evasive and unsatisfactory.

Humbly

Recognize the limitations of your own mind and knowledge, and do not for a moment imagine that there is no solution just because you have found none. There is, in all probability, a straightforward answer, even when you can find no solution at all.

Determinedly

Make up your mind that you will find the solution if you can by buying out a respectable amount of study time and complex thinking. The difficulties of the Bible are our heavenly Father's challenge to us to set our brains to work. Do not give up searching for a solution because you cannot find it in five minutes or ten minutes. Ponder over it and work over it for days if necessary. The work will be more beneficial than the solution does. There is a solution somewhere, and you will find it if you only search for it long enough and hard enough.

Fearlessly

Do not be frightened when you find a difficulty, no matter how unanswerable or how insurmountable it appears at first sight. Thousands of men have encountered just such difficulties, and still, the old Book has withstood the test of time, being the bestseller that will never be touched, in the untold billions of copies. The Bible that has stood eighteen centuries of rigid examination and incessant and awful assault is not likely to go down before your discoveries or before the discharges of any modern critical guns. To one who is at all familiar with the history of critical attacks on the Bible, the confidence of those contemporary critics who think they are going to annihilate the Bible, at last, is simply amusing.

Patiently

Do not be discouraged because you do not solve every problem in a day. If some difficulty persistently defies your very best efforts at a solution, lay it aside for a while. Later it will likely be resolved, and you will wonder how you were ever perplexed by it.

Scripturally

Nothing explains Scripture like Scripture. If you find a difficulty in one part of the Bible, look for another Scripture to throw light upon it and dissolve it. People repeatedly came to me with some problem in the Bible that had greatly staggered them and asked for a solution. I have given a reasonable, rational answer by simply asking them to read some other chapter and verse, and the simple reading of that scripture has thrown such light upon the passage in question that all the mists have disappeared. The truth has shone as clear as day.

Prayerfully

It is simply incredible how difficulties dissolve when one looks at them on his knees. Not only does God open our eyes in answer to prayer to behold beautiful things out of His Word, but He also opens our eyes to look straight through a difficulty that seemed impenetrable before we prayed. Remember, this is no miracle planting the answer to the Bible difficulty in your mind. It is you buying out the time to research in the Bible and Bible study tools while the Holy Spirit guides (not inspires) you along, and at some point, the light will come on for you. One great reason why many modern Bible scholars have learned to be destructive critics is that they have forgotten how to pray.

YOUR GUIDE FOR DEFENDING THE BIBLE

SECTION 5 HOW TO STUDY THE BIBLE

Digging Deeper

We put books here on this subject if one is interested in taking the subject deeper. This section gives you foundational knowledge to evangelize or engage people in conversation.

HOW TO STUDY YOUR BIBLE: Rightly Handling the Word of God by Edward D. Andrews (2017)

ISBN-13: 978-1945757624

https://www.amazon.com/dp/B075HZX1Y7

HOW to STUDY: Study the Bible for the Greatest Profit by R A Torrey and Edward D Andrews (2016)

ISBN-13: 978-1945757112

https://www.amazon.com/dp/1945757116

DEEP Bible STUDY: The Importance and Value of Proper Bible Study by R A Torrey and Edward D Andrews (2016)

ISBN-13: 978-1945757129

https://www.amazon.com/dp/1945757124

CHAPTER 20 Unlocking the Treasures of Scripture

The Art of Bible Study: Techniques and Approaches

Bible study is not just an academic exercise; it is a sacred endeavor aimed at understanding the mind of God as revealed in the Scriptures. This journey for truth involves specific techniques and approaches that allow us to unlock the treasures found within the Bible's pages. Adhering to a conservative, literal translation philosophy and the Historical-Grammatical method of interpretation, we aim to be both accurate and faithful to the original text.

Textual Analysis

Textual analysis is an indispensable first step in Bible study. This involves examining the words and phrases in their original languages—Hebrew for the Old Testament and Greek for the New Testament. Tools like lexicons, interlinear Bibles, and concordances can be immensely helpful in this regard. For example, the Greek word "agapé" often translated as "love," conveys the essence of moral goodwill. Knowing the specific kind of love can enrich our understanding of passages like John 3:16, "For God so loved (agapé) the world, that he gave his only Son, that whoever believes in him should not perish but have eternal life" (ESV).

Contextual Study

Understanding the context is pivotal in Bible study. This means not only looking at the verses surrounding a passage but also understanding the historical, cultural, and social background. For example, when studying the book of Daniel, knowing the Babylonian exile's historical context aids in comprehending why Daniel and his friends were in Babylon in the first place.

Linguistic Features

Identifying linguistic features like idioms, parallelism, and chiasmus can also offer deeper insights. In Psalm 19:1, "The heavens declare the glory of God, and the sky above proclaims his handiwork" (ESV), the parallelism serves to emphasize the universal testimony of creation to the greatness of God.

Comparing Scripture with Scripture

The principle of "Scriptura Scripturae interpres" (Scripture interprets Scripture) is vital. Scripture is a unified whole, and one part can illuminate another. For example, Isaiah 53's prophecy finds its fulfillment in the New Testament descriptions of Christ's suffering and death, providing a coherent understanding of God's redemptive plan.

Exegetical Approach

Exegesis involves explaining or interpreting the Bible text. Here, the Historical-Grammatical method is crucial, which means we take into account the original languages' syntax and grammar, and we also consider the historical context. For example, understanding the cultural context of 1 Corinthians 11:2-16, which discusses head coverings, helps us differentiate between the timeless principles and the cultural specifics.

Avoiding Eisegesis

Eisegesis is the practice of reading one's own preconceived notions into the text. This is to be avoided at all costs. For example, we must refrain from attributing modern-day geopolitical events to apocalyptic biblical prophecies without thorough exegetical support.

The Use of Commentaries

Commentaries should be used cautiously. While they can provide valuable insights, they should never replace the text of the Scripture itself. Given the wide range of commentaries available, it is advisable to use those aligned with a conservative, literal approach to Scripture.

Application of Doctrine

Understanding the doctrine is essential for practical Christian living. The Epistles, for instance, are rich in doctrine and offer guidelines on how early Christians should conduct themselves. These principles remain relevant today. In studying these doctrinal portions, one should rely on a literal, word-for-word translation to capture the author's intended meaning accurately.

Reliance on Prayer and Humility

The intellectual endeavor should be balanced with spiritual openness. While we don't believe in the indwelling of the Holy Spirit, we do believe that prayerful humility allows us to be guided by the Spirit-inspired Word of God.

In conclusion, the art of Bible study involves a multi-faceted approach that respects the original text and seeks to uncover its meanings faithfully. A conservative, literal translation, like the Updated American Standard Version (UASV), aligned with the Historical-Grammatical method of interpretation, provides the most reliable pathway for this noble endeavor. By diligently applying these techniques and approaches, one can truly unlock the treasures of the Scripture.

Choosing the Right Bible Version: Translation Considerations

Bible translation is a matter of serious import for it deals with the very words of God. The primary concern should always be fidelity to the original languages—Hebrew, Aramaic, and Greek. In line with this, let's look at some key considerations when choosing a Bible version suitable for deep study.

Literal Translation Philosophy

It is imperative to select a translation grounded in a literal, or word-for-word, translation philosophy. The reader should be given what God said through His human authors, as opposed to what a translator believes God meant. This approach respects the reader's role in interpretation and recognizes the significance of each word in the original languages. A literal translation like the Updated American Standard Version (UASV) maintains the complexity and depth of the original text, providing a robust basis for exegesis.

Language Level and Readability

Though a literal translation aims to be as faithful to the original text as possible, it should also be intelligible to the modern reader. A suitable version should be written on a 10th-12th grade level, expecting the readers to invest time to understand the Scripture. After all, spiritual nourishment isn't fast food; it requires thoughtful chewing. Readability, however, shouldn't compromise accuracy.

Textual Basis

Ensure that the translation you choose relies on the best available manuscripts. The importance of this cannot be overstated. The text should be in line with the earliest and most reliable Hebrew and Greek manuscripts. While the Masoretic Text is standard for the Old Testament, the New Testament ideally should be translated from the critical text, which takes into account the most reliable early manuscripts like the Codex Sinaiticus and Codex Vaticanus.

Translator's Credentials and Methodology

While many translations are produced by committees from various denominations, there's a need for caution. Non-denominational efforts focused purely on a rigorous, scholarly translation free from ecumenical or interfaith influences are often the most reliable. The translators should be experts in the biblical languages and conservative in their theology, acknowledging the inerrancy and authority of Scripture.

Doctrinal Neutrality

A good translation doesn't insert doctrinal bias into the text. While complete objectivity is difficult, the translation should minimize interpretation in favor of letting the text speak for itself. For example, translating the Greek word 'gehenna' literally as 'Gehenna' instead of interpreting it as 'hell' allows the reader to investigate its meaning, which may not align with traditional notions of eternal torment but rather eternal destruction.

Annotations and Study Aids

Although this focuses mainly on the text, it's worth mentioning that some Bible versions come with annotations, cross-references, and other study aids. These should be used cautiously and should not replace the text as the primary source of truth. They can, however, provide useful historical and grammatical context that aids in a historical-grammatical method of interpretation.

Examples

1. **Literal Translation**: The UASV renders 2 Timothy 3:16 as, "All Scripture is breathed out by God and profitable for teaching, for reproof, for correction, and for training in righteousness." The phrase "breathed out by God" is a literal translation of the Greek 'theopneustos,' providing a clear basis for understanding the divine origin of Scripture.

2. **Language Level**: The UASV maintains readability without compromising textual integrity. Consider its rendering of Romans 5:12: "Therefore, just as through one man sin entered into the world, and death through sin, and so death spread to all men because all sinned." It's understandable yet preserves the complexities of the original text.

3. **Textual Basis**: The UASV uses the Masoretic Text for the Old Testament and the critical text for the New Testament. This can be seen in how it

handles Old Testament prophecies and New Testament citations, ensuring continuity and fidelity to the most reliable manuscripts.

4. **Doctrinal Neutrality**: An example would be the UASV's handling of passages that discuss the nature of hell. It avoids theological baggage and remains close to what the text actually says, allowing the reader to engage in unbiased study.

In summary, the Bible version you choose should be a literal translation based on the most reliable manuscripts, translated by qualified individuals, and free from doctrinal bias. Only such a version can serve as a reliable basis for unlocking the treasures of Scripture through in-depth study.

Tools for Deeper Understanding: Bible Dictionaries and Encyclopedias, Commentaries, and More

In the endeavor to accurately understand and interpret the Scriptures, having the right tools at one's disposal is vital. These tools, like skilled craftsmen's instruments, help to chisel away human ignorance and prejudice, revealing the raw, untampered truth of God's Word. Below is an overview of some essential resources for rigorous, textual study: Bible dictionaries and encyclopedias, commentaries, and other vital tools for deeper understanding.

Bible Dictionaries and Encyclopedias

Understanding the language, culture, geography, and historical context is paramount for accurate exegesis. Bible dictionaries and encyclopedias are invaluable in this regard. They help clarify terms, provide cultural insights, and often delve into the etymology of words to expose their full range of meaning. For instance, while studying the term "justification" as used by Paul in Romans 5:1 ("Therefore, since we have been justified by faith, we have peace with God through our Lord Jesus Christ."), one can consult a reputable Bible dictionary to understand its Greek root, "dikaios," its historical usage, and its theological implications.

Commentaries

Commentaries offer exegetical insights and scholarly perspectives on individual books or the entire canon of Scripture. However, the utility of a commentary is directly related to the theological perspective and methodological rigor of its author. Given that we approach the text from a literal translation philosophy and the objective Historical-Grammatical method, it is advisable to consult commentaries that also adhere to these principles. Commentaries that offer a verse-by-verse exposition are particularly useful. For example, if one is studying Ephesians 2:8-9, a commentary can elucidate the concept of grace, show how it contrasts with works, and delineate its significance in the larger Pauline corpus.

Lexicons and Interlinear Bibles

If the "primary goal is to be accurate and faithful to the original text," then lexicons and interlinear Bibles are indispensable. Lexicons provide the original Greek or Hebrew words along with their possible meanings. Interlinear Bibles show the English text aligned with the original language text, allowing for immediate comparison. For instance, studying the Greek word "agapé" (love) in 1 Corinthians 13 with the aid of a lexicon can deepen one's understanding of the apostolic concept of love as distinct from other forms of love like "storgé" (familial love) or "philía" (friendship).

Concordances

Concordances list the occurrences of words throughout Scripture, facilitating thematic studies or comprehensive understanding of specific terms. If one wants to study the concept of "faith" throughout Paul's epistles, a concordance makes this task manageable and precise.

Software and Online Resources

In the modern age, various software packages and online resources provide comprehensive tools for Bible study. Software like Logos or Accordance have sophisticated search algorithms, original language tools, and extensive libraries that provide a treasure trove of scholarly resources. However, the theological perspectives of these databases and the works they include should be considered critically.

Importance of Peer-reviewed Journals

Scholarly journals that uphold a high view of Scripture and maintain rigorous peer-review processes are also indispensable tools. They keep the scholar abreast of the latest research and discussions in the field of Biblical Studies.

An accurate understanding of the Scriptures is not a casual undertaking but involves an investment of time and resources. The individual reader must make the commitment to engage with the text thoroughly, employing the best tools available to unpack its rich, multifaceted truths. These tools—Bible dictionaries, commentaries, lexicons, interlinear Bibles, and more—are integral to a rigorous and disciplined study that honors the inerrancy and authority of God's Word. By properly using these resources, one can faithfully uncover the treasures that are waiting to be discovered in the Holy Scriptures.

Creating a Study Plan: Organizing Your Bible Study

A meticulously planned Bible study is essential for extracting the profound treasures that Scripture holds. It allows you to delve deeply into God's Word, examining the text in its original languages, understanding its historical context, and interpreting it correctly through the lens of the Historical-Grammatical method. Let's break down the components of a robust study plan that aids in organizing your Bible study.

1. Determine Your Goals

Before you start with the actual study, it's crucial to articulate your goals. Are you looking to improve your doctrinal understanding, investigate a particular topic, or gain a more profound appreciation for the Biblical text? Identifying the goals sets the direction for your study.

2. Choose the Scripture Portion

Based on your goals, select a specific section of the Bible for detailed study. If you're aiming to dig deep into doctrine, Paul's epistles like Romans or Ephesians could be a starting point. For historical narratives, the books of Samuel or Kings would be beneficial.

3. Translation Selection

For accuracy and fidelity to the original languages, it's best to use a literal translation of the Bible. The Updated American Standard Version (UASV) is one of the most reliable choices, as it provides the reader with what God said via the human authors.

4. Create a Timeline

Your study plan should have a realistic and achievable timeline. Whether it's a 3-month or a 6-month plan, it should be structured but flexible, allowing for an in-depth study without rushing through the text.

5. Gather Study Tools

a) Bible Dictionaries and Encyclopedias: These resources provide lexical and etymological details for keywords in the text. For example, understanding the term "justification" in its original Greek context could be enlightening when studying Romans.

b) Interlinear Bible: An interlinear Bible shows the original language beside the English translation, aiding in word-for-word comparisons.

c) Commentaries: Use conservative commentaries that apply the Historical-Grammatical method. They can provide insights into the cultural and historical context without diluting the authority of Scripture.

d) Concordances: These tools help you locate where specific words appear in the Bible, facilitating thematic studies.

6. Preliminary Reading

Before diving into the text, get an overall grasp by doing a cursory reading. Take note of recurring themes, patterns, or specific words that stand out.

7. In-Depth Study

a) Lexical Analysis: Examine the meaning of key words in the original languages. Use your Bible dictionary and interlinear Bible for this.

b) Contextual Analysis: Consider the historical context of the text. Who was the author, what was the purpose of the writing, and who were the intended readers? For example, understanding the Jewish culture is crucial when studying the Old Testament.

c) Thematic Study: Use your concordance to find other passages that discuss similar themes or ideas. This will offer a well-rounded understanding of the subject matter.

8. Interpretation

Apply the objective Historical-Grammatical method to interpret the text. The meaning of the text is bound by its historical setting and grammatical rules. Take into account the literary style, whether it's poetic, narrative, or epistolary.

9. Synthesis and Application

Having dug deep into the text, summarize your findings. How do they align with broader Scriptural themes? More importantly, what implications do they have for your life?

10. Record Your Insights

Document your observations, findings, and interpretations. These will be valuable for future reference and for sharing your insights with others who seek to delve into the richness of Scripture.

Organizing your Bible study in this systematic manner will not only make your learning experience rewarding but also maintain the integrity of Scripture, honoring its Divine authorship. Remember, we are not reading the Bible to make it align with our beliefs; we are studying it to align our beliefs with its divinely inspired teachings.

Edward D. Andrews

CHAPTER 21 Digging Deeper: Advanced Bible Study Methods

Bible Background and Historical Settings: Understanding the Times

The journey through Biblical exegesis demands more than a mere surface reading of the text. A crucial layer of this complex process involves understanding the Bible against the backdrop of its historical settings. This approach adheres to the objective Historical-Grammatical method of interpretation, emphasizing the importance of the historical context in deciphering the text's original meaning. The aim is to grasp what the text meant to its original audience and thereby appreciate what it means for us today. Let's delve into why background and historical settings are paramount and provide specific examples to elucidate this.

Importance of Background and Historical Settings

The original authors of the Bible did not write in a vacuum; they were influenced by their cultural, political, and historical environments. Understanding these factors can greatly enrich our interpretation of the Scriptures. Without this, we risk anachronism—projecting our own cultural norms and understandings back onto Biblical events, thereby distorting their actual significance.

1. **Cultural Context**: Knowing the social norms, values, and practices of a particular time helps us better understand the actions and words of Biblical figures. For example, Jesus' use of parables had a particular resonance and comprehensibility for His first-century Jewish audience that might be lost to modern readers if the cultural background is not considered.

2. **Political Context**: This often shapes the struggles and aspirations of the people within the Biblical narrative. Take, for instance, the Israelites' exodus from Egypt. Understanding the political oppression they were under adds depth to the story and highlights the magnitude of Jehovah's deliverance.

3. **Geographical Context**: Geography can dictate lifestyles and events. The location of ancient Israel between major empires like Egypt and Mesopotamia had a profound influence on its history and its relationship with Jehovah.

Examples

1. **The Sermon on the Mount (Matthew 5-7)**: Jesus' teachings here were radical within the context of Jewish legalism. Understanding the Pharisaic rigidity of the law helps us see how revolutionary His message of inner purity over external conformity truly was.

2. **Paul's Mars Hill Address (Acts 17:16-34)**: To fully grasp the profundity of Paul's sermon, it's useful to understand the Athenian culture that venerated multiple gods and esteemed philosophical debate. Paul tapped into this context by starting his sermon with a reference to an "unknown god," a tactic that could be missed without understanding the cultural backdrop.

3. **The Book of Daniel**: Daniel is set in the Babylonian exile. This historical setting reveals how radical Daniel's refusal to eat the king's food was (Daniel 1:8). His actions and visions can only be fully appreciated against the backdrop of an oppressive foreign empire that sought to wipe out his religious identity.

4. **The Johannine Letters**: Knowing that the early church was struggling with false teachers, especially Gnosticism, illuminates why John emphasized the physicality of Jesus Christ in his letters.

5. **Paul's Letter to the Romans**: Written to a church in the capital of an empire that would soon ramp up its persecution of Christians, the epistle addresses both the doctrinal foundations of the faith and practical ways to live it out in a hostile environment.

Methodology

To effectively utilize historical background in Bible study, here are some suggested methods:

1. **Utilize Reliable Historical Sources**: Archaeological findings, ancient texts, and credible historical documents can provide invaluable context.

2. **Linguistic Study**: Languages evolve over time, and a word's meaning can change. An understanding of Koine Greek or Biblical Hebrew could offer fresh insights.

3. **Consult Conservative Scholarship**: Choose commentaries and articles that uphold the inerrancy and authority of the Scriptures. This ensures a more accurate and reverential approach to Biblical study.

4. **Compare Scripture with Scripture**: Often the Bible itself provides the best historical context for understanding a passage. Use cross-references to shed light on difficult texts.

5. **Prayer and Reflection**: Though not a "method" per se, prayer is a vital component, asking for divine wisdom to understand the Word better.

In summary, delving into the historical settings of the Bible provides a richer, more nuanced understanding of its text. This not only aids in more accurate interpretation but also enhances the application of Biblical truths to our contemporary lives. Following a consistent, conservative, and historical-grammatical approach ensures a deeper and more authentic engagement with the living Word.

Theological Analysis: Unpacking Doctrines and Themes

Theological analysis in Bible study is an intricate, yet crucial, part of understanding the Scriptures holistically. It allows us to dissect doctrines, study themes, and situate them in their appropriate contexts. By doing this, we unveil the depth of the divine message, which is foundational to Christian belief and practice. A conservative approach that honors the text's historical and grammatical context helps maintain fidelity to the intended meaning.

Why Theological Analysis is Important

Theology matters because it's the study of God as He has revealed Himself in Scripture. The study of doctrines provides the scaffolding for our understanding of the Biblical text and helps us integrate what we learn into a coherent framework. This approach eliminates the chance of taking a single verse out of context to construct an entire doctrine, a mistake that could have serious implications for faith and practice.

Methodology for Theological Analysis

The foundational principle here is the Historical-Grammatical method, which aims to uncover the original intent of the author by considering the historical and cultural context, the meaning of words in their original languages, and the grammatical structure of the sentences. This method eschews the pitfalls of subjective interpretation.

1. **Identifying Doctrines**: The first step in theological analysis is identifying the doctrines that a particular passage or book of the Bible addresses. These could range from soteriology (the study of salvation) to eschatology (the study of end times).
2. **Contextual Analysis**: After identifying the doctrine, it's essential to examine the immediate and broader context. What is the cultural

background? What covenant is in place? What has been revealed about this doctrine elsewhere in Scripture?

3. **Lexical Study**: Research the original languages. Greek and Hebrew lexicons can be of immense help. A literal translation like the Updated American Standard Version (UASV) can assist this effort, aiming for word-for-word accuracy.

4. **Cross-Referencing**: It's important to compare Scripture with Scripture. However, ensure the cross-references are genuinely parallel passages that speak to the same topic or theme.

5. **Consult Trusted Commentaries**: Finally, turn to sound theological commentaries and dictionaries to aid your understanding, but be discerning about the source.

Examples of Theological Analysis

1. **Doctrine of Salvation (Soteriology)**
   - **Text**: Ephesians 2:8-9
   - **Context**: Written by Paul to the church in Ephesus, under the New Covenant.
   - **Lexical Study**: The term "grace" (Gr: charis) is central to this text. It is an unmerited favor, not something one can earn.
   - **Cross-Referencing**: Romans 6:23, Titus 3:5
   - **Conclusion**: Salvation is by grace through faith and not by works. This is consistent throughout the New Testament.

2. **Doctrine of the Resurrection**
   - **Text**: 1 Corinthians 15:20-22
   - **Context**: Paul addresses the Corinthians, who were confused about the resurrection.
   - **Lexical Study**: "Firstfruits" (Gr: aparchē) suggests that Christ's resurrection is a precursor to the general resurrection.
   - **Cross-Referencing**: Acts 24:15, John 5:28-29
   - **Conclusion**: Christ's resurrection ensures and precedes the resurrection of believers, which is a critical Christian doctrine.

3. **Doctrine of Divine Sovereignty**
   - **Text**: Romans 9:20-21

- **Context**: Addressed to the church in Rome, discussing God's sovereign choice.
- **Lexical Study**: "Potter" (Gr: kerameus) symbolizes God's authority over creation.
- **Cross-Referencing**: Isaiah 45:9, Jeremiah 18:1-6
- **Conclusion**: God is sovereign over His creation, including human beings, yet this does not negate human responsibility.

Theological analysis is not an optional extra but an essential aspect of serious Bible study. By carefully unpacking doctrines and themes, we come closer to a fuller, more faithful understanding of God's Word, enhancing both our intellectual grasp and spiritual depth. With the objective Historical-Grammatical method as our guide, we can navigate the complexities of Biblical text, confident that our findings will be both rigorous and reliable.

Topical Bible Study: Navigating Key Topics

In the realm of biblical studies, a topical study allows us to explore a subject across the entirety of the biblical canon, tracing it from Genesis to Revelation. The advantage of a topical Bible study is that it helps us to understand the Bible's unified teaching on particular doctrines or themes. This study format acknowledges the coherence and unity of the Scriptures as inspired by God, thereby providing a comprehensive overview of the topic. Let's go through some crucial steps and examples to understand how to undertake a topical study with the rigor it demands.

Step 1: Identify the Topic

The first step in a topical study is to identify the topic of interest. Topics can range from theological doctrines like justification, sanctification, and the nature of God, to ethical issues like abortion or marital roles, to eschatological themes like the return of Christ.

Step 2: Initial Scripture Collection

Once you have a topic, gather initial passages that directly address it. Utilize a reliable concordance or a Bible software that relies on a word-for-word translation like the Updated American Standard Version (UASV).

Example: Justification

For instance, if your topic is "Justification," initial passages might include Romans 3:21-26; 5:1, Galatians 2:16, and Ephesians 2:8-9.

Step 3: Contextual Examination

Study the context of the identified verses. A word or concept may take on slightly different nuances in different contexts. Read chapters and books in their entirety to get the broader picture.

Example: Romans 3:21-26

In Romans 3, Paul argues that justification comes through faith in Jesus Christ and not through works of the Law. Understanding the Judaic context against which Paul is speaking enhances our comprehension of justification as a theological concept.

Step 4: Lexical Analysis

Consult Greek or Hebrew lexicons to study key terms in your selected verses. This brings depth and richness to your study.

Example: The Greek Word "Dikaioō"

In the case of justification, the Greek word "dikaioō" often translated as "justify," is crucial. It means "to declare righteous," and not to make righteous. This distinction is vital for a proper understanding of the doctrine.

Step 5: Cross-References

Check for parallel passages, quotations, or references in other books of the Bible. These can either reinforce or shed additional light on the topic under study.

Example: James 2:24

James 2:24 says, "You see that a person is justified by works and not by faith alone." This seems to contrast Paul's teaching, but a closer look shows that James and Paul are addressing two sides of the same coin—Paul focuses on justification before God, while James focuses on the demonstration of that justification before men.

Step 6: Consult Commentaries

Refer to reliable commentaries that follow a historical-grammatical interpretation. This will give you a broader understanding and address complexities you might not be able to resolve independently.

Example: Justification Commentaries

Consult commentaries that delve deeply into the Pauline epistles or into systematic theology works that address justification, ensuring they adhere to historical-grammatical methods.

Step 7: Synthesize Findings

Compile your findings in a structured manner. Identify where the Bible is clear and straightforward on your topic, and note areas where Scripture offers principles rather than specific teachings.

Step 8: Application

The final step is personal application. After understanding the biblical doctrine, the next question is, "How does this affect my life as a follower of Christ?"

A topical Bible study is a significant endeavor that requires methodical and focused effort. It is a tool that provides us with a holistic understanding of Scriptural teachings on key topics, doctrines, and themes. This method strengthens our convictions and deepens our relationship with God by aligning us more closely with His revealed truth. It stands as a pillar for anyone committed to a serious and objective study of the Scriptures, illuminating the way in which we should walk and the truths we should uphold.

Verse-by-Verse Exegesis: In-Depth Analysis of Scripture

Verse-by-verse exegesis is a detailed and systematic examination of each individual verse of a biblical text. Unlike a topical study or thematic analysis, verse-by-verse exegesis is focused on understanding each verse in its immediate context, as well as within the broader scope of Scripture. The aim is to uncover the original meaning of each verse as intended by the human author and by extension, the divine Author, Jehovah.

Steps in Verse-by-Verse Exegesis

1. **Choose a Passage**: Select a specific chapter or section of verses that you wish to examine closely.
2. **Textual Criticism**: Establish the most reliable text based on the manuscript evidence. This is critical in ensuring that you are studying a text as close to the original as possible.

3. **Translation Choice**: Use a translation that is faithful to the original text. The Updated American Standard Version (UASV) would be recommended for this kind of rigorous study.
4. **Historical Context**: Familiarize yourself with the cultural, historical, and societal factors that influenced the text. This helps to understand idioms, metaphors, and specific terms used in the text.
5. **Grammatical Analysis**: Examine the grammar and syntax of the verse. This includes understanding the role played by each word in a sentence—nouns, verbs, adjectives, etc.
6. **Lexical Study**: Investigate the original Hebrew or Greek words to grasp their full semantic range.
7. **Theological Implications**: Recognize and note the doctrinal or theological principles the verse is highlighting.
8. **Cross-References**: Link the verse with other verses in the Bible to create a more comprehensive understanding. This is often facilitated by a thorough understanding of biblical theology.
9. **Commentary Consultation**: Consult trusted, conservative commentaries for different perspectives and further insights, but always test these against the Scriptures.
10. **Application**: Finally, seek to apply the insights gained from the exegesis to your life or to the life of the Church.

Example: Romans 5:1

Let's take Romans 5:1 as an example: "Therefore, since we have been justified by faith, we have peace with God through our Lord Jesus Christ."

1. **Textual Criticism**: The verse is well-supported by early and reliable manuscripts.
2. **Translation Choice**: The UASV's rendering closely mirrors the original Greek and is therefore suitable for this study.
3. **Historical Context**: The book of Romans was written by the Apostle Paul to address the church in Rome, which had a mix of both Jewish and Gentile believers.
4. **Grammatical Analysis**: The verb "justified" is in the passive voice, suggesting that the action is done to us—we are not the ones justifying ourselves. The noun "faith" is the means by which this justification is attained.

5. **Lexical Study**: The Greek word for "justified" is "dikaioō," meaning to declare righteous. It's a legal term used in the courtroom setting.
6. **Theological Implications**: The concept of justification by faith alone is being emphasized, which is foundational to Protestant theology.
7. **Cross-References**: Ephesians 2:8-9; Galatians 2:16
8. **Commentary Consultation**: Various conservative commentaries like that of John Stott or F.F. Bruce affirm the understanding that justification is an act of God's grace, made possible through faith in Jesus Christ.
9. **Application**: The immediate implication is the assurance of peace with God, which should instill in believers a sense of gratitude and responsibility to live out their faith.

By following this process, you can perform an in-depth analysis of individual verses, gaining a rich and comprehensive understanding of Scripture. This will not only deepen your own faith but also equip you to teach and guide others in their spiritual journey. Remember, the objective is always to arrive at the most accurate understanding of the text, respecting its original context and intended meaning. Therefore, your study is not only an academic exercise but a spiritual discipline that brings you into closer alignment with the truths of God's Word.

CHAPTER 22 Applying God's Word to Your Life

Practical Application: Making Scripture Relevant

Studying the Bible is more than an academic exercise; it is an endeavor that should influence every aspect of your life. Practical application is the bridge that connects biblical exegesis and daily living, translating what has been gleaned through careful study into actions, attitudes, and insights that shape one's character and choices. This is the realm where head knowledge transforms into heart transformation and hands-on experience.

Key Principles for Practical Application

1. **Know the Context**: Context is king when interpreting Scripture, and this holds true when making it relevant for your life. Understand the background, original audience, and purpose of the text. This contextual comprehension sets the stage for accurate application.

2. **Interpret Before You Apply**: Use the objective Historical-Grammatical method to get at the original meaning of the text. Interpretation precedes application; hence, the reader must first ascertain what the text meant to its original audience before determining its meaning for today.

3. **Universal Truths**: Identify principles that are universally applicable. While some parts of Scripture were specific to a particular time, place, or people, universal principles are truths that can be applied across cultures and timelines.

4. **Personal Relevance**: Ask probing questions like, "What does this Scripture reveal about God? What does it say about human nature or the human condition? How can this truth be implemented in my life today?"

5. **Be Honest and Self-Critical**: The Bible often serves as a mirror reflecting the state of our soul. Be honest and open to conviction, which may involve the need for repentance, transformation, or even simple affirmation of an ongoing practice.

Examples of Practical Application

- **James 1:22**: "But be doers of the word, and not hearers only, deceiving yourselves." (UASV)
    - **Interpretation**: James is exhorting his readers to put their faith into action. This was critical because faith without works is essentially dead, according to James 2:17.
    - **Application**: Don't just read Scripture or attend church services; implement biblical principles in your life. This could mean serving others, engaging in genuine worship, or even disciplining oneself in areas like finance or relationships in accordance with biblical teachings.
- **Matthew 5:44**: "But I say to you, Love your enemies and pray for those who persecute you," (UASV)
    - **Interpretation**: Jesus is challenging the conventional wisdom of His day, teaching that love should extend even to enemies. This was revolutionary and went against natural instincts.
    - **Application**: Consider how you can show love to people who are difficult to love in your life. Rather than retaliating or harboring grudges, try to respond in love and kindness, praying for their well-being.
- **1 Corinthians 10:31**: "So, whether you eat or drink, or whatever you do, do all to the glory of God." (UASV)
    - **Interpretation**: Paul is encouraging the Corinthians to live in a manner that honors God in all things, even in seemingly mundane activities like eating and drinking.
    - **Application**: Make it a point to consciously dedicate all your activities to God. From your work to your social interactions, seek to give glory to God in all you do.

Take Action

The most robust theology is not merely understood; it is lived out. After identifying the principles and assessing their relevance, you must put them into practice. This is the crux of practical application. The aim is not merely to know more but to become more like Christ.

Remember, the Bible is not a mere book of information but a transformational text designed to change lives. Your engagement with Scripture should lead to a greater understanding and, most importantly, a deeper relationship with God. This change occurs when we move from reading to doing, from understanding to living out what we understand. In this way, the Scripture becomes deeply relevant, shaping us to be the people God has called us to be.

Devotional Study: Deepening Your Spiritual Life

Devotional study is an indispensable aspect of spiritual formation and maturity for every believer. Unlike academic or topical study, the primary aim of devotional study is not to gain information but to facilitate an intimate and transformative encounter with God. Here, the focus is on "heart-knowledge," a genuine and experiential awareness of God's nature, character, and work. Let's delve deeper into this vital practice.

The Essence of Devotional Study

Devotional study aims to foster a personal relationship with Jehovah. While recognizing the crucial role of intellectual engagement, devotional study prioritizes the transformation of the heart and soul. One of the principal ways this occurs is through Scripture, "For the word of God is living and active, sharper than any two-edged sword, piercing to the division of soul and of spirit, of joints and of marrow, and discerning the thoughts and intentions of the heart" (Hebrews 4:12, UASV).

Communion with God

At the core of devotional study is communion with God through His Word and prayer. This study fosters a space where the believer can hear from Jehovah and respond in faithfulness. The Psalms, for instance, are excellent examples of the human experience in communion with Jehovah, where cries for help and songs of thanksgiving reverberate in one volume.

The Importance of Context and Literal Interpretation

While the devotional approach can often lean towards personal applications, it must be grounded in the correct understanding of the text. Understanding a passage's context and what it meant to its original audience is essential. The aim is always to bridge the ancient text's cultural and historical gap to its application in today's context. A text can never mean what it never meant.

Strategies for Devotional Study

1. **Prayerful Approach**: Before you begin your study, pray for illumination. Ask God to open the eyes of your understanding.
2. **Choose a Passage**: This can be a chapter, a portion of a chapter, or even just a verse. Consider following a reading plan or a particular book of the Bible.
3. **Observation**: Read the passage slowly. Take note of keywords, phrases, and the general flow of the passage.
4. **Interpretation**: Here, the objective historical-grammatical method comes into play. Ask questions like, "What did this mean to the original audience?" and "What is the main point of this passage?"
5. **Application**: How does this passage apply to your life? What is God speaking to you about through this text?
6. **Prayer and Reflection**: Respond to God in prayer. Thank Him for His Word and ask for strength to apply it. Spend a few moments reflecting on the truths you have gleaned.
7. **Journaling**: Writing down what you've learned, questions you may have, and prayers can solidify your understanding and provide a reference for future studies.
8. **Accountability**: Sharing what you've learned with trusted believers can provide additional insights and mutual encouragement.

The Need for a Reliable Translation

Using a reliable translation like the Updated American Standard Version (UASV) ensures that the text you are studying is as close to the original languages as possible. It serves the purpose of being both accurate and faithful to the original text, thereby giving the reader the best opportunity to interpret God's Word correctly.

Potential Pitfalls

1. **Over-Personalization**: Avoid reading your circumstances into every text.
2. **Neglect of Study**: Devotion should not replace the deep study of the Word. Both are necessary for a balanced Christian life.
3. **Avoiding Difficult Passages**: Don't skip over passages that are hard to understand or that challenge your lifestyle or beliefs.

Devotional study is not an isolated discipline but an integral part of our spiritual life that significantly impacts our worldview, ethical choices, and relationship with

God. Done correctly, it can result in a life that is continually being conformed to the image of Christ (Romans 8:29). Therefore, approach it with the seriousness it deserves, guided by proper hermeneutical principles and an unwavering commitment to the authority and inerrancy of Scripture.

Teaching and Sharing: Communicating Biblical Truth

In the journey of faith, one cannot underestimate the value of teaching and sharing the Biblical truth. It is not sufficient to merely acquire knowledge; the mandate from Scripture is clear—believers are to be "doers of the Word, and not hearers only" (James 1:22, UASV). Moreover, the Apostle Paul writes to Timothy, "Preach the word; be prepared in season and out of season; reprove, rebuke, and exhort, with complete patience and teaching" (2 Timothy 4:2, UASV). These directives underline the imperative of not just internalizing God's Word, but also effectively communicating it to others.

The Importance of Faithful Communication

The foremost task in teaching and sharing is faithful communication of God's Word. Accuracy and fidelity to the original text of Scripture are non-negotiables. This is why a faithful translation like the Updated American Standard Version (UASV) can be instrumental. It gives us what God said through His human authors, allowing us, as interpreters, to grapple with the meaning of those words. Every word in Scripture is divinely inspired (2 Timothy 3:16), and thus it is essential to relay these words as accurately as possible.

Building Competence

An effective communicator must first be a competent student. The Bereans are cited as an exemplary model because they "received the word with all eagerness, examining the Scriptures daily to see if these things were so" (Acts 17:11, UASV). This model should compel us to be diligent students of the Bible, equipped to "rightly handling the word of truth" (2 Timothy 2:15, UASV). This requires a commitment to the objective Historical-Grammatical method of interpretation, which takes into account the historical setting, literary context, and grammatical structure, while honoring the authority and inerrancy of Scripture.

The Pedagogical Approach

Once we've established the importance of competent study, the question turns to how best to communicate this knowledge. We are exhorted to "let your speech always be gracious, seasoned with salt, so that you may know how you ought to answer each person" (Colossians 4:6, UASV). Effective teaching engages the mind but also resonates with the heart. It should be done with "complete patience and teaching," as per 2 Timothy 4:2, without compromise on core doctrines or dilution through interfaith perspectives.

Leveraging Modern Tools

In today's interconnected world, opportunities for teaching and sharing are not restricted to pulpits or community gatherings. Social media, blogs, and other digital platforms can be employed to spread the Word. However, while the medium may change, the message must remain the same. Technology should serve as a tool for dissemination, not as a platform for distortion.

Challenges and Pitfalls

While teaching and sharing are rewarding, they are not without challenges. A notable one is the cultural climate that often promotes relativism and is averse to absolute truth claims. We must be prepared to encounter opposition or apathy, but we should take comfort in the words of Jesus, who said, "If the world hates you, know that it has hated me before it hated you" (John 15:18, UASV).

Another pitfall is the temptation to accommodate or dilute Biblical teachings for broader appeal. This is not just a disservice to the audience but also a disobedience to God. Scripture exhorts us to be vigilant, "holding fast the faithful word which is in accordance with the teaching, so that he will be able both to exhort in sound doctrine and to refute those who contradict" (Titus 1:9, UASV).

Teaching and sharing are not optional activities for the believer but are inherent to the Christian calling. As we commit to being lifelong learners and faithful communicators of God's Word, let us remember Paul's charge to Timothy, "What you have heard from me in the presence of many witnesses entrust to faithful men, who will be able to teach others also" (2 Timothy 2:2, UASV). This stewardship of truth is not just a personal blessing but a communal mandate, extending the life-changing power of God's Word to a world in dire need of it.

Living Out Your Faith: Putting God's Word into Action

The transformational power of Scripture is not in merely reading it, but in applying its truths to our lives. Living out one's faith is the true manifestation of understanding the Word of God. But how does one successfully transition from biblical understanding to lived practice?

YOUR GUIDE FOR DEFENDING THE BIBLE

The Primacy of the Word

First and foremost, it's crucial to recognize the primacy of Scripture as God's revealed truth. The apostle Paul, in his second letter to Timothy, reminds us that all Scripture is "inspired by God and profitable for teaching, for reproof, for correction, for training in righteousness" (2 Timothy 3:16, UASV). The original languages of the Bible are essentially God speaking to us; therefore, each word is of paramount importance. As believers, we have an obligation to be faithful to these words, which act as the bedrock upon which our faith rests.

The Role of Interpretation

The interpretation of Scripture is essential for correct application. The objective Historical-Grammatical method guides us to understand the text as the original audience would have. It requires careful analysis of language, historical context, and the grammatical construction of the text. This methodology avoids the pitfalls and biases present in subjective approaches to interpretation, which distance biblical understanding from truth.

Meditating and Internalizing

David, the man after God's own heart, stressed the importance of meditating on God's law. "I will meditate on Your precepts and regard Your ways," he says in Psalm 119:15 (UASV). Meditating isn't just thinking; it's dwelling upon, internalizing, and allowing the Scripture to saturate your mind and soul. The outcome of this meditation is a life that exemplifies biblical truths.

Practical Steps for Application

1. **Prayerful Reading**: Start your reading with prayer, asking God for wisdom and understanding.

2. **Identify Principles**: Recognize the moral and ethical teachings in the text.

3. **Personalize**: Examine how these principles relate to your personal life.

4. **Commit to Action**: Determine concrete steps to implement these principles.

5. **Accountability**: Engage in fellowship with other believers who can help you stay on course.

The Danger of Unapplied Knowledge

James warns against being mere hearers and not doers of the Word (James 1:22, UASV). Unapplied knowledge puffs up and leads to spiritual stagnation. A disconnect between one's understanding of Scripture and one's life practice is a perilous position for any Christian. It can also send misleading signals to those observing the Christian community from outside.

The Witness of a Transformed Life

Living out the Word of God is a powerful witness to its truth and efficacy. When people see a life changed by the Word, they are more likely to be open to its message. This is fulfilling the Great Commission as Jesus commanded in Matthew 28:19-20, where he instructed his followers to make disciples, teaching them to observe all that he had commanded.

Courage Amidst Challenges

Living a biblical life is neither easy nor popular. It often involves making choices that are counter-cultural and can lead to social ostracism or even persecution. But as Paul reminds us, the present sufferings are not worth comparing with the glory that will be revealed in us (Romans 8:18, UASV). Therefore, it's essential to remain steadfast, drawing strength from the Holy Spirit inspired Word of God and the hope of eternal life with Christ.

Applying God's Word in daily life is a dynamic process that involves diligent study, prayerful reflection, and, most importantly, courageous action. The objective is not merely to increase knowledge but to effect a transformation that aligns us more closely with God's will. This lived faith, then, becomes both our spiritual act of worship and our greatest witness to the world.

YOUR GUIDE FOR DEFENDING THE BIBLE

SECTION 6 CHRISTIAN APOLOGETICS

Digging Deeper

We put books here on this subject if one is interested in taking the subject deeper. This section gives you foundational knowledge to evangelize or engage people in conversation.

CHRISTIAN APOLOGETICS: Answering the Tough Questions: Evidence and Reason in Defense of the Faith by Edward D. Andrews (2023)

ISBN-13 : 979-8376868072

https://www.amazon.com/dp/B0BVD1VVDF

THE CHRISTIAN APOLOGIST: Always Being Prepared to Make a Defense by Edward D. Andrews (2016)

ISBN-13: 978-1945757273

https://www.amazon.com/dp/1945757272

Edward D. Andrews

CHAPTER 23 Introduction to Christian Apologetics

The Biblical Basis for Christian Apologetics: Understanding 1 Peter 3:15

The task of defending the Christian faith, also known as apologetics, has a well-grounded biblical basis. One key Scripture frequently cited in this regard is 1 Peter 3:15, which in the Updated American Standard Version (UASV) reads, "But sanctify Christ as Lord in your hearts, always being prepared to make a defense to anyone who asks you for a reason for the hope that is in you; yet do it with gentleness and respect."

Contextualizing 1 Peter 3:15

Understanding 1 Peter 3:15 requires acknowledging its immediate and broader context. The Apostle Peter writes this letter to various churches under the umbrella of suffering for righteousness, and he calls upon believers to conduct themselves in a manner worthy of their calling, even in the face of persecution. The term "defense" used here is the Greek word "apologia," from which we derive the term "apologetics." This indicates a structured, reasoned argument or justification for the Christian worldview.

Sanctifying Christ as Lord in Your Hearts

The verse starts by urging believers to "sanctify Christ as Lord in your hearts." To sanctify means to set apart as holy. To have Christ as Lord in our hearts means to have Him as the authoritative figure in our lives. This sanctification serves as the foundational mindset for Christian apologetics. We engage in apologetics not as an intellectual exercise but out of a sanctified relationship with Christ. In other words, our apologetics is an outpouring of our committed relationship to Christ, who is the ultimate truth.

YOUR GUIDE FOR DEFENDING THE BIBLE

Being Prepared

Peter exhorts believers to be "always prepared." This is a call to diligent study, understanding, and internalization of Scripture and Christian doctrine. The Christian must be well-versed in biblical truths to offer an intellectual and spiritually rich response to those who question their faith. This level of preparedness is possible through consistent and earnest study of the Scriptures, applying the objective Historical-Grammatical method of interpretation to gain an accurate understanding of the text.

To Whom and Why?

The instruction is to be prepared "to make a defense to anyone who asks you for a reason for the hope that is in you." Apologetics, therefore, is not only for public debates or academic forums but also for everyday interactions where questions about faith and hope in Christ might arise. Our hope is based on the resurrection of Jesus Christ, God's promises, and the guidance provided by Scripture. Given the exclusive claims of Christianity concerning salvation and God's nature, apologetics becomes a necessary endeavor for the Church.

Gentleness and Respect

It is crucial to note that Peter instructs us to make our defense "with gentleness and respect." Apologetics isn't about winning arguments but about guiding people toward the truth of the Gospel. An apologist must be careful to maintain a respectful and gentle demeanor, avoiding a contentious or confrontational attitude.

Counter to Modern Trends

Given the post-Enlightenment skepticism and proliferation of ideologies that challenge Christian doctrines, 1 Peter 3:15 serves as an essential verse for believers today. Modern trends of interfaith and ecumenism dilute the distinctiveness of Christian doctrine. The nature of Christian apologetics stands counter to these trends. Apologetics preserves the doctrinal purity of the Church, ensuring that its teachings remain undiluted by external influences.

An Antidote to Unbelief

Furthermore, 1 Peter 3:15 serves as an antidote to the damaging influences of flawed interpretative methodologies that have undermined confidence in the Bible and its teachings. In a world increasingly hostile to Christian beliefs, being unprepared is not an option. The verse serves as a wake-up call for equipping oneself intellectually and spiritually to "give an answer," providing a robust defense of one's faith.

Understanding 1 Peter 3:15 is paramount for anyone engaging in Christian apologetics. This verse encompasses the spiritual, intellectual, and emotional dimensions of defending the Christian faith. It is a call to set Christ apart as Lord in our hearts, prepare ourselves intellectually and spiritually, and engage in respectful dialogue with those who challenge or question our faith. All this is performed with the ultimate goal of leading people to the saving knowledge of Jesus Christ. Thus, apologetics is not an optional activity for a believer but a Scripturally mandated task, central to the Christian life and mission.

Colossians 4:6 – Know How You Ought to Answer Each Person

Colossians 4:6 from the Updated American Standard Version (UASV) instructs Christians, "Let your speech always be gracious, seasoned with salt, so that you may know how you ought to answer each person." This verse stands as a critical guidepost in the realm of Christian apologetics, emphasizing the importance of both the content and the manner in which believers engage in defense of the faith.

Contextual Understanding

To fully grasp the implications of this verse for apologetics, we must understand the context within which it was penned. The Apostle Paul wrote Colossians while in prison, addressing a church facing heretical teachings that sought to corrupt the purity of Christian doctrine. Paul is thus concerned not only with correct teaching but also with the way that teaching is conveyed.

Speech "With Grace"

Paul begins by advising that speech must always be "with grace." In the New Testament, grace often connotes undeserved kindness or favor. In the apologetic context, this implies a dialogue that is respectful and kind, devoid of arrogance or hostility. This runs counter to the confrontational and aggressive styles of argumentation prevalent in society today. Instead, it aligns with other Scriptural admonitions that call for gentleness and respect in our interactions with others, even when defending the faith (1 Peter 3:15).

"Seasoned with Salt"

The phrase "seasoned with salt" suggests speech that is not only palatable but also worthy of consumption, so to speak. In the ancient world, salt was used not just for flavor but also for preserving food. Applied to speech, this could mean words that preserve the integrity of the Gospel message. When engaged in apologetics, Christians are to offer arguments that are intellectually rigorous and Scripturally faithful, preserving the "saltiness" of the Christian message.

Knowing "How You Ought to Answer"

The verse closes with the admonition that Christians should know "how you ought to answer each person." This is not a call for a "one size fits all" approach but suggests that apologetics is a nuanced endeavor. People come from various backgrounds, hold different objections, and are at diverse stages in their spiritual journeys. As such, knowing how to answer each person means we should be attentive to the individual's particular questions, doubts, or misconceptions.

Relevance for Apologetic Methodology

Colossians 4:6 has far-reaching implications for the methodology employed in Christian apologetics.

First, it echoes the Historical-Grammatical method of interpretation. This approach seeks to understand the original intent of the Scriptural text within its historical and grammatical context, resisting the speculative tendencies of modern biblical criticism. It aims to preserve the Scriptural "saltiness" by staying faithful to the original languages and the author's intent, treating every word as divinely inspired and therefore of utmost importance.

Second, the verse aligns with the importance of using a literal translation of the Bible. Literal translations, such as the UASV, aim to be as close as possible to the original languages, allowing the reader the opportunity to delve into the richness and complexity of the text. The verse underlines the significance of presenting God's word as it was originally given, enabling the reader to decide what the author meant, thus underscoring the importance of a translation philosophy that prizes accuracy over readability.

Finally, the verse upholds the exclusive claims of Christianity. It assumes that there is a correct way to answer questions about the faith, standing in direct opposition to modern pluralistic notions that all religions lead to the same truth. Therefore, the verse tacitly refutes interfaith or ecumenical attempts to dilute or compromise Christian doctrines.

Colossians 4:6 serves as a valuable guide for the practice of Christian apologetics. It teaches us that defending the faith is not just about what we say but also how we say it. It instructs us to be gracious in our dialogue, rigorous in our arguments, and sensitive to the unique needs and questions of each individual. Moreover, it reinforces the importance of sticking closely to Scriptural truths as they were originally conveyed, making it a bedrock text for anyone engaged in the serious business of Christian apologetics.

The Primary Problem in Christian Apologetics Today

Christian apologetics involves the defense and articulation of the Christian faith against objections, misconceptions, and misunderstandings. It aims to provide a rational basis for the Christian faith and offer answers to questions about Christian doctrine and practice. While Christian apologetics has a rich history, it faces certain challenges today that can undermine its effectiveness and relevance. The primary problem in Christian apologetics today is not necessarily the strength of the arguments posed by skeptics or other religious systems, but the internal issues among Christian apologists and believers. Specifically, the dilution of doctrinal integrity, the loss of focus on the authority of Scripture, and the influence of secular humanistic ideologies are posing serious threats.

Dilution of Doctrinal Integrity

One significant problem lies in the dilution of doctrinal integrity. The apostle Paul warned Timothy that the time would come when people would not endure sound teaching (2 Timothy 4:3-4). This prophecy is strikingly accurate today. The inclination towards ecumenism and interfaith dialogue has led to the watering down of essential Christian doctrines. Instead of standing firm on doctrines clearly laid out in the Scriptures, there is a growing acceptance of heterodox views for the sake of unity. This is problematic because when essential doctrines are compromised, the very foundations of the Christian faith are shaken.

Loss of Focus on the Authority of Scripture

Another major issue is the loss of focus on the authority of Scripture. The Bible repeatedly claims that every one of its words (in the original languages) is a word spoken to us by God and is therefore of utmost importance. In light of this, it is concerning to see some Christian scholars and apologists leaning towards critical methodologies that undermine the authority and inerrancy of the Scriptures. The objective Historical-Grammatical method of interpretation, which takes the text seriously and aims to understand it within its original context, is often sidelined in favor of critical methodologies that are fundamentally flawed and speculative. As a result, the authority of Scripture is diminished, and the reliability of Christian doctrine is called into question.

Influence of Secular Humanistic Ideologies

Finally, the influence of secular humanistic ideologies like relativism, pluralism, and naturalism has crept into Christian apologetics. Some apologists are increasingly relying on human reasoning and philosophy, often neglecting the role of Scripture in shaping Christian thought. This is dangerous because it aligns the apologists more with the values of the world than with the teachings of the Bible.

The primary problem in Christian apologetics today is not necessarily external but internal. The dilution of doctrinal integrity, the loss of focus on the authority of the Bible, and the growing influence of secular humanistic ideologies are weakening the efficacy and credibility of Christian apologetics. These issues demand urgent attention. The apostle Peter urged Christians to be prepared to make a defense to anyone who asks for the reason for the hope that is within us (1 Peter 3:15). To do this effectively, Christian apologists must be rooted in the authority of the Scriptures, hold firmly to sound doctrine, and be aware of the ideological shifts that could compromise their mission. Without these pillars, Christian apologetics risks becoming a hollow exercise, devoid of the transformative power of the Gospel. Therefore, it is imperative for those engaged in Christian apologetics to address these internal issues to be truly effective in their divine calling.

Addressing Common Objections to the Christian Faith: Doctrine, Ethics, and Science

Apologetics is the rational defense of the Christian faith against its critics. Given the range of criticisms targeting Christian doctrine, ethics, and the perceived tension between faith and science, it becomes imperative to address these objections through a carefully laid out apologetic approach. The focus here is to ground this defense in sound, literal translation of the Bible, upholding the authority and inerrancy of Scripture.

Objections to Christian Doctrine

1. **The Trinity**: Skeptics often point out that the term "Trinity" is not found in the Bible. It's essential to clarify that while the term isn't used, the concept is indeed Scriptural. Matthew 28:19 instructs to baptize "in the name of the Father and of the Son and of the Holy Spirit," implying a unified nature.

2. **Salvation through Faith, Not Works**: Critics argue that Christianity presents an "easy way out" by emphasizing faith over moral action. Ephesians 2:8-9 clarifies that faith leads to salvation, but James 2:17-18

argues that faith without works is dead. Thus, true Christian faith naturally results in moral uprightness.

3. **Exclusive Salvation**: Questions arise about the fate of those who haven't heard the Gospel. Romans 1:20 holds that God's qualities are evident through creation, leaving no one with an excuse. Acts 4:12 asserts the exclusive path to salvation through Christ, highlighting the necessity of mission work.

Objections in Ethics

1. **The Problem of Suffering**: Why would a good God allow suffering? The Bible maintains that suffering is the result of sin and a fallen world (Romans 5:12). God allows suffering but also offers comfort and ultimate justice (Revelation 21:4).

2. **Ethical Standards in the Old Testament**: Critics frequently cite harsh Old Testament laws. It's important to distinguish between moral, civil, and ceremonial laws, recognizing that many were specific to Israel's historical and cultural context.

3. **Sexual Ethics**: Christianity's stance on issues like homosexuality and premarital sex is often deemed outdated. However, the New Testament promotes a high moral standard (1 Corinthians 6:18-20), not to oppress, but to free individuals for godly living.

Objections from Science

1. **Creation vs. Evolution**: Critics argue that belief in creation is scientifically untenable. However, the Bible isn't a science textbook. Genesis 1-2 outlines a purposeful creation by a personal Creator, which doesn't necessarily contradict scientific theories that align with a purposeful, guided process.

2. **Miracles**: Scientific skepticism often dismisses the possibility of miracles. Yet, the point of miracles in the Bible isn't to defy science but to affirm God's dominion over creation (John 20:30-31).

3. **Historical Accuracy**: Doubts are cast on the historical reliability of Biblical accounts. Archaeological findings, however, have consistently corroborated Scriptural records, affirming the Bible's historical integrity.

Apologetics is not about winning arguments but about faithfully representing Christian truth claims, grounded in a rigorous and literal understanding of Scripture. While objections will persist, a nuanced, compassionate, and scholarly apologetic approach can help remove intellectual barriers to faith. By addressing objections related to doctrine, ethics, and science, believers can present a more complete, coherent, and compelling case for the Christian worldview.

YOUR GUIDE FOR DEFENDING THE BIBLE

A Closer Look at Faith and Reason: Complementary, Not Contradictory

In the world of religious discourse, one of the most enduring debates centers on the relationship between faith and reason. Some see the two as inimical, claiming that faith is the antithesis of reason, or vice versa. However, this perspective is misguided. A closer examination of Scripture and Christian doctrine reveals that faith and reason are not mutually exclusive but are, in fact, complementary forces that enrich one another.

The Scriptural View of Faith and Reason

Starting from a biblical standpoint, we see that faith is not portrayed as a blind leap into the dark. Hebrews 11:1 states, "Now faith is the assurance of things hoped for, the conviction of things not seen." The term "assurance" implies a rational basis, a conviction that is not arbitrary but based on evidence, albeit not always empirical in nature.

Reason, on the other hand, is neither scorned nor dismissed in Scripture. In Isaiah 1:18, Jehovah invites His people to "come now, let us reason together." The Apostle Paul, a learned man, regularly engaged in reasoned discourse to explain and defend the Christian faith (Acts 17:2-4; Acts 18:4). Clearly, the Bible does not portray reason as the enemy of faith.

The Theological Framework

Christian doctrine, when properly understood, likewise does not create a chasm between faith and reason. The doctrine of God's omniscience means that God is the ultimate source of all truth—whether discovered through faith or reason. There is no real conflict because both originate from the same Divine source. Theologians like Thomas Aquinas have painstakingly articulated how faith and reason can coexist harmoniously, with reason helping to elucidate elements of faith, and faith enriching reason by providing it with its ultimate context—God's revelation.

Contemporary Objections

In today's secularized culture, three common objections arise against integrating faith and reason:

1. **Science Disproves Religion**: Some argue that scientific discoveries have made religious faith obsolete. Yet, they overlook that many groundbreaking scientists were devout Christians—Isaac Newton, Johannes Kepler, and Francis Collins to name a few. The proper interpretation of Genesis is not

in conflict with the established facts of science, given that the text focuses on the "who" and "why" of creation, not the "how."

2. **Faith is Irrational**: Some critics posit that faith is irrational because it believes in the unseen. This is a misconception. For example, love or justice are also "unseen," yet they are very real and universally accepted. Faith, similarly, is a conviction based on evidence not visible to the naked eye, like the wind that we feel but cannot see (John 3:8).

3. **Incompatibility of Old Testament Laws with Modern Ethics**: Critics frequently claim that Old Testament laws are outdated and incompatible with modern ethics. They forget the cultural and historical context of these laws. What was given to ancient Israel was appropriate for its time and should not be misunderstood as universal moral prescriptions.

Examples from Church History

The Church Fathers, medieval scholars, and Reformers all saw faith and reason as partners. Augustine, Anselm, and Aquinas never saw a need to divorce faith from reason. Even Martin Luther, who emphasized sola fide (faith alone), never discounted the role of reason; he merely posited that reason must be subservient to Scripture.

Contrary to popular belief, faith and reason are not contradictory but complementary aspects of the Christian experience. Both are gifts from God, designed to be used in understanding the Divine, the world, and our place in it. Far from being adversaries, they are allies in the quest for truth. Utilizing reason to explore and articulate faith not only deepens one's relationship with God but also equips the believer to "always be prepared to make a defense to anyone who asks you for a reason for the hope that is in you" (1 Peter 3:15).

CHAPTER 24 Being Prepared to Make a Defense

The Armor of God: Spiritual Readiness through Scripture and Prayer

In the realm of Christian apologetics, the Bible speaks in military terms of "waging the fine warfare" (1 Timothy 1:18, UASV) and being "a soldier of Christ Jesus" (2 Timothy 2:3, UASV). Why such martial language? We are in a spiritual struggle. The battle is real, though not against flesh and blood. It's against worldviews, ideologies, and spiritual confusion. Therefore, it's essential to understand the Biblical concept of "the armor of God," outlined in Ephesians 6:10-18. Understanding and applying the armor of God is pivotal for spiritual readiness and can effectively serve the apologist in the mission to defend the faith.

The Belt of Truth

The first component of the armor is the belt of truth. In a world of fake news, ideological agendas, and relativism, truth is often compromised or ignored. The Bible, however, emphasizes that Jehovah is a "God of truth" (Psalm 31:5, UASV), and Jesus proclaimed that He is "the way and the truth and the life" (John 14:6, UASV). Apologists must be grounded in truth, which begins by a commitment to Biblical inerrancy and an adherence to the objective Historical-Grammatical method of interpretation. For the apologist, the belt of truth enables us to discern accurate knowledge and make sound arguments based on Scripture, thus providing the undergirding for all apologetic efforts.

The Breastplate of Righteousness

The breastplate of righteousness refers to the moral integrity required of a Christian apologist. Without righteousness, even the most articulate defense of the Gospel will lack credibility. Being rooted in the right standing with God, we can offer apologetics from a position of moral clarity and ethical integrity. Righteousness here isn't just a personal attribute but aligns with God's moral standards as revealed in Scripture. It serves as a safeguard for the heart (Proverbs 4:23, UASV), protecting us from falling into errors or moral pitfalls that could discredit our testimony and apologetic efforts.

The Gospel Shoes

Being prepared with the Gospel of peace involves the readiness to engage others about the message of Christ. In apologetics, this entails being equipped to explain the Gospel clearly and concisely, anticipating objections, and offering reasonable responses. For instance, when Paul stood before King Agrippa, he was prepared to articulate his faith and offer a reasoned defense, even aiming to persuade Agrippa towards Christianity (Acts 26:28, UASV). The Gospel is our ultimate peace treaty with God; therefore, we should be quick to share it.

The Shield of Faith

In spiritual warfare, the apologist is often the target of "the flaming arrows of the evil one" (Ephesians 6:16, UASV). These might come in the form of intellectual challenges, doubts, or even personal attacks. It's faith that enables us to quench these attacks. This isn't a blind faith but a reasoned trust based on evidence and the reliability of Scripture. In apologetics, faith serves as the shield that provides confidence in the arguments we present and the doctrines we defend.

The Helmet of Salvation

The helmet of salvation points to the importance of a sound mind secured by the assurance of eternal life. Apologists can carry out their duties effectively only when they have a clear understanding of the doctrine of salvation as taught in Scripture. Knowing that we have been justified through faith in Christ, and recognizing that there is no universal salvation, equips us with a mental fortitude that shields against discouragement and ideological attacks.

The Sword of the Spirit

This is the only offensive weapon in the armor—a double-edged sword, referring to the Word of God. In apologetics, the Scripture is our ultimate authority for defending the faith. When Jesus was tempted by Satan, He countered each temptation with "it is written" (Matthew 4:4, 7, 10, UASV). Similarly, a well-equipped apologist must be skilled in "rightly dividing the word of truth" (2 Timothy 2:15, UASV) and should be adept at using Scripture to refute false doctrines, answer objections, and guide people toward the truth.

Prayer

Finally, the armor is ineffective without prayer. Paul ends his description by urging "all kinds of prayers and supplications" (Ephesians 6:18, UASV). Prayer not only invites divine assistance but also serves as a tool for clarity and wisdom. In apologetics, prayer should precede, accompany, and follow every endeavor. It's through prayer that we receive the wisdom and courage to defend the faith effectively.

To summarize, each element of the armor has apologetic relevance and application. In our efforts to make a defense for the hope that is within us, so that we may know how we ought to answer each person. (1 Peter 3:15, Colossians 4:6 UASV), being girded with this spiritual armor provides the readiness, resilience, and resources necessary to stand firm in the faith and successfully counter ideological and spiritual challenges.

Understanding the Landscape: Identifying Common Challenges and Skepticism

As followers of Jesus Christ, believers must be prepared to make a defense for the hope that is within them, doing so with gentleness and respect. In a world increasingly hostile to the Christian worldview, this task may be daunting. However, before rushing into the battlefield for the defense of the faith, one must first understand the landscape. This involves identifying common challenges and skepticism that often confront Christian beliefs. The terrain is fraught with objections ranging from the intellectual to the emotional, from attacks on the integrity of the Scriptures to questions about the existence and character of God.

The Bible's Historicity and Reliability

One of the primary areas of skepticism is the historicity and reliability of the Scriptures. Skeptics often argue that the Bible is a collection of myths, legends, and contradictions. To counter this claim, a believer should be well-equipped with evidence demonstrating the historical accuracy of the Bible. For example, archaeology has confirmed numerous biblical accounts, such as the existence of King David, the Hittites, and many other historical figures and places mentioned in the Bible. Manuscript evidence, particularly the Dead Sea Scrolls, also attests to the reliability and preservation of the Old Testament text. For the New Testament, the sheer number of early manuscripts, some dating within a generation of the original authors, bolster its textual integrity.

Existence of God

Another frequent challenge is the question of God's existence. Atheists and agnostics might argue from a naturalistic worldview, suggesting that everything in existence can be explained without invoking a supernatural deity. The cosmological, teleological, and moral arguments can be particularly useful here. For example, the cosmological argument points to the origin of the universe as evidence for a First Cause or an Uncaused Cause, identified as God. The teleological argument looks at the design, complexity, and order in the universe as indicative of a Designer. The moral argument postulates that the universal moral law that people instinctively recognize implies a Moral Lawgiver.

Problem of Evil and Suffering

The problem of evil and suffering is another significant challenge often used against the Christian faith. Skeptics question how a loving, omnipotent, and omniscient God could allow evil and suffering in the world. The Christian response involves multiple facets, including the concept of free will and the resultant human responsibility for sin, which is the root cause of evil and suffering. Another aspect to consider is God's sovereign plan, which includes allowing suffering for reasons that may be beyond human comprehension but ultimately contribute to a greater good or divine purpose.

The Exclusivity of Christ

Some people find the Christian claim that Jesus is the only way to God (John 14:6) to be exclusionary or intolerant. This objection often arises in pluralistic societies that endorse relativistic views on truth and morality. To address this, Christians can emphasize the uniqueness of Jesus' claims, His resurrection, and the transformative power of His teachings. The argument here is not one of intolerance but of distinctive truth claims that have stood the test of scrutiny and time.

Skepticism About Miracles

The Bible is replete with accounts of miraculous events, leading some skeptics to discount it as mere folklore. However, one must remember that if God exists and created the universe, miracles are not only possible but would be expected as acts of divine intervention in the natural order. For example, if the resurrection of Jesus Christ can be defended historically, as many scholars argue, then the plausibility of other biblical miracles increases.

Reliability of Eye-Witness Testimony

Skeptics often question the reliability of eye-witness testimony in the Bible. The Gospel accounts, for instance, are frequently scrutinized for alleged contradictions. A robust defense here involves underscoring the criterion of embarrassment, multiple attestation, and the lack of legendary embellishment, all of which lend credence to the Gospel writers' accounts as reliable eye-witness testimony.

In conclusion, understanding the landscape involves being aware of these and other challenges to the Christian faith. It's crucial to not only identify these common objections but also to be prepared to address them thoughtfully and respectfully, equipped with both Scriptural knowledge and apologetic arguments. This preparation allows Christians to navigate through the complexities of modern skepticism and to make a compelling case for the veracity of their faith. Being prepared, therefore, is not just a recommendation; it is an essential part of being a follower of Christ in a world that desperately needs to hear His message of hope and salvation.

Practical Tools for Defense: Evidences, Arguments, and Factual Support

When Christians are called upon to "to make disciples ... teaching them" (Matthew 28:19-20, UASV), they engage in a form of apologetics. This term comes from the Greek "apologia," which signifies a reasoned defense. Thus, to be effective apologists for the Christian faith, believers should have practical tools in their arsenal, such as evidence, logical arguments, and factual support. Below are some vital tools to consider:

Scriptural Evidence

Scripture is the cornerstone of Christian belief and should serve as the primary foundation in apologetics. Use well-defined references to support your positions. For example, when speaking about the resurrection, one might cite 1 Corinthians 15:3-8 as a straightforward passage that highlights the essential nature of this event and provides historical validation through eyewitness accounts. When the authority of the Bible itself is under scrutiny, one can highlight its historical reliability, internal consistency, and prophetic accuracy. In line with the Apostle Paul's method, 'reasoning from the Scriptures' helps make a compelling case (Acts 17:2, 3).

Archaeological and Historical Facts

Physical evidence outside of the Bible provides robust support for the biblical record. The Dead Sea Scrolls, for example, lend credence to the accurate transmission of the Old Testament. Archaeological finds such as the Tel Dan Stele or the Moabite Stone corroborate biblical accounts and peoples, thereby strengthening the Scripture's historical reliability.

Philosophical Arguments

Logical reasoning also has a role in Christian apologetics. Arguments such as the Cosmological Argument (arguing for a First Cause) and the Moral Argument (arguing for an objective moral lawgiver) can be helpful in discussions concerning the existence of God. While these philosophical tools are not replacements for the revealed truth in Scripture, they serve to counter objections and to prepare the intellectual ground for the acceptance of faith.

Scientific Evidences

While science cannot 'prove' God in the way it proves a mathematical formula, it can point to God's existence and attributes. For instance, the complexity of DNA or the fine-tuning of the universe's constants can be considered pointers to a Designer. Again, these should not replace Scriptural truth but can support it, particularly in discussions with those who highly regard scientific evidence.

Testimonies and Personal Experiences

While subjective and thereby not decisive proof, personal experiences and testimonies can have a powerful role in apologetics. Whether it's the transformative power of the Christian faith in a person's life or experiences that affirm the existence and goodness of God, these accounts offer 'real-world' validation of Christian beliefs. However, they should be used cautiously and in conjunction with objective evidence to prevent emotionalism from clouding reasoned judgment.

Responding to Common Objections

It's also essential to understand the common objections raised against Christianity to respond effectively. Objections might come in the form of supposed contradictions in the Bible, the existence of evil in a world made by a good God, or challenges to the exclusive claims of Christianity. In such cases, being versed in apologetics means not only presenting arguments for the faith but also refuting opposing viewpoints with sound reasoning and evidence.

Hermeneutic Principles

Understanding the principles of interpretation, especially the objective Historical-Grammatical method, is crucial for the defense of the Christian faith. It ensures the accurate handling of Scriptural texts, which is pivotal in any form of Christian defense or proclamation. Using this method prevents eisegesis—reading one's own ideas into the text—enabling one to confront criticisms rooted in misinterpretation or ignorance of these principles.

Countering Modern Criticism

Many criticisms of Christianity are rooted in flawed methodologies, such as the Historical-Critical Method and other liberal-moderate biblical criticism approaches. It's essential to expose these for what they are: ideologically driven interpretations that deviate from a commitment to the authority and inerrancy of Scripture.

Being equipped with a robust set of tools—Scriptural, logical, and factual—profoundly enhances the Christian's ability to "demolish arguments and every pretension that sets itself up against the knowledge of God" (2 Corinthians 10:5, UASV). Indeed, apologetics is not merely an intellectual exercise but a form of spiritual warfare, grounded in truth and aimed at the salvation of souls. Therefore, it is of utmost importance for Christians to be diligently prepared in their apologetics endeavors.

Case Studies: Successfully Navigating Real-World Scenarios and Conversations

Engaging in Christian apologetics is not just an intellectual exercise. It has real-world applications that can either fortify or undermine a believer's faith. The Apostle Peter exhorted us to "always be prepared to make a defense to anyone who asks you for a reason for the hope that is in you" (1 Peter 3:15, UASV). Let us delve into a few case studies that demonstrate how to navigate conversations and scenarios, maintaining faithfulness to the Scriptures.

Case Study 1: "Is the Bible Just Another Book?"

In an academic setting, you might encounter claims that the Bible is a "collection of myths" or "just like any other ancient literature." Here's how you could respond:

1. **Scriptural Anchoring**: Paul reminded Timothy that "all Scripture is inspired by God" (2 Timothy 3:16, UASV). Highlight this verse and explain its significance.

2. **Factual Support**: Refer to archaeological evidences like the Dead Sea Scrolls, which not only confirm the Bible's preservation but also its historical accuracy.

3. **Reasoning**: Pose questions to challenge the interlocutor's view. If the Bible is just another book, why has it endured intense scrutiny and still remains the best-selling book of all time?

Case Study 2: "Aren't All Religions the Same?"

1. **Scriptural Anchoring**: Assert the unique claim of Jesus: "I am the way, and the truth, and the life. No one comes to the Father except through me" (John 14:6, UASV).

2. **Logical Argument**: Point out the contradictory tenets of different religions. If all paths lead to the same God, wouldn't that God be self-contradictory?

3. **Reasoning**: Use Paul's example in Athens, reasoning from the Scriptures and using cultural points to bring the audience to the truth (Acts 17:22-31).

Case Study 3: "Why Is There Suffering?"

1. **Scriptural Anchoring**: Explain that God did not create suffering; it is a result of human sin (Romans 5:12). God allows it but promises to end it (Revelation 21:4).

2. **Factual Support**: Bring up historical instances where suffering led to positive change or drew people closer to God.

3. **Reasoning**: A loving parent allows a child to face challenges to grow; similarly, God permits suffering for reasons we may not fully understand but can trust are ultimately for our good (James 1:2-4).

Case Study 4: "The Bible Promotes Intolerance"

1. **Scriptural Anchoring**: Clarify that the Bible teaches to "love your neighbor as yourself" (Matthew 22:39, UASV).

2. **Logical Argument**: Explain the difference between moral judgments and personal attacks. The Bible does not promote hate but does stand firm on moral issues.

3. **Reasoning**: Mention how the early Christians were willing to die rather than compromise their standards, demonstrating conviction, not intolerance (Acts 7:54-60).

Each case study follows a pattern: Scriptural anchoring, factual support, and reasoning. This triad equips the believer to make a well-rounded defense. In this way, one can fulfill the mandate of 1 Peter 3:15 in diverse situations, ranging from academic debates to everyday discussions.

Remember, apologetics is not about winning an argument; it's about faithfully representing the Christian message. The goal is to provide enough compelling evidence and reason for someone to consider the message of the Bible seriously, and ultimately, make an informed decision to follow Christ. It is about planting and watering the seed; God is responsible for the growth (1 Corinthians 3:6-7).

CHAPTER 25 Contend for the Faith

The Imperative of Jude 1:3: Understanding the Call to Contend for the Faith

In the epistle of Jude, the half-brother of Jesus issues a clarion call to the early Christian community. Jude 1:3 in the Updated American Standard Version reads, "Beloved, although I was very eager to write to you about our common salvation, I found it necessary to write appealing to you to contend earnestly for the faith that was once for all delivered to the saints." The call to 'contend earnestly for the faith' resonates deeply with the contemporary Christian's responsibility and aptly encapsulates the essence of Christian apologetics. But what exactly does Jude mean by this, and how should a modern believer understand and apply it?

The Context of Jude 1:3

To begin with, it's imperative to consider the historical backdrop against which Jude writes. His community was replete with internal threats of apostasy and heresy. These heretics were, as Jude describes, "ungodly people, who pervert the grace of our God into sensuality and deny our only Master and Lord, Jesus Christ" (Jude 1:4, UASV). This underscores the seriousness of contending for the faith; it is not merely an intellectual exercise but a spiritual battle with eternal ramifications.

Unpacking the Language

In Jude 1:3, the term 'contend earnestly' comes from the Greek word 'epagōnizomai,' a compound verb that invokes the imagery of intense struggle or combat. It is the same word used to describe an athlete's exertion in a competition. This suggests that defending the faith is not a passive endeavor but one that requires effort, skill, and fervor.

Faith "Once for All Delivered"

Jude is specific that it's the "faith that was once for all delivered to the saints" we must fight for. He refers to the body of Christian doctrine, the truths of Scripture, that are unchanging and have been fully revealed. This sets the boundaries for our contention; it is a fight for established, biblical truths, not personal opinions or cultural ideologies. We don't defend a "progressive" or "evolving" faith, but the faith "once for all delivered."

Literal Translation and Accurate Interpretation

Given that our primary goal is to be accurate and faithful to the original text, applying a word-for-word, or 'literal,' translation method, such as found in the UASV, supports the urgency of Jude's message. A literal translation brings to light the weightiness of the original language, allowing the reader to engage more deeply with the text and draw out its intended meaning.

Methods of Contention

Our methods of contention should mirror those of Jesus and the apostles, who anchored their teaching in Scripture. When Jesus was confronted, he responded with, "It is written" (Matthew 4:4, 7, 10). Paul also "reasoned from the Scriptures, explaining and proving by references" what he taught (Acts 17:2-3). These methods are not only biblically prescribed but also intellectually robust, engaging both the heart and the mind in the process.

Avoiding Ecumenism and Interfaith Compromises

It's crucial to note that the faith Jude urges us to defend is neither ecumenical nor interfaith in nature. The first-century Christians were distinct in their beliefs, claiming an exclusive truth not open to synthesis with other faiths or denominations. In contending for the faith, we do not seek a diluted, palatable version that caters to a pluralistic society but the unadulterated truth of the Gospel.

Objective Historical-Grammatical Method of Interpretation

When contending for the faith, our interpretative methodology matters significantly. The objective Historical-Grammatical method allows for a nuanced, contextually accurate understanding of Scripture, devoid of the speculative tendencies prevalent in liberal-moderate biblical criticism. This is in contrast to subjective methods like the Historical-Critical Method, which often erode the authority and inerrancy of the Scriptures.

The imperative of Jude 1:3 to "contend earnestly for the faith" is not just a first-century exhortation but a timeless principle that applies to every believer. This is not an option but an obligation—driven not by intellectual vanity but by a love for the truth and an earnest desire to see it upheld for the glory of God and the edification of His people. It is a call to defend the uncompromised, biblical faith against both internal and external threats through accurate translation, diligent study, and bold proclamation.

Thus, in an age of skepticism and spiritual compromise, Jude's words ring out as a solemn charge to each of us, stirring us to action in the defense and affirmation of the unchanging truth of God's Word.

Develop Ability as a Teacher

As an apologist who defends the Christian faith, one could say that the role of teaching within a Christian setting is multifaceted. Whether you are newly committed to evangelism, an experienced teacher, or perhaps even a parent, the ultimate goal remains the same: to effectively impart knowledge and spiritual understanding that brings people closer to God.

Learning from Jesus, the Master Teacher

Jesus Christ serves as the ideal model for teaching. His words were not just well-spoken but were also impactful, stimulating the minds of His listeners and providing them with practical applications they could immediately incorporate into their lives. So, if you wish to develop your teaching abilities, look no further than Christ's method.

Relying on Jehovah

Jesus was an extraordinary teacher because of His close relationship with Jehovah and the guidance He received through God's spirit. Prayer should be an essential component of your teaching practice, asking Jehovah for the wisdom and words to effectively educate and spiritually nourish those you are teaching.

Utilize Scripture Effectively

In addition to prayer, leveraging the power of God's Word, the Bible, is crucial. Scripture is God-breathed and useful for teaching, rebuking, correcting, and training in righteousness (2 Tim. 3:16-17). The more adept you become at applying Scripture in your lessons, the more effective your teaching will be.

Honoring Jehovah in Teaching

While skill in public speaking is beneficial, it is essential to remember that the focus should always be on glorifying Jehovah. This principle guides not just what is said, but also how it's said. Your teaching should lead people closer to God, not merely entertain or draw attention to yourself.

Clarity through Contrast

To make your teachings impactful, make sure to elucidate how Biblical truths differ from worldly beliefs or misunderstandings. Differentiating between the sacred and the secular helps your audience understand the significance of following God's commandments.

Encourage Independent Thought

A good teacher doesn't just dispense information; they cultivate thinking skills in their students. Employ open-ended questions and discussions that encourage your audience to think critically about Biblical principles and how to apply them in their lives.

Reach the Heart

True faith is not just about intellectual understanding but also involves the heart. Teaching should reach people on an emotional and spiritual level, encouraging a genuine relationship with God that goes beyond mere rule-following.

Practical Application

Finally, teaching must go beyond theoretical knowledge to practical application. Your audience should leave with a clear sense of how to apply what they've learned in their day-to-day lives. The Apostle Peter's sermon at Pentecost serves as an excellent example, as it led the people to ask, "What shall we do?" (Acts 2:37).

In summary, to be an effective Christian teacher, focus on following Christ's example, rely on Jehovah through prayer, make purposeful use of Scripture, aim to honor God, employ contrast for clarity, encourage critical thinking, reach the heart, and provide practical applications. This approach will help you fulfill your role as a spiritual guide, whether you are a parent, an evangelist, or an aspiring church leader.

The Importance of Reasoning Manner in Religious Discussions

Why Should We Care?

We all have a vested interest in helping others understand the transformative power of Scripture and its teachings. Our convictions about the Bible aren't just theoretical; they bear practical implications for everyone's life and eternal future

(Matt. 7:13, 14; John 12:48). While our passion for the truth is commendable, the *way* we express that truth matters just as much as the truth itself.

Limitations of a Dogmatic Approach

Merely stating a belief, even if supported by multiple passages from Scripture, often fails to resonate with people. A direct assault on someone's cherished beliefs is rarely effective and often closes the door to future discussions. *Being reasonable and considerate* can make your points more palatable and persuasive. James 3:17 highlights that divine wisdom is "peaceable, reasonable," emphasizing the interrelationship between these two qualities. Similarly, Titus 3:2 and Philippians 4:5 instruct us to be mild and known for our "reasonableness."

Tailoring the Approach: Know Your Audience

The Apostle Paul, a seasoned communicator, adapted his approach depending on his audience. When speaking in a synagogue, Paul leveraged the audience's respect for the Hebrew Scriptures, "explaining and proving by references that it was necessary for the Christ to suffer and to rise from the dead" (Acts 17:2, 3). Conversely, when addressing Greeks who weren't versed in the Scriptures, Paul anchored his arguments in their own cultural references (Acts 17:22-31). Today, with billions of people unfamiliar with the Bible, *beginning with shared concerns* may open the door for deeper conversations.

Addressing Sensitive Beliefs

When confronting others about their long-held religious beliefs, it's crucial to be *mindful of their emotional investment*. For instance, if a person has recently discovered truths in the Bible that contradict his family's beliefs, it's essential to communicate this change delicately to avoid causing undue offense or estrangement.

The Value of Yielding

Jehovah himself shows exemplary reasonableness, accommodating individual needs as demonstrated in the story of Lot's escape from Sodom (Gen. 19:17-30). *Being adaptable does not mean compromising on Scriptural principles*, but rather it entails knowing when to press an issue and when to retreat for the sake of a more meaningful future conversation (Prov. 16:23; 19:11).

Freedom of Choice

Jehovah respects the free will he has given us (Josh. 24:15). Similarly, when we discuss matters of faith, *we must remember that others also have the right to make their own choices*.

Engaging Through Questions

Jesus was a master at drawing people into productive conversations. He used questions to provoke thought and to understand where people were coming from. *Questions are powerful tools for mutual understanding* and should not be underestimated.

Explaining Rationale

When referring to Scripture, take the extra step to clarify your interpretation. Explain key phrases and provide additional scriptural references if possible. *A complete explanation, supported by evidence, leaves a more significant impact* than mere statements (Acts 17:1-4).

How To Do It

- **Assess the background and attitude of your listeners** before launching into your discussion.
- **Don't challenge every wrong statement.** Choose your battles wisely.
- **Speak with conviction** but acknowledge the freedom others have to make their own choices.
- **Prompt reasoning** through questions and illustrations, not just quick answers.
- **Detail your interpretation of a scripture**, using supporting evidence or analogies to clarify its meaning.

Exercises

1. Analyze your previous conversations with individuals who have strong views. Assess the evidence you presented, the questions you asked, and your consideration of their background.
2. Plan how you would reason with someone who is considering doing something wrong, either a peer or a child. Apply these guidelines to your hypothetical conversation.

YOUR GUIDE FOR DEFENDING THE BIBLE

By taking a reasoned, Scripturally grounded approach in our discussions, we not only honor Jehovah but also open up a pathway for others to receive the life-changing teachings of the Bible.

Principles of Sound Argumentation

The Imperative of Evidential Support

Why is evidence important? Whenever you make a claim, your audience has every right to question its validity: "Why is that true? What proof do you have?" You bear the responsibility, as the speaker or teacher, to either answer these questions or guide your audience toward the answers. If your argument hinges on a particular point, ensure you provide compelling reasons for its acceptance. Doing so elevates the persuasive power of your message.

The Apostle Paul, a master of rhetoric, employed logical reasoning, sound argumentation, and impassioned pleas to encourage a shift in his listeners' perspectives (*Acts 18:4; 19:8*). However, beware: not all uses of persuasion serve the truth. Some employ faulty premises, biased sources, superficial reasoning, or emotional manipulation to deceive (*Matt. 27:20; Acts 14:19; Col. 2:4*).

Anchored in Divine Truth

What should be the foundation of our arguments? Any teaching we present should not stem from human innovation but from Scriptural truths. Influential Christian literature can aid us in understanding the Bible, but these should guide us back to Scripture. Our aim is not self-justification but an earnest wish to let others discern what the Bible itself declares. Aligning with Christ's assertion, "Your word is truth" (*John 17:17*), we affirm that the ultimate authority is Jehovah, the Creator of all. Arguments grounded in His Word stand unassailable.

For those unfamiliar with or skeptical about the Bible, exercise discretion in introducing Scriptural support. The goal is to lead them to this unparalleled resource as soon as is reasonable. A mere citation of Scripture may not suffice; sometimes you may need to clarify its context or provide additional Scriptural evidence to fortify your claim. *Be cautious not to overstate what a Scripture proves*; your audience should clearly see how it substantiates your point.

Strengthened by Supplementary Evidence

When should you use additional evidence? At times, corroborative data from reliable, non-Biblical sources can further emphasize the reasonableness of the Scriptures. You might cite the intricacies of the universe as evidence of a Creator or mention natural laws to suggest a Lawgiver. These are valid arguments as long as they are consistent with the teachings of the Bible (*Job 38:31-33; Ps. 19:1; Rom. 1:20*).

However, while scholars and scientific data can complement Scriptural arguments, they should not replace the Bible as the foundational authority. Base your claims on the firm foundation of God's Word, then use scientific or other forms of evidence to support, not to establish, your arguments.

Tailoring Your Approach

Different audiences may require different forms of evidence. Analogies can illuminate the logic behind a concept, as long as they align with Scriptural teachings. Personal experiences, too, can underline the applicability and wisdom of Scriptural guidance, though these should be used sparingly to avoid drawing attention to oneself. Always adapt your reasoning to the needs and perspectives of your audience, as advised by *Proverbs 16:23*: "The heart of the wise one causes his mouth to show insight, and to his lips it adds persuasiveness."

Practical Steps for Effective Argumentation

1. **Offer concrete evidence**: Don't just make claims; support them with evidence.
2. **Ground arguments in the Scriptures**: Ensure your main points are Biblically supported.
3. **Employ supplementary evidence wisely**: Use additional data as needed to meet the expectations and questions of your audience.

Exercises for Further Study

1. **Examine the Scripture**: Look at how Jesus Christ and the Apostle Paul reasoned from the Scriptures. Pay attention to the questions they raised and how they answered them, focusing on Scriptural emphasis.
2. **Study Persuasive Techniques**: Observe how both effectively employed persuasive arguments during their interactions.

By adhering to these principles and Scriptural guidelines, your ability to present sound, convincing arguments will be greatly enhanced.

CHAPTER 26 Reasoning from the Scriptures

Effort to Reach the Heart of Your Listeners

Focus on how individuals feel about the topics at hand and help them form motivations that lead them closer to God.

To align with God's will, it is essential that people **implant God's Word deep within their hearts**. In addition to sharing the message of the Scripture, strive to connect with people's inner selves or figurative "hearts." This is the core of who they are—their emotions, thoughts, and motivations. This is where the seeds of truth take root (Matt. 13:19), and from where obedience to God must arise (Prov. 3:1; Rom. 6:17).

Objectives for Deep Connection

1. Understand what has already influenced your listener's heart.
2. Bolster positive qualities like love and godly fear.
3. Inspire listeners to scrutinize their inner motives to be pleasing to God.

Using Discernment

People have various reasons for not yet embracing the truth. Be discerning to understand their objections and barriers. **Discernment is the ability to understand what isn't immediately obvious**, requiring a keen sense of observation and a genuine caring attitude (Prov. 20:5).

Non-verbal cues like facial expressions or tone changes offer valuable insight. Pose well-chosen questions to reveal what's truly in someone's heart. However, exercise caution and sensitivity when probing into personal matters (1 Pet. 4:15).

Stirring Up Beneficial Feelings

Once you understand someone's beliefs, work on that foundation. Encourage feelings of love and godly fear by emphasizing God's character and what He values in them as individuals. Reference passages like Psalm 139:1-3, Luke 21:1-4, and John 6:44 to deepen their understanding of God's enduring love.

Fostering godly fear can inspire actions otherwise thought impossible (Ps. 111:10; Rev. 14:6, 7). Remind your listeners that their actions significantly affect God and that living by His principles benefits them (Isa. 48:17).

Helping Others to Make an Examination

Assist your listeners in becoming aware of their inner selves. **The Bible is not just a historical record but a mirror reflecting God's own thinking** (James 1:22-25). Encourage them to consider how their lives align with God's teachings (Heb. 4:12; Rom. 15:4).

Address potential barriers, like societal pressure or fleshly desires, and point out the dangers of indecision (1 Ki. 18:21). Encourage self-examination and prayer for inner refinement (Ps. 26:2; 139:23, 24).

Wholehearted Service

Teaching the person that you are speaking with to serve God with their "whole heart" means aligning their feelings, desires, and motives with God's ways (Luke 10:27). When someone develops a personal relationship with God, obedience flows naturally out of faith. Such heartfelt obedience is pleasing to God (Prov. 23:15).

Remember, it is God who examines hearts and draws people to Him (Prov. 21:2; John 6:44). Our role is merely to cooperate in this divine process (1 Cor. 3:9). By taking these steps, you can work toward not just reaching minds, but more importantly, hearts, thereby aiding individuals in forming a closer, more obedient relationship with God.

Using the Art of Persuasion (Acts 18:4, 13; 26:28; 28:23)

The art of persuasion is a vital skill for anyone engaging in Christian apologetics. The Apostle Paul was a master of this art, utilizing it effectively as he "reasoned in the synagogue every Sabbath, and tried to persuade Jews and Greeks" (Acts 18:4, UASV). In the book of Acts, we find additional instances where persuasion played a crucial role. For example, Acts 26:28 highlights King Agrippa's interaction with Paul, where Agrippa admits, "In a short time you would persuade me to become a Christian." Paul's efforts at persuasion also extended to "explaining and solemnly testifying about the kingdom of God" from "morning until evening" (Acts 28:23, UASV).

The goal of persuasion in Christian apologetics is not merely to win an argument but to guide individuals toward a transformative understanding of

Scriptural truths. The objective is ultimately spiritual, aimed at capturing the heart, enlightening the mind, and steering the will toward God's intended purpose.

Elements of Persuasion

1. **Reasoning from the Scriptures**: Paul, the master apologist, often employed a method known as 'dialegomai' in Greek, which means 'to reason' or 'to converse.' Acts 17:2-3 reveals his approach: "And Paul went in, as was his custom, and on three Sabbath days he reasoned with them from the Scriptures, explaining and proving that it was necessary for the Christ to suffer and to rise from the dead, and saying, 'This Jesus, whom I proclaim to you, is the Christ.'"

2. **Use of Sound Arguments**: A well-reasoned argument is often a convincing one. In Acts 18:13, the Jews accused Paul of persuading people to worship God contrary to the law. Paul's persuasive techniques, however, were based on the sound interpretation of the Law and the Prophets, highlighting the fulfillment of Messianic prophecies in Jesus Christ.

3. **Appeal to Conscience**: In Acts 24:25, Paul reasoned with Felix regarding "righteousness, self-control, and the judgment to come." His argument was not merely intellectual; it also aimed at the conscience, which is a fundamental aspect of effective persuasion.

Examples of Persuasion in Scripture

1. **The Resurrection Argument**: One of Paul's primary persuasive arguments was the resurrection of Jesus Christ. In Acts 17:31, he states, "because he [God] has fixed a day on which he will judge the world in righteousness by a man whom he has appointed; and of this he has given assurance to all by raising him from the dead." The resurrection is not only a historic event but also a central tenet that validates Christian faith.

2. **The Argument from Prophecy**: Isaiah 53 was often cited as a Messianic prophecy fulfilled in Jesus. Paul could use such Scriptures to demonstrate the consistency and reliability of God's Word, thereby persuading Jews who revered these texts.

3. **The Moral Argument**: In Romans 2:14-15, Paul argues that the Gentiles, who do not have the Law, demonstrate the work of the Law written in their hearts. Their conscience and moral inclinations bear witness to a moral lawgiver—God.

4. **The Argument from Fulfillment**: In Acts 13:27-33, Paul persuades his audience by explaining that the residents of Jerusalem unwittingly fulfilled the prophecies about Jesus by condemning him. He then demonstrates how the resurrection is the ultimate fulfillment of God's promises.

The effectiveness of persuasion is not solely determined by the persuader's skill but also relies on the work of the Holy Spirit. While it is essential to be adept in the art of persuasion, relying on human wisdom alone is insufficient. As Paul said, "My speech and my preaching were not with persuasive words of wisdom, but in demonstration of the Spirit and of power" (1 Corinthians 2:4, UASV).

Christian apologetics is a domain where skill in persuasion intersects with divine truth. The apologist's task is not to manipulate but to present the Gospel persuasively, following the pattern of reasoning set by Jesus Christ and His apostles. As we engage in this vital task, let us continually seek to hone our skills in the art of persuasion, always aiming for the greater objective—the transformation of souls through the life-changing message of the Gospel.

The Art of Effective Communication: Biblical Principles for Answering Questions

Understanding the Complexity of Questions

Sometimes, questions can serve as the tip of an iceberg, hiding the crux of the issue beneath the surface. Even a seemingly straightforward inquiry may entail a layered meaning or ulterior motive. It's crucial to employ discernment to gauge not just what should be said but *how* it should be presented. Scripture provides guidance in this area: "Let your speech always be gracious, seasoned with salt, so that you may know how you ought to answer each person" (Col. 4:6 ESV).

Perception of the Inquirer

Christ demonstrated the importance of understanding the inquirer's point of view when He was questioned by the Sadducees about the resurrection (Luke 20:27-40). By pinpointing their disbelief in the resurrection, He masterfully provided an answer that addressed their underlying assumptions, silencing any further queries.

Adapting to the Context

When confronted with questions, it's pivotal to discern the motivations and concerns of the questioner. Responses should be crafted based on the particular context. For example, answering a query about not celebrating Christmas may necessitate identifying the questioner's motivation. This understanding allows for a tailored response that may even educate the questioner on the Bible's stance on specific celebrations.

YOUR GUIDE FOR DEFENDING THE BIBLE

Navigating Tricky Situations

Occasionally, you may encounter questions designed to test or challenge your beliefs. In such instances, it's beneficial to preface your answers with remarks that address common misconceptions, thereby creating a more receptive environment for a fruitful discussion. Your response could serve to enlighten your audience, offering them valuable information while clarifying the Scriptural basis for your beliefs.

Interacting with Authorities

When dealing with figures of authority, it's imperative to offer responses that reflect a "mild temper and deep respect," as Scripture advises (1 Pet. 3:15). By understanding their concerns and respectfully acknowledging them, you are more likely to find a common ground.

Considering Scriptural Authority

The authority your questioner places on Scripture also affects how you should answer. Christ, for instance, used references familiar to the Sadducees in order to substantiate His arguments. Should your listener not hold the Bible as authoritative, you may follow the example of the Apostle Paul, who in Acts 17:22-31 conveyed Scriptural truths without direct quotations.

Grace in Speech

Being gracious in our speech, reflecting God's own graciousness, is a Scriptural command. In a world rife with rudeness and hostility, a gentle response can diffuse tension and open doors for constructive discussion (Prov. 15:1; 25:15).

Advising on Personal Choices

When asked for advice on personal matters, instead of providing a direct answer, you could guide the person to Bible principles and examples that can help him make a wise decision. This respects individual autonomy and places the responsibility for decision-making where it belongs: on the individual (Gal. 6:5).

Participating in Church Discussions

Preparing Ahead

Advanced preparation can significantly enhance your contributions during church meetings, thereby encouraging your fellow believers.

Strategies for Commenting

When called upon, aim for clarity and brevity. This allows others to participate and contribute their insights as well.

Key Takeaways Before Responding

- Assess the motivation behind the question.
- Consider laying a foundation for better understanding of your answer.
- Show respect for the other person's concerns.
- Communicate with kindness and conviction.

In Summation

Answering questions effectively requires more than knowing the answer; it demands discernment and a thoughtful approach. But when our responses are both sincere and considerate, the resulting dialogue can prove deeply rewarding for everyone involved (Prov. 15:23).

Practical Application: How to Employ Scriptural Reasoning in Everyday Conversations

Mastering the art of Scriptural reasoning is essential for any Christian who aims to "always [be] prepared to make a defense to anyone who asks you for a reason for the hope that is in you" (1 Peter 3:15, UASV). The Scriptures are not a detached, academic subject; they are the living Word of God, intended to guide every facet of our lives. Let's delve into some methods to employ Scriptural reasoning in everyday conversations.

Initiate With Respect

Before you can reason from the Scriptures, you must establish a respectful and receptive environment. The apostle Paul "reasoned in the synagogue with the Jews and the devout persons, and in the marketplace every day with those who happened to be there" (Acts 17:17, UASV). Whether in a religious setting or daily life, respect is foundational. Use polite language, active listening, and non-confrontational body language.

YOUR GUIDE FOR DEFENDING THE BIBLE

Start With Common Ground

Find a mutual concern or question to begin the conversation. The apostle Paul, when in Athens, started with a local altar to an "Unknown God" (Acts 17:22-23). He used this as a stepping stone to introduce the concept of Jehovah, the true God.

Use Clear and Understandable Terms

Employ language that is accessible and relatable to the individual you are talking to. Christ Himself made use of parables—earthly stories with a heavenly meaning—to make His teachings more relatable to everyday people (Matthew 13:10-17).

Cite Scriptural References

Always back your reasoning and assertions with clear Scriptural references. Take the example of Jesus, who responded to Satan's temptations by saying, "It is written..." followed by Scriptural quotations (Matthew 4:4, 7, 10).

Explain, Don't Just Quote

Paul, in reasoning with the Jews, was "explaining and proving by references" (Acts 17:2-3). Merely quoting a verse is rarely sufficient. Explain the historical context, the grammatical structure, and how the passage fits within the broader biblical message.

Incorporate Questions

Asking questions can engage the other person's thought processes and open up new avenues for Scriptural reasoning. Jesus was a master of this, often responding to questions with questions of His own (e.g., Matthew 21:24-27).

Apply the Scripture to Modern Contexts

Scriptures were written long ago, but their teachings are timeless. Show how Scriptural principles can be applied to contemporary issues. For example, the principle found in Galatians 6:7 ("Do not be deceived: God is not mocked, for whatever one sows, that will he also reap") can be applied to discussions about ethical behavior, personal responsibility, and even environmental stewardship.

Use Analogies and Illustrations

Just like Jesus used parables, employing analogies and illustrations can help clarify Scriptural teachings. For example, the relationship between Christ and the church can be likened to that of a husband and wife, as Paul does in Ephesians 5:22-33.

Be Humble and Willing to Learn

In the course of your discussions, you may find yourself challenged or questioned. Take this as an opportunity to delve deeper into Scripture. Peter advised Christians to make their defense "with gentleness and respect" (1 Peter 3:15).

Know When to Pause or Stop

Discernment is vital. Not every conversation will result in a conversion or even an agreement. Like Jesus instructed, if a place does not receive you or listen to your words, "shake off the dust from your feet" (Matthew 10:14).

In conclusion, reasoning from the Scriptures in everyday conversations is not merely a skill but a Christian duty. The above guidelines do not offer a one-size-fits-all approach, but they provide a structured and respectful way to bring the Word of God into your everyday interactions. As Paul wisely observed, "Let your speech always be gracious, seasoned with salt, so that you may know how you ought to answer each person" (Colossians 4:6, UASV).

YOUR GUIDE FOR DEFENDING THE BIBLE

SECTION 7 CHRISTIAN EVANGELISM

Digging Deeper

We put books here on this subject if one is interested in taking the subject deeper. This section gives you foundational knowledge to evangelize or engage people in conversation.

CONVERSATIONAL EVANGELISM: Defending the Faith, Reasoning from the Scriptures, Explaining and Proving, Instructing in Sound Doctrine, and Overturning False Reasoning by Edward D. Andrews (2017)

ISBN-13: 978-1945757372

https://www.amazon.com/dp/B01N7OQY16

THE EVANGELISM HANDBOOK: How All Christians Can Effectively Share God's Word in Their Community by Edward D. Andrews (2017)

ISBN-13 : 978-1945757389

https://www.amazon.com/dp/B01N7PWS3R

REASONING WITH The WORLD'S VARIOUS RELIGIONS: Examining and Evangelizing Other Faiths by Edward D. Andrews (2018)

ISBN-13: 978-1945757815

https://www.amazon.com/dp/B07B44G924

CHAPTER 27 Using Persuasion to Reach the Heart of Our Listeners

The Role of Persuasion in the New Testament: Insights from Pauline Epistles

The act of persuading someone to adopt a particular belief or course of action is not merely a modern tool of rhetoric; it's a scriptural imperative. The Apostle Paul, a leading figure in the New Testament, provides us with invaluable insights on the role of persuasion in Christian discourse. By examining Paul's epistles, we can understand not just the art of persuasive communication but also its scriptural grounding, thereby equipping us for impactful evangelism.

Pauline Principles of Persuasion

Paul's life provides a study in contrasts, from persecuting Christians to becoming one of its most powerful spokesmen. He was not just a passive conveyor of theological concepts but an active persuader for Christ. In his epistles, Paul's persuasive tactics are often clear and purposeful. He employed logic, moral principles, and emotions to address the whole person—mind, heart, and will.

Ethos: Building Credibility

Paul recognized the importance of ethos, the ethical appeal, in persuasion. He often started his letters by establishing his credentials as an apostle "not sent from men nor through the agency of man, but through Jesus Christ and God the Father" (Galatians 1:1, UASV). This was not to boast, but to build credibility with his audience, thereby strengthening the persuasiveness of his message.

Logos: Reasoning from Scriptures

Paul's letters are characterized by strong logical reasoning. For example, in Romans, he meticulously lays out the case for the universality of sin (Romans 3:23), justification by faith (Romans 5:1), and the transformative power of the Gospel (Romans 12:2). He reasoned from the Scriptures, explaining and proving what he taught (Acts 17:2-3).

Pathos: Emotional Appeal

While reason forms the backbone of Paul's argumentation, he does not neglect the emotional dimension. Take the case of Philemon; Paul could have ordered him to accept Onesimus back, but instead, he appealed to his sense of compassion, stating, "I preferred to do nothing without your consent in order that your goodness might not be by compulsion but of your own accord" (Philemon 14, UASV).

Employing Persuasion in Everyday Conversations

Ask Provocative Questions

Paul often used questions to stimulate thought. In Romans 6:1, he asks, "What shall we say then? Are we to continue in sin that grace may abound?" This question makes the reader ponder the implications of grace and confront their own behavior.

Adapt to Your Audience

Paul adapted his message to his audience without compromising the Gospel. For example, to the Jews, he became as a Jew (1 Corinthians 9:20). His speech in Athens (Acts 17:22-34) demonstrated cultural understanding, yet didn't dilute the message of Christ's resurrection.

Use Real-World Examples

Paul often used real-world examples to illustrate spiritual principles. In 1 Corinthians 9:24-27, he used the metaphor of an athlete to discuss self-discipline. By doing so, he related the message to experiences that were familiar to his audience.

Testify from Personal Experience

Your own testimony is a powerful tool of persuasion, as seen when Paul recounts his personal encounter with Christ (Acts 26:12-18). Sharing how you have personally been impacted by the Gospel can be instrumental in reaching the hearts of your listeners.

Paul's epistles offer a wealth of insights into the biblical art of persuasion. By understanding and implementing these principles, we are better equipped to communicate the Gospel effectively. Remember that we are not simply disseminating information but engaging in the transformational act of guiding souls towards salvation in Christ. So let us take our cues from Paul and engage in purposeful, Scripture-based persuasion, applying it diligently in our everyday conversations to the glory of God.

Balancing Logic and Emotion: Crafting Messages that Appeal to Mind and Heart

A well-crafted message doesn't merely address the intellect; it also appeals to the heart. Achieving the balance between logic and emotion is a delicate dance, especially in the realm of Christian Apologetics. While it's vital to present arguments grounded in Scripture and reason, a mechanical approach devoid of emotional connection can be alienating. Here, insights from Paul's epistles serve as a model for balancing the cerebral and the emotional in our persuasive efforts.

Leveraging Logic: Intellectual Integrity of Paul's Messages

Paul was a man of robust intellectual credentials. Trained under Gamaliel, one of the leading Jewish scholars of his day, Paul knew how to formulate and present logical arguments. His letters brim with theological richness, presenting foundational doctrines with intellectual rigor. In Romans, for example, Paul lays out the logical arguments for justification by faith. With precision, he draws from the Old Testament, quoting Genesis and Psalms to substantiate his case (Romans 4:1-8, UASV).

It is also essential to note Paul's method of 'reasoning from the Scriptures,' as he did in Thessalonica for three weeks, explaining and proving that it was necessary for the Christ to suffer and rise from the dead (Acts 17:2-3). This reliance on Scripture reinforces the intellectual integrity of Paul's messages and encourages us to ground our persuasive tactics in Biblical truth.

Emotional Resonance: Paul's Relational and Compassionate Approach

However, Paul was not a dry intellectual. His letters are steeped in emotion and relational language. Who can forget his poignant words in 1 Corinthians 13, extolling love as the greatest of virtues? Or his touching words to the Philippians, "For to me, to live is Christ and to die is gain" (Philippians 1:21, UASV)?

In 2 Corinthians, he opens his heart and shares his afflictions and fears, emphasizing the comfort he finds in God (2 Corinthians 1:3-11). This emotional vulnerability does more than just add color to his letters; it builds a relational bridge between him and his readers, making his intellectual arguments more accessible and relatable.

YOUR GUIDE FOR DEFENDING THE BIBLE

Case Study: Paul's Address to the Athenians

One of the most remarkable instances of Paul's persuasive mastery is his speech at the Areopagus (Acts 17:22-31). Here, Paul starts by acknowledging the Athenians' religiosity, thus creating emotional goodwill. He then introduces the concept of the 'Unknown God,' logically progressing to the nature and demands of this God. While making rational appeals, he doesn't shy away from tapping into the Athenians' fear of ignorance or their desire for spiritual completeness. It's a striking balance between rational argument and emotional appeal.

Why Both Are Necessary

Engaging only the intellect or only the emotions is an incomplete approach. A message that's all intellect risks becoming a sterile exercise in syllogistic reasoning. On the other hand, an emotionally laden message without substantive intellectual content may sway the emotions momentarily but lacks the staying power to bring about genuine transformation.

Scripture insists that we should love God with all our mind and heart (Matthew 22:37). Persuasion, therefore, should be a holistic exercise engaging both. Emotional resonance brings down the defenses and opens the heart to receive the seed of the Word. Intellectual rigor ensures that the seed finds good soil to take root, grow, and bear fruit.

Practical Steps

1. **Scripture First**: Anchor your message in Scripture, letting it guide both the intellectual and emotional dimensions of your message.
2. **Know Your Audience**: Tailor your message to meet the intellectual and emotional needs of your audience, as Paul did with his diverse audiences.
3. **Personal Testimony**: Don't underestimate the power of personal stories. Paul often shared his own experiences to make abstract truths relatable.
4. **Be Authentic**: Authenticity is the key to emotional resonance. Be true to your faith and convictions; it will shine through your message.

By mastering the art of balancing logic and emotion, we not only follow in the footsteps of great Biblical communicators like Paul but we also become more effective in fulfilling our Christian mandate to "make disciples" (Matthew 28:19, UASV). In doing so, we contribute to the vital task of not merely informing but also transforming hearts in alignment with Biblical truth.

The Ethics of Persuasion: Truthfulness, Integrity, and Respect in Apologetics

In the realm of Christian apologetics, persuasion plays an essential role. Nevertheless, persuasion must be tempered by ethical considerations: namely, truthfulness, integrity, and respect. These elements should be woven into the very fabric of our apologetic endeavors, for they mirror the character of God, who embodies these virtues.

Truthfulness

At the core of apologetics is the assertion that Christian faith rests on objective, verifiable truths. As 1 Peter 3:15 reminds us, we should always be prepared to give a defense for our faith, doing so with "gentleness and respect." A persuasively crafted message that lacks truth is not just an oxymoron but a betrayal of the Christian calling. Truthfulness is the first, indispensable criterion for ethical persuasion.

- **Example 1**: When defending the Resurrection, it would be unethical to ignore or dismiss alternative explanations given by skeptics, even if they do not align with Christian beliefs. These counterarguments should be fairly presented and then refuted, supporting the veracity of the Resurrection event.

- **Example 2**: Citing textual reliability, scholars often refer to the vast number of New Testament manuscripts. While this argument is valid, one must not exaggerate or misconstrue the numbers merely to bolster the point. Truthfulness requires presenting facts as they are, even if they do not make for a more dramatic argument.

Integrity

Integrity in apologetics is closely linked to truthfulness but goes beyond it. This speaks to the honesty, ethical uprightness, and moral character of the apologist themselves. It's not just what is said, but how it's said and the motives behind saying it. The Apostle Paul, in 2 Corinthians 4:2, asserts that he "renounced the things hidden because of shame, not walking in craftiness or adulterating the word of God, but by the manifestation of truth commending ourselves to every man's conscience in the sight of God."

- **Example 1**: You might be posed with a difficult question you can't answer. Integrity means admitting your limitations rather than faking an answer.

This also gives you an opportunity to research and return with a well-considered response.

- **Example 2**: When reasoning with others, avoid the temptation to "win" an argument at the expense of the other person. Do not cut corners theologically or engage in personal attacks. Our goal is to win souls, not arguments. Apologetics is not a conquest; it is an aspect of discipleship.

Respect

Respect is the third pillar of ethical persuasion. It involves recognizing the dignity and worth of every individual as made in the image of God (Genesis 1:27). In practice, this means listening carefully, avoiding a demeaning tone, and never manipulating or coercing someone into belief. The Parable of the Sower (Matthew 13:1-23) reminds us that the role of the Christian is to sow seeds; it is God who causes growth.

- **Example 1**: If someone is struggling with the issue of suffering, it's not respectful to dismiss their pain by providing pat theological answers. Be empathetic, validate their feelings, and then carefully lead them through the Scriptures that address suffering, acknowledging that while answers may exist, pain is still real.

- **Example 2**: If engaging with someone from another faith, respect doesn't mean you have to agree with their views, but it does require acknowledging their right to hold these views. We must remember Peter's counsel to share the reasons for our hope "with gentleness and respect."

In summary, persuasion in apologetics must be a marriage of both style and substance, characterized by an unwavering commitment to truthfulness, integrity, and respect. It's not enough to be right; we must also be good in our rightness. By upholding these ethical standards, we do more than bolster the integrity of our message; we reflect the very character of God to those with whom we engage. This is perhaps the most persuasive argument we could ever make.

Techniques and Best Practices: Proven Methods for Effective Persuasion in Apologetics

The task of an apologist extends far beyond intellectual argumentation; it involves reaching the hearts of the listeners. To achieve this, persuasive techniques that maintain the integrity of the message are indispensable. Here are some proven methods that align well with a conservative, literal understanding of the Scriptures.

Cite Scriptural Authority

In apologetics, Scripture remains the ultimate source of authority. Paul reasoned "from the Scriptures, explaining and proving by references" (Acts 17:2-3 UASV). Our persuasive techniques should be deeply rooted in the Scriptures, and we should be prepared to cite them effectively.

Example:

When discussing salvation, instead of resorting to emotional anecdotes, focus on what the Bible says. For instance, you might say, "Ephesians 2:8-9 makes it clear that we are saved by grace through faith, not by works. How does your view align with this Scripture?"

Employ Logical Reasoning

Scriptural argumentation should be logical and sound. Avoid logical fallacies like straw man arguments, ad hominem attacks, or appeals to emotion that distort the message.

Example:

If discussing why hell is not eternal torment, instead of painting grotesque images, logically explain that words like "Sheol" or "Hades" in the Scriptures represent the grave or death, and not a place of eternal suffering.

Appeal to Shared Beliefs and Values

Common ground serves as a foundation for building persuasive arguments. You might appeal to shared human experiences, a collective sense of morality, or even mutual acknowledgment of historical events. But the conversation should always lead back to what the Bible actually says.

Example:

If you are talking with someone who values justice, you might discuss God's ultimate plan for justice as presented in the Book of Revelation, and how it provides a solution for the problem of evil in the world.

Use Analogies and Parables Wisely

While Jesus used parables to convey complex truths, it is important to remember that these analogies should not distort Scriptural truths. They should help illuminate them.

Example:

If discussing God's sovereignty, you might use the analogy of a potter and clay as found in Romans 9:21, emphasizing that the potter has the right to make out of the same lump of clay one vessel for honorable use and another for dishonorable use.

Ask Provocative Questions

Questions engage the listener's mind and invite them to think critically. Jesus often used questions to challenge prevailing thoughts.

Example:

In discussing the resurrection, one might ask, "If Christ has not been raised, then what is the foundation of Christian hope?" This could lead to a discussion of 1 Corinthians 15 where Paul argues the necessity of the resurrection.

Utilize Testimonials Strategically

While personal experiences can be impactful, they should never replace Scriptural evidence. They should instead serve to complement and reinforce the Scriptural message.

Example:

One could share how understanding the Scriptural teaching that we do not have a soul, but we are souls (Gen 2:7), revolutionized their approach to life and spirituality, leading them to prioritize Scriptural values.

Maintain a Respectful Tone

Persuasion is not just about what is said, but how it is said. Respect for one's audience is paramount. Paul, when addressing the Athenians, acknowledged their religiosity before presenting the truth about the "unknown god" they were worshiping (Acts 17:22-31).

The art of persuasion in apologetics is a delicate balancing act. While employing these techniques, we must remain unwaveringly committed to Scriptural truth. Techniques should serve to enhance the delivery of the message, not dilute or compromise it. Being effective in persuasion requires a robust understanding of the Bible, skilled communication, and, above all, a prayerful reliance on God for wisdom and guidance.

Edward D. Andrews

CHAPTER 28 Speak the Word of God with Boldness

The Biblical Mandate for Boldness: Lessons from the Acts of the Apostles

In an era of religious pluralism and moral relativism, boldness in proclaiming Scriptural truth is more crucial than ever. While the world offers a cacophony of viewpoints, the unchanging Word of God stands as the authoritative standard. This is why the early followers of Jesus were commanded and exemplified a sense of utter boldness in proclaiming God's messages. Particularly, the Book of Acts serves as a rich repository of lessons in Christian boldness.

The Apostolic Blueprint

From the moment the apostles received the Holy Spirit at Pentecost, they displayed an audacity that startled both their supporters and adversaries. Acts 4:31 (UASV) tells us, "And when they had prayed, the place where they had gathered together was shaken, and they were all filled with the Holy Spirit and began to speak the word of God with boldness." This boldness wasn't a result of emotional hype but the consequence of being filled with the Holy Spirit.

Peter and John, once cowering in fear during Jesus' trial, became paragons of boldness. When warned not to speak about Jesus, they replied, "Whether it is right in the sight of God to listen to you rather than to God, you judge; for we cannot but speak of what we have seen and heard" (Acts 4:19-20, UASV). They recognized the urgency and the unparalleled significance of their message, setting a precedent for Christians today.

Boldness Despite Opposition

Not only were the apostles bold in the face of religious authorities, but they also displayed this trait when confronted by society at large, and even when facing mortal danger. For example, Stephen, full of the Holy Spirit, confronted the Sanhedrin with a profound Scriptural history lesson before openly rebuking them for their hard-heartedness (Acts 7). His fate was martyrdom, yet his boldness had an immeasurable impact—planting seeds of truth in the heart of Saul of Tarsus, a future apostle.

The Role of Reasoning and Proof

Boldness did not negate the need for reasoned argument and proof from the Scriptures. Paul, an intellectual giant of his age, exemplified this perfectly. Acts 17:2-3 (UASV) states that Paul "reasoned with them from the Scriptures, explaining and proving that it was necessary for the Christ to suffer and to rise from the dead." This method of 'reasoning from the Scriptures' underscores the necessity for deep Scriptural knowledge and intellectual engagement with the content of our faith, all while maintaining the imperative of bold proclamation.

The Necessity of Clarity and Conviction

The apostles did not mince words or dilute their message to make it more palatable to the masses. Acts 2:38-39 (UASV) shows Peter proclaiming, "Repent, and each of you be baptized in the name of Jesus Christ for the forgiveness of your sins; and you will receive the gift of the Holy Spirit." There was no room for ambiguity or compromise. This demands that modern Christians not only understand their message clearly but also possess the conviction to proclaim it without dilution or hesitation.

A Balanced Boldness

While the apostles were bold, they were not brash or arrogant. Their boldness was coupled with genuine love and concern for those they were reaching. As Paul told the Thessalonians, "But having the same boldness in God to speak to you the gospel of God amid much opposition. For our encouragement did not come from error or impurity or by way of deceit; but just as we have been approved by God to be entrusted with the gospel, so we speak, not as pleasing men, but God who examines our hearts" (1 Thess. 2:2-4, UASV). This balanced boldness stems from the nature of the message itself—a message of eternal life and hope.

The Book of Acts sets a powerful precedent for the kind of boldness that should typify followers of Jesus Christ. This boldness is fueled by the Holy Spirit, sustained by a firm grasp of Scriptural truth, and guided by love for God and neighbor. It is a call to defy societal norms and religious traditions that run counter to the unchanging Word of God. To be a Christian, according to the apostolic model, is to embrace the command to speak the Word of God with boldness. This is not an optional attribute; it's a Biblical mandate. Therefore, let the lessons from the Acts of the Apostles serve as our guide as we navigate through the complexities of a world in dire need of the simple, yet profound, truth of the Gospel.

Overcoming Barriers: Fear, Uncertainty, and the Challenges to Bold Speech

The bold proclamation of the Word of God is not merely an option but a mandate for Christians. From the apostolic examples in the book of Acts, we discern that courage was a defining characteristic of those who effectively communicated the divine message. Yet, contemporary Christians often find themselves hesitant, anxious, or even fearful when opportunities arise to speak forth the eternal truths of Scripture. To walk in the footsteps of the apostles, we must identify and confront the barriers to bold speech—namely, fear, uncertainty, and the various challenges that stifle our courage.

Fear: The Invisible Handcuff

Fear has been the nemesis of bold proclamation since the earliest days of the Christian Church. Even the apostle Peter, who would later become a stalwart advocate of the faith, initially denied Jesus out of fear (Matthew 26:69-75). Yet, he transformed into a fearless proclaimer of the Gospel (Acts 4:8-12). How? Through prayer and reliance on God's promises. He knew the cost but also understood the gravity of withholding the truth. Thus, fear must be replaced with faith. "For God gave us a spirit not of fear but of power and love and self-control," as Paul reminds Timothy (2 Timothy 1:7, UASV).

Uncertainty: The Quagmire of Inaction

Another crippling factor is uncertainty. Doubts often flood the mind when we contemplate speaking for God. "What if I misinterpret the Scripture?" "What if I don't have all the answers?" These questions sap our courage. Paul, in his mission at Athens, models a profound solution (Acts 17:16-34). He did not have the luxury of knowing how his message would be received, yet he was deliberate, reasoned from the Scriptures, and stood his ground. Preparation and grounding in the Word help dissipate uncertainty. Paul advises in 2 Timothy 2:15, "Do your best to present yourself to God as one approved, a worker who has no need to be ashamed, rightly handling the word of truth" (UASV).

Societal and Cultural Challenges

In a society that increasingly leans toward moral relativism and secularism, speaking the absolute truths of the Bible can be an uphill battle. However, societal trends should not dissuade Christians from the task at hand. Stephen, the first Christian martyr, knew the hostility he faced. His audience was diametrically opposed to his views (Acts 7:54-60). Yet, he stood firm and even prayed for his persecutors as he was being stoned. We may not face physical stones, but the proverbial stones of ridicule, ostracization, and contempt are real. The apostles rejoiced that they were counted worthy to suffer dishonor for the name (Acts 5:41). Can we do less?

Strategies for Overcoming Barriers

1. **Prayer and Dependence on God**: Before Peter and John spoke to the Sanhedrin, the early Church engaged in earnest prayer for boldness (Acts 4:29-31). Prayer is the Christian's greatest weapon against fear and uncertainty.

2. **Studious Preparation**: Paul's model of 'reasoning from the Scriptures' (Acts 17:2-3, UASV) sets an example. A thorough understanding of the Bible will arm us against both internal doubts and external criticisms.

3. **Wisdom and Discernment**: Jesus said, "Behold, I am sending you out as sheep in the midst of wolves, so be wise as serpents and innocent as doves" (Matthew 10:16, UASV). Know when to speak, what to say, and whom to address. Wisdom can be your shield in hostile territories.

4. **Cultivate Courage through Small Steps**: Take gradual steps in sharing the Gospel. Start with your immediate circles and then broaden your scope. Each successful interaction builds confidence for more significant endeavors.

5. **Partnership and Accountability**: Paul seldom worked alone; he had Barnabas, Silas, Timothy, and others. Surrounding oneself with like-minded believers offers emotional and spiritual support.

6. **Rest in God's Sovereignty**: Ultimately, the results are not in our hands but God's. As Paul stated, "I planted, Apollos watered, but God gave the growth" (1 Corinthians 3:6, UASV).

In conclusion, boldness in speech is not an innate quality but a cultivated virtue. The barriers can be formidable but are not insurmountable. The apostles, as described in the book of Acts, offer timeless lessons in overcoming fear, uncertainty, and the unique challenges posed by different cultural and societal contexts. They leaned not on their own understanding but on the immutable Word and promises of God. So must we.

The Power of Scriptural Authority: Standing Firm on the Inspired Word of God

For a Christian, the Bible is not just a collection of ancient texts but the inspired, inerrant Word of God. When it comes to sharing the Christian faith or contending for its truths, the authority of Scripture serves as an unshakeable foundation. The boldness in proclaiming God's Word is deeply rooted in its divine authorship and the historical reliability of its content. In this chapter, we explore why standing firm on the authority of the Bible empowers believers to speak with conviction and resolve. We will delve into the critical aspects that reinforce our boldness and dispel barriers like fear and doubt.

Why the Authority of Scripture Matters

1. **Divine Authorship**: The Bible asserts that "All Scripture is inspired by God" (2 Timothy 3:16, UASV). When Christians proclaim its messages, they are effectively communicating divine truths. This element of divine authorship imbues the Scriptures with unparalleled authority, enabling the believer to speak without the ambivalence that often accompanies human opinions.

2. **Consistency and Unity**: Despite being penned by different authors over centuries, the Bible displays an extraordinary consistency in its messages. This unity stems from its divine origin, strengthening our conviction in its truths.

3. **Objective Truth**: The Bible does not offer a buffet of truths to suit varying palates. It lays down objective truths rooted in historical facts. Objective truth needs no consensus; it stands firm irrespective of popular opinion.

The Importance of Literal Translation Philosophy

A literal translation like the Updated American Standard Version adheres closely to the original languages, enabling readers to delve deeper into the text. Such translations respect the words of the human authors and, by extension, God himself. They challenge the reader to invest time and effort to mine the riches of Scripture. This fosters a profound respect for the text, making the reader's proclamation of it rooted in sound understanding.

Barriers to Standing on Scriptural Authority

1. **Cultural Challenges**: Living in a pluralistic society, we often encounter objections like "That's your truth" or "Who says your book is right?" Here, grounding in Scriptural authority becomes pivotal. Paul confronted such challenges by "reasoning from the Scriptures" (Acts 17:2, UASV).

2. **The Pull of Emotionalism**: Many prefer subjective experiences over objective truths. However, feelings can be fleeting and deceptive. A stand on Scriptural authority provides an anchor beyond the changing tides of emotion.

3. **Academic Skepticism**: Critics often employ methodologies that aim to dissect the Bible, questioning its reliability. By adhering to an objective, historical-grammatical approach, we can confidently refute such criticisms, relying not on the shifting sands of academic trends but on the enduring Word of God.

Practical Steps for Standing Firm on Scriptural Authority

1. **Be Thoroughly Equipped**: Understand the central doctrines and historical background of the Bible. Know why you believe what you believe.

2. **Utilize Apologetics**: Learn basic apologetics to provide reasoned defenses for your faith.

3. **Pray for Courage**: Despite having unshakable truths, we may still falter due to human weakness. Paul asked the Ephesians to pray that he might proclaim the Gospel "with all boldness" (Ephesians 6:19, UASV).

4. **Cultivate Humility**: Being firm in your beliefs does not mean being abrasive. Peter advises that our defense of the faith should be done with "gentleness and respect" (1 Peter 3:15, UASV).

Conclusion

The authority of Scripture is not merely an abstract concept; it is a transformative truth that should permeate our preaching and daily living. As the psalmist beautifully puts it, "Your word is a lamp to my feet and a light to my path" (Psalm 119:105, UASV). By standing firm on the inspired Word of God, we are not only fortified against societal pressures but also emboldened to speak life-transforming truths to a world desperately in need of them.

Real-world Examples: Instances of Boldness Making a Difference in Apologetic Outreach

There is an indispensable quality that each believer ought to cultivate for effective apologetic outreach: boldness. This is not a brash or arrogant attitude but a courageous willingness to speak the truth uncompromisingly. A crucial component in apologetic outreach, boldness has a biblical foundation that Christians can look to for inspiration and guidance.

The first account of Christian boldness comes immediately after Pentecost when Peter and John were arrested for healing a man and proclaiming the resurrection of Jesus Christ. As recorded in Acts 4:13 (UASV), "Now when they saw the boldness of Peter and John, and understood that they were uneducated and untrained men, they were amazed, and began to recognize them as having been with Jesus." Peter and John were neither intimidated nor silenced by religious and political authorities. They recognized the supreme authority of God's word and acted upon it.

Then, there's the Apostle Paul, who, despite experiencing beatings, imprisonments, and shipwrecks, proclaimed the gospel relentlessly. When in Athens, Paul did not shy away from confronting a culture steeped in idol worship. Acts 17:22-23 (UASV) captures Paul's fearless apologetic approach: "So Paul stood in the midst of the Areopagus and said, 'Men of Athens, I observe that you are very religious in all respects. For while I was passing through and examining the objects of your worship, I also found an altar with this inscription, "TO AN UNKNOWN GOD." Therefore what you worship in ignorance, this I proclaim to you.'"

Today's apologetics also offers instances of such boldness making a difference. Consider the case of a Christian lecturer at a secular university. Despite an overwhelmingly atheistic environment, he regularly hosts discussions on the evidence supporting the Resurrection, the authenticity of Scriptures, and the historicity of Jesus. By fearlessly putting forth a case for the Christian worldview, he has seen students turn from skepticism to faith.

Another example comes from a Christian woman living in a predominantly non-Christian community. She holds Bible study classes in her home, despite facing hostility and isolation from her neighbors. Using carefully chosen Scripture passages and historical evidence, she explains the plan of salvation and Christian doctrines. Over time, she has seen the group grow and several people commit their lives to Christ.

Modern technology has also provided platforms for bold apologetic outreach. Blogs, podcasts, and YouTube channels are being used to defend the Christian faith. A noteworthy instance is a YouTube channel dedicated to refuting atheistic claims. Despite receiving constant backlash, the channel's creators stand firm, offering sound biblical and historical evidence to counter atheistic arguments. Many viewers, initially staunch atheists or agnostics, have expressed a change of heart after watching these well-reasoned videos.

What can we glean from these examples? First, the authority and the inspiration of Scriptures are foundational to bold apologetic outreach. No man-made argument can substitute the intrinsic power of God's word. Second, boldness emanates from a deep conviction and commitment to the truth of the Gospel, a commitment to stand firm even in the face of ridicule or persecution. Third, bold apologetics is not just the purview of theologians and scholars. It is the calling of every Christian who believes in the authority of the Bible.

Boldness in apologetic outreach is not just a New Testament phenomenon or a modern-day marvel. It is a timeless principle, deeply embedded in the fabric of authentic Christian living. This does not mean being confrontational but rather willing to confront the confrontable: false ideas, untruths, and spiritual deceit. Boldness, driven by an unwavering allegiance to the inspired Word of God, will always make a difference in apologetic outreach. The Apostle Paul's words in Romans 1:16 (UASV) still resonate profoundly today, "For I am not ashamed of the gospel, for it is the power of God for salvation to everyone who believes."

Let these real-world examples serve as a clarion call for all believers to speak the Word of God with boldness. Not only will you be obeying the Great Commission, but you'll also be participating in the transformative power of the Gospel, a power that has been changing lives for nearly two millennia and continues to do so today.

CHAPTER 29 Skillfully Using the Word of God

The Sword of the Spirit: Understanding the Transformative Power of Scripture

Scripture is not merely a repository of historical accounts, ethical guidelines, or theological insights; it possesses transformative power. Ephesians 6:17 designates the Word of God as "the sword of the Spirit," illustrating its active, penetrative characteristics. When wielded skillfully, this sword can dissect the complexities of human experience, judgment, and motive, laying bare the very essence of our beings (Hebrews 4:12).

One reason for the transformative power of Scripture is its divine origin. According to 2 Timothy 3:16-17, "All Scripture is inspired by God and profitable for teaching, for reproof, for correction, for training in righteousness; so that the man of God may be adequate, equipped for every good work." This divine imprint gives Scripture an authoritative and active role in the lives of believers, impacting both their personal spiritual development and their apologetic outreach.

Understanding the Transformative Power

The transformative power of Scripture does not reside in the ink and paper, but in its ability to accurately convey God's character, will, and purposes. When believers immerse themselves in the objective understanding of the Word, aided by the Historical-Grammatical method of interpretation, they are exposing themselves to the very mind of God (1 Corinthians 2:16). It is this direct exposure to divine truths that ignites transformation.

For example, consider how the Apostle Paul skillfully used Scripture in his ministry. Acts 17:2-3 tells us that Paul "reasoned from the Scriptures, explaining and proving" the truth about Jesus Christ. In other words, he employed Scripture not merely as a passive set of documents but as an active tool for transformation. When defending the resurrection, Paul didn't appeal to abstract philosophy but relied on the Old Testament prophecies to validate his arguments.

YOUR GUIDE FOR DEFENDING THE BIBLE

Scripture in Apologetic Outreach

The powerful efficacy of Scripture is also evident in apologetic endeavors. For instance, Peter urges Christians to "always be prepared to make a defense to anyone who asks you for a reason for the hope that is in you" (1 Peter 3:15). This defense is substantially founded on Scripture, the most credible testimony to God's interaction with mankind.

Scripture empowers believers to tackle challenging questions about God's nature, human suffering, and ethical dilemmas. Take the problem of evil, for instance. While various philosophical arguments may offer some comfort, it is the clear declarations in the Book of Job, Romans, and other passages that provide the most profound answers. The sufferer finds solace in knowing that God is in control and has a purpose behind the adversities (Romans 8:28).

The transformative power is not limited to intellectual enlightenment but also results in behavioral changes that further bolster apologetic outreach. For example, the Corinthian church was marked by divisions and immorality. Yet, Paul's first letter to them, grounded in authoritative Scripture, initiated a transformative process that resulted in their repentance and renewal (2 Corinthians 7:11).

Skillful Usage Requires Diligence

To wield the sword of the Spirit effectively requires diligence and competence. 2 Timothy 2:15 admonishes believers to be diligent workmen, "accurately handling the word of truth." The Greek term "orthotomounta" implies cutting something straight, like a master carpenter who makes precise, intentional cuts. Thus, understanding the text's grammar, historical context, and immediate circumstances is vital for accurate interpretation and application.

For example, the doctrine of salvation is often twisted into various human-centered philosophies. Yet, a careful, literal reading of Ephesians 2:8-9, Romans 6:23, and other related texts quickly dispels such distortions, affirming that salvation is a gift of God and not a result of human works.

The Word of God, as the sword of the Spirit, possesses transformative power that extends beyond personal edification to apologetic efficacy. The key to unlocking this power lies in a deep, objective, and skillful understanding of Scripture. Only then can believers not merely defend their faith but also "destroy arguments and every lofty opinion raised against the knowledge of God" (2 Corinthians 10:5), thereby fulfilling the Great Commission in a world increasingly hostile to divine truths.

Proper Exegesis: The Importance of Accurate Interpretation Using the Historical-Grammatical Method

Interpreting Scripture is an awe-inspiring responsibility that carries eternal consequences. There are many methodologies of Biblical exegesis, but the one that stands as robust, objective, and faithful to the original text is the Historical-Grammatical Method (HGM). This method emphasizes the historical context, grammatical structure, and literary form of the text, striving to ascertain the author's original intent. The significance of adhering strictly to this method cannot be overstated, especially considering the fact that the Bible is not merely another piece of literature but the divinely inspired Word of God. The integrity of our faith hinges on our understanding and application of Scripture, and any deviation from an accurate, literal interpretation can be eternally damaging.

Why the Historical-Grammatical Method?

1. **Honoring the Original Context**: The Bible was written over a span of about 1,600 years by different human authors, each influenced by their own historical circumstances. Understanding this historical backdrop is crucial for a correct interpretation. For instance, when reading Paul's letters, knowing the socio-political landscape of the first-century Roman Empire can enlighten the reader about the urgency and focus of his messages.

2. **Literal Interpretation**: The HGM is concerned with extracting the plain sense of the text. In contrast to methods like allegorical interpretation, the HGM keeps the reader from imposing external ideologies onto the text. Each word is of utmost importance and should be carefully scrutinized. For example, when interpreting the Creation account in Genesis, a literal reading demands six 24-hour days of creation, as the text is clear and unambiguous in its wording.

3. **Grammatical Considerations**: It pays attention to language structure, syntax, and semantics. Knowing the rules of Hebrew and Greek grammar allows us to dig deeper into the text. For instance, the use of the present tense in Romans 6:14, "For sin will have no dominion over you," shows that Paul isn't promising an instant eradication of sin but a continuous, ongoing process.

4. **Consistency and Unity of Scripture**: This method acknowledges the coherent and unified message of the Bible. While human authors may differ in style and focus, they were all inspired by the Holy Spirit. Therefore, any interpretation that seems to pit one part of Scripture against another is likely misguided.

YOUR GUIDE FOR DEFENDING THE BIBLE

Examples of Proper Exegesis Using HGM

1. **Understanding the Sermon on the Mount**: When interpreting the Beatitudes (Matthew 5:3-12), HGM discourages us from seeing them as "laws" to be obeyed. A study of the historical context reveals that Jesus was correcting the legalistic interpretations of the Pharisees, and hence, the focus should be on the heart condition rather than mere external compliance.

2. **The Role of Faith and Works in James and Paul**: A common theological tension arises when comparing James' emphasis on works (James 2:24) and Paul's focus on faith (Romans 3:28). The HGM helps resolve this by considering the unique circumstances and audiences of each author. Paul was addressing a legalistic Jewish audience, while James was cautioning against an empty faith devoid of good works. Both were presenting two sides of the same coin.

3. **Interpreting Revelation**: The book of Revelation, teeming with symbolic language, can tempt one to drift into allegorical interpretation. However, HGM requires a scrutiny of the genre and historical context. When John mentions Babylon, he might be alluding to the Roman Empire—the superpower of his day known for its persecution of Christians.

4. **Examining Conditional Salvation**: Passages like Hebrews 6:4-6 and 2 Peter 2:20-22 speak about the possibility of falling away after coming to the knowledge of truth. Using the HGM, we find that these warnings are to be taken seriously and literally, without resorting to theological systems that promise eternal security.

In conclusion, skillful use of the Word of God requires a commitment to proper exegesis and the most objective and reliable method is the Historical-Grammatical Method. It respects the historical context, grammatical rules, and literary forms, aiming to grasp the original intent of the authors who were inspired by God. Only by adhering to this method can we hope to attain an accurate understanding of God's will as expressed in the Scripture, thereby safeguarding our faith and practice from errant teachings and ideologies.

Addressing Common Misconceptions: How to Correctly Handle Difficult Passages

The task of biblical interpretation is not for the faint-hearted. The task of navigating through difficult passages is even more demanding, requiring careful handling, scrutiny, and a sober awareness of the principles of interpretation. The objective Historical-Grammatical method offers an invaluable guide for this task. While it may be tempting to evade difficult texts or apply subjective explanations, this does a disservice both to Scripture itself and to those seeking a clearer understanding of God's word. This section aims to outline how to address common misconceptions and correctly handle challenging passages.

The Dangers of Eisegesis

Before delving into methods of proper exegesis, it's important to highlight the pitfalls of eisegesis—the projection of one's own ideas or cultural perspectives onto the text. For example, some people read the narrative of David and Goliath as merely a motivational tale for overcoming life's challenges, neglecting its broader context within the historical and spiritual landscape of Israel. This sort of eisegesis can be misleading and detracts from the original purpose and message of the text.

Framework for Correct Handling

The objective Historical-Grammatical method should be our primary lens for understanding Scripture. This means considering the historical circumstances, language, grammar, and literary genre of the text.

1. **Historical Context**: Understanding the culture, norms, and historical events at the time of writing. For example, the claim that "there is no God" in Psalm 14:1 is clarified when understanding it as a poetic structure and as a description of a fool's beliefs, not a theological statement on atheism.

2. **Lexical Analysis**: Study the original Hebrew or Greek terms. Using a lexicon can help to pinpoint the most accurate meaning of a word. For instance, understanding the word "logos" in John 1:1 as "word," "reason," or "divine expression" can shed light on the complexities of this passage.

3. **Grammatical Structure**: Scrutinizing the grammatical arrangement of sentences can help clarify meaning. For example, the Greek term "pisteuo eis" in John 3:16, generally rendered as "believe in," has implications beyond mere intellectual assent—it signifies an entrusting or commitment to Jesus Christ.

4. **Literary Genre**: Recognizing the genre can guide us in how to read the text. Poetic language in Psalms shouldn't be read in the same way as legal code in Leviticus.

The Word of God is replete with profound wisdom and complex ideas that require diligent study and understanding. One cannot underestimate the importance of approaching Scripture with not just a devotional mindset but also with scholarly rigor. An accurate and faithful understanding of the Bible requires attention to detail and a commitment to integrity in interpretation. This is why the Updated American Standard Version (UASV) is a valuable resource, as it adheres to the principle of giving the reader what God said through His human authors, in a literal translation form. Below are ways to address common misconceptions and handle difficult passages.

Use the Historical-Grammatical Method

A disciplined approach to Bible study entails using a sound method of interpretation, such as the objective Historical-Grammatical method. This method involves studying the text within its historical setting and understanding the language, syntax, and grammar used by the original authors. This helps us avoid eisegesis—the imposition of our ideas onto the text—and allows for sound exegesis—drawing the correct meaning from the text itself.

For example, the phrase "sons of God" in Genesis 6:2 has been understood in various ways. Some view these as fallen angels, based on Jude 6-7 and 2 Peter 2:4-5, which seem to confirm this. Others, citing passages like Hosea 1:10, believe they are descendants of Seth. But the Historical-Grammatical method, scrutinizing the original language and corroborating scripture, supports the idea that these are indeed fallen angels. The term "sons of God" in other Old Testament instances often refers to angelic beings, and New Testament texts confirm this understanding.

Context is King

One of the most common reasons for misinterpretation is taking verses out of context. We must always consider the literary context (what comes before and after a verse), the historical context (the circumstances at the time), and the canonical context (how it fits within the whole counsel of God's Word).

Consider Philippians 4:13: "I can do all things through Him who strengthens me." Some may claim this as a guarantee for any personal endeavor, but the context reveals that Paul is speaking about contentment in times of need or plenty. The "all things" he refers to are situations he might find himself in, not any and every individual aspiration.

Lexical Precision

Understanding the original language can drastically change one's interpretation of a text. Greek and Hebrew are far more expressive languages than English, and nuances can be lost in translation. Therefore, it is sometimes necessary to consult lexicons and original language tools.

For instance, many misunderstand the concept of hell due to translation discrepancies. While some translations use the word "hell" for various Greek and Hebrew terms like Hades, Sheol, Gehenna, and Tartarus, understanding each term in its original language helps clarify that hell is not a place of eternal torment, but rather a place of eternal destruction.

Scriptural Harmony

Another vital aspect is ensuring that interpretations do not conflict with other Scriptures. Contradictory interpretations often signify a lack of understanding or a flawed exegesis.

Take, for instance, the issue of eternal security, which suggests "once saved, always saved." Verses like Romans 8:38-39 are often cited in support. However, this contradicts other passages like Hebrews 6:4-6, which warn against falling away. True scriptural harmony acknowledges the necessity of enduring faithfulness and obedience to God, negating the idea of eternal security.

Confronting Misconceptions Head-On

Misconceptions can sometimes be so entrenched that they become traditional interpretations. In these instances, it is crucial to be equipped with a comprehensive understanding of Scripture, supported by the original languages, to confront these misunderstandings respectfully and effectively. The pattern to follow here is the one provided by Jesus and His apostles, who reasoned from the Scriptures to correct misconceptions (Matt. 12:1-12; Acts 17:2-3).

Summary

The integrity of Scripture mandates that we approach it with the utmost respect and academic rigor. This involves choosing the right translation, utilizing the objective Historical-Grammatical method, and applying principles that ensure sound interpretation. Misconceptions can be corrected and difficult passages understood when we allow the text to speak for itself, using these tools and principles.

In this effort, it is imperative to steer clear of compromised methods of interpretation and translation efforts that involve ecumenical or interfaith alliances. A non-denominational effort, grounded in a faithful and literal translation like the UASV, aligns most closely with a biblically conservative approach. Such an approach stands as a bulwark against the flawed methodologies and ideological biases that have plagued modern biblical scholarship, equipping us to engage effectively in a world increasingly hostile to the Word of God.

Application in Apologetics: Skillfully Employing Scripture in Defense of Christian Beliefs

In the realm of Christian apologetics, one's proficiency in utilizing the Scriptures is tantamount to a swordsman's skill with his blade. Paul wrote in 2 Timothy 2:15 (UASV), "Be diligent to present yourself approved to God as a workman who does not need to be ashamed, accurately handling the word of truth." This handling is not merely for personal edification but extends to our responsibility to "demolish arguments and every pretension that sets itself up against the knowledge of God" (2 Corinthians 10:5, UASV).

Know the Context

Before employing a Scripture in defense of doctrine, it is essential to have a thorough understanding of its context. A common fallacy made by both believers and skeptics is proof-texting, wherein a verse is isolated from its context to justify a particular point of view. For example, critics often cite 1 Timothy 6:10, "For the love of money is a root of all kinds of evil," to argue that the Bible condemns wealth. However, it condemns not money but the "love of money."

The Importance of Original Language

When involved in more in-depth apologetics, the ability to reference the original Hebrew and Greek languages can be invaluable. For instance, Jehovah says in Exodus 3:14, "I AM WHO I AM." The phrase "I AM WHO I AM" is derived from the Hebrew verb "to be" and **is foundational for the Christian belief in the eternality and self-existence of God**. This detail can be crucial to those focused on theology when translating the Word of God in their discussions about the nature of God.

Their reasoning seems to be theology and not actual biblical Hebrew. They reason: "The phrase "I AM WHO I AM" is derived from the Hebrew verb "to be" and is foundational for the Christian belief in the eternality and self-existence of God." We do not render the Word of God based on theology, or our favorite doctrinal beliefs.

The Hebrew phrase אֶהְיֶה אֲשֶׁר אֶהְיֶה ('Ehyeh Asher 'Ehyeh) found in Exodus 3:14 can be more accurately rendered as "I will be what I will be" or "I will prove to be what I will prove to be." The Hebrew verb form used here is indeed in the imperfect tense, signifying incomplete or future action.

The phrase speaks to Jehovah's dynamic ability to become whatever is necessary to fulfill His purposes and promises, rather than being an ontological statement about self-existence. It's a self-designation that highlights Jehovah's actions towards His creation in line with His will, rather than a statement of His eternal nature per se. I appreciate the opportunity to correct this aspect.

In the context of Exodus 6:3, Jehovah is making it clear that He would now manifest His name — that is, His reputation or His actions — in a way that had not been previously manifested to Abraham, Isaac, and Jacob. The focus is on God's purpose and what He will cause to be, aligning with the historical-grammatical method of interpretation. So why did the Updated American Standard Version (UASV) render it is "I am what I am"? They did so because there are 31,102 verses in the Bible and they chose to retain the traditional rendering in a handful of Bible verse, so the Bible would not be neglected by the masses over theological bias. But in these handful of verse, the alternative readings are given. For example, the footnote on Exodus 3:14 reads, "Or, based on grammar and context, an alternative reading could be, *I will be what I will be.*" I will show you the footnotes for some of the other renderings below.

Use Parallel Verses for Corroboration

In addressing doctrinal issues, never rely on a single verse. The principle of "Scripture interprets Scripture" is valuable here. To argue for the deity of Jesus, one can start with John 1:1, "In the beginning was the Word, and the Word was with God, and the Word was God." However, this should be corroborated with other passages like Titus 2:13, "our great God and Savior, Christ Jesus," (Footnote in UASV reads, "Or, based on grammar and context, an alternative reading could be, *of the great God and our Savior.*") and Romans 9:5, "Christ, who is God over all." (Footnote in UASV reads, "Or, an alternative reading, *Christ, who is God over all, blessed forever.*")

Addressing Misconceptions

It is crucial to dispel common misconceptions. For instance, the doctrine that hell signifies eternal torment is widespread. Yet, by scrutinizing words like "Gehenna" and "Hades" and using verses such as Matthew 10:28, which says, "fear Him who can destroy both soul and body in hell," one can present a Scriptural argument that hell signifies eternal destruction, not everlasting torment.

Leverage Historical and Cultural Insights

Familiarity with the customs, history, and culture of the biblical world can add depth to your apologetics. Take, for instance, the concept of "faith." In the Greco-Roman world, "faith" (pistis in Greek) included the idea of loyalty and commitment, not just intellectual assent. This helps us better understand passages like James 2:24: "You see that a person is justified by works and not by faith alone."

Address the Counterarguments

In apologetics, always be prepared for counterarguments. For example, skeptics often use the Canaanite genocide to attack the Bible's moral framework. The objective Historical-Grammatical method requires us to consider that the Canaanites were not innocent but engaged in practices such as child sacrifice, and their destruction was a divine judgment. Relevant Scriptures like Deuteronomy 9:4 can be cited to show that the Israelites were not entitled but were also under divine scrutiny.

Be Christ-like in Presentation

Last but not least, the manner in which we present our apologetics should reflect the humility and love of Christ. The apostle Peter reminds us to "always be prepared to give an answer to everyone who asks you to give the reason for the hope that you have. But do this with gentleness and respect" (1 Peter 3:15, UASV).

The objective is not to win arguments but to guide seekers of truth toward the salvation that is found only in Christ Jesus. The Scriptures are "God-breathed" and therefore the final authority on all matters of faith and doctrine (2 Timothy 3:16, UASV). Skillful use of the Word, thus, not only strengthens personal faith but serves as a compelling testimony to its divine authorship and the truths it contains.

CHAPTER 30 Giving Reasonable, Rational, and Persuasive Answers When We Share God's Word

Biblical Foundations for Reasoned Apologetics: Examining Verses that Advocate for a Thoughtful Faith

Christianity has always been rooted in reasoned thought, and this is especially evident when we turn to Scripture. Far from promoting blind faith, the Bible encourages believers to employ their intellect in their quest for truth. As we strive to follow the pattern set by Jesus Christ and His apostles, who 'reasoned from the Scriptures' (Acts 17:2, UASV), we should be aware of various key verses that emphasize the role of reason and intellect in the Christian faith.

1 Peter 3:15

The apostle Peter admonishes Christians to "always be prepared to make a defense to anyone who asks you for a reason for the hope that is in you; yet do it with gentleness and respect" (1 Peter 3:15, UASV). This verse is often considered a cornerstone text for Christian apologetics. The term 'defense' here is translated from the Greek word "apologia," from which we get 'apologetics.' It refers to a reasoned argument or writing in justification of something. It is an invitation, and indeed a command, to engage intellectually with the world concerning the tenets of our faith.

Isaiah 1:18

Jehovah Himself encourages reason as a pathway to spiritual clarity, stating, "Come now, let us reason together, says Jehovah" (Isaiah 1:18, UASV). This verse demonstrates that Jehovah, the Creator of the universe, values intellectual engagement and rational discourse. He invites His creation into a logical dialogue to understand His standards and moral principles.

YOUR GUIDE FOR DEFENDING THE BIBLE

Acts 17:11

Paul's interactions with the Bereans provide another example. Luke tells us that the Bereans were "more noble" than those in Thessalonica because "they received the word with all eagerness, examining the Scriptures daily to see if these things were so" (Acts 17:11, UASV). This highlights the importance of scrutinizing teachings against the standard of Scripture, using it as the ultimate filter for truth. It's noteworthy that the Bereans are commended not for their blind faith, but for their reasoned, investigative approach to the Gospel message.

Romans 12:2

Paul also urges the Roman believers to be "transformed by the renewal of your mind, that by testing you may discern what is the will of God, what is good and acceptable and perfect" (Romans 12:2, UASV). The term 'testing' here refers to the idea of proving or verifying something by subjecting it to an examination. It is not an emotional or baseless acceptance, but a calculated and reasoned approach to discerning truth.

Proverbs 14:15

Wisdom literature also contributes to the discussion. Proverbs 14:15 advises, "The simple believes everything, but the prudent gives thought to his steps" (Proverbs 14:15, UASV). This verse pits naive credulity against reasoned faith. It cautions against believing something solely because it was spoken or presented persuasively, endorsing instead a prudent, analytical approach to claims and teachings.

2 Timothy 2:15

Finally, Paul counsels Timothy: "Do your best to present yourself to God as one approved, a worker who has no need to be ashamed, rightly handling the word of truth" (2 Timothy 2:15, UASV). The term 'rightly handling' is crucial here, for it implies that the Word of God can be mishandled. The onus is on Christians to be diligent, engaging intellectually with Scripture to accurately present its teachings.

The Bible is not a book for the naive or the intellectually lazy. It's a complex, multi-genre, historical document that lays out a comprehensive worldview. Rational engagement is not only encouraged but also expected. By relying on a rigorous, objective historical-grammatical method of interpretation, and by using a translation committed to the original text such as the UASV, Christians can ensure that they are engaging with God's Word as He intended.

In summary, Christianity and its foundational text, the Bible, advocate for a faith that is thoughtful, reasoned, and intellectually engaging. Faith is not an abandonment of reason, but the act of placing reasoned trust in the truth claims set forth in the Scriptures. Therefore, when we are called to defend our faith, we should draw upon these biblical foundations, using reason and intellect to provide rational, persuasive answers.

The Role of Logic and Rationality: Employing Sound Arguments in Apologetics

When it comes to the task of defending the faith, an understanding of logic and rationality is essential. It is not sufficient to only possess a fervent zeal for the things of God; rather, that zeal must be guided by sound thinking. As believers, we are exhorted in 1 Peter 3:15 to "always [be] prepared to make a defense to anyone who asks you for a reason for the hope that is in you; yet do it with gentleness and respect." This passage illuminates the need for Christians to engage in reasoned apologetics with a disposition of humility.

The Importance of Sound Reasoning

In the realm of apologetics, employing sound reasoning can separate persuasive arguments from mere opinion. The Apostle Paul exemplified this method when he argued persuasively about the Kingdom of God in Acts 19:8, "And he entered the synagogue and for three months spoke boldly, reasoning and persuading them about the kingdom of God." He wasn't merely content with offering platitudes; he presented reasoned arguments that aimed to persuade his listeners.

Types of Logical Arguments

Deductive Reasoning: Deductive reasoning seeks to establish a conclusion that is necessarily true if its premises are true. It is common in the writings of Paul. For instance, Romans 6:23 states, "For the wages of sin is death, but the free gift of God is eternal life in Christ Jesus our Lord." Paul's argument here can be formulated deductively as follows:

1. The wages (or consequence) of sin is death (Premise).
2. All humans have sinned (Premise, Romans 3:23).
3. Therefore, all humans face death as the consequence of sin (Conclusion).

Inductive Reasoning: Unlike deductive reasoning, inductive reasoning seeks probable conclusions based on observations. For example, the Apostle Peter appeals to the observation of fulfilled prophecy as evidence for the divine inspiration of Scripture in 2 Peter 1:19–21.

Abductive Reasoning: This involves forming a conclusion from the available information. For example, the Resurrection accounts can be examined abductively. The empty tomb, the transformation of the apostles, and the testimony of hundreds of eyewitnesses provide a reasonable basis for inferring the Resurrection of Jesus as the best explanation for these facts.

Logical Fallacies to Avoid

Being well-versed in logical fallacies can help not only in identifying them in opponents but also in avoiding them oneself.

1. **Strawman Fallacy:** Misrepresenting the opponent's position and then attacking it is dishonest and does not lead to a productive conversation.
2. **Ad Hominem:** Attacking the character of your opponent instead of their argument.
3. **Appeal to Authority:** Using an authority as evidence in your argument when the authority is not an expert on the facts relevant to the argument.

The Balance of Faith and Reason

While reason is vital, it is not the ultimate arbiter of truth. Faith has a substantial role in the life of the believer. Hebrews 11:1 defines faith as "the assurance of things hoped for, the conviction of things not seen." Nevertheless, faith is not blind but is grounded in the evidential truths of Scripture, making it both reasonable and rational.

To be an effective apologist for the Christian faith, employing logic and rationality is indispensable. When Paul was in Athens, he engaged with Epicurean and Stoic philosophers, not merely asserting his beliefs but reasoning from the Scriptures (Acts 17:2-3). Similarly, Christians today are called to not only share the Gospel but also provide sound, logical reasons for the hope they possess, thereby embodying a thoughtful faith.

Engaging in reasoned apologetics does not mean diluting the faith or compromising on the core doctrines. Rather, it means being like the Bereans who "received the word with all eagerness, examining the Scriptures daily to see if these things were so" (Acts 17:11). Therefore, the application of sound reasoning and logic should be seen as tools that aid in the delivery and defense of the unchangeable truths contained in Scripture.

Building a Persuasive Case: How to Assemble Evidence in a Cohesive and Compelling Manner

The Apostle Paul urged Timothy to "Do your best to present yourself to God as one approved, a worker who has no need to be ashamed, rightly handling the word of truth" (2 Timothy 2:15, UASV). A cornerstone of effective apologetics lies not only in having a sound argument but in presenting that argument in a persuasive, coherent manner. The task demands logical acumen, biblical fidelity, and an ability to make complex truths understandable. Here are ways to achieve this:

Start with a Strong Thesis Statement

A thesis should be a clear, concise, and defendable statement that outlines the main point of the argument. For example, if discussing the deity of Christ, one's thesis could be, "The Bible teaches the deity of Christ through direct statements, titles attributed to Him, and His actions."

Employ Exegetical Precision

Engage the biblical text in its original languages, paying close attention to grammar, syntax, and context. When Paul reasoned with the Bereans, the Scriptures mention they "examined the Scriptures every day to see if what Paul said was true" (Acts 17:11, UASV). Good apologetics always ties back to careful interpretation of the Bible.

Cite Multiple Lines of Evidence

A persuasive case doesn't rely on a single line of argument but assembles multiple strands of evidence. Using the same example of Christ's deity, one could cite Scriptural affirmations (John 1:1), divine prerogatives (forgiving sins, Mark 2:5-7), and Old Testament prophecies fulfilled (Isaiah 9:6).

Address Counter-Arguments

Preemptively address counter-arguments to demonstrate thoroughness and to prevent your case from appearing one-sided. When Jesus was questioned about the greatest commandment, He not only answered but also connected His response to another Scriptural truth, silencing His critics (Matthew 22:34-46).

Use Analogies and Illustrations

Jesus often used parables to make profound truths more accessible. Analogies and illustrations help to bridge the gap between unfamiliar concepts and the listener's own experience. For instance, explaining the Trinity might be aided by certain analogies (though all analogies are limited).

YOUR GUIDE FOR DEFENDING THE BIBLE

Provide Historical and Cultural Context

Arguments become more convincing when rooted in the cultural and historical context within which the biblical text was written. For example, understanding the concept of "Messiah" in first-century Judaism can lend tremendous weight to the prophecies Jesus fulfilled.

Logical Consistency

It's crucial to ensure that your arguments are logically sound and free from fallacies. For example, avoid circular reasoning, which is often a pitfall when interpreting prophetic or doctrinal passages.

Conclude by Reinforcing Your Thesis

A persuasive case needs a strong conclusion that circles back to the thesis. This reaffirms the arguments made and leaves no room for ambiguity.

Engage Emotionally without Manipulation

While logic is paramount, emotional resonance shouldn't be neglected. The apostle Paul, while maintaining logical rigor, also employed emotional appeals to his audience (e.g., Acts 20:19-21).

Call to Action

Lastly, a persuasive argument usually concludes with a call to action, asking the listener to respond in some way to the truth presented. This could be a call to repentance, further study, or even simply to ponder the implications of the truth being discussed.

In sum, the goal of assembling evidence in a persuasive manner is to engage the mind, will, and emotions of the listener, so that they can see the biblical truth clearly and compellingly. It's not merely about winning an argument, but about guiding others to the understanding and acceptance of what God has revealed in His Word.

Edward D. Andrews

Addressing Moral and Ethical Questions: Providing Balanced Answers Based on Scripture

In an increasingly complex and morally ambiguous world, questions of ethics and morality often arise when we engage in sharing God's Word. These questions can pertain to a wide range of issues, from sexual ethics to questions about justice and fairness. The challenge is to provide answers that are not only scripturally sound but also reasonable, rational, and persuasive to the listener.

Framework for Addressing Questions

Paul's method provides an exemplary model for how to approach such issues. Acts 17:2-3 tells us that Paul "reasoned from the Scriptures, explaining and proving by references" what he taught. Thus, our first point of reference for addressing any moral or ethical question should always be the Scriptures. The objective Historical-Grammatical method allows us to interpret these Scriptures as they were intended by their original authors, thus serving as a reliable foundation for ethical reasoning.

The Importance of Context

When using Scripture to address moral or ethical questions, context is critical. Take, for example, the issue of abortion. While the Bible does not explicitly discuss abortion, Scriptures like Psalm 139:13-16 speak of God's role in forming us in the womb, which can be reasonably extended to a pro-life viewpoint. To argue persuasively, one should present these Scriptures in the broader context of biblical teachings on the sanctity of life, such as in Genesis 9:6 and Exodus 20:13. This contextual approach adds weight to the argument, showing that the position is not based on isolated texts but is consistently supported throughout Scripture.

A Balanced View

Scripture often provides principles that can be applied to various situations rather than explicit commands for every ethical scenario we might encounter. For instance, questions about the ethical implications of new technologies like gene editing can be addressed through broader biblical principles about the sanctity of life and the limitations of human authority over creation (Genesis 1:27; Romans 12:1-2).

A balanced scriptural response acknowledges the complexities of modern life but maintains the integrity of biblical principles. For example, in discussing the ethics of war, one can bring in the Sixth Commandment ("You shall not murder," Exodus 20:13) and Jesus' teachings on love and non-resistance (Matthew 5:43-48). While these Scriptures can be seen to promote a position of pacifism, one should also consider texts that permit the use of force in certain circumstances, like Romans 13:4. A balanced view considers all relevant Scriptures, holding them in tension where necessary, to present an ethical position that is both nuanced and scripturally sound.

Providing Concrete Examples and Analogies

Jesus frequently used parables to illustrate complex spiritual truths. Similarly, the use of concrete examples or analogies can be helpful in making a scriptural point about a moral or ethical question. For instance, if discussing the morality of wealth and poverty, the parable of the rich man and Lazarus (Luke 16:19-31) could serve as a powerful illustration.

The Tone of the Conversation

The tone with which we present our scripturally-based arguments is also crucial. Colossians 4:6 advises, "Let your speech always be gracious, seasoned with salt, so that you may know how you ought to answer each person." Being confrontational or judgmental will close doors and ears. Thus, even as we hold firm to scriptural truths, we must present them in a manner that is winsome and gracious, respecting the freedom God has given each individual to choose whether to accept or reject His teachings.

Addressing moral and ethical questions in a persuasive manner requires a deep understanding of Scripture, interpreted through a reliable method, and presented in a balanced and gracious manner. By approaching moral and ethical questions in this way, we can honor the pattern set by Jesus Christ and His apostles, equipping ourselves to provide reasonable, rational, and scripturally sound answers in our evangelistic efforts.

Responding to Cultural and Philosophical Challenges: Navigating Topics Relevant to Contemporary Audiences

In a cultural climate increasingly divergent from biblical truth, Christians face significant hurdles in sharing the Word of God. Topics such as morality, sexuality, and religious pluralism are often at odds with Scriptural teachings, making it imperative for believers to navigate these sensitive issues with grace, clarity, and sound reasoning. Adhering to Paul's advice to Timothy, "Do your best to present yourself to God as one approved, a worker who has no need to be ashamed, rightly handling the word of truth" (2 Timothy 2:15, UASV), let's delve into how to address these challenges based on Scripture.

Moral Relativism

Today's society often adheres to a kind of moral relativism that asserts that "what's true for you may not be true for me." To counteract this notion, Christians can point to the objective moral law detailed in Scripture. For example, the Ten Commandments (Exodus 20:1-17) present an unwavering moral code. The emphasis on moral absolutes could be illustrated by Jesus' own words in Matthew 5:17-18, where He confirms that not even a "jot or tittle" would disappear from the Law until all is fulfilled.

Sexual Ethics

Another challenging area is sexual ethics, particularly around issues like homosexuality and transgenderism. Rather than simply quoting Leviticus 18:22, a nuanced approach can involve explaining the biblical design for marriage and sexual relations as elucidated in Genesis 2:24, Matthew 19:4-6, and Ephesians 5:31-33. It's crucial to delineate that the biblical stance is not about hatred or discrimination, but about God's design for human flourishing.

Religious Pluralism

The modern emphasis on religious pluralism suggests that all religions lead to God. However, Scripture is clear that salvation is through Christ alone (Acts 4:12; John 14:6). To be compelling, one can elucidate that if all paths led to the same truth, there would be no need for Christ's crucifixion. Thus, the exclusivity of the Christian faith is not a sign of intolerance, but a logical necessity based on the life and teachings of Jesus Christ.

The Problem of Evil

An evergreen topic is the Problem of Evil, or why a loving God would allow suffering. Romans 8:28 tells us that "all things work together for good to them that love God." This doesn't mean that evil comes from God but that He can bring good out of evil circumstances. Job's story serves as a potent narrative that God allows suffering for reasons that may be beyond human understanding, yet within His sovereign plan.

YOUR GUIDE FOR DEFENDING THE BIBLE

Science and Faith

In an age where science is often pitted against faith, Christians can point to the intricate design of the universe as evidence of a Creator. Romans 1:20 informs us that "his invisible attributes, namely, his eternal power and divine nature, have been clearly perceived, ever since the creation of the world, in the things that have been made." By appreciating science as the study of God's creation, believers can engage in meaningful dialogue about the compatibility of science and faith.

Social and Political Issues

Christians are also frequently asked to weigh in on political or social issues, such as abortion or social justice. In these cases, a balanced answer based on Scripture—like Jeremiah 1:5 for the sanctity of life or Micah 6:8 for the importance of justice—can serve as an effective witness. Christians should avoid becoming overtly partisan, focusing instead on the overarching biblical principles that apply to the situation.

In conclusion, to navigate the cultural and philosophical challenges of our times effectively, it's imperative for Christians to equip themselves with a sound understanding of Scripture, and an ability to "reason from the Scriptures" as did Paul (Acts 17:2, 3). The aim is not to win debates but to faithfully represent the truths of God's Word in a compelling manner. The ultimate goal is to glorify God and perhaps plant seeds that the Holy Spirit might water in due time, leading to the repentance and salvation of those who hear.

Real-life Scenarios: Effective Communication and Application of Reasoned Apologetics in Diverse Situations

Effective apologetics is more than just reciting Bible verses and theological axioms; it's about contextually and culturally relevant communication. As Paul advised Timothy, "Preach the word; be ready in season and out of season; reprove, rebuke, and exhort, with complete patience and teaching" (2 Timothy 4:2, UASV). Here, we will consider real-life scenarios where reasoned apologetics can be applied.

Scenario 1: The Problem of Suffering

When confronted with the issue of suffering and evil, it is tempting to become defensive, but consider approaching the subject empathetically. Acknowledge the reality of suffering but steer the conversation toward the Biblical perspective that

God allows suffering due to human free will and the sinful state of the world (Romans 5:12). Stress that God promises an end to all suffering (Revelation 21:4).

Scenario 2: Scientific Challenges

In a world enthralled by science, Christians often face criticisms that faith is "unscientific." However, the Bible is not a science textbook, but it is scientifically accurate. Cite examples such as the Bible's reference to the "circle of the earth" in Isaiah 40:22, long before the earth was universally recognized as a sphere. Always remember to maintain the authoritative stance of Scripture while appreciating the scientific method.

Scenario 3: Relativism

The notion that "all truths are equal" permeates the culture. Navigate this by referencing Jesus' claim in John 14:6: "I am the way, and the truth, and the life. No one comes to the Father except through me." Unlike relativistic philosophies, Biblical truth claims are not subjective but are grounded in the person and work of Jesus Christ.

Scenario 4: Exclusivity of Salvation

Many find the doctrine of exclusive salvation in Christ intolerant. Point to Acts 4:12, which asserts that "there is salvation in no one else, for there is no other name under heaven given among men by which we must be saved." The exclusivity is not a matter of intolerance but one of revealed truth from God.

Scenario 5: Sexual Morality

In a world with evolving views on sexual morality, stay anchored to the Bible's teachings. Reference Romans 1:26-27 and Matthew 19:4-6 when discussing topics like homosexuality and marriage. It's crucial to differentiate between upholding Biblical standards and showing love and grace to those who disagree.

Scenario 6: The Resurrection

Skeptics often question the Resurrection. A reasoned approach includes pointing to the historical evidence, such as empty tombs and eyewitness accounts (1 Corinthians 15:3-8). These are not just religious claims but historical events scrutinized through the lens of objective evaluation.

Scenario 7: "The Bible is Just Another Book"

Some people claim that the Bible is nothing more than human literature. Here, a solid response would involve pointing to its unique prophetic accuracy, internal consistency over centuries of its writing, and its unparalleled impact on humanity. These factors attest to divine authorship.

Scenario 8: Atheism and Agnosticism

When engaging with atheists or agnostics, it's often beneficial to turn the tables and ask them to provide evidence for their own worldview. This can lead to more equal dialogue and allow room to insert sound Biblical reasonings.

Scenario 9: End Times Skepticism

People often mock the Biblical view of end times. A rational response would involve discussing the increasing fulfillment of Bible prophecies and the "signs of the times" Jesus mentioned (Matthew 24).

Remember, the objective is not to win an argument, but to faithfully declare the truth of God's Word in a way that it can be understood and accepted. By applying reasoned apologetics wisely in these diverse situations, not only do we obey the Scriptural mandate to defend the faith, but we also do it in a manner that is most likely to win souls for the Kingdom of God.

In all of these scenarios, keep in mind the pattern set by Jesus and his apostles, who 'reasoned from the Scriptures, explaining and proving by references' the veracity of their teachings (Acts 17:2, 3). The objective Historical-Grammatical method of interpretation, along with a commitment to the authority and inerrancy of Scripture, provides a robust foundation for addressing these challenges effectively.

Edward D. Andrews

SECTION 8 BIBLICAL ARCHAEOLOGY

Digging Deeper

We put books here on this subject if one is interested in taking the subject deeper. This section gives you foundational knowledge to evangelize or engage people in conversation.

ARCHAEOLOGY & THE OLD TESTAMENT by Edward D. Andrews (2023)

ISBN-13: 979-8378333448

https://www.amazon.com/dp/B0BW2LXP8W

ARCHAEOLOGY & THE NEW TESTAMENT by Edward D. Andrews (2023)

ISBN-13: 979-8385984442

https://www.amazon.com/dp/B0BW385FXR

THE BIBLE AS HISTORY: A Historical Journey Through the Bible by Edward D. Andrews (2023)

ISBN-13: 979-8392220793

https://www.amazon.com/dp/B0C39FLM3Y

CHAPTER 31 Unearthing the Past: Introduction to Biblical Archaeology

The Significance of Biblical Archaeology: Connecting Scripture and History

Biblical archaeology is the study of the Bible's people and events through the physical evidence buried in the ground. Archaeologists excavate and analyze rock, ruined walls and buildings, shattered cities, pottery, clay tablets, written inscriptions, tombs, and other ancient remains, or artifacts, to glean information. These studies often enhance our understanding of the circumstances under which the Bible was written, the lives of ancient men of faith, and the languages they and their neighbors spoke. They have expanded our knowledge of all the regions touched by the Bible: Palestine, Egypt, Persia, Assyria, Babylonia, Asia Minor, Greece, and Rome.

Biblical archaeology is a relatively new science. It was only in 1822 that the decipherment of the Rosetta Stone unlocked Egyptian hieroglyphics. Assyrian cuneiform was decoded more than 20 years later. Systematic excavations in Assyria began in 1843 and in Egypt in 1850.

Major sites and finds

Archaeology has confirmed many historical features of the biblical account of these lands and substantiated points once questioned by modern critics. Skepticism about the Tower of Babel, denials of the existence of a Babylonian king named Belshazzar and an Assyrian king named Sargon (whose names were not found in independent sources until the 19th century CE), and other adverse criticisms of biblical data relating to these lands have all been shown to be unfounded. On the contrary, a wealth of evidence has been unearthed that fully harmonizes with the scriptural account.

Biblical archaeology serves as an invaluable scholarly discipline that aims to bring the ancient world of the Bible to life. Its significance is not solely academic; it's a field that can resonate deeply with those who view Scripture as a divinely inspired text, providing an indispensable backdrop against which the eternal truths of the

Bible can be understood. In fact, the preeminence of the Bible as a source of truthful knowledge and guidance is amplified when it is corroborated by archaeology. In this sense, the field serves as an auxiliary light, illuminating what we already accept on the basis of faith, and rendering the Bible "more intelligible through a fuller knowledge of its background and setting."

Unveiling Historical Accuracy

One of the most pivotal roles of biblical archaeology is its ability to substantiate the historical claims made in the Scriptures. Time and again, archaeological discoveries have validated the Bible's historical and chronological accounts, fortifying its integrity as a document of divine origin. For example, the existence of Pontius Pilate, the Roman governor who ordered the crucifixion of Jesus, was verified through the discovery of the "Pilate Stone" in 1961 at Caesarea Maritima. The stone bears an inscription mentioning "Pontius Pilate, Prefect of Judea," giving external evidence to the New Testament narrative.

Confirming Geographical Details

Archaeology provides geographical clarity, corroborating the places mentioned in Scripture. The city of Jericho serves as a case in point. The archaeological digs led by Kathleen Kenyon in the 1950s revealed that the walls of Jericho had indeed collapsed outward, as mentioned in the Book of Joshua. Though some archaeological interpretations can be disputed, the overall evidence supports the biblical account, giving the reader a real-world context in which to place the Scriptural narratives.

Identifying Cultural Contexts

Understanding the cultural backdrop of biblical events enriches our grasp of Scripture. For instance, the discovery of the Ebla tablets has brought clarity to the patriarchal period, affirming the names and places cited in the early chapters of Genesis. This discovery has equipped biblical scholars with a greater understanding of the vocabulary, idioms, and legal practices of the period, thereby facilitating a more nuanced reading of the Scriptural texts.

Distinguishing Factual Accounts from Myth

In a world increasingly skeptical of the Bible's historical claims, archaeology serves to affirm the reality of the events it describes. The discovery of the Hittite civilization, once thought to be a mythical people mentioned only in the Bible, affirmed the existence of this ancient empire and substantiated the biblical accounts that mentioned them.

A Balanced Perspective

However, it's critical to remember that archaeology is not an infallible field. Findings are subject to interpretation and are often debated among scholars. Therefore, while it often harmonizes with biblical accounts, there may be instances where findings appear contradictory due to current limitations in our understanding or the data available. Even in such cases, the faith of the believer should not rest on archaeology but on the inspired, inerrant Word of God.

Biblical archaeology, when approached using a rigorous historical-grammatical method, significantly contributes to our understanding of Scripture. It provides a tangible and contextual stage upon which the biblical drama unfolded. It doesn't merely serve to affirm what is already accepted by faith but adds layers of meaning and context that enrich our comprehension of God's revelation to humanity. Archaeological findings amplify the voice of history, allowing it to resonate with the eternal truths of Scripture.

Thus, the significance of biblical archaeology lies in its capacity to act as a bridging discipline—connecting Scripture with history, theology with fact, and faith with empirical evidence. While the ultimate authority for faith and doctrine remains the divinely inspired Scriptures, the discipline of biblical archaeology provides a robust, empirical witness to the trustworthiness and enduring relevance of the Bible. It also serves as a formidable defense against critics who question the Bible's historical accuracy. Hence, this discipline remains an invaluable tool for anyone committed to a serious study and faithful understanding of the Scriptures.

Methods and Approaches: How Archaeologists Investigate the Bible's World

The science of biblical archaeology is not a random dig into the sands of time but rather an intricate discipline that employs a broad spectrum of methodologies and approaches to unlock the ancient world. The objective is to gain insights that contribute to our understanding of the biblical text—its history, culture, and geography. However, as those who view the Bible as the inspired, inerrant Word of God, it is crucial to note that while archaeology can provide supportive evidence, our faith ultimately rests on the Scriptures themselves.

The Excavation Process

Excavation is the most fundamental aspect of archaeology, and its goal is often to unearth artifacts, inscriptions, and other forms of material culture. This process is meticulously planned and executed, often beginning with a survey to identify the most promising dig sites. Once a site is chosen, archaeologists employ stratigraphy—the study of layers of soil—to help date their finds and reconstruct the sequence of human activity over a period of time.

Typology

Archaeologists use typology to categorize artifacts based on form and function, which often correspond to specific time periods. For example, the style of pottery shards can provide clues about the time when they were made, thereby helping scholars estimate the age of other artifacts and structures found in the same layer of soil. This can aid in dating biblical events within their historical contexts.

Epigraphy and Palaeography

Inscriptions provide firsthand accounts that can confirm, elaborate, or clarify biblical narratives. Epigraphy is the study of inscriptions, while palaeography focuses on ancient writing styles. These are invaluable for dating manuscripts and understanding the languages of the biblical world. The Dead Sea Scrolls, for instance, were authenticated and dated using palaeographic techniques, and their contents have significantly contributed to our understanding of the Hebrew Bible and the world of Second Temple Judaism.

Carbon-14 Dating

This dating technique measures the decay of carbon isotopes in organic materials. While it's not perfect, and its reliability diminishes for samples dating back beyond a few thousand years, it can still offer valuable data. For example, the age of the Dead Sea Scrolls was partially determined using Carbon-14 dating.

Contextual Analysis

Context matters not just in interpretation but also in archaeology. The location where an artifact is found, its relation to other items, and the type of soil it's found in can all offer clues. For instance, seals and bullae (clay lumps with seal impressions) found in administrative buildings can indicate a place's significance in official or royal contexts, thereby corroborating its mention in biblical records.

Comparative Studies and Extra-Biblical Texts

Comparative studies involve examining biblical artifacts and sites in the light of similar finds in the broader ancient Near Eastern world. For instance, the legal codes found in the Pentateuch can be better understood when compared with other ancient

Near Eastern legal traditions, like the Code of Hammurabi. Extra-biblical texts such as the Assyrian Annals can also shed light on biblical events.

Archaeological Ethics

While the goal of biblical archaeology is to enlighten our understanding of the Scriptures, this must be done ethically. Looted artifacts, for example, lose their context, making them far less valuable for scholarly analysis. Furthermore, the potential for sensationalized finds that can capture the public imagination must not divert the scholarly rigor that the field demands.

The Limitations of Archaeology

Though archaeological evidence often supports the historical narratives in the Bible, the field has its limitations. For instance, the absence of evidence is not evidence of absence. Also, findings are subject to interpretation, which can vary among experts. Moreover, archaeological data rarely offer conclusive proofs but rather lend weight to particular viewpoints.

The Intersection of Faith and Archaeology

For the believer, biblical archaeology can serve as a reinforcing discipline. While the Scriptures stand authoritative on their own merit, corroborative evidence from archaeology can bolster faith and offer powerful rebuttals against critics who dismiss the Bible's historical accuracy.

Understanding the methods and approaches in biblical archaeology equips us to more thoughtfully engage with discoveries that intersect with the biblical record. Employing a rigorous historical-grammatical method in both the exegetical and archaeological disciplines allows us to navigate the complexities of each field, all while upholding the integrity and authority of Scripture. As we continue to unearth remnants of the ancient world, we gain additional perspectives that enrich our understanding of the eternal Word of God, knowing well that while archaeology can inform our faith, it is the Scriptures that form its foundation.

Key Discoveries: Notable Finds that Illuminate Biblical Narratives

While faith rests on the authority of Scripture, archaeological findings often serve to corroborate the biblical narratives, providing tangible evidence that substantiates the historical and geographical claims made in the Bible. In this section, we'll explore some key discoveries that have made significant contributions to our understanding of the biblical world.

The Dead Sea Scrolls

Uncovered between 1947 and 1956 in eleven caves around the site of Qumran, the Dead Sea Scrolls include copies of almost every book of the Old Testament. Notably, they contain a full manuscript of the Book of Isaiah, which closely aligns with the Masoretic Text, affirming the reliability of the Scriptures that have been passed down to us. These scrolls also provide valuable insights into Second Temple Judaism, thereby illuminating the religious context of the New Testament.

The Rosetta Stone and the Decipherment of Hieroglyphics

Although not a biblical artifact per se, the discovery of the Rosetta Stone in 1799 dramatically impacted biblical archaeology by providing the key to deciphering Egyptian hieroglyphics. Once this script was understood, scholars were able to read various Egyptian texts and inscriptions that clarified the historical framework of ancient Egypt—a significant player in the Old Testament narrative.

The Moabite Stone (Mesha Stele)

Discovered in 1868 in Dhiban, Jordan, the Moabite Stone dates back to around the 9th century B.C.E. and confirms the existence of Moabite King Mesha, who is mentioned in 2 Kings 3. The inscription speaks of Mesha's revolt against Israel, thereby providing an external corroboration of the biblical narrative.

The Taylor Prism

This Assyrian cuneiform prism describes the campaigns of King Sennacherib, including his siege of Jerusalem during the reign of King Hezekiah, as recorded in 2 Kings 18-19 and Isaiah 36-37. Although the prism claims that Hezekiah was "shut up like a caged bird," it makes no mention of the city falling, which aligns with the biblical account where an angel of Jehovah struck down the Assyrian army, saving Jerusalem.

The Cyrus Cylinder

This clay cylinder found in the ruins of Babylon contains an account by Cyrus the Great, detailing his conquest of Babylon in 539 B.C.E. and his subsequent policy of allowing conquered peoples to return to their homelands. This corroborates the biblical account in the Book of Ezra, where Cyrus permits the Jews to return to Jerusalem and rebuild their temple.

YOUR GUIDE FOR DEFENDING THE BIBLE

The Pilate Stone

Found in the coastal city of Caesarea Maritima, this limestone block contains an inscription referring to "Pontius Pilate, Prefect of Judea." For a long time, skeptics questioned the existence of Pilate, but this discovery affirms his historicity and his role as the Roman official who presided over the trial of Jesus, as mentioned in the Gospels.

The Caiaphas Ossuary

Discovered in Jerusalem, this limestone burial box (ossuary) bears the inscription "Joseph son of Caiaphas," possibly referring to the high priest who played a crucial role in the arrest and trial of Jesus. The ossuary provides a tangible link to the biblical narrative, confirming the existence of characters mentioned in the New Testament.

The Tel Dan Inscription

This fragmented stele, found at the site of Tel Dan in northern Israel, refers to the "House of David," providing the first historical evidence of King David outside the Bible. It dates to the 9th century B.C.E. and likely commemorates a military victory.

The Pool of Siloam

Excavations in Jerusalem have uncovered a pool described in John 9, where Jesus healed a man born blind. The discovery of the Pool of Siloam confirms the geographical details in John's Gospel, adding a layer of historical credibility.

Goliath Inscription

A shard of pottery discovered at the site of ancient Gath contains an inscription with the name "Goliath" or a similar name, dating to roughly the same period as the biblical account of David and Goliath. While it doesn't prove the biblical story, it suggests that the name and locale are historically plausible.

These are just a few examples, but they serve to illustrate how archaeology can provide valuable corroborative evidence for the biblical narratives. While these finds are subject to human interpretation and may not offer unequivocal proofs, they nonetheless contribute to a cumulative case that upholds the historical reliability of the Scriptures. As we delve into the material culture of the ancient world, these tangible pieces of history offer us additional avenues to understand and affirm the eternal truths enshrined in the Word of God.

Challenges and Controversies: Navigating Debates in Biblical Archaeology

Biblical archaeology, despite its rich and illuminating contributions to understanding the Scriptures, is not without its challenges and controversies. These complexities often stem from various factors, such as interpretive frameworks, emerging methodologies, and even ideological or theological predispositions.

Authenticity Debates

The first layer of challenge involves the authenticity of discovered artifacts. For instance, the James Ossuary, which bears the inscription "James, son of Joseph, brother of Jesus," stirred both excitement and controversy. Skepticism arose around the possibility of forgery, especially concerning the latter part of the inscription. Ultimately, the debates over authenticity impact how these findings corroborate the biblical narratives.

Minimalist vs. Maximalist Perspectives

Another dimension of controversy is the divergent approaches of "minimalists" and "maximalists." Minimalists tend to be skeptical of the Bible's historical accounts, often relegating them to the realm of mythology or ideological literature. Maximalists, on the other hand, are more inclined to accept the Bible's historical narratives and seek to corroborate them with archaeological evidence. This dichotomy sometimes results in widely varying interpretations of the same set of data.

Chronological Challenges

Chronology is another challenging area. Differing dating methods and frameworks can either affirm or challenge the biblical timeline. For example, the dating of the Exodus event varies widely, with some scholars placing it in the 15th century B.C.E., while others propose a 13th-century date. Such discrepancies can have far-reaching implications for the historicity of biblical events.

Archaeological Silence

Archaeology doesn't always provide evidence for every biblical account, a phenomenon often termed "archaeological silence." For example, the lack of direct archaeological evidence for figures like Abraham or Moses has led some to question the historical reliability of these characters. However, the absence of evidence is not evidence of absence.

Geopolitical Sensitivities

Archaeological activities in the Middle East often intersect with modern geopolitical issues, adding another layer of complexity. Territorial disputes can limit excavation opportunities or even result in the destruction of valuable sites. This compromises the comprehensiveness and integrity of archaeological research in biblically significant regions.

Conflicts with Secular History

Sometimes, biblical accounts appear to conflict with what is considered established secular history, requiring scholars to navigate carefully. For instance, the Bible suggests a significant Assyrian presence in Israel during the 8th century B.C.E., yet some historians propose a later timeline based on Assyrian records. Such discrepancies necessitate thoughtful consideration and balanced scholarship.

Ethical Concerns

There are also ethical dimensions to biblical archaeology. The looting of artifacts and illegal excavations are unfortunate realities in the field. Such activities not only damage the historical record but also raise serious ethical questions about the acquisition and ownership of cultural heritage.

Theological Implications

Archaeological findings can sometimes challenge long-standing theological positions. For example, the discovery of household idols in ancient Israelite dwellings complicates simplistic understandings of Israelite monotheism. While the Bible remains the authoritative standard for doctrine, archaeological evidence can push scholars to reconsider interpretive traditions.

Intersection with Textual Criticism

Finally, archaeological discoveries often intersect with the discipline of textual criticism. Ancient manuscripts, like the Dead Sea Scrolls, not only illuminate the world of the Bible but also raise questions about the text's transmission and reliability.

Navigating the challenges and controversies in biblical archaeology requires a balanced, methodological approach that respects both the integrity of the archaeological record and the authoritative status of the Bible. Despite the complexities, the endeavor is worthwhile. Each shard of pottery, each inscription, and each ancient wall can serve as a tangible touchpoint to the world of the Scriptures, providing additional contexts and perspectives for a more nuanced understanding of the biblical text.

In sum, while archaeology may have its own set of limitations and challenges, its contributions are invaluable for anyone committed to understanding the Bible more deeply. It is not the final word on matters of faith and doctrine but serves as a useful tool in exploring the rich tapestry of the biblical narrative.

YOUR GUIDE FOR DEFENDING THE BIBLE

CHAPTER 32 Exploring Ancient Sites: Archaeological Excavations

Digging into History: The Process of Archaeological Excavations

Prominent Biblical Sites: Uncovering the Cities and Places of Scripture

Archaeological Tools and Technologies: Advancements in Unearthing the Past

Interpreting Artifacts: Understanding What Ancient Objects Reveal

Edward D. Andrews

CHAPTER 33 Biblical Archaeology and Faith: Implications for Believers

Faith and Evidence: How Biblical Archaeology Supports Belief

Archaeological excavations offer us an exceptional window into the world of the biblical past. Far more than just unearthing ancient artifacts, the process of excavation seeks to reconstruct history, providing context and tangible evidence that illuminate our understanding of the Scriptures. Let's delve into the complex and fascinating process of archaeological excavations and how this endeavor enhances our appreciation for the biblical narrative.

Initial Planning and Surveys

Archaeological endeavors don't just begin with a shovel in hand; they often start years before any soil is turned. An exhaustive review of existing literature, prior excavations, aerial surveys, and even the study of ancient texts help in deciding the location and scope of the dig. Sites with potential biblical connections are especially significant, making the planning phase critical for theological as well as historical inquiries.

Stratigraphy and Grid System

One of the most crucial principles in archaeology is stratigraphy—the study of the sequence of human activity over time. Different layers (or "strata") in a dig represent different periods of occupation or use. To keep track of these layers, a grid system is often employed, dividing the site into squares to maintain a record of where each artifact is found. This is essential for understanding the chronology and context of each find.

The Excavation Process

The actual digging is a meticulously slow process. Spades and trowels are used more frequently than large shovels. Each layer of soil is removed and sifted to ensure that even the smallest items—be they pottery shards, ancient coins, or fragments of bone—are collected. Notably, the Tel Dan inscription, which provided the first historical evidence of King David outside the Bible, was discovered in such a methodical manner.

Documentation and Analysis

Each find is catalogued, often with the aid of technology like GPS to accurately pinpoint its location within the grid. Photographs are taken, sketches are made, and a detailed log is maintained. Proper documentation is crucial for the subsequent analysis phase, where artifacts are dated and studied in labs to gather as much information as possible. This is also when experts will engage in paleography, the study of ancient writing, to interpret any inscriptions. For example, the Dead Sea Scrolls were subjected to extensive analysis, which has proven invaluable in understanding the textual history of the Old Testament.

Specialized Techniques

Modern archaeology also employs specialized techniques like carbon-14 dating, spectrography, and DNA analysis to gain further insights. While these methods offer additional avenues for understanding the past, they are not without their limitations and debates, especially when they seem to challenge established biblical chronologies.

Interpretation and Peer Review

The final step involves synthesizing all the data into a coherent narrative or hypothesis about the site. Peer review by other experts in the field ensures that the interpretations are sound and reliable. This is not merely an academic exercise but can have significant implications for our understanding of the biblical text. The excavation of Jericho, for example, sparked extensive debates about the historicity of the biblical account of its fall.

Ethical Considerations

Beyond the academic and scientific aspects, archaeological digs are fraught with ethical considerations. Who has the right to excavate and possess artifacts, especially when the lands are subject to political conflict? Respect for the cultural heritage of the areas being excavated is paramount.

Public and Scholarly Engagement

Finally, the findings are often shared with the public through academic papers, museum exhibits, and lectures. These serve educational purposes but also allow for a wider scrutiny and appreciation of the archaeological endeavor.

Conclusion

The process of archaeological excavation is an intricate blend of science, history, and often, theology. From planning to execution and interpretation, each phase involves a careful set of methodologies aimed at unveiling the most accurate picture of the past. While archaeology is not without its challenges and controversies, when conducted rigorously, it provides an invaluable complement to biblical scholarship. By unearthing the material culture of ancient civilizations, archaeology brings the biblical world to life, enriching our understanding and appreciation of the divinely inspired Scriptures. Each artifact discovered and each layer unearthed adds nuance and depth to the biblical narrative, helping us to engage more profoundly with the Word that "is alive and exerts power."

Archaeology does not serve to prove the Bible but can affirm its historical reliability, providing tangible links to the events, places, and people described in the Scriptures. It enhances our understanding of the Bible's rich history and deepens our faith in its divine message. Therefore, despite its challenges, the process of archaeological excavation remains a vital and rewarding discipline for anyone interested in the authentic, historical context of the biblical world.

Historical Accuracy: Confirming the Bible's Trustworthiness

The discipline of archaeology has frequently found itself intersecting with biblical scholarship, given that the territories explored often overlap with regions discussed in the Bible. A large body of archaeological evidence demonstrates that the Scriptures are grounded in real places, times, and events. As we turn our attention to this aspect of the archaeological enterprise, we can appreciate how the material remains unearthed provide substantive corroboration for the biblical record.

The City of Jericho

Jericho's fame stems primarily from the biblical account of its walls collapsing after the Israelites marched around the city (Joshua 6). Kathleen Kenyon's excavations during the 1950s cast doubt on the Bible's account due to her dating of the wall's collapse. However, further review of her findings by scholars like Bryant Wood, who reconsidered the pottery chronology, provided a date compatible with the biblical account, renewing confidence in the Scripture's historical narrative.

Hezekiah's Tunnel

The tunnel described in 2 Kings 20:20 and 2 Chronicles 32:30 was indeed discovered in Jerusalem, confirming the accounts about King Hezekiah's efforts to safeguard the city's water supply during the Assyrian siege. An inscription was found inside the tunnel, which matches the biblical description of how the tunnel was built.

The Tel Dan Inscription

The Tel Dan inscription, discovered in 1993 in northern Israel, was groundbreaking because it offered the first epigraphic evidence for the Davidic dynasty. Critics had long argued that King David was merely a legendary figure, but the inscription referring to the "House of David" gives external corroboration for David's historical existence.

YOUR GUIDE FOR DEFENDING THE BIBLE

The Hittites

At one time, skeptics questioned the existence of the Hittite people mentioned in the Bible (Genesis 23:10; 2 Kings 7:6) because there was no external evidence for them. However, subsequent discoveries in modern-day Turkey have validated their existence, culture, and interactions with other civilizations mentioned in the Bible.

The Moabite Stone

Also known as the Mesha Stele, this artifact corroborates the Bible's account of the Moabite revolt against Israel as found in 2 Kings 3. It is a rare example of an event recorded both in the Bible and an external source, reinforcing the credibility of the biblical account.

Cyrus Cylinder

The Persian king Cyrus is favorably portrayed in the Bible (Ezra 1:1-4; Isaiah 44:28; 45:1). The Cyrus Cylinder discovered in Babylon provides external testimony to Cyrus's policy of religious tolerance and his decree to allow captive peoples to return to their homelands, just as described in the Book of Ezra.

Names and Titles

Archaeology has also validated the use of specific names and titles mentioned in the Bible. For example, the title "tetrarch" was initially considered anachronistic in the New Testament but was later verified through inscriptions. Similarly, the name Caiaphas, the high priest during Jesus' trial, was confirmed through an ossuary bearing his name.

The Dead Sea Scrolls

Although not a traditional archaeological 'find,' the Dead Sea Scrolls significantly contribute to our confidence in the Bible. They offer us manuscripts of the Old Testament that are over a millennium older than what had been the oldest known manuscripts, affirming the remarkable textual preservation of the Scriptures.

Limitations and Interpretation

While archaeological evidence often aligns well with the biblical narrative, it's crucial to remember that archaeology is not without its limitations. First, not all archaeological finds directly relate to the Bible. Second, even when they do, they are subject to interpretation. Lastly, absence of evidence is not evidence of absence; many biblical accounts may yet receive future archaeological corroboration.

Edward D. Andrews

Against the Critics

Skeptics often hastily conclude that discrepancies between archaeological findings and the Bible disprove its historical reliability. However, what often occurs is that later discoveries or reinterpretations of existing data align more closely with the biblical text. Over the years, many "biblical problems" raised by critics have found solutions, courtesy of the spade and brush.

Archaeological discoveries offer invaluable insights into the people, places, and events described in the Bible. While archaeology is not designed to prove faith, the discipline provides substantial evidence that the Bible describes actual historical events. Numerous finds have given scholars reason to trust the Bible, not only as a religious text but also as a document that interacts with the same history and geography that we can touch, see, and explore through archaeological endeavors. The material culture unearthed from the ancient Near East and surrounding regions often harmonizes with what we find in the Scriptures, thereby serving as external witnesses to the Bible's trustworthiness.

Therefore, those who seek to understand the Bible can be encouraged by the wealth of archaeological data that supports its historical narratives. Even though faith rests on the inherent authority and trustworthiness of God's Word, the corroborative power of archaeology serves to affirm that the events detailed in the Scriptures are not mere fables but are grounded in historical reality. Thus, as we continue to dig into both the ground and the Scriptures, we find that the two frequently complement each other, enriching our understanding of each and fortifying our confidence in the eternal truths contained in the Bible.

Archaeology and Apologetics: Defending the Faith with Archaeological Insights

In contemporary discussions concerning the veracity and reliability of the Christian faith, the question often arises: How can we be sure the biblical accounts are historically accurate? Here, the intersection of archaeology and apologetics becomes a critical arena for thoughtful dialogue. Apologetics, the rational defense of the faith, is significantly bolstered by archaeological findings that affirm the historical reliability of the Scriptures. Though our faith rests on the inherent authority and veracity of God's Word, archaeological insights serve as supportive external evidence that the biblical narrative is grounded in historical fact.

YOUR GUIDE FOR DEFENDING THE BIBLE

Verifying Biblical Personalities

Skeptics have often denied the historical existence of biblical figures. For example, for many years, critics questioned the existence of King David until the Tel Dan Stele was discovered in 1993. This inscription from the 9th century B.C.E. refers to the "House of David," providing external confirmation of the Davidic dynasty and effectively silencing the naysayers.

Corroboration of Biblical Events

Archaeological findings also validate specific events mentioned in the Bible. For instance, the Moabite Stone (or Mesha Stele) corroborates the Moabite revolt against Israel as mentioned in 2 Kings 3. The Cylinder of Cyrus, in the British Museum, confirms the Biblical account of the Persian king Cyrus allowing the Jews to return to their land and rebuild their temple (Ezra 1:1-4).

Artifacts and Daily Life

The discovery of everyday items like pottery, coins, and household implements in places mentioned in the Bible, such as Capernaum or Bethsaida, provide a tangible link to the biblical narrative. They help us understand the culture and daily life during biblical times, enriching our interpretation and appreciation of the Scripture. For example, discoveries in Jerusalem from the time of Jesus give us insights into the political and religious climate in which He conducted His ministry.

Codifying Laws and Treaties

The discovery of ancient law codes like the Code of Hammurabi has offered comparative insights into biblical laws. While the Code of Hammurabi and the Mosaic Law are distinct, the fact that comprehensive legal codes existed in the ancient Near East during the time the Torah was written adds plausibility to the biblical accounts of Moses receiving laws from Jehovah on Mount Sinai.

Archaeological Silence

One of the important aspects to consider in the apologetic use of archaeology is that absence of evidence is not evidence of absence. Some critics hastily point to the lack of archaeological evidence for certain biblical narratives as proof against their historical reliability. This is a fallacious argument. The discipline of archaeology is still in progress, and new discoveries are continually coming to light.

Understanding Limitations

While archaeology can offer external validation for biblical accounts, it is not without its limitations. The archaeological record is incomplete, and interpretations are subject to human error. Moreover, archaeology deals primarily with material culture, which can only provide partial insights into the spiritual truths conveyed in the Scriptures.

Responding to Criticism

Critics often use archaeology to cast doubt on the Bible, cherry-picking instances where findings appear to contradict biblical narratives. However, these contradictions are often resolved through subsequent discoveries or more nuanced interpretations of the data. In many cases, what was once considered a problem becomes an affirmation of the biblical account.

The conjunction of archaeology and apologetics provides a robust defense for the Christian faith. Archaeological findings serve as corroborative evidence for the biblical narratives, affirming that the people, places, and events described in the Scriptures are not mythical constructs but rooted in historical reality. These discoveries, therefore, serve as valuable tools in the apologist's arsenal, reinforcing the Bible's claims and answering its critics.

While faith in Jehovah God and His Word does not rest on archaeology, the latter serves as a helpful handmaid to the former. The evidence uncovered from the dust of the ancient world often aligns with the biblical account, providing a tangible connection to the world of the Bible. As a result, those who are earnest in defending the faith find in archaeology a supportive field of study that adds layers of understanding and credibility to the Scriptural record.

So, while we emphasize that faith is based on the inherent truthfulness of God's Word, we can also acknowledge that archaeology has a significant role to play in Christian apologetics. As we dig deeper, both in the soil and in the Scriptures, we often find that the two are in harmony, enhancing our confidence in the historical reliability and thus the divine inspiration of the Bible. This dual pursuit not only enriches our understanding of the biblical text but also equips us to "always be prepared to make a defense to anyone who asks you for a reason for the hope that is in you" (1 Peter 3:15).

Ethical Considerations: Respecting Sacred Sites and Cultures

The field of biblical archaeology is not merely an academic exercise in unearthing ancient artifacts or validating historical texts. At its core, it intersects with real communities, faiths, and cultural heritage. Therefore, the ethical dimensions of archaeological practice are of paramount importance, especially when it comes to respecting sacred sites and cultures. This goes beyond mere legal obligations and taps into the moral and spiritual responsibilities that come with excavating land that holds significant religious and cultural meaning.

The Stewardship Mandate

The Christian worldview posits that humans have been given a mandate of stewardship over the earth (Gen 1:28). This sense of stewardship extends to how we treat archaeological sites. Delving into these sites isn't merely a matter of "finders keepers"; it is a serious responsibility that requires ethical deliberation. This stewardship involves not just preserving the physical artifacts but also respecting the cultural and religious sensitivities associated with them.

Cultural Sensitivity and Collaboration

Local communities often have a profound spiritual and cultural connection to archaeological sites. It is, therefore, crucial to involve these communities in the decision-making process, considering their perspective and traditional knowledge. This shows respect for their history and often aids in a more accurate understanding of the site itself. Whether in Israel, Turkey, or Jordan, collaborative efforts can be a win-win situation, enriching the archaeological work while ensuring community concerns are addressed.

Recognizing Sacred Ground

Sites mentioned in the Bible, such as Jerusalem, Hebron, or Bethel, hold spiritual significance not just for Christians but often for Jews and sometimes for Muslims as well. In such multi-faith contexts, it is essential to approach excavation projects with heightened sensitivity. Even within Christian circles, places like the Church of the Holy Sepulchre or the supposed site of Jesus' baptism hold varying degrees of reverence among different traditions. Understanding and respecting these viewpoints are vital in conducting ethical archaeological work.

Preservation Over Treasure Hunting

The impulse to make groundbreaking discoveries should never override the importance of preserving the integrity of the site and its artifacts. "Looting" is anathema in responsible archaeological circles for good reason: it disrespects the cultural and often spiritual significance of artifacts, reducing them to mere commodities. The emphasis should always be on preservation for the sake of knowledge and cultural heritage, not personal or institutional gain.

Respect for Human Remains

Perhaps one of the most sensitive issues in biblical archaeology is the handling of human remains. Whether it's the ossuaries in Jerusalem or burial sites elsewhere in the ancient Near East, these are not just archaeological specimens but individuals who were part of communities with beliefs about death and the afterlife. Proper care, respectful handling, and, where appropriate, reburial, should be the standard procedures.

Public Sharing and Education

Once findings have been documented and analyzed, ethical considerations extend to how these are presented to the public. Sensationalism, particularly in the media, can often distort the actual findings and their significance. This can harm not only the scientific integrity of the archaeological work but also risk offending the religious and cultural groups connected to the site.

Ethical Dilemmas and Decision-making

Archaeologists often face ethical dilemmas, such as whether to excavate a site that is in danger of being destroyed by construction projects. In such cases, the decision to proceed should be made cautiously, considering both the potential gains in knowledge and the ethical implications concerning sacred sites and local communities.

Academic Integrity

Lastly, biblical archaeologists must adhere to high standards of academic integrity. This involves acknowledging the limitations of one's findings, avoiding overstated claims, and crediting collaborative or precedent work. Archaeology's role is to add layers of understanding to the biblical text, not to rewrite it according to one's biases or preconceived notions.

In conclusion, ethical considerations in biblical archaeology serve as both a constraint and an opportunity. While they set boundaries that limit what can be done, they also provide a framework within which meaningful, respectful, and enriching work can take place. In aligning with these ethical norms, archaeologists do not merely pay lip service to modern standards of conduct; they reflect a more profound ethical and spiritual commitment that honors both God and neighbor. Therefore, as we dig into the past, let us do so with an eye toward the ethical implications of our work, recognizing that what we unearth is not merely matter but meaning, not just relics but repositories of faith and culture that deserve our deepest respect.

CHAPTER 34 Some Major Sites and Finds

The Dead Sea Scrolls: Unlocking Ancient Manuscripts

One of the most impactful archaeological discoveries of the 20th century was the unearthing of the Dead Sea Scrolls. This collection of manuscripts, hidden in the cliffs of Qumran near the Dead Sea, has given biblical scholars, theologians, and historians invaluable insights into the Jewish world of the Second Temple period. This find has significantly affected the field of biblical archaeology, and it has implications that echo through textual criticism, the study of ancient languages, and our understanding of early Judaism and Christianity.

Discovery and Initial Exploration

The Dead Sea Scrolls were initially discovered in 1947 by a Bedouin shepherd. What started as a casual exploration of a cave led to one of the most momentous archaeological finds ever. The caves would eventually yield a treasure trove of texts: fragments from every book of the Hebrew Bible, except for Esther, as well as numerous other Jewish writings and documents of the time.

Significance for Textual Criticism

Before the discovery of the Dead Sea Scrolls, the oldest complete Hebrew Bible manuscript dated to around the 10th century C.E., known as the Aleppo Codex. The Dead Sea Scrolls pushed that date back by about a thousand years, providing manuscripts from as early as the 2nd century B.C.E. This is crucial for textual critics, as it allows for a more accurate reconstruction of the original text of the Hebrew Bible. These ancient manuscripts serve as a vital checkpoint for assessing the fidelity of later copies, substantiating the meticulous nature of Jewish scribes in transmitting the text. The Isaiah Scroll, one of the most complete scrolls found, is a prime example. When compared to the Masoretic Text, the canonical text for Rabbinic Judaism, the scroll showed astonishingly few variations, affirming the text's high degree of preservation over the centuries.

Insights into Second Temple Judaism

The Dead Sea Scrolls not only contain biblical texts but also other Jewish writings, often referred to as sectarian documents. These include commentaries, hymns, and legal texts that shed light on the beliefs and practices of a particular Jewish group, often thought to be the Essenes. The "Community Rule" and the "War Scroll" are examples of such texts, offering scholars insights into the sectarian life and eschatological expectations of this Jewish community. Understanding this context is pivotal for interpreting the New Testament, as Jesus and his followers existed within the religious and social landscape shaped by Second Temple Judaism.

Illuminating Early Christianity

There is no direct evidence of Christian writings among the Dead Sea Scrolls, but the findings do illuminate the world in which Christianity emerged. Texts like the "Psalms of Solomon" and the "Book of Enoch," although not canonical, were known to early Christian writers and offer insights into messianic expectations and angelology that were prevalent in the period. While none of these texts are part of the New Testament canon, they serve as cultural and theological background against which the New Testament events unfolded.

Controversies and Ethical Questions

While the Dead Sea Scrolls have been a monumental contribution to biblical archaeology and scholarship, they have not been without controversy. Issues related to the scrolls' initial acquisition, their subsequent publication, and even their authenticity have been matters of academic debate. However, it's vital to remember that archaeology is not a field settled in absolutes. The interpretation of findings can change with new discoveries and evolving methodologies.

Implications for Apologetics

While faith must ultimately rest on the enduring Word of God, archaeological findings like the Dead Sea Scrolls serve to buttress the historical reliability of Scripture. These ancient manuscripts offer a tangible link to the world of the Bible, serving as external corroborations of its textual integrity and its depiction of Second Temple Judaism. They also provide scholars with more resources to counter critics who doubt the Bible's historical veracity.

The discovery of the Dead Sea Scrolls is a watershed moment in the fields of biblical archaeology and textual criticism. It provides a direct window into the religious life, scriptural interpretations, and even the languages of the Second Temple period, making the biblical narrative more vivid and grounded in its historical context.

Moreover, the scrolls reinforce the high level of care with which these sacred texts were transmitted, supporting the notion that what we have today is a faithful representation of the original manuscripts. While faith does not rest on archaeology, such discoveries offer additional layers of confirmation and richness to our understanding of the Scriptures and their historical backdrop. Therefore, the Dead Sea Scrolls remain an indispensable resource for anyone committed to the rigorous study of the Bible, its world, and its enduring message.

Babylonia Excavations

Babylonia has long captivated the imaginations of historians, scholars, and religious enthusiasts alike. The ancient civilization, located in what is modern-day Iraq, not only holds a prominent place in Mesopotamian history but also features significantly in the Bible. Babylonia and its greatest king, Nebuchadnezzar, are frequently mentioned, especially in the context of the Babylonian exile of the Israelites. The excavations carried out in Babylonia offer a fascinating intersection of biblical history and archaeology, providing both challenges and affirmations to the Scriptural record.

Babylon: The Legendary Capital

Babylon, the capital city, has been the focal point of numerous excavations. The remnants of the city walls, the Ishtar Gate, and the foundations believed to be the Tower of Babel all attest to Babylon's grandeur. Of particular interest is the discovery of the famed Babylonian ziggurats, stepped pyramidal structures that resemble the biblical description of the Tower of Babel (Genesis 11:1–9).

The Nebuchadnezzar Chronicles

Archaeological finds relating to King Nebuchadnezzar have been particularly illuminating. Tablets describing his reign, military campaigns, and building projects offer insights into this king who played a pivotal role in Israelite history. One of the key finds has been the "Babylonian Chronicles," a series of tablets that outline significant events during Nebuchadnezzar's reign. These chronicles corroborate the Bible's account of his siege of Jerusalem in 587/586 B.C.E., further affirming the historical reliability of books like Jeremiah and 2 Kings.

Nabonidus and Belshazzar: The Mystery Resolved

For years, skeptics pointed out that there was no extrabiblical evidence to support the existence of Belshazzar, the Babylonian king mentioned in the Book of Daniel (Daniel 5). However, archaeological finds have validated the Bible's account. Tablets discovered indicate that Belshazzar was the son of Nabonidus and served as a co-regent during his father's prolonged absence. This neatly explains why Daniel was offered the position of "third highest ruler in the kingdom" (Daniel 5:16), as Nabonidus and Belshazzar would have been the first and second.

The Cyrus Cylinder and the Return of the Exiles

The Cyrus Cylinder, discovered in the ruins of Babylon, records the conquest of Babylon by Cyrus the Great and his policy of allowing conquered peoples to return to their lands and rebuild their temples. This edict was instrumental in ending the Babylonian Captivity of the Israelites, as recorded in Ezra 1:1-4. The cylinder serves as a significant extrabiblical corroboration of the Biblical narrative.

The Code of Hammurabi

Though not directly related to biblical events, the discovery of the Code of Hammurabi has provided scholars with a comprehensive look at Babylonian law and social norms. Some laws resemble those in the Torah, affirming the historical backdrop against which the Mosaic Law was given.

Controversial Interpretations and Limitations of Archaeology

Archaeological findings in Babylonia, while providing significant insights, are subject to interpretation. The so-called "House of the New Year," for instance, has been variously identified as the Tower of Babel, though this is debated. Archaeology is not an exact science, and interpretations may shift as new discoveries are made. It's also crucial to keep in mind that the absence of evidence is not evidence of absence. Many events and figures mentioned in the Bible have not yet been confirmed through archaeology but that does not necessarily invalidate the Biblical account.

YOUR GUIDE FOR DEFENDING THE BIBLE

The Apologetic Value of Babylonian Archaeology

While the final foundation of Christian faith rests on the divine authority and enduring nature of the Scriptures, archaeological discoveries in Babylonia have often served to affirm the Bible's historical narratives. These findings provide a tangible connection to the world described in the Old Testament, offering an external line of evidence that bolsters the case for the Bible's reliability. Particularly in an age of skepticism, these excavations offer robust responses to critics who question the historicity of the Bible.

Babylonia, with its rich history intertwined with biblical narratives, remains an intriguing field for archaeologists and scholars. Excavations have unearthed monumental structures, royal edicts, and legal codes that collectively affirm the cultural and historical backdrop of biblical events. While not every biblical detail has archaeological corroboration, the excavations in Babylonia have often provided supportive evidence for the Bible's historical reliability.

Though we must not base our faith solely on archaeological findings, these discoveries enhance our understanding of the Scriptural text. They also provide a powerful tool for apologetics, reinforcing the trustworthiness of the Bible. The Babylonia excavations remain a testament to the intricate tapestry of history, faith, and scholarly endeavor, underscoring the enduring relevance of exploring our ancient past to enrich our understanding of the Scriptures and fortify our faith in its divine Author.

Assyria Excavations

The realm of Assyria, an ancient empire whose heartland was located in what is today northern Iraq and southeastern Turkey, has long been the subject of archaeological investigation. Notably aggressive and expansive, Assyria has a storied history documented not just in its own cuneiform records but also significantly in the Bible. Its interactions with Israel and Judah—capturing the Northern Kingdom of Israel and laying siege to Jerusalem—make the Assyrians a key player in biblical history. Excavations in Assyria have brought to light various aspects of the empire that enrich our understanding of the Bible's historical setting.

Nineveh: The Mighty Capital

Nineveh, perhaps the most famous Assyrian city, is extensively mentioned in the Bible, particularly in the book of Jonah and Nahum. The city was rediscovered in the 19th century and has since yielded magnificent palaces and a library containing thousands of clay tablets. These include administrative documents, letters, and texts on divination and rituals. The layout and monumental structures corroborate the biblical description of Nineveh as a "great city" (Jonah 1:2).

Ashurbanipal's Library

One of the most critical finds was the royal library of King Ashurbanipal. The library contained a wealth of information, including the famous Epic of Gilgamesh, but for biblical studies, the chronicles detailing Assyrian campaigns are most illuminating. These texts confirm Assyrian military activities during the period of biblical history, such as the siege of Lachish vividly portrayed in the book of Isaiah (Isaiah 36:2).

Tiglath-Pileser III and Israel

Tiglath-Pileser III is a king of note, as he was instrumental in the downfall of the Israelite kingdom. The Bible records that he took people from Israel and moved them to Assyria (2 Kings 15:29). Inscriptions discovered from his reign verify his campaign into Israel and his policy of deportation, thus affirming the biblical account.

The Siege of Jerusalem: Sennacherib's Prism

Sennacherib's Prism, another archaeological find, provides an Assyrian perspective on the siege of Jerusalem as recorded in 2 Kings 18-19 and Isaiah 36-37. While Sennacherib claims to have trapped King Hezekiah of Judah "like a bird in a cage," he notably does not claim to have captured Jerusalem. This absence of a claim aligns remarkably well with the biblical narrative, which details how the Assyrian army was divinely thwarted from conquering Jerusalem.

The Black Obelisk and Jehu

Another intriguing artifact is the Black Obelisk of Shalmaneser III, which depicts Israelite tribute bearers and identifies one figure as Jehu, King of Israel. This provides extrabiblical evidence of Jehu's existence and pays homage to Shalmaneser III, thereby substantiating accounts in 2 Kings 9-10.

Archaeological Confirmations and Limitations

As in Babylonia, the archaeology of Assyria has its limitations. Sometimes inscriptions appear boastful or propagandistic, and not all details align neatly with the biblical narrative. Nonetheless, the broad strokes often do, reinforcing the historical reliability of the Bible's account of Assyrian interactions with Israel and Judah.

YOUR GUIDE FOR DEFENDING THE BIBLE

Apologetic Value of Assyrian Archaeology

In an era where the Bible's historicity is often called into question, Assyrian excavations and finds offer substantive external corroborations. The Assyrian records not only affirm the existence of biblical figures and events but also provide a geopolitical and cultural backdrop against which these events occurred. This has significant apologetic value, offering robust responses to critics and skeptics alike who challenge the Bible's historical accuracy.

The landscape of Assyrian archaeology is both complex and fascinating. From the royal palaces and libraries of Nineveh to the inscriptions detailing military campaigns and political intrigues, the excavated artifacts serve as a tangible link to the world of the Old Testament. These findings, while not always offering a perfect match, lend substantial credibility to the biblical narrative and fortify the case for its historical reliability.

The importance of Assyrian archaeology, however, extends beyond merely authenticating specific people or events. It provides an enriched context within which the biblical narrative unfolds, helping us better appreciate the complexities faced by figures like Hezekiah and prophets like Jonah and Nahum. While archaeology alone is not the foundation for faith, these discoveries certainly contribute to a more robust understanding of the Scriptures and reaffirm their enduring relevance and reliability.

Persia Excavations

The Persian Empire holds a significant place not only in world history but also in the narrative of the Bible. Ranging from Cyrus the Great's decree permitting the Jews to return to Jerusalem to rebuild the temple, to the intrigue-laden court of King Ahasuerus in the book of Esther, the empire appears in several biblical books, including Ezra, Nehemiah, Esther, and Daniel. Archaeological work in areas once under Persian rule has produced a wealth of material culture that illuminates the world behind the biblical text. This archaeological evidence provides a powerful testimony to the historical reliability of the Bible.

Persepolis: The Ceremonial Capital

Excavations at Persepolis, the ceremonial capital of the Achaemenid Empire, have unearthed several palaces and a grand terrace adorned with detailed sculptures and reliefs. Inscriptions in Old Persian, Elamite, and Akkadian can be found throughout the site. These inscriptions often detail the extent of the empire and the subjugated peoples, including references to areas familiar from the biblical narrative, like Judah. The site complements our understanding of the lavish royal setting described in books like Esther.

The Cyrus Cylinder

Among the most famous discoveries is the Cyrus Cylinder, unearthed in Babylon. This artifact contains a decree from Cyrus, detailing his conquests and his policy of allowing conquered peoples to return to their homelands and restore their places of worship. While the cylinder does not mention the Jews explicitly, the policy aligns remarkably well with the biblical account of Cyrus allowing the Jewish exiles to return to Jerusalem and rebuild their temple (Ezra 1:1-4).

Behistun Inscription

The Behistun Inscription is another essential find. Carved into a cliff, the inscription contains a trilingual account of Darius I's achievements. Apart from its value for deciphering cuneiform, the text mentions several regions and kings subdued by Darius, offering insights into the political environment of the early Persian period. This broader context aids in the understanding of the empire as it interacted with the biblical characters.

Elephantine Papyri

Though not in Persia proper, the Elephantine Papyri from Egypt contain Aramaic letters and legal documents from a Jewish military colony situated on the Elephantine Island. These texts, dating from the 5th century B.C.E., offer firsthand accounts of Jewish life under Persian rule. They include references to religious practices and, importantly, correspondence seeking permission to rebuild a Jewish temple in Elephantine, echoing the official support that Ezra and Nehemiah received for their endeavors in Jerusalem.

The Royal Road

Archaeological evidence of the Royal Road, stretching from Sardis to Susa, amplifies the biblical description of the Persian communication and governance system, such as the use of mounted couriers (Esther 8:10,14). Understanding this logistical marvel adds layers of meaning to scenes like Esther's two banquets, which would have involved extensive planning and resources.

Archaeology and Interpretation

While the material culture unearthed provides compelling evidence supporting the Bible's historical accounts, it's essential to approach these findings with caution. Interpretations can change, and archaeology is not an infallible discipline. However, the significant agreement between archaeological finds and the biblical record bolsters the Bible's credibility.

YOUR GUIDE FOR DEFENDING THE BIBLE

Apologetic Significance of Persian Archaeology

In an era when skepticism regarding the Bible's historical veracity is on the rise, the archaeological finds related to the Persian Empire offer a potent counter-argument. These discoveries have a powerful apologetic function, standing as external witnesses to the biblical narrative. Skeptics often posit that biblical accounts are late constructs devoid of historical truth. However, the correspondence between Persian-period archaeology and the biblical record refutes such notions.

While the field of archaeology can only go so far in confirming the biblical record, it has indeed provided supportive material when it comes to the Persian Empire as depicted in Scripture. These findings do not merely add a veneer of credibility; they allow for a deeper, more nuanced understanding of the Bible's accounts. They offer a window into the world of Ezra, Nehemiah, Esther, and Daniel, providing tangible links to the settings in which these individuals lived, prayed, struggled, and triumphed.

Archaeology, then, does not serve as a substitute for faith in the Scriptures, but rather enhances our understanding of its background and context. This allows us to appreciate the divine hand at work, not just in monumental events, but also in the intricate details of history and human experience. By doing so, archaeology serves to strengthen our conviction in the Scriptures as not only a document of spiritual truth but also one of historical reliability.

Mari and Nuzi Excavations

In the landscape of biblical archaeology, few sites have proven as insightful for understanding the world of the Old Testament as the excavations at Mari and Nuzi. While these ancient city-states may not appear directly in the Bible, they provide a unique window into the social, economic, and legal contexts that parallel the early periods of biblical history.

Mari: The Kingdom on the Euphrates

Located on the western bank of the Euphrates River in modern-day Syria, Mari was a bustling trade center. Excavated primarily from the 1930s onward, the site revealed a grand palace complex with over 300 rooms. But what sets Mari apart is the discovery of nearly 20,000 cuneiform tablets. These tablets provide invaluable data on the political, economic, and social conditions of the time.

The tablets speak to the administration of law, the organization of trade, and the particulars of everyday life. They are chronologically situated around the time of the patriarchs, particularly Abraham, and the Amorite milieu of the tablets resonates with the Amorite background cited in the Bible (Gen. 10:16; 1 Chron. 1:13-16).

One notable correspondence is the practice of adopting a servant as an heir in the absence of offspring. This is strikingly parallel to Abraham's lament that Eliezer of Damascus would be his heir (Gen. 15:2-3). Moreover, the tablets contain names that are etymologically akin to biblical names, further accentuating the cultural and linguistic similarities between Mari and the world of the patriarchs.

Nuzi: Unveiling the Hurrians

Located in northeastern Iraq, Nuzi was part of the Hurrian civilization. The excavations conducted in the 1920s and 1930s uncovered private homes and a vast array of legal documents and family records. These documents have illuminated the domestic and civil laws, some of which closely parallel legal practices and social customs described in Genesis.

For instance, the Nuzi tablets describe laws and customs concerning marriage, inheritance, and adoption that have uncanny resemblances to those found in the patriarchal narratives. A well-known example is the practice of a barren wife giving a maidservant to her husband to produce offspring, similar to the story of Sarai, Abram, and Hagar (Gen. 16:1-4).

Archaeology and Interpretation

While both Mari and Nuzi offer tantalizing correlations with the Bible, a measured approach is necessary. It is vital to affirm that even if the Bible did not have this external validation, it would still remain a reliable document due to its divine origin. Moreover, it should be remembered that archaeology is not infallible and that human interpretation of archaeological data can be fraught with error.

However, the finds from Mari and Nuzi certainly contribute to a robust understanding of the Bible's historical and cultural background. In essence, they function as pieces of a complex puzzle that, when assembled with care, reveal a vibrant picture of life in the ancient Near East.

Apologetic Implications

Mari and Nuzi serve as powerful apologetic tools against skeptics who claim the Bible is a mere collection of myths. The excavations and their corresponding tablets affirm that the customs, laws, and practices described in the Old Testament are rooted in historical realities.

While it may be tempting to sensationalize the findings from Mari and Nuzi as "proving" the Bible, we must resist this impulse. What these sites do offer is a wealth of information that complements our understanding of the biblical world and thereby enriches our reading and interpretation of Scripture.

Archaeology, then, serves as an auxiliary lens through which to view the biblical text. By providing contextual grounding for understanding the lives of the patriarchs and the ancient Near Eastern world they inhabited, Mari and Nuzi become valuable assets for both scholars and laypeople committed to a nuanced and informed reading of Scripture. These sites and their treasures fortify our confidence not only in the historical reliability of the Bible but also in its enduring message for today's world.

Egypt Excavations

Egypt occupies a unique and complex space in the context of biblical history. From Joseph's rise to power to Moses' leading of the Israelite Exodus, Egypt has been an epicenter for some of the Bible's most critical events. Archaeological excavations in Egypt have garnered much attention, given their potential to inform our understanding of the biblical narrative. The findings unearthed across various sites, ranging from monumental structures to papyrus documents, offer a textured background to the characters and stories in Scripture.

The Rosetta Stone and Egyptian Language

Perhaps one of the most significant archaeological discoveries in Egypt, the Rosetta Stone has been instrumental in deciphering Egyptian hieroglyphs. Uncovered in 1799, the stone presented a text in three different scripts: Greek, Demotic, and hieroglyphic. Because Greek was well-understood, scholars could unravel the Egyptian texts, subsequently opening up an enormous range of Egyptian records and inscriptions for interpretation. This discovery has had a profound impact on how we read ancient documents that correlate with the Bible's timeline, thereby refining our understanding of the Egyptian empire's intricacies.

City of Ramses and the Exodus

One excavation site that has been closely scrutinized is the ancient city of Pi-Ramesses, often equated with the biblical city of Ramses mentioned in the Exodus account (Exodus 1:11). The city, discovered in the Nile Delta, was the capital during the reign of Pharaoh Ramesses II. Artifacts and structures found here have provided insights into the grandeur of the city, fitting well with the narrative of a prosperous and robust Egyptian kingdom from which the Israelites fled.

The Amarna Letters

The Amarna Letters, discovered in the late 19th century, consist of a collection of clay tablets written primarily in Akkadian cuneiform. These correspondences between Egyptian Pharaohs and various vassal rulers and kingdoms offer a glimpse into the geopolitical climate of the ancient Near East during the Late Bronze Age. They bear on biblical history, particularly on the Egyptian influence over Canaan before the Israelite conquest. While they don't specifically mention Israelites, they provide the larger political and military context of that period.

The Merneptah Stele

An intriguing artifact that has received attention is the Merneptah Stele. Dating back to the end of the 13th century B.C.E., this granite slab contains the earliest known reference to Israel outside of the Bible. Pharaoh Merneptah inscribed his conquests, mentioning Israel as a people already living in Canaan. This find has implications for the dating of the Israelite settlement and serves as a form of extrabiblical evidence for their presence in the land.

Joseph and Grain Storage

Another fascinating parallel between Egypt's archaeological record and the Bible's account is the evidence for large-scale grain storage during years of plenty. While there's no definitive evidence linking such storage to the Joseph narrative in Genesis 41, these findings resonate with the biblical account of Joseph's foresight in storing grain to prepare for seven years of famine.

Archaeology and Interpretation

As with all archaeological data, care is needed in interpretation. These findings can provide contextual background that enriches our understanding of Scripture, but they don't serve as direct proof of the biblical accounts. The Bible stands on its own merits as the inspired Word of God, and while archaeological finds can provide context or even corroboration, they are not the foundation of our faith.

Apologetic Implications

Egyptian archaeology does offer a robust defense against criticisms of the Bible's historical reliability. Skeptics often posit that the biblical stories are ahistorical or evolved from myths. However, the coherence between the archaeological findings and the Scriptural accounts serves to discredit such claims.

Egyptian archaeology enriches our understanding of the world of the Bible. It offers tangible points of contact with the stories and characters of Scripture, even as it opens up avenues for further study and interpretation. While the primary foundation of our faith is not in the shifting sands of archaeological data but in the unchanging Word of God, these archaeological finds from Egypt offer an auxiliary, yet invaluable, means to delve deeper into the Scriptures. In doing so, they not only enhance our historical understanding but also serve as a tool for apologetics, underscoring the Bible's reliability and its enduring message.

Palestine Excavations

The land of Palestine, comprising modern-day Israel, the Palestinian territories, parts of Jordan, and adjoining regions, has an inextricable relationship with biblical history. The Bible itself offers a historical and cultural geography of Palestine, but the monumental task of archaeology seeks to unearth and elucidate material remains of this past. Here, we will discuss some major sites and finds in Palestine that offer valuable perspectives into the historical background of the Bible.

Jerusalem: The Heart of Three Religions

Jerusalem is more than just a city; it's a repository of millennia of religious, historical, and cultural heritage. Excavations here have turned up evidence from the First and Second Temple periods, including the Western Wall, Hezekiah's tunnel, and the Siloam Pool, where Jesus reportedly healed a blind man (John 9:1-7). These finds give life to the narrative canvas of both the Old and New Testaments.

Jericho: The City of Palms

Jericho is one of the oldest continuously inhabited cities in the world. The site holds significance for understanding the Israelite conquest of Canaan. The layers of fallen walls support the biblical account of the walls tumbling down after the Israelites encircled the city, blowing trumpets (Joshua 6). However, scholars differ on correlating the archaeological evidence with the biblical chronology.

Qumran and the Dead Sea Scrolls

Perhaps the most famous discovery related to biblical archaeology, the Dead Sea Scrolls were found in the caves near Qumran between 1947 and 1956. The scrolls contain copies of almost all the Old Testament books, apocalyptic writings, and community rules, providing invaluable insights into the text of the Hebrew Bible and the religious milieu at the time of Jesus.

Megiddo: A Strategic City

Megiddo is known for its military history and as a symbol of final, apocalyptic battle in Revelation (Har Megiddo or Armageddon). Excavations have revealed twenty layers of ruins, providing insights into various periods of occupation, including the time of King Solomon, who fortified the city (1 Kings 9:15).

Hazor: A Canaanite Stronghold

Excavations at Hazor have shed light on the city's significance as a Canaanite center before its destruction by the Israelites (Joshua 11:10-13). The presence of large gates and fortifications also resonate with descriptions found in the Scriptures.

Bethsaida: The City of Fishermen

Located near the Sea of Galilee, Bethsaida is frequently mentioned in the New Testament as the hometown of Peter, Andrew, and Philip. Excavations have revealed an ancient fishing village, offering insights into the daily lives and occupations of some of Jesus' earliest followers.

Dan: Idolatry and Apostasy

Tel Dan, in northern Israel, offers a glimpse into the idolatrous practices that led the northern kingdom astray. An inscription mentioning the "House of David" was discovered here, providing extrabiblical evidence for the Davidic dynasty.

Apologetic Considerations

The findings from these sites contribute to the larger dialogue about the Bible's historical accuracy. Critics often discount the Bible as myth or allegory, but the physical evidence unearthed often correlates well with the biblical record, effectively countering such skepticism.

The Limitations and Strengths of Archaeology

It is imperative to approach archaeological data with nuance. The findings can supplement, contextualize, and sometimes even validate biblical history, but they should not supersede Scripture as the ultimate source of truth.

Palestinian archaeology serves a twofold purpose. First, it enriches our understanding of the Bible, grounding the events, characters, and teachings of Scripture in a tangible reality. Second, it provides additional substantiation for the biblical accounts, countering critics who question the historical reliability of Scripture.

Through meticulous study and scholarly integrity, archaeology in Palestine continues to contribute to biblical studies. While the field has its limitations, often due to the interpretive constraints and ongoing debates among archaeologists, it serves as a crucial discipline for anyone interested in the historical and cultural world behind the biblical narrative. The convergences between archaeology and the Bible affirm the latter's enduring reliability and divine inspiration, strengthening our faith and understanding of God's revelation to humanity.

Syria Excavations

The modern territory of Syria encompasses an area that is deeply ingrained in the biblical narrative. This region played host to a number of pivotal events and characters, stretching from the times of the Patriarchs to the early Christian church. Hence, archaeological investigations in Syria bear relevance not just to a historical or cultural understanding, but also to a deeper comprehension of the Scriptures.

Ebla: The Ancient Archive

The ancient city of Ebla, discovered in northern Syria, has been one of the most monumental finds, revealing an extensive archive of cuneiform tablets. These tablets not only provide insights into early Semitic languages but also bear names and places that resonate with the biblical text. While Ebla is not directly mentioned in the Bible, the discovery of its archive has illuminated the broader ancient Near Eastern context in which biblical events unfolded.

YOUR GUIDE FOR DEFENDING THE BIBLE

Mari: Along the Euphrates

Mari was another significant city-state located on the Euphrates River. Excavations have unearthed a grand palace, several temples, and a vast number of cuneiform tablets. Mari was a thriving commercial hub with cultural and possibly political contacts with the biblical patriarchs, particularly Abraham, who hailed from Ur of the Chaldeans, not far from Mari. Although Mari itself is not mentioned in the Bible, its archaeological discoveries have shed light on the socio-political landscape of the early second millennium B.C.E., corresponding to the patriarchal period.

Tell Brak: The Nagar of Scriptures?

Though not definitively identified, Tell Brak in northeastern Syria is believed by some scholars to be the biblical Nagar, referenced in Genesis 24:10. While not explicitly mentioned again in the biblical text, the city could provide valuable insights into the regions from which Rebekah, Isaac's wife, originated.

Dura-Europos: A Mosaic of Cultures

The site of Dura-Europos, located along the Euphrates River, is significant for its diverse religious landscape during the Hellenistic and Roman periods. Notably, a Christian house church was discovered with a baptistry room containing early Christian frescoes, which offer important glimpses into early Christian worship practices. Although not directly tied to biblical events, findings at Dura-Europos expand our understanding of early Christian communities.

Laodicea ad Libanum: Not the Laodicea of Revelation

While Laodicea ad Libanum is not the same as the Laodicea mentioned in the book of Revelation, it is still of historical interest. The site, situated in western Syria, has Greco-Roman ruins that help us understand the blend of cultures prevalent during the time of the New Testament.

Palmyra: A Desert Oasis

Palmyra is not directly mentioned in the Bible but stands as an example of the kind of cosmopolitan, caravan cities that could have had indirect interactions with biblical figures, particularly in trade networks. The site is renowned for its spectacular architecture and inscriptions.

Apologetic Considerations

While Syria doesn't often feature as prominently as Palestine in the biblical record, the archaeological discoveries from this region have nonetheless contributed significantly to our understanding of the Scriptures. Various artifacts, inscriptions, and structures unearthed in Syrian excavations have corroborated aspects of the biblical narrative, reaffirming the historical reliability of the Bible against its critics.

Limitations and Strengths of Archaeology

Archaeological evidence is not without its limitations. Conclusions drawn from excavations are subject to interpretation and can be revised as new evidence comes to light. However, when wielded carefully, archaeology serves as a robust auxiliary to the study of Scriptures. The archaeology of Syria, for instance, offers a broader lens through which to interpret the events, characters, and teachings of the Bible.

The archaeological landscape of Syria is as rich and complex as its history, offering a fertile ground for the scholarly investigation of biblical times. It's worth noting that faith is not solely based on material discoveries; it's anchored in the power and reliability of God's Word. However, archaeological endeavors in Syria continue to enrich our understanding of the historical and cultural backdrop against which the biblical narrative unfolded. Even when not directly cited in Scripture, the cities and regions excavated in Syria provide valuable context for the biblical events that took place in neighboring areas.

Through diligent study, grounded in a conservative approach to both biblical exegesis and archaeological methodology, the excavations in Syria serve to elucidate the complexities of the world of the Bible. They offer valuable contributions to the fields of biblical studies, Near Eastern archaeology, and apologetics. These finds, while not serving as a foundation for faith, certainly offer supportive evidence that contributes to a robust, well-informed faith. In doing so, they reveal the intricate tapestry of divine providence woven through the history and geography of the lands of the Bible.

Bibliography

Andrews, E. (2020). *FROM SPOKEN WORDS TO SACRED TEXTS: Introduction-Intermediate New Testament Textual Studies.* Cambridge: Christian Publishing House.

Andrews, E. D. (2016). *INTERPRETING THE BIBLE: Introduction to Biblical Hermeneutics.* Cambridge, OH: Christian Publishing House.

Andrews, E. D. (2016). *THE CHRISTIAN APOLOGIST: Always Being Prepared to Make a Defense [Second Edition].* Cambridge, OH: Christian Publishing House.

Andrews, E. D. (2016). *THE COMPLETE GUIDE to BIBLE TRANSLATION: Bible Translation Choices and Translation Principles [Second Edition]* . Cambridge: Christian Publishing House.

Andrews, E. D. (2017). *CONVERSATIONAL EVANGELISM: Defending the Faith, Reasoning from the Scriptures, Explaining and Proving, Instructing in Sound Doctrine, and Overturning False Reasoning [Second Edition].* Cambridge, OH: Christian Publishing House.

Andrews, E. D. (2018). *REASONING WITH THE WORLD'S VARIOUS RELIGIONS: Examining and Evangelizing Other Faiths.* Cambridge, OH: Christian Publishing House.

Andrews, E. D. (2019). *INTRODUCTION TO THE TEXT OF THE NEW TESTAMENT: From The Authors and Scribe to the Modern Critical Text.* Cambridge, Ohio: Christian Publishing House.

Andrews, E. D. (2023). *ARCHAEOLOGY & THE NEW TESTAMENT.* Cambridge, Ohio: Christian publishing House.

Andrews, E. D. (2023). *ARCHAEOLOGY & THE OLD TESTAMENT.* Cambridge, Ohio: Christian Publishing House.

Andrews, E. D. (2023). *BIBLICAL EXEGESIS: Biblical Criticism on Trial.* Cambridge, OH: Christian Publishing House.

Andrews, E. D. (2023). *CHRISTIAN APOLOGETICS: Answering the Tough Questions: Evidence and Reason in Defense of the Faith.* Cambridge, Ohio: Christian Publishing House.

Andrews, E. D. (2023). *HOW WE GOT THE BIBLE*. Cambridge, OH: Christian Publishing House.

Andrews, E. D. (2023). *INTRODUCTION TO OLD TESTAMENT TEXTUAL CRITICISM*. Cambridge, OH: Christian Publishing House.

Andrews, E. D. (2023). *INTRODUCTION TO THE TEXT OF THE OLD TESTAMENT: From the Authors and Scribes to the Modern Critical Text.* Cambridge, OH: Christian Publishing House.

Andrews, E. D. (2023). *INTRODUCTION TO THE TEXT OF THE OLD TESTAMENT: From the Authors and Scribes to the Modern Critical Text.* Cambridge, OH: Christian Publishing House.

Andrews, E. D. (2023). *THE BIBLE AS HISTORY: A Historical Journey Through the Bible.* Cambridge, Ohio: Christian Publishing House.

Andrews, E. D. (2023). *THE BIBLE ON TRIAL: Examining the Evidence for Being Inspired, Inerrant, Authentic, and True.* Cambridge, Ohio: Christian Publishing House.

Andrews, E. D. (2023). *THE MACCABEES: The Hasmonaean Dynasty between Malachi and Matthew.* Cambridge, OH: Christian Publishing House.

Andrews, E. D. (2023). *THE OLD TESTAMENT: Commentary, Background, & Bible Difficulties (Introduction to the Old Testament).* Cambridge, OH: Christian Publishing House.

Andrews, E. D. (2023). *THE SCRIBE AND THE TEXT OF THE NEW TESTAMENT: Scribal Activities in the Transmission of the Text of the New Testament.* Cambridge, Ohio: Christian Publishing House.

Archer, G. L. (1982). *New International Encyclopedia of Bible Difficulties, Zondervan's Understand the Bible Reference Series.* Zondervan Publishing House: Grand Rapids, MI.

Comfort, P. W. (1992). *Early Manuscripts & Modern Translations of the New Testament.* Wheaton, IL: Tyndale House Publishers.

Comfort, P. W. (1992). *The Quest for the Original Text of the New Testament.* Eugene, Oregon: Wipf and Stock Publishers.

Comfort, P. W. (2005). *ENCOUNTERING THE MANUSCRIPTS: An Introduction to New Testament Paleography and Textual Criticism.* Nashville, TN: Broadman & Holman.

Comfort, P., & Barret, D. (2019). *THE TEXT OF THE EARLIEST NEW TESTAMENT MANUSCRIPTS: Papyri 1-72, Vol. 1* . Grand Rapids, MI: Kregel Academic.

Comfort, P., & Barret, D. (2019). *THE TEXT OF THE EARLIEST NEW TESTAMENT MANUSCRIPTS: Papyri 75-139 and Uncials, Vol. 2.* Grand Rapids, MI: Kregel Academic.

Elwell, W. A., & Comfort, P. W. (2001). *Tyndale Bible Dictionary.* Wheaton: Tyndale House Publishers.

Geisler, D. a. (2009, 2014). *Conversational Evangelism.* EUGENE, OREGON: Harvest House Publishers.

Howe, T. A. (2015). *Objectivity in Biblical Interpretation.* Seattle: CreateSpace.

Howe, T., & L., G. N. (1992). *BIG BOOK OF BIBLE DIFFICULTIES, The: Clear and Concise Answers from Genesis to Revelation.* Grand Rapids, MI: Baker Books.

MacArthur, J. F. (2011). *Evangelism: How to Share the Gospel Faithfully (MacArthur Pastor's Library).* Nashville, TN: Thomas Nelson.

Metzger, B. M. (1964, 1968, 1992). *The Text of the New Testament: Its Transmission, Corruption, and Transmission.* New York: Oxford University Press.

Metzger, B. M. (1994). *A Textual Commentary on the Greek New Testament (2nd ed.).* New York: United Bible Society.

Metzger, B. M. (2001). *The Bible in Translation: Ancient and English Versions.* Grand Rapids, MI: Baker Academic.

Ramm, B. (1999). *Protestant Biblical Interpretation: A Textbook of Hermeneutics, 3rd rev. ed.* Grand Rapids, MI: Baker.

Ryken, L. (2002). *The Word of God in English. Wheaton.* Wheaton: Crossway Books.

Ryken, L. (2008). *Choosing a Bible: Understanding Bible Translation Differences.* Wheaton: Crossway Books.

Ryken, L. (2009). *Understanding English Bible Translation: The Case for an Essentially Literal Approach.* Wheaton: Crossway Books.

Stein, R. H. (2011). *A Basic Guide to Interpreting the Bible: Playing by the Rules.* Grand Rapids: Baker Books.

Terry, M. S. (2022). *Biblical Hermeneutics: A Treatise on the Interpretation of the Old and New Testaments.* Cambridge, OH: Christian Publishing House.

Thomas, R. L. (2002). *Evangelical Hermeneutics.* Grand Rapids: Kregel Publications.

Virkler, H. A., & Ayayo, K. G. (1981, 2007). *Hermeneutics: Principles and Processes of Biblical Interpretation.* Grand Rapids, MI: Baker Academic.

Wayne, G., & J. I., P. (2005). *Translating Truth: The Case for Essentially Literal Bible Translation.* Wheaton, IL: Good News Publishers/Crossway Books.

Zuck, R. B. (1991). *Basic Bible Interpretation: A Practical Guide to Discovering Biblical Truth.* Colorado Springs: David C. Cook.